Prized Possessions DUTCH PAINTINGS FROM NATIONAL TRUST HOUSES

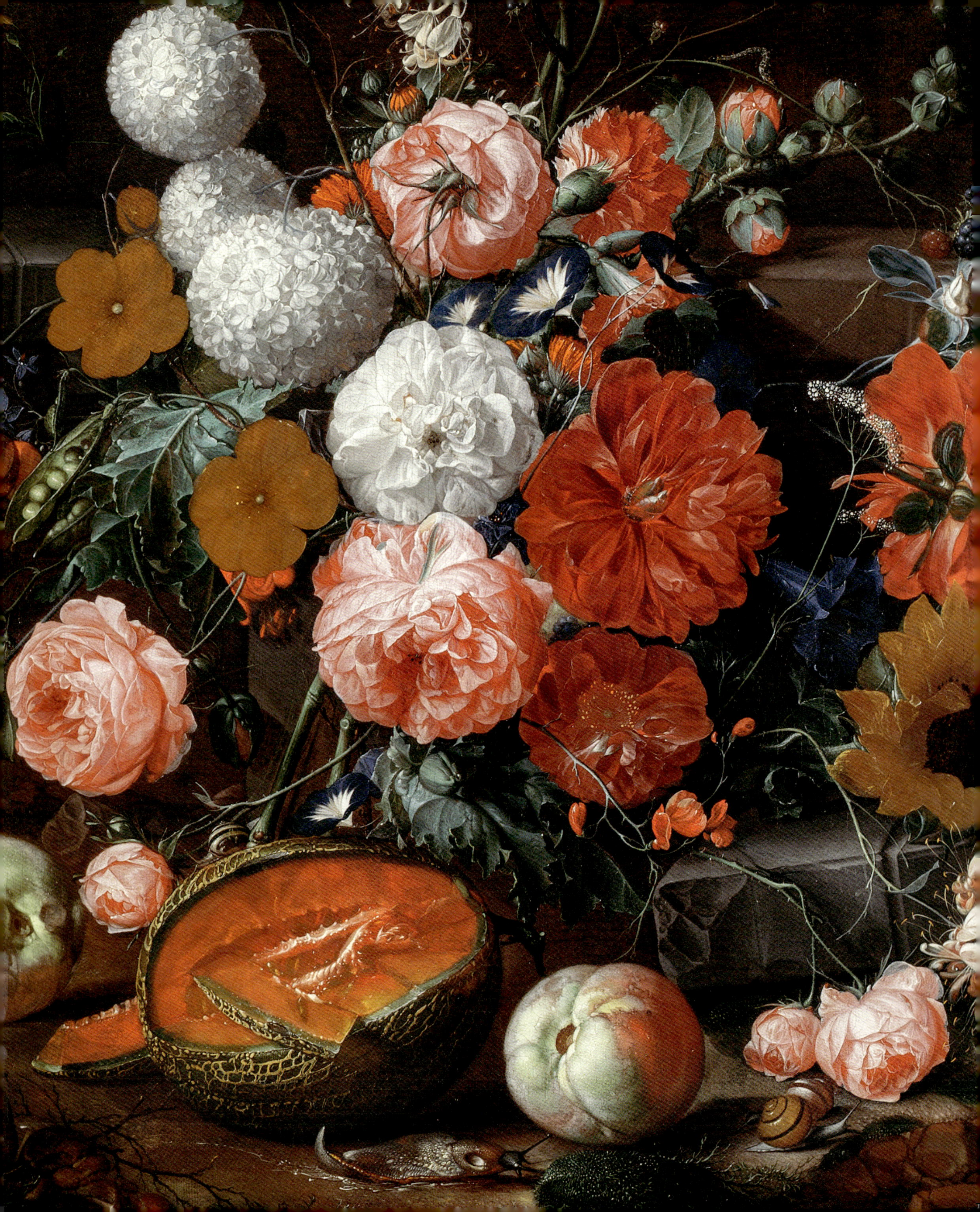

Prized Possessions DUTCH PAINTINGS FROM NATIONAL TRUST HOUSES

EDITED BY
Rupert Goulding and David A.H.B. Taylor

ESSAYS BY
Quentin Buvelot and David A.H.B. Taylor

NATIONAL TRUST
in association with
PAUL HOLBERTON PUBLISHING

Published to coincide with the exhibition

Prized Possessions DUTCH PAINTINGS FROM NATIONAL TRUST HOUSES

The Holburne Museum, Bath
25 May – 16 September 2018

Royal Picture Gallery Mauritshuis, The Hague
11 October 2018 – 6 January 2019

Petworth House, West Sussex
26 January 2019 – 24 March 2019

ISBN 978 1 911300 24 3

British Library Cataloguing in Publication Data

A catalogue record for this book is available from the British Library

Produced by Paul Holberton Publishing
89 Borough High Street, London SE1 1NL
WWW.PAULHOLBERTON.COM

Designed by Laura Parker

Printing and reproductions by E-Graphic, Verona

FRONT COVER: Gabriel Metsu, *The Duet ('Le corset bleu')*, *c.*1660 (cat. 15), detail
BACK COVER & FRONTISPIECE: Cornelis de Heem, *A Still Life of Flowers and Fruit Arranged on a Stone Plinth in a Garden*, *c.*1685 (cat. 7), detail
PAGE 6: Pieter Saenredam, *Interior of the Church of St Catherine, Utrecht* (cat. 19), detail

Contents

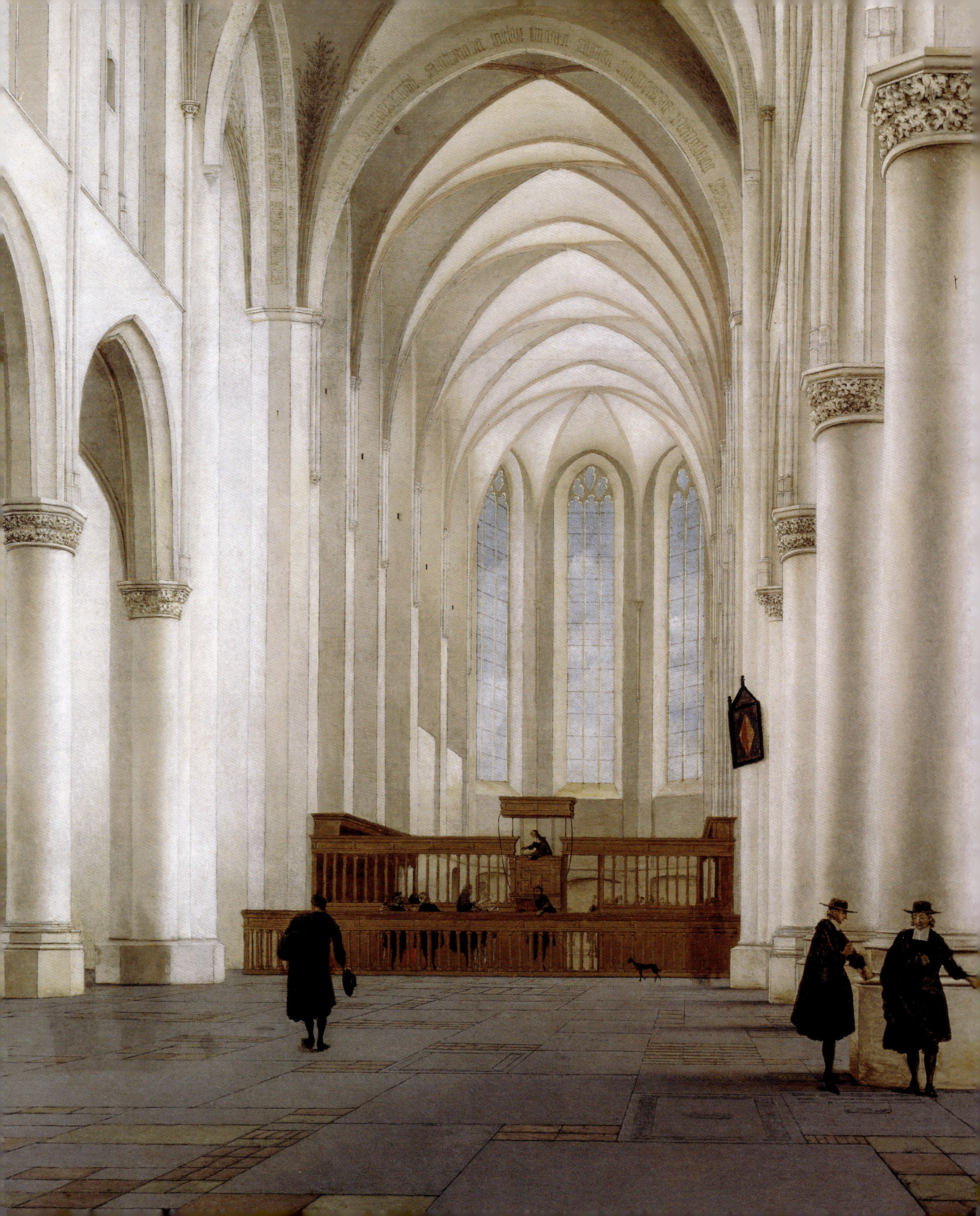

CLARENCE HOUSE

The National Trust's wonderful collection of paintings includes impressive works by some of the best-loved artists of the Dutch Golden Age. I am delighted that this has inspired the Trust to create the first exhibition of National Trust pictures for twenty-two years. 'Prized Possessions: Dutch Paintings from National Trust Houses' celebrates the British fondness for collecting Dutch pictures, with examples collected by some of the Nation's most important patrons and displayed in some of our greatest houses.

The range of artists represented in the exhibition naturally includes Rembrandt and Cuyp, as well as émigré artists who came to work in England, including Jan Lievens and Peter Lely, and others who are less well-known today. The wide variety of works – portraits, landscapes, religious pictures, still lives, subject pictures and seascapes – have been chosen to illustrate the breadth of seventeenth-century Dutch painting.

The exhibition will be touring to three separate venues, all of which are the sites of important historic collections, and the inclusion of one of the venues, the Mauritshuis in The Hague, particularly underlines the significant cultural links between the United Kingdom and the Netherlands.

I very much hope that this exhibition will open visitors' eyes to this less well-known aspect of the National Trust's art collection, and excite, intrigue and move in equal measure. I wish the exhibition every possible success.

Charles

Acknowledgements

The National Trust is extremely grateful for the generous loan from the Earldom of Jersey Trust and for the support from our donor, historic and tenant families. We gratefully acknowledge a generous bequest from the late Mr and Mrs Kenneth Levy that has supported costs in preparing this book. The National Trust is likewise grateful for the generous support in the acquisition of certain paintings featuring in this exhibition: from the National Heritage Memorial Fund, the Mr and Mrs Kenneth Levy bequest, the Art Fund, a fund set up by the late Hon. Simon Sainsbury, the Royal Oak Foundation, the Ulster Land Fund, and private donations.

Many National Trust staff and advisors, both current and former, have contributed in considerable ways. The general managers (and their collection teams), curators and conservators responsible for the lending properties have all been unwaveringly supportive of the exhibition, for which we are hugely grateful. The various contributing authors have all taken much time and trouble to share their expert knowledge here – including Emile de Bruijn, Simon Chesters-Thompson, Patricia F. Ferguson, Allison Goudie, Tim Pye, James Rothwell and Christopher Rowell. We would particularly like to thank Claire Forbes, National Trust Specialist Publications, and Susannah Stone, picture researcher, for all their work on the catalogue. Thanks, too, go to Lynne Richards for translating Quentin Buvelot's essay, and to Diane Webb for translating his and Charlotte Rulkens's catalogue entries. Special thanks go to David Adshead, Elizabeth Alcock, Katya Belaia, John Chu, Tarnya Cooper, Alison Dalby, Helen Ghosh, Claire Hollinghurst, Helen Lloyd, Holly Lopez, Phoebe Meiklejohn-McLaughlin, Hilary McGrady, Simon Murray, Sandy Nairne, John Orna-Ornstein, Francesca Roberts, Craig Robson, Christine Sitwell, Fernanda Torrente and Cara Wallace. Other thanks are due for support and advice from Jennifer Scott, former director of the Holburne Museum, and to Karen Hearn and Robert Wenley.

We would like to thank all the staff members of the three exhibition venues who have helped with the catalogue and exhibition, in particular, at the Holburne Museum in Bath, Chris Stephens, Spencer Hancock, Nina Harrison Leins, Katie Jenkins, Vanessa Wells and Amina Wright; at the Mauritshuis in The Hague, Emilie Gordenker, Quentin Buvelot and Charlotte Rulkens; and at Petworth House, Joanna Cartwright, Anna Connolly and Andy Loukes.

Our very grateful thanks go to Paul Holberton, Laura Parker and Katherine Bogden Bayard at Paul Holberton Publishing, for all their work on the production of this catalogue.

Our final and heartfelt thanks go to Helen Goulding and Nick Bridgland for their patient and enduring support throughout this whole project, without which it would have been an impossible task.

RUPERT GOULDING & DAVID A.H.B. TAYLOR

Introduction

RUPERT GOULDING & DAVID A.H.B. TAYLOR

Prized Possessions brings together some of the National Trust's best-loved works of seventeenth-century Dutch art to celebrate the enduring appeal of two great achievements of European culture, Dutch Golden Age painting and the British country house.

The purpose of the National Trust, from its foundation in 1895, has been to preserve places of historic interest and natural beauty for the benefit of the nation. Spread across the length and breadth of England, Wales and Northern Ireland, its country houses contain an extraordinarily diverse collection of almost one million individual items. Each house's collection tells its own unique story but within this vast assemblage are alternative groups of related works of art which, together, can be counted among the finest in the world. Its exceptional Dutch paintings are one such group. This exhibition is a rare opportunity to view twenty-two highlights of the National Trust's Golden Age pictures in one place, assembled from houses as far apart as Castle Ward in Northern Ireland, Felbrigg Hall in Norfolk, Buckland Abbey in Devon and Petworth in West Sussex.

Dutch paintings have entered British country houses via many routes, spanning periods of both conflict and alliance between these neighbouring countries. In some cases they were purchased directly from their makers by seventeenth-century patrons and collectors, leaving an unusually complete picture of the influence of Dutch taste on the British at a particular moment in time. Contemporary Dutch paintings, for example, were integral to the original decorative schemes at both Ham House and Dyrham Park. Ashdown House has many Dutch ties through its architectural designers and its portrait collection. Gerrit van Honthorst's portrait of Elizabeth Stuart, the 'Winter Queen', which pre-dates the construction of the mansion, is a memorial to Anglo-Dutch dynastic bonds during that century. The bird's-eye view of Dunham Massey by Adriaen van Diest is a testament to the steady flow of artistic talent from the Low Countries to the British Isles.

Golden Age art continued to be collected throughout the eighteenth century. Willem van de Velde's *Battle of Texel*, for example, was purchased in 1752 for Felbrigg Hall by William Windham, reflecting his seafaring and military interests. The 3rd Earl of Egremont, who became one of the great patrons of British Romantic art, bought the somewhat louche portrait of Prince Rupert for Petworth in 1786. As the art market developed in the nineteenth century, wealthy industrialists and financiers competed to acquire Dutch masterpieces from existing collections. Towards the end of the century, William McEwan bought *The Colf Players* and *The Introduction* on the advice of specialist art dealers and bequeathed both to his daughter, the society hostess Dame Margaret Greville, along with Polesden Lacey. Lord Bearsted bought both *The Tired Traveller* and *The Duet* for Upton House in 1924, while Anthony de Rothschild acquired Aelbert Cuyp's exquisite view of Dordrecht in 1928 for Ascott.

Country house collections are rarely static, and works have continued to be acquired even after properties passed into the National Trust's care. Acquisitions such as the Cornelis de Heem flower painting for Dyrham in 2015 have been made in order to return to their historic homes works of art which were lost through sale or inheritance. Occasionally the National Trust is also the grateful recipient of bequests of paintings without historic connections to its houses but of significance in their own right. In 2010, for example, it accepted the Rembrandt *Self-portrait* from the estate of Edna, Lady Samuel of Wych Cross, and allocated it for display at Buckland Abbey.

Prized Possessions highlights the sheer variety of Golden Age pictures that have entered British country house collections by these different routes. The celebrated genre paintings stand out with their captivating narratives and technical mastery – nowhere clearer than in Metsu's brilliant layering of ermine and satin in *The Duet*. In the field of still life, Ambrosius Bosschaert's blackbird is captured with charming delicacy while De Heem balances accuracy with a bravura display. Seascapes of the period are represented in *The Battle of Texel* by Willem van der Velde, which, though illustrative of Anglo-Dutch military conflict, captures the shared maritime history of these nations. Landscapes extend from the depictions of far-flung Brazil to the more familiar Dutch countryside and the British country estate. Religious works are represented in *The Baptism of Christ* by Abraham Bloemaert and also in the more mystical *Magus at a Table* by Jan Lievens. The perspectival control displayed by Pieter Saenredam in his *Interior of the Church of St Catherine, Utrecht* creates an impression of air and space only surpassed by the romantic mastery of light in Aelbert Cuyp's *View of Dordrecht*. In portraiture, the likenesses of historic owners of National Trust houses are captured by Sir Peter Lely and Cornelius Johnson; kings and princes are represented by Jan de Baen and Simon Verelst. Jan Lievens's mysterious *Unknown Woman in a Green Velvet Hood* can be compared to a *Self-portrait* by Rembrandt van Rijn, one of the most recognisable Dutchmen of them all.

For all its richness, *Prized Possessions* is by no means comprehensive of all the great works of the Dutch Golden Age within the National Trust collections. Limitations of space and the challenges of conservation mean that many works have been omitted which would otherwise certainly warrant inclusion. The flower painting of Rachel Ruysch at Dudmaston Hall, Melchior d'Hondecoeter's huge *trompe-l'oeil* at Belton House, the perspective views by Samuel van Hoogstraten at Dyrham Park and Philips Wouwerman's *Conversion of Saint Hubert* at Penrhyn Castle would each justify a visit to those houses in their own right.

Though the exhibition is concerned with Golden Age paintings, the National Trust's collections are a treasure trove of a much wider range of seventeenth-century material culture of Dutch influence or creation. To give a flavour of these holdings and an historical context for the variety of fine objects that so often appear in the pictures themselves, National Trust curators and advisors have contributed short entries on other categories of art. Patricia Ferguson describes the National Trust's world-class collection of the celebrated tin-glazed earthenware known in England as 'Delftware'. Simon Chesters-Thompson describes a clock of 1658 at Lyme Park, Cheshire, which is England's earliest surviving pendulum clock – a technology invented in the Netherlands and swiftly imported to Britain. Tim Pye's overview of the large holding of Dutch books in National Trust houses highlights the importance of Low Countries publications for the dissemination of knowledge in the British Isles during that period. James Rothwell uncovers the presence of Dutch silver and its influence, while Christopher Rowell discusses the migration of craftsmen and styles through an examination of furniture and decorative schemes. The competing interests of the Dutch and English East India Companies in global luxury markets throughout the seventeenth century are described by Emile de Bruijn. David Taylor explains the opportunities afforded by print culture with examples from National Trust collections. Rupert Goulding explores the cross-pollination of garden design and the influence of Anglo-Dutch personal connections on architecture.

Two essays explore the wider context for the artworks within this exhibition. David Taylor examines the taste for Golden Age Dutch pictures across the National Trust's collection while Quentin Buvelot offers a Dutch perspective on seventeenth-century Dutch paintings in England. Two short articles conclude the catalogue and provide an overview of the Dutch collections at the exhibition partners. The Holburne Museum is a Victorian gentleman's townhouse collection of rare quality and breadth, containing Dutch pictures and many of the other collection categories described above. The Mauritshuis is a royal collection of global significance, a collection of remarkable depth and quality, and containing pictures of international fame, none more so than Vermeer's *Girl with a Pearl Earring*.

Together, these essays and articles attempt to tell the rich and multifaceted story of Dutch Golden Age art in the British country house.

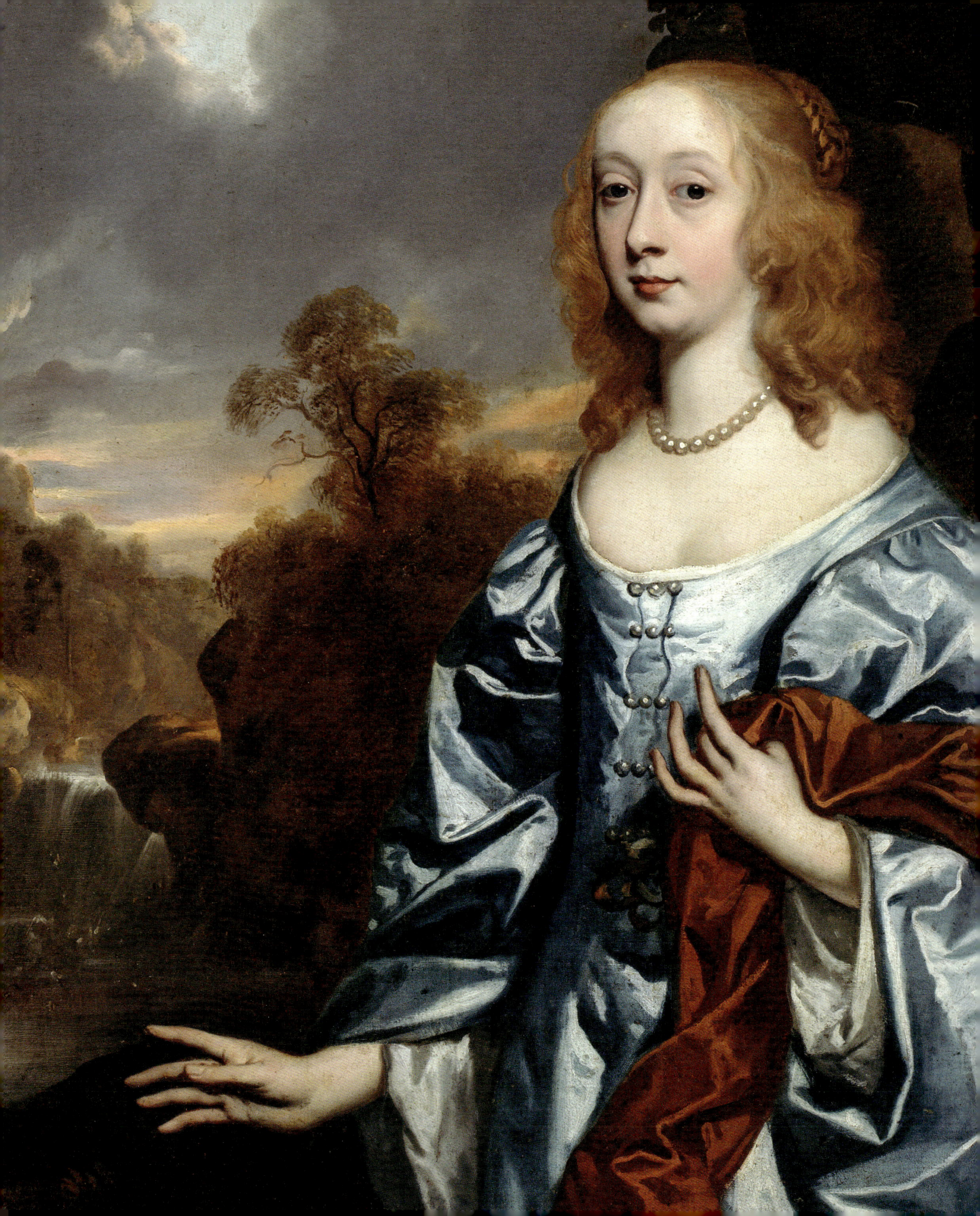

A Taste for the Golden Age
Dutch Pictures in the National Trust's Collection

DAVID A.H.B. TAYLOR

The National Trust has more than 13,000 oil paintings in its care. The many discrete collections, across England, Northern Ireland and Wales, that make up this number illustrate the evolution of British picture-collecting tastes over six centuries. Many of the pictures still hang in rooms in which they were displayed historically, some even in spaces or within decorative schemes for which they were first commissioned or collected. In sum, these collections, in which portraiture predominates, provide a unique record of many of the nation's most important patrons, collectors and sitters.

Beyond this, there are particular strengths in individual collections, such as the Spanish pictures at Kingston Lacy, Dorset, or the cycle of First World War paintings by Stanley Spencer at the Sandham Memorial Chapel, Hampshire, but one of the greatest strengths, in terms of number and quality, is in Dutch pictures, among which can be counted some of the best examples of 'Golden Age' Dutch painting in Britain – that is, those painted in the long seventeenth century. The Dutch pictures are displayed in houses across the country, though some of the best examples are grouped in a small number of specific collections, such as those at Ham House, Surrey, at Upton House, Warwickshire, and notably those at Ascott House, Buckinghamshire. The greater part of the collection of works of art at Ascott, together with the house and grounds, were given to the National Trust in 1949 by the banker and philanthropist Anthony de Rothschild (1887–1961), and that included one of the masterpieces now in the Trust's care, the magnificent *View of Dordrecht* by Aelbert Cuyp (cat. 5). This essay considers the enthusiasm for collecting Dutch pictures exhibited by a number of families associated with houses now in the Trust's stewardship, whether by seventeenth-century patrons then collecting contemporary pictures or by those in later centuries. The Trust has itself 'repatriated' to its properties a number of Dutch pictures, the most recent acquisitions being made in the twenty-first century.

In 1648, following the end of the Eighty Years' War, the Dutch Republic was finally recognised by Catholic Spain and a prosperous period of financial stability and growth ensued. The consequent rise of a confident and affluent middle class eager to acquire works of art – previously the preserve of a privileged elite – led to an increase in the production of paintings. The Reformation marked a cultural as well as religious transformation in many parts of Western Europe, and, while the production of devotional painting declined, other forms such as portraiture and genre painting increased in popularity. In Britain, despite the tumultuous events of the seventeenth century, which included civil war, the execution of a king, an interregnum and a revolution, middle-class wealth increased, as did an appetite for the manufacture, acquisition and display of luxury items, not least among which were paintings. Following the Reformation, portraiture became and has remained the most popular art form in the British Isles; foreign

Detail of cat. 12 (Lely, *Elizabeth Murray*)

artists, mostly from the Low Countries, dominated the production of pictures from the end of the fifteenth century and into the seventeenth century.

During the seventeenth century there were various reasons why artists from the Netherlands might travel to England to work, or wish to have their pictures displayed in this country. Some came to escape religious persecution or economic uncertainty, others were attracted by the lure of potential business in a nation whose courtiers at least clearly wanted to spend money to establish collections of art. The Earl and Countess of Arlington were a case in point. In 1665 the English statesman Henry Bennet, later 1st Earl of Arlington (1618–1685), married a Dutch woman, Isabella van Nassau-Beverweerd (1631–1718). She sat to a number of important Dutch artists – in 1651 to Gerrit van Honthorst (Netherlands Institute for Cultural Heritage, Amsterdam)[1] and in 1672, whilst travelling in the Netherlands, to Caspar Netscher (private collection) with her husband and daughter. The display by the Arlingtons of their collection of portraits, of family members, royalists and politicians, at their country seat, Euston Hall in Suffolk, was no doubt influenced by the portrait series that the countess would have been familiar with in the Netherlands. Similarly, Edward Hyde, Lord Clarendon (1609–1674), Charles II's Lord Chancellor, had a celebrated portrait gallery in Clarendon House, his townhouse on Piccadilly, London. It included portraits of himself and his daughter Anne Hyde, Duchess of York (1637–1671), which had been painted in The Hague by Adriaen Hanneman when they were exiled there before the Restoration (both private collection). Such galleries of '*uomini famosi*' in the houses of prominent courtiers were well-known and would have been seen by associates of the Clarendons, such as Elizabeth Murray, Countess of Dysart in her own right and later Duchess of Lauderdale (1626–1698), one of the great patrons of seventeenth-century England.

Following her father's death Elizabeth inherited his title as well as Ham House, his Thames-side palace outside Richmond in Surrey, which was presented to the National Trust in 1948. It was at Ham, and predominantly in the Long Gallery there, that Elizabeth displayed a collection of portraits by Peter Lely, which, commissioned over several decades, depict various family members and political allies. She was an important and influential courtier and her relationship with Lely helped secure that artist's reputation in England in the 1640s (see cat. 12). Lely's work became highly fashionable, especially after the Restoration, and, following his appointment as Charles II's Principal Painter, sitting to him and giving him commissions was also a way a courtier could display loyalty to the king. Another important patron was Sir Ralph Bankes (1631–1677), whose collection of portraits by Lely, displayed at Kingston Hall, Dorset – rechristened Kingston Lacy during its rebuilding in the late 1830s – included one of himself, which now hangs in the Library (fig. 1).[2] All remained in the family until bequeathed to the National Trust by (Henry John) Ralph Bankes (1902–1981), together with the estate and the rest of the house's contents.[3]

As well as portraits, Bankes also bought one of Lely's earlier subject pictures, a full-length depiction of *The Penitent Magdalen*. Lely only painted around

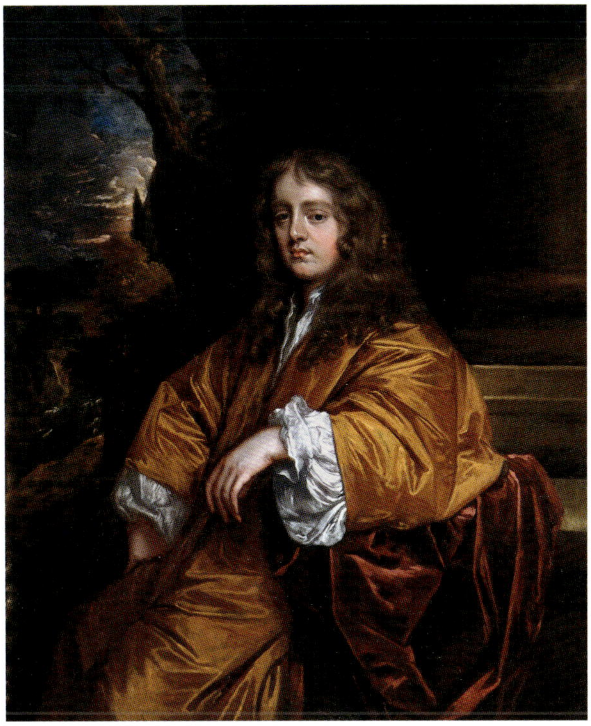

FIG. 1
Sir Peter Lely (1618–1680)
Sir Ralph Bankes (1631–1677), c.1655
Oil on canvas, 127 × 102.9 cm
National Trust, Kingston Lacy, Dorset
(NT 1257049)

thirty subject pictures after his arrival in England in the 1640s, depicting religious, mythological, pastoral or musical themes. The woman in the picture, playing the role of the repentant prostitute Mary Magdalen, was probably a member of one of Lely's circles of actor and musician associates. She is recognisable as the nymph being carried off in the artist's *Rape of Europa* (Chatsworth) and as the woman playing a guitar in *The Music Lesson* (a version of which, from the Earl of Jersey's collection, now hangs in the National Trust's Osterley House, Middlesex). The picture, which shows the saint in a cave, contemplating a crucifix, was described by Bankes in a 1659 list as 'A Magdelen of m^{r} lillys', and cost £20, including its frame.[4] The picture was then kept in Bankes's rooms at Gray's Inn, where he had been admitted as a member in 1656, until it was moved to Kingston Hall.[5] A recent rediscovery is the artist's signature, comprising his initials in monogram, inscribed on the reverse. Revealed during cleaning in 2017, it was clearly known to the maker of the 1835 inventory: 'Sir P. Lely's Cipher is on this Picture'.

Lely was involved in the acquisition of one of the finest Dutch pictures now at Kingston Lacy, the Haarlem painter Nicolaes Berchem's magnificent, brooding *Landscape with Herdsmen*, signed and dated 1655 (fig. 2). Bought by Bankes with Lely's help, this is an unusually large canvas for the artist, and was presumably made for a specific space; it was also kept at Gray's Inn before Bankes took it to Kingston Hall.

The majority of Berchem's pictures are Italianate landscapes – pastoral scenes with rural figures, like the present picture, in which the landscape is lit by the warm colours of the early evening while herdsmen bring their animals down a rocky path. Lely also helped Bankes acquire a copy of the Leiden painter Gerrit Dou's *Two Lovers Singing*, which shows a couple at a table in a dark, candlelit room, with a third person entering the room behind them through a door.[6] This was traditionally thought to have been after the Dou original bought by James II and still in the Royal Collection, but this second picture is now considered to be a copy too.[7]

Painted seven years after Berchem's *Landscape with Herdsmen*, one of the most enduringly popular pictures in the National Trust's care is Samuel van Hoogstraten's great 'threshold picture', his 1662 *View through a House*,[8] displayed in a closet at the end of an enfilade at Dyrham Park, Gloucestershire. It makes spectacularly full use of the *trompe l'oeil* effect to delight. Visitors to the house, if seeing the picture for the first time, are as intrigued by the clever composition as are the painted dog, parrot and cat in the picture to see them (fig. 3). The picture was painted in London for Thomas Povey (1613/14–*c.*1705) in 1662,

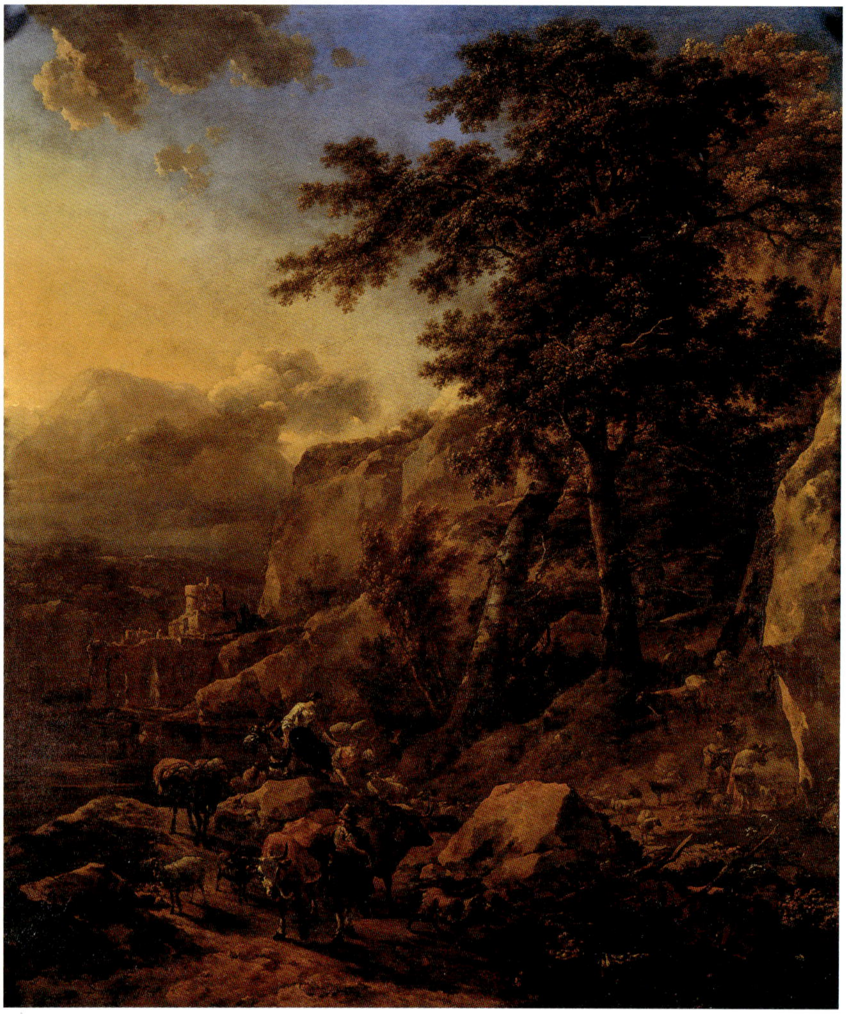

FIG. 2
Nicolaes Berchem (1620–1683)
Landscape with Herdsmen, 1655
Oil on canvas, 218.4 × 182.9 cm
National Trust, Kingston Lacy, Dorset
(NT 1257110)

and it is mentioned several times in Samuel Pepys's famous diary. On first seeing it at Povey's London house, Pepys noted: '... he after dinner showed me, from room to room, so beset with delicate pictures, and above all a piece of Perspective in his closett in the low parler' (19 January 1663). During a return visit later that same month he wrote: 'But above all things I do most admire his piece of perspective especially' (26 January 1663). Povey sold the picture to his nephew, William Blathwayt, William III's Secretary at War and so-called 'imperial fixer', who filled Dyrham with Dutch pictures and decorative art (see cat. nos. 1 and 7). It stayed in the family, by descent, until it was sold at Sotheby's on 29 February 1956 (lot 51). It was bought by Colnaghi & Co. and then by the Ministry of Works, before being transferred to the National Trust in 1961.[9]

There is another, larger picture by Hoogstraten at Dyrham, his *c.*1664 *Perspective View of a Courtyard of a House*, also bought by Blathwayt from his uncle Thomas around 1693.[10] The 'Great Perspective' was bought to add to the collection at Dyrham, a house he had acquired through his marriage to the heiress Mary Wynter in 1686. The enigmatic picture shows a courtyard, with steps down from an Ionic colonnade, and with various doorways and windows through which we get tantalising glimpses of the outside

FIG. 3
Samuel van Hoogstraten (1627–1678)
A View through a House, 1662
Oil on canvas, 264.2 × 136.5 cm
National Trust, Dyrham Park, Gloucestershire (NT 453733)

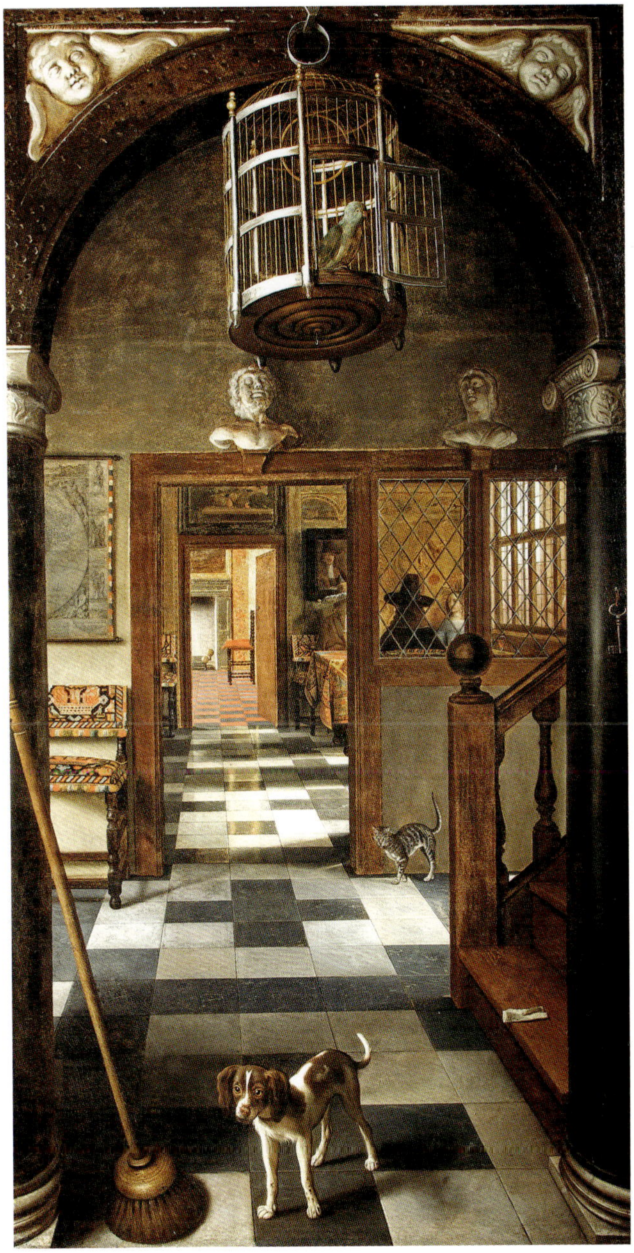

world. A boy, who turns his back to the viewer, has taken off his hat to sit on the steps and read. A spaniel lies sleeping nearby, a cat tentatively peers around the base of one of the columns and in the background a cockatoo and a monkey sit decoratively on a balustrade before a doorway. The size of the picture made its display a considerable problem, and in December 1701 Blathwayt's cousin, and latterly brother-in-law, John Povey, who also worked as his clerk, noted: '… there is a necessity of placing it on one side of the Best Stair case where after all by the Elevation and the proper placing of it, it promises a Wonderfull Effect'.

Blathwayt's close association with William III has resulted in Dyrham being the National Trust's most Williamite house, and one that clearly looked to the Netherlands for its cultural influences, not least in the formation of its art collection. It was the so-called Glorious Revolution of 1688 that saw the overthrow of the Catholic King James II by his Protestant son-in-law and eldest daughter Mary, the Prince and Princess of Orange, who then became co-regnant monarchs of England, Scotland and Ireland as William III and Mary II. After their arrival from the Netherlands there was an inevitable growth of interest in, and consumption of, Dutch culture. While Mary II's well-known love for blue-and-white Dutch Delftware stimulated an English response (for example in the collecting of tulip vases) there was also a reinvigorated interest in collecting and displaying pictures that had either been made in the Netherlands or painted in England by Dutch artists. Although émigré artists from the Low Countries had dominated the production of paintings in England from the sixteenth century, this renewed interest demonstrated loyalty to the new royal house.

In 1692, four years after the Glorious Revolution, the Dutch painter Godfried Schalcken travelled to England. During his four-year sojourn in the country he painted the new king, a picture which remains one of the Trust's more unusual portraits (fig. 4). Schalcken

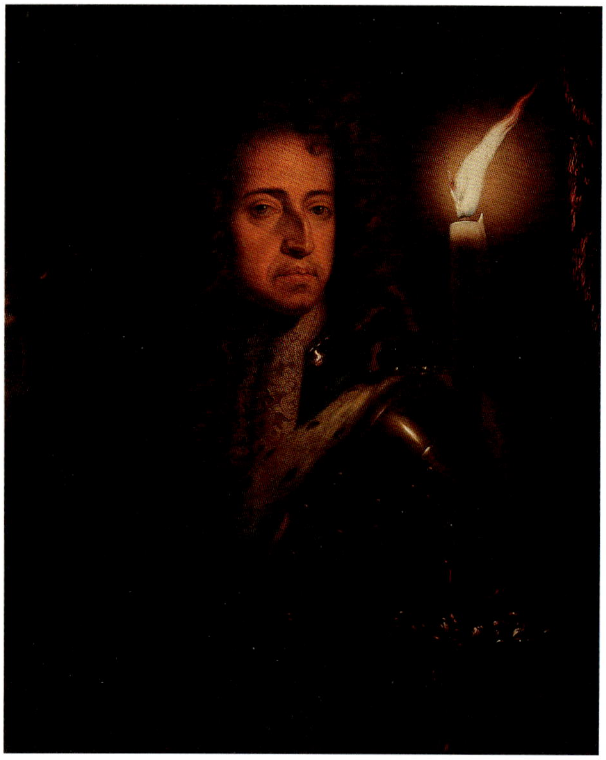

FIG. 4
Godfried Schalcken (1643–1706)
King William III by Candleight, *c.*1692–96
Oil on canvas, 74.9 × 62.2 cm
National Trust, Attingham Park,
Shropshire (NT 609007)

specialised in candlelit scenes, which he produced by placing whomever or whatever he was painting inside a darkened room lit by a candle, while he remained outside, painting in daylight, and observing his subject through a small hole. His unusual depiction of the king showed him wearing a perfectly regal costume of an ermine-lined cloak over a suit of armour, but in a dark interior with his face illuminated by the light of a prominent, flickering candle. A probably apocryphal account of the picture by Horace Walpole claimed that Schalcken 'once drew King William; but, as the piece was to be by candlelight, he gave up his majesty the candle to hold, till the tallow ran down upon his fingers'.[11] The portrait apparently caused a sensation[12] and several versions survive, including another signed canvas (Rijksmuseum, Amsterdam).[13]

The portrait, *King William III by Candlelight*,[14] is displayed at Attingham Park, Shropshire, where it is first recorded in the 1847 catalogue of pictures. It is the most important of the three portraits of the king there – the other two were painted, respectively, in the studio of Peter Lely and by an unknown Dutch artist.[15] A fourth portrait of William III has since left the collection. It is thought that the pictures were all acquired by different family members. Attingham, the home of the Berwick family, was bequeathed to the National Trust by Thomas Henry Noel-Hill, 8th Baron Berwick (1877–1947).

While Attingham has a large picture collection of high quality (and a top-lit picture gallery designed by the Regency architect John Nash), for a British collection of its type is has remarkably few Dutch pictures. Its strengths lie in its French and Italian holdings, the latter representing the remnants of two collections that were partly acquired in Italy by Thomas Noel-Hill, 2nd Baron Berwick (1770–1832) during his Grand Tour and by his brother William Noel-Hill, 3rd Baron Berwick (1773–1842) during his ambassadorships in Cagliari and Turin. Of the Dutch pictures, however, it is believed that the 3rd Lord Berwick purchased Jacob van Strij's *Cattle in a Landscape* of 1800.[16] While not a Golden Age painter, Van Strij (1756–1815) was an imitator of Aelbert Cuyp, and his pictures were particularly popular with English aristocratic collectors.

Of the other Dutch pictures at Attingham, an Italianate *Landscape with Huntsmen* by Adam Pynacker is probably the finest piece,[17] followed by a Willem Wissing and a studio portrait of Laurence Hyde, 1st Earl of Rochester (1642–1711), the uncle of Mary II and Queen Anne, depicted in his Garter robes (the original of which is in the Holburne Museum, Bath).[18] A seventeenth-century picture of *Two Cocks Fighting*, in the style of Melchior d'Hondecoeter,[19] bought

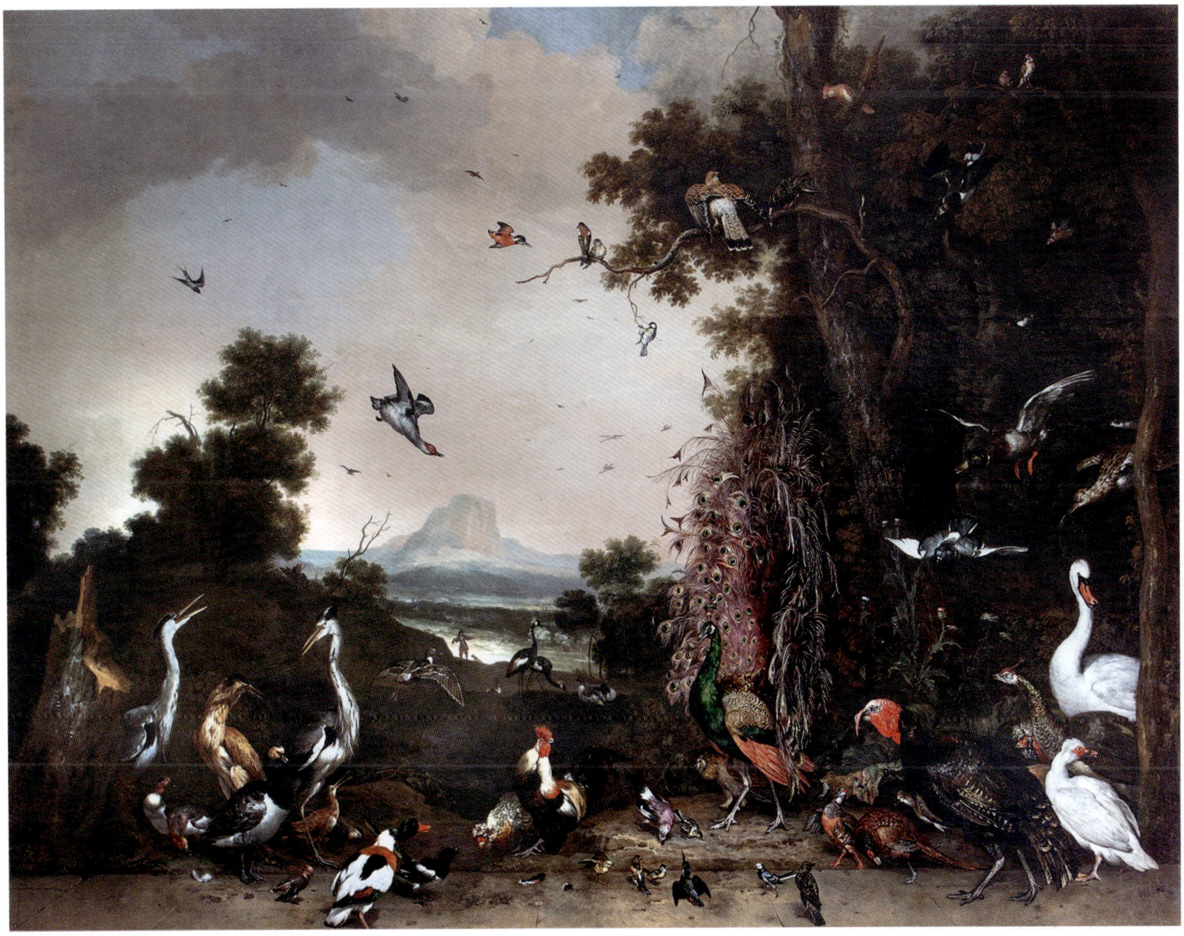

FIG. 5
Melchior d'Hondecoeter (1636–1695)
Open Landscape with Poultry and Waterfowl, *c.*1670–80
Oil on canvas, 362 × 535.9 cm
National Trust, Belton House, Lincolnshire
(NT 436163)

by Colonel William Noel-Hill, 6th Baron Berwick (1802–1882), and a *Classical Landscape* in the style of Melchior's grandfather Gillis Claesz d'Hondecoeter (*c.*1575/80–1638) complete the Dutch pictures at Attingham.[20]

One of the National Trust's exceptional groupings of Dutch pictures is in the dining room at Belton House, Lincolnshire. It is also known as the 'Hondecoeter Room' because it is dominated by three huge canvases by Melchior, 'the supreme specialist in decorative bird paintings' of the Dutch Golden Age.[21] Painted by the artist in the 1670s, the canvases comprise *A View of a Terrace with a Page Descending* and *A View of a Park with Swans and Ducks* (which flank a fireplace surmounted by another bird picture, of a dead swan and a peacock, painted by Jan Weenix, who was Hondecoeter's cousin), and the monumental *Open Landscape with Poultry and Waterfowl* (fig. 5).

It is not known for which house in the Low Countries the Hondecoeters were painted, or indeed if they were originally intended as a set (although a similar set exists in the Alte Pinakothek, Munich).

Their early provenance remains unknown, although they were possibly owned by a G. Crawford of Drumsoy, a Scottish businessman living in Holland, who appears to have sold Dutch and Flemish pictures at Christie's in 1806.[22] In 1867 they were offered for sale by a private owner in a letter sent by Rutley & Son to Lady Marian Alford, the mother of the 2nd and 3rd Earls of Brownlow. It would, however, be another six years before they were bought, for £1,500, from an unnamed vendor, through Christie's, by Adelbert Wellington Brownlow Cust, 3rd Earl Brownlow (1844–1921), the then owner of Belton. By that date the canvases had already been cut down, presumably to fit their previous location. At Belton, between 1876 and 1878, the library on the principal floor was refurbished as a dining room and the canvases were incorporated into the panelling. A fourth picture that was bought as part of the group, and that was hung in an adjoining serving room, depicted Orpheus playing his lyre to a group of animals (now in a private collection in the United States). In 1984 Edward John Peregrine Cust, 7th Baron Brownlow (born 1936) gave Belton, its garden and some of its contents to the National Trust. A grant from the National Heritage Memorial Fund secured further parts of the collection, including the three Hondecoeters.

In the *Open Landscape* canvas we see a large and unlikely grouping of wild and domestic birds appearing at the edge of a forest. A moralising message about the dangers of vanity might have been intended, for Hondecoeter includes a peacock standing proudly with his tail feathers outstretched, who is largely ignored by his fellow birds, while in the background, under a distant mountain, the figure of a hunter approaches.

It was probably Hondecoeter's membership of the artists' society Confrerie Pictura, in The Hague, that brought him to the attention of William III, who commissioned pictures from him to display in his residences at Honselaarsdijk, Soestdijk and Het Loo. These included the artist's most famous bird picture, *The Floating Feather* of *c.*1680 (Rijksmuseum, Amsterdam). The influence of this patronage can be seen in Williamite houses in Great Britain, such as Dyrham, where a number of fine Hondecoeters survive. The British love of animals, and of hunting animals, may also account for the number of Hondecoeters, and pictures by other Golden Age Dutch bird painters, that remain in public and private collections in this country.

Despite the destruction of many country houses in the twentieth century (more than 1,000 country houses have been demolished in England alone since 1900)[23] and the pressures of increased taxation and death duties which have seen the partial or complete dispersal of some collections, there were those who had the means to continue the taste for collecting Dutch pictures into the twentieth century. A particularly fine example of a seventeenth-century self-portrait that was acquired by an important National Trust donor family member is the signed and dated *Self-portrait at the Age of Thirty-two* (fig. 6) by Frans van Mieris the Elder, one of the *fijnschilders* ('fine painters') for which Leiden was famous. It was bought through Agnew's by Margaret Greville (1863–1942) for 700 guineas in 1919. Greville bequeathed Polesden Lacey, Surrey, to the National Trust in 1942, stipulating that 'a Picture

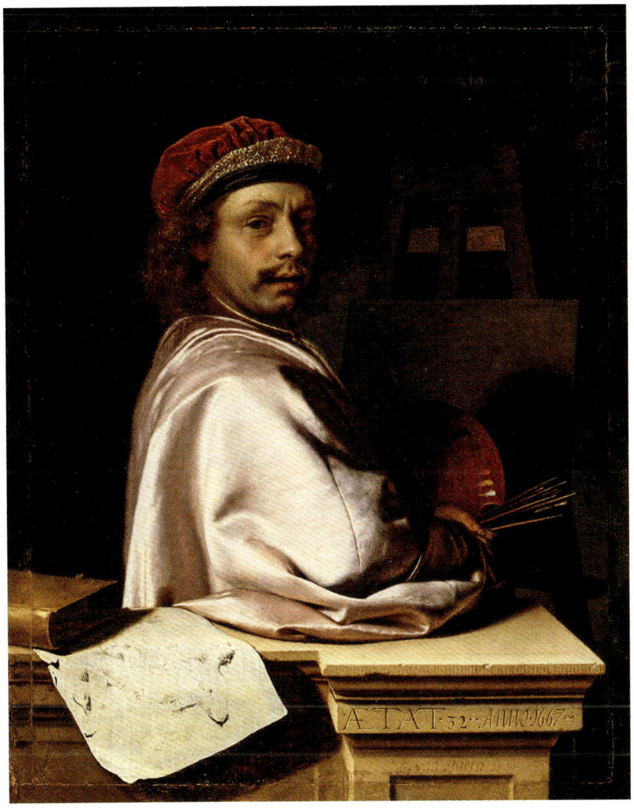

FIG. 6
Frans van Mieris the Elder (1635–1681)
Self-portrait at the Age of Thirty-two, 1667
Oil on panel, 45 × 39 cm
National Trust, Polesden Lacey, Surrey
(NT 1246501)

and Art Gallery' be created there in memory of her father, William McEwan MP (1827–1913). It was the first property that the Trust accepted on the quality of its collection.

McEwan was himself an avid picture collector and he acquired several of the better Dutch works at Polesden Lacey, such as Gerard ter Borch's *Officer Making his Bow to a Lady*, Pieter de Hooch's *Colf Players* (both in the exhibition, cat. nos. 3 and 10) and Adriaen van Ostade's 1668 *Peasants Before a Fire in an Inn*.[24] The Dutch pictures that Greville bought were mostly portraits, such as an *Unknown Boy, Aged Ten* by Willem van der Vliet and an *Unknown Woman* by Isaack Luttichuys, but she also acquired other kinds of pictures, such as Jan van Goyen's 1655 *River Estuary* and Jan van der Heyden's *Church at Maarsen*.[25]

Van Mieris's *Self-portrait* is certainly one of the best pictures acquired by Greville. Dated 1667, it is full of confidence and swagger, despite its small size. The beautifully observed and highly finished depiction of the various materials and the play of light on different surfaces are typical of his work. Dressed in expensive clothes, displaying his success (and therefore his skill) as a painter, Van Mieris shows himself to his viewers (and potential patrons) as 'self-confident and distinguished, at the pinnacle of his fame'.[26] Certainly he painted more self-portraits than any other Dutch artist at the time except for Rembrandt. Turning from his easel to face the viewer, he has his mouth open as if caught in the middle of a conversation with us, and despite his inappropriate clothes he holds his loaded palette and brushes. He leans upon a stone balustrade, with a painted inscription of his age and date as well as his signature. Behind him are a book and piece of paper showing a drawing of a nude figure, alluding to the intellectual approach to painting, and this knowledge is conveyed in his self-assured pose. It is one that derives, via Rembrandt's *Self-portrait at the Age of Thirty-Four*, from Titian's *Man with a Blue Sleeve* (both National Gallery, London) – and probably also relates to Bartholomeus van der Helst's 1654 *Portrait of Paulus Potter* (Mauritshuis), in which again the artist at his easel turns to face the viewer.[27]

One of the finest collections of pictures in the National Trust is at Upton House, Warwickshire. It was bought in 1927 by Walter Samuel, 2nd Viscount Bearsted (1882–1948), who gave the house to the National Trust shortly before his death. Samuel's father Sir Marcus Samuel, 1st Viscount Bearsted (1853–1927), founder of the Shell Transport & Trading Co. Ltd, and the company's chairman until 1921, had an impressive art collection, which included pictures such as Jan van Goyen's 1643 *River Scene*,[28] a characteristically muddy brown panel painting, showing a ferry, carrying cattle, pushing off from a riverbank by a village, while eel fishermen sit in a boat on the water nearby. It was bought, through a third party, from the sale of Sir George Drummond's Canadian collection of important European pictures (sold Christie's, 26 June 1919, lot 179).[29]

Upton was also seen as a suitable venue in which to display the 2nd Lord Bearsted's own, growing collection, as well as offering good hunting, something he was passionate about and which is reflected in the sporting pictures that he bought. He also bought pictures by Stubbs, Devis and Hogarth, amongst others, before turning his attention to Continental pictures, buying from the art dealer Knoedler, and then increasingly from smaller dealers and auction houses, acquiring Italian, Spanish and Netherlandish paintings and Golden Age Dutch pictures.[30] Amongst the finest of his Dutch pictures are the works in this exhibition – Jan Lievens's *Magus at a Table*, Pieter Jansz Saenredam's *Interior of the Church of St Catherine, Utrecht*, Jan Steen's *Tired Traveller* and Gabriel Metsu's *Duet* (cat. nos. 14, 19, 20 and 15).[31] While we are unsure when exactly some of the Dutch pictures came into the collection at Upton – such as Philips Wouwerman's *Landscape with Dunes and Figures*, showing dogs greeting travellers on a stormy day outside a cottage and a ramshackle shelter[32] – other works demonstrate how Bearsted bought his Dutch pictures.

Melchior d'Hondecoeter's 1672 *Cock Turkey and Other Birds in a Garden*,[33] for example, which had previously been in the collection of Henry Labouchere, 1st Baron Taunton (1798–1869), was sold by his grandson E.A.V. Stanley (1879–1941) and bought by Lord Bearsted from Knoedler in July 1920, for £1,250. Or Jan Steen's four panels of the senses (*The Sense of Hearing*, *Sense of Sight*, *Sense of Smell* and *Sense of Taste*),[34] all scenes of single peasants sitting next to tables – a complete set of five when they were apparently sold in Amsterdam in 1695, but reduced to four when they were sold at Sotheby's on 3 November 1926 (lot 107), having apparently been owned by Prince Leopold – were bought for Upton from the dealer Jacques Goudstikker in Amsterdam in 1928.[35]

Jacob van Ruisdael's magnificent landscape '*Le coup de soleil*' shows a village in the tree-covered sand dunes of Overveen in north Holland, complete with cottages, windmill, church tower and a ruined castle.[36] In the middle distance the flat fields are momentarily illuminated by sunlight breaking through rainclouds. At least two thirds of the canvas is made up of sky and a huge, shifting cloudscape (an example of so-called 'Dutch mountains', which was a speciality of Ruisdael's), while the distant horizon is punctuated by the Groote Kerk in Haarlem, the subject (both its exterior and its interior) of so many seventeenth-century Dutch pictures. The picture had been in the collection of Count Charles de Mornay (1803–1878), from which it was sold (Philips, 20 June 1848, lot 39) and bought by Sir George Holford (1860–1926), the son of the great art collector Robert Stayner Holford and inheritor of Westonbirt House in Gloucestershire and Dorchester House in Park Lane, London – who also owned Aelbert Cuyp's *View of Dordrecht* (cat. 5). In the

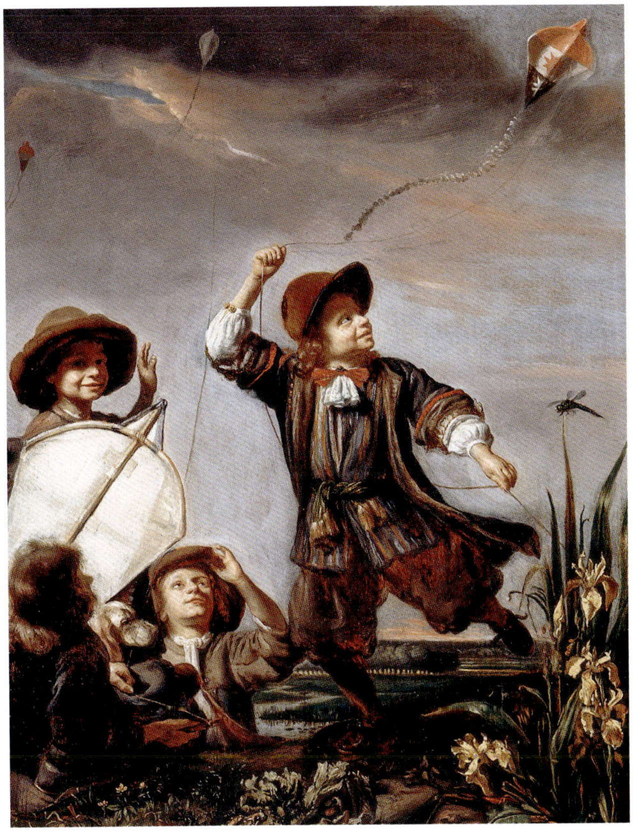

FIG. 7
Probably by Justus de Gelder (1650–1707)
Boys Flying Kites, *c.*1670–75
Oil on panel, 44.4 × 34.3 cm
National Trust, Upton House, Warwickshire (NT 446734)

1928 sale of Holford's important collection the picture was bought by Knoedler on behalf of Lord Bearsted (Christie's, 17 May 1928, lot 400) for £6,930.

One of the pictures bought for Lord Bearsted from an auction house by a third party, in this case from Christie's (15 May 1936, lot 99) by Sir Alec Martin, the fine art auctioneer and chairman of the National Art Collections Fund, was Adriaen van der Venne's 1633 grisaille panel *Peasants Dancing*, in which we see a group of men and women trapped in a seemingly endless dance, a nearby barrel and an overturned flagon alluding to the source of their woes.[37]

The attribution of a charming picture of *Boys Flying Kites* (fig. 7) has long been a matter of debate.[38] Amongst the group playing with their kites in front of a distant polder landscape is a fashionably dressed boy, who, running in the centre of the composition, looks up at his toy, which appears to be decorated with (indecipherable) family arms.[39] It is currently thought to have been painted by Godfried Schalcken, although it was sold to Lord Bearsted as by Nicolaes Maes. Schalcken's signed 1670 *Boy Fishing in a Landscape* (Gemäldegalerie, Berlin) is very similar to the Upton picture, including the yellow flag irises in the foreground (that have butterflies resting on the flowers in the same way that the Upton picture has a dragonfly perching on the tallest leaf).[40] Another picture that is particularly similar in style and mood is the canvas *Children Bathing* in the Louvre, currently attributed to a follower of Maes, but incorporating the remnant of a signature that starts with an 'S',[41] and one more is *The Pancake Maker*, in the Museum of Fine Arts, Boston, previously also thought to be by a follower of Maes, but now attributed to Justus de Gelder.[42] Alastair Laing has posited that the Upton *Boys Flying Kites*, along with the Louvre and Boston pictures, form a group that represent Schalcken's 'earliest manner, after he had been taught by [Samuel van] Hoogstraten, but before he had come under the influence of [Gerrit] Dou and his *fijnschilderij*', with the Berlin picture being produced slightly later.[43] However, León Krempel suggests De Gelder as the most likely artist responsible for the Upton picture.[43a]

The earliest provenance for this picture is the collection of Jean-Gilles-Marie-Joseph Schamp d'Averschoot (1765–1839), and it first arrived in London after being bought from the sale of his collection in Ghent on 14 September 1840 (lot 116) following his death. It was in the collections of the 1st and 2nd Lords Aldenham, and following the death of the latter it was bought by the London dealers Pawsey & Payne, on

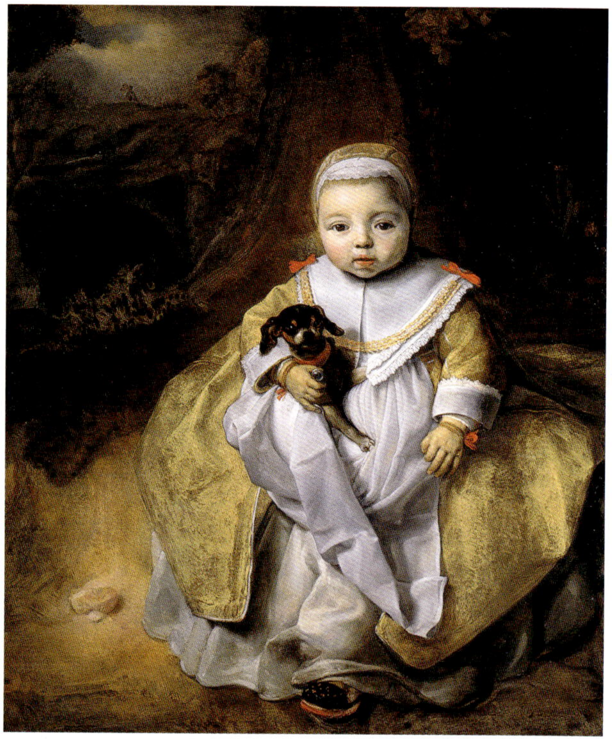

FIG. 8
Attributed to Govaert Flinck (1615–1660)
A Child holding a Dog, *c.*1640–42
Oil on canvas, 91.4 × 75.5 cm
National Trust, Upton House, Warwickshire (NT 446720)

behalf of Lord Bearsted, at Sotheby's on 24 February 1937 (lot 15), as by Nicolaes Maes.

A Rembrandtesque portrait of an *Unknown Woman*,[44] currently attributed to Rembrandt's pupil Isaac de Jouderville, was thought to be autograph (a painted Rembrandt 'RHL' monogram – 'Rembrandt, son of Harmen, from Leiden' – had been added on the middle right of the panel) when Lord Bearsted bought it for 900 guineas from the sale of works owned by Sir Berkeley Sheffield, Bt (1876–1946) of Normanby Park in Lincolnshire (Christie's, 16 July 1943, lot 108).[45]

One of the most charming portraits of a child in the National Trust's collections is a picture at Upton whose authorship, despite its quality, remains a matter for debate. The image, of *A Child Holding a Dog* (fig. 8),[46] shows a toddler sitting on a bank under a tree, wearing a fine yellow coat with a white collar, apron and skirts, and a lace cap.[47] The child holds a tiny dog under its right arm, whose red collar, with a bell, matches the ribbon bows on the costume. It was painted *c.*1640–42, and is currently attributed to Govaert Flinck, who had been a pupil of Rembrandt's in Amsterdam, although it has also been considered to be by Jacob Gerritsz Cuyp, the father of Aelbert Cuyp. Some art historians now believe the author to be Aelbert Cuyp himself, whose authorship had been suggested in the past and indeed when the picture was last sold, in 1947, to Lord Bearsted.[48] It was previously in the collection of Edward Law, 1st Earl of Ellenborough (1790–1871) at Southam Delabere in Gloucestershire, then it descended through the family until it was sold at Sotheby's (11 June 1947, lot 39), where it was bought by the fine art dealers Leggatt, who in turn sold it to Lord Bearsted.

Another example of twentieth-century patronage, at Dudmaston, Shropshire, a property that came to the National Trust in 1978, is one of a particularly interesting collection that, as well as historical pictures, includes important modern art, such as a group of mid-twentieth-century dissident works from Francoist Spain, assembled by the then owner Sir George Labouchere (1905–1999) during his time on diplomatic service. Amongst the other, more traditional pictures is a collection of flower paintings that includes Rachel Ruysch's *Still Life with Fruit, Bird's Nest and Insects* (fig. 9).[49] It was painted by the Amsterdam artist Ruysch in either 1710 or 1716 – the last numeral of the date on the canvas is indecipherable – and shows a typical composition of flowers and fruit placed at the bottom of an architectural detail, including details such as rotting fruit and a lizard raiding an egg from a bird's nest (although this was painted in the early

FIG. 9
Rachel Ruysch (1664–1750)
Still Life with Fruit, Bird's Nest and Insects,
1710 or 1716
Oil on canvas, 76.2 × 57.1 cm
National Trust, Dudmaston, Shropshire
(NT 814164)

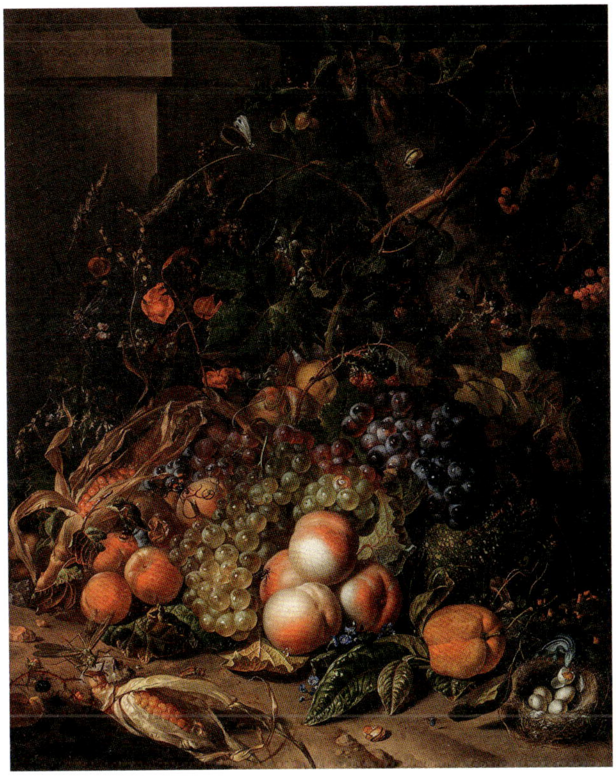

eighteenth century, Ruysch was selling pictures from the early 1680s, and so she should still be seen as a Golden Age flower painter).

Ruysch had trained with the still-life painter Willem van Aelst and she was celebrated for her attention to the depiction of light falling on colourful profusions of fruit and flowers. She was the first female member of the Confrerie Pictura in The Hague, an academic club formed in 1656 by a number of artists who were dissatisfied with the organisation of the Guild of St Luke in that city. In many ways her choice of career was unsurprising: her maternal grandfather was the architect and painter Pieter Post, and her father Frederik Ruysch (1638–1731) was a famous anatomist and botanist, and professor at Amsterdam's botanic gardens, the Hortus Botanicus.

The picture was previously in the collection of Francis Darby (1783–1850) of Sunnyside, Coalbrookdale, one of the Quaker family of ironmasters who played a prominent role in the Industrial Revolution. His great-great-granddaughter Rachel Hamilton-Russel, Lady Labouchere (1908–1996), who rather aptly trained as a botanical artist, transferred the house and estate to the National Trust in 1978, and continued to live there until her death.

Dutch pictures lost from its houses have also been 'repatriated' by the National Trust in recent years. These may have been purchased by private treaty sale or at auction or have been allocated through the government's Acceptance in Lieu scheme by which nationally significant works of art can be transferred into public ownership in lieu of inheritance tax. There is a sense of poignancy when a painting returns to its natural home and it adds to the excitement of being able to rearrange a historical hang – just as when a picture is reattributed or the sitter in a portrait is identified. Both help us to understand our collection better and reinterpret it in a meaningful way. An example of this kind was the purchase of Cornelis de Heem's spectacular late 1680s *Still Life of Flowers and Fruit Arranged on a Stone Plinth in a Garden* (cat. 7),[50] probably bought by William Blathwayt in the 1690s and by 1703 likely hanging in 'The Greate Roome above the Stairs'. It stayed in the Blathwayt family until it was sold in 1956, then bought back by the Trust in 2015.[51]

Some pictures have instead come into the collections as gifts. The Rembrandt *Self-portrait* (cat. 18) that came in 2010 was part of the provision of the will of Edna Nedis, Lady Samuel of Wych Cross, who generously left three pictures to the National Trust. The government's Cultural Gifts Scheme provides another route. It allows for nationally important works to be donated

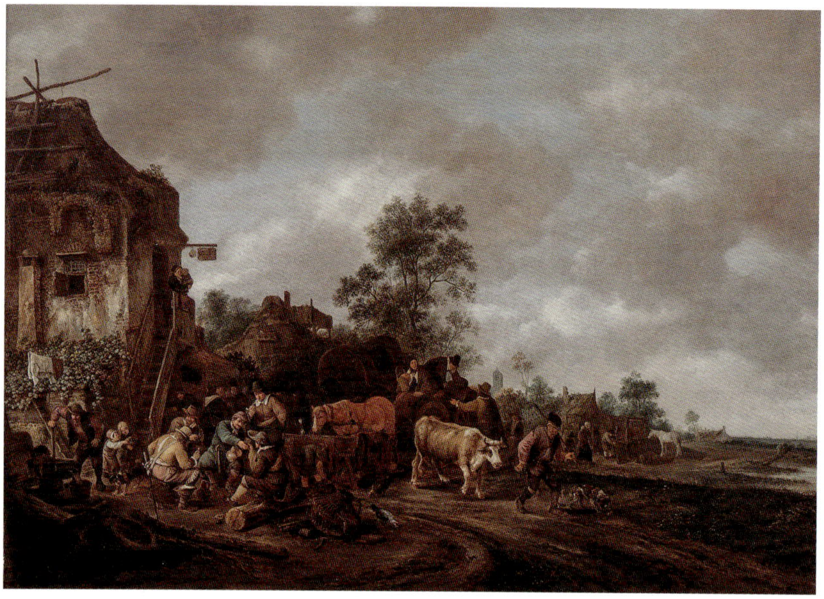

FIG. 10
Isack van Ostade (1621–1649)
Figures outside an Inn, 1647
Oil on canvas, 103 × 142 cm
National Trust, Waddesdon, Buckinghamshire
(Accepted under the Cultural Gifts Scheme by HM Government and allocated to the National Trust, 2016; acc. no. 259)

to the nation in return for a tax reduction based on a percentage of the value of the object. A recent Dutch addition to the collection that was generously gifted by the present Lord Rothschild using that mechanism is Isack van Ostade's 1647 painting *Figures outside an Inn* (fig. 10).[52] Isack, who trained under his brother the genre painter Adriaen van Ostade, is best known for his landscapes (in particular for winter scenes), such as the present picture of figures and animals that have stopped outside a country inn. This late painting from the artist's short career is one of his finest works. It was in a succession of French collections from the late eighteenth century, until bought by Frederick Perkins, the head of the Barclay, Perkins & Co. brewery, in the mid-nineteenth century. It was displayed in the Morning Room at Waddesdon in the late nineteenth century, and it is listed in Baron Ferdinand de Rothschild's privately printed *Red Book* (1897).[53]

Dutch pictures continue to be added to the National Trust's collection, including works of the quality of the above-mentioned De Heem and Van Ostade, which are worthy of a national picture collection, and which serve to emphasise that the Dutch paintings the National Trust cares for, for all our various audiences, can be living, changeable things. They allow us the same sense of excitement and wonder as must have been felt by the first Golden Age collectors, by their successors who pursued them in the sale rooms, and by the many visitors who have gazed upon them down through the centuries since.

NOTES

1 Judson and Ekkart 1999, p. 303, no. 435.
2 A second version of Lely's portrait of Sir Ralph Bankes is in the collection of the Yale Center for British Art, New Haven (B1978.22), which includes a dog with *Sr RB* inscribed on its collar.
3 The group of Lely portraits at Kingston Lacy comprises seven autograph works, three copies of autograph works, and one picture painted in his studio.
4 See Laing 1993, p. 123, no. 13.
5 Foster 1889, p. 277.
6 NT 1257090.
7 RCIN 404653.
8 NT 453733.
9 McCabe 2015, p. 156.
10 NT 453771.
11 Walpole 1849, II, p. 616.
12 See Ingamells 2009, p. 332, listed under 1692.
13 Beherman 1988, pp. 183–84, no. 84.
14 NT 609007.
15 Compiled under Richard Noel-Hill, 4th Baron Berwick (1774–1848).
16 NT 608973.
17 NT 608996.
18 NT 609013.
19 NT 609075.
20 NT 609079.
21 Rikken 2008, p. 38.
22 See Laing 1991, pp. 172–73.
23 Worsley 2002, p. 7.
24 NT 124691, NT 1246485 and NT 1246490.
25 NT 1246489, NT 1246483, NT 1246496 and NT 1246495.
26 Buvelot 2005, p. 181.
27 See Naumann 1981, I, p. 71; Laing 1995, p. 186, no. 68; Van Suchtelen 2015, p. 96, no. 17.
28 NT 446722.
29 Beck 1972, p. 232, no. 492.
30 Amongst the highlights of the non-Dutch Continental works bought by Lord Bearsted are *The Adoration of the Magi* by Jheronimus Bosch (and workshop), Gerard David's *Madonna and Child with Two Music-Making Angels*, Jan Provost's *The Nativity at Night*, El Greco's *El Espolio*, Pieter Bruegel the Elder's grisaille *The Death of Virgin* and Hans Holbein the Younger's miniature *A Young Man with a Pink*.
31 NT 446728, NT 446733, NT 446735 and NT 446725.
32 NT 446741.
33 NT 446719.
34 NT 446736, NT 446739, NT 446738 and NT 446737.
35 Van Westrheene 1856, p. 156, no. 437; De Groot 1907–28, I, nos. 104–08.
36 NT 446731.
37 NT 446740.
38 NT 446734.
39 Fila and Dekker 2013, pp. 76 and 82.
40 Gemäldegalerie, Staatliche Museen zu Berlin, inv. 837.
41 Musée du Louvre, Paris, RF 2132; see Laing 1995, p. 188, no. 69.
42 Museum of Fine Arts, Boston, inv. 57.199.
43 Laing 1995, p. 188, no. 69.
43a Krempel 1999, p. 367, no. F6.
44 NT 446730. It was bought by someone named 'Betts', who was probably an agent working for Lord Bearsted, or even Lord Bearsted himself.
45 Anon. 1944, pp. 62–63; Van Gelder 1953, p. 37.
46 NT 446720.
47 See Wenley et al. 2015, p. 8, no. 7.
48 The author thanks Robert Wenley, Deputy Director at the Barber Institute of Fine Arts, University of Birmingham, for this information.
49 NT 814164.
50 NT 2900107.
51 It was sold at Sotheby's, 29 February 1956 (lot 44), and acquired by the National Trust in 2015, with funds from the National Heritage Memorial Fund, the Mr and Mrs Kenneth Levy bequest, the Art Fund, a fund set up by the late Hon. Simon Sainsbury, the Royal Oak Foundation and a private donation.
52 NT 259.
53 Rothschild 1897, pp. 50–51.

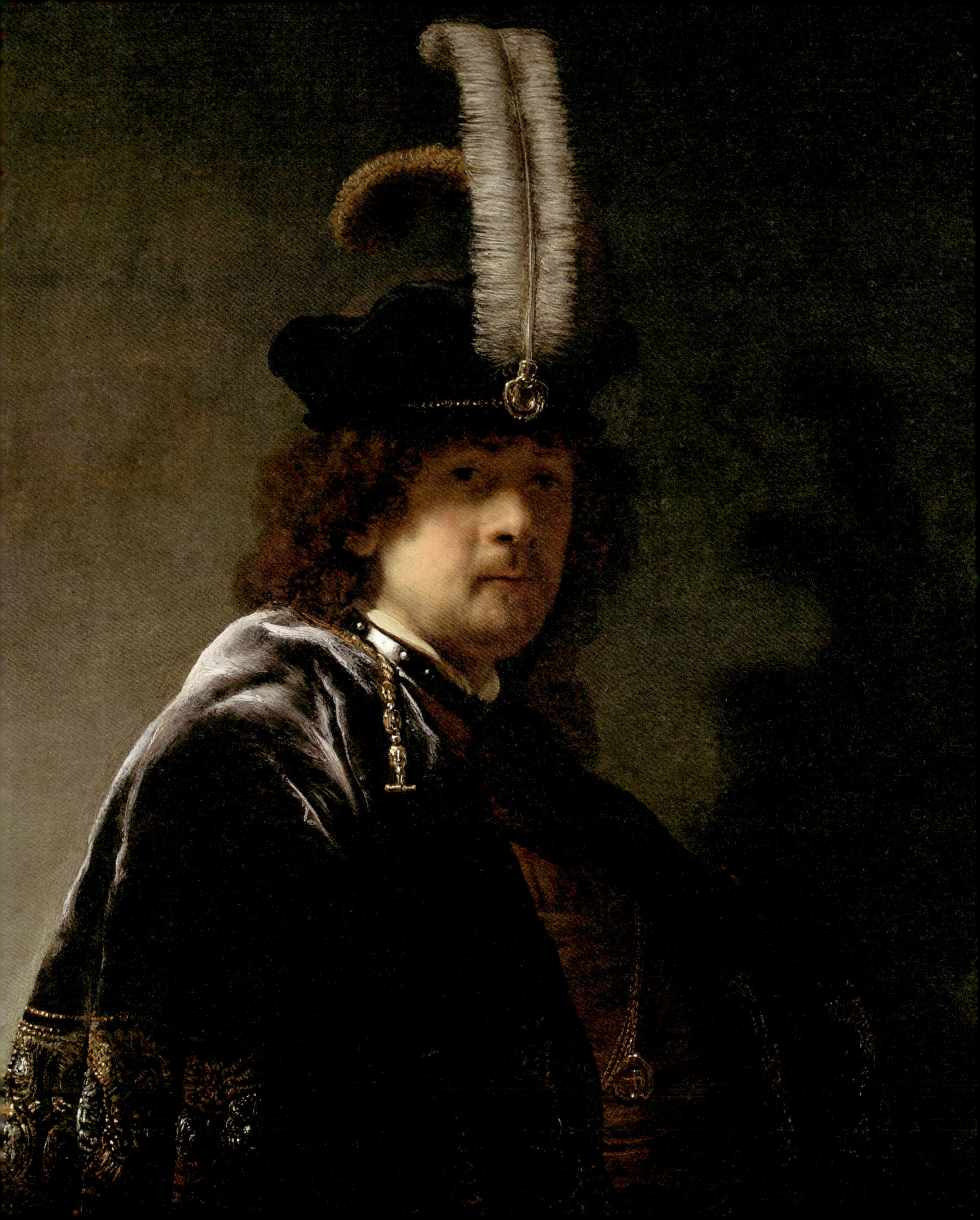

Ambassadors for the Netherlands
Seventeenth-century Dutch Paintings in England

QUENTIN BUVELOT

The presence of so many seventeenth-century Dutch paintings in England is not simply explained by the great passion for collecting evinced by the British in centuries past,[1] it is also the result of direct patronage, a fact often overlooked on the European continent. For a long time, England had to rely on artists from the Low Countries, who were initially employed almost exclusively to meet the great demand for portraits from members of the royal family and the aristocracy. The ties between England and the Republic of the Seven United Provinces, roughly the present-day Netherlands, date from the sixteenth century. It was a significant moment when in 1585 Queen Elizabeth I expressed her support for the revolt of the Northern Netherlands against the Spanish occupation at the Treaty of Nonsuch, because 'one [country] cannot well live without friendship of the other', as the queen's advisors told her – advice that still resonates today.[2] Even before this important moment in the relations between the two countries, Dutch artists were working in England, among them the renowned history and portrait painter Cornelis Ketel of Gouda, who for financial reasons worked in London for several years from 1573 onwards; in 1581 he settled in Amsterdam because he did not want to confine himself solely to portraiture.[3]

Although the focus in this essay is almost exclusively on paintings by seventeenth-century artists whose roots lay in the Dutch Republic, in England at that time virtually no distinction was made between artists from the Northern or Southern Netherlands (roughly present-day Belgium or 'Flanders'), who came from neighbouring regions speaking the same language. In the absence of good home-grown artists, many commissions in the seventeenth century were given to artists from the Continent, including several Dutch artists who lived in England for varying lengths of time. Most of these 'Dutch' paintings made in England, of wildly differing quality, have never left the country where they were painted.

The Dutch Golden Age

It was in the seventeenth century that the Dutch Republic enjoyed an immense explosion in painting talent in a relatively short space of time,[4] a phenomenon never since repeated in Europe. Rembrandt heads the field as the most versatile and influential painter (cat. 18); his work is characterised by unsurpassed technique and reveals a profound psychological insight. He was rivalled, however, by extraordinarily talented and productive artists like the portrait painter Frans Hals, born to an Antwerp family who moved to Haarlem when he was a small child, and whose inimitable swift, assured brushstroke brought him great fame. Then there were the painter of landscape and animals Paulus Potter (see fig. 24), the genre and history painter Jan Steen (see cat. 20) and last but not least the now universally acclaimed Johannes Vermeer, who concentrated in his relatively small oeuvre on scenes from everyday life (see fig. 22).

Detail of cat. 18 (Rembrandt, *Self-portrait*)

As far as we know, none of these painters, so celebrated in the Republic, ever set foot in England.

In a situation not dissimilar to that in England after King Henry VIII had proclaimed himself head of the Church in 1534, Protestantism in the Republic, too, had put an end to the Church's role in commissioning altarpieces and other painted decorations.[5] What was unusual in the Republic was the gradual emergence of a large group of new buyers – citizens who became very wealthy as the country's economy boomed. People of relatively modest means could afford paintings – something that constantly amazed foreign visitors, including the English.[6] Huge numbers of paintings were made in the Republic, almost all for the open market, save for portraits, and never before were so many of those created as in the Dutch Golden Age (see cat. nos. 1, 9, 11).[7] They were notable for their realism and immense variety; as well as individual portraits there were many double portraits, family portraits, children's portraits and group portraits (see fig. 100), including the specifically Dutch genre of paintings of members of the civic guard or the administrators of charitable and correctional institutions. The quality of all these different types of portraits is almost without exception remarkably high, something that can generally be said about most seventeenth-century Dutch paintings.

Dutch painters of the Golden Age typically looked for their subjects close to home, in their own surroundings. They found new ideas in the landscape around them – possibly the most popular subject of the period. Painters pictured literally every aspect of the Dutch landscape – the rivers and woodlands (cat. 8), the sea and the seashore, the towns and cities and the buildings in them (cat. 5). Some travelled to Italy to study the work of their predecessors and incorporated the hills and the warm sunlight they found there into their paintings (cat. 16). Others went even further afield, among them Frans Post, whose South American landscapes gave him a unique selling point (cat. 17). Churches were depicted inside and out by painters like Pieter Saenredam (cat. 19). Other favourite subjects were still lifes of flowers and other products of nature. Lavish displays of food were popular, and these, along with countless other motifs, were painted in a manner that suggested the artist had simply chanced across them (cat. nos. 4, 7). There were also genre works reflecting everyday life, often with recognisable anecdotes put across with humour and an eye for detail, and sometimes with a hidden meaning that conveyed a warning message (cat. nos. 3, 10, 15, 20). These are scenes of people going about their day-to-day affairs, from peasants in inns and mothers and children in an intimate setting to elegant gatherings paying court to one another in well-appointed interiors. Traditional subjects based on Bible stories and classical mythology, which required considerable knowledge and a lively imagination on the part of the artist, also featured (cat. nos. 2, 14). Sometimes commissioned for one of their palaces by the Princes of Orange and their families, or by an institution for a public building, they were, however, greatly outnumbered by other kinds of subjects.

Beyond the Dutch borders

For various reasons Dutch artists sought to make their living abroad.[8] Some felt the effects of increasing competition in the Republic, where more and more artists were offering good, affordable paintings; others were simply looking for a new challenge. Any investigation of the presence of Dutch artists on English soil rapidly arrives at the English royal house, since many Dutch artists supplied paintings to the court, some specially commissioned. In 1618 the eminent diplomat Constantijn Huygens (1596–1687) visited Whitehall Palace in London, where he looked at paintings collected by the late Crown Prince Henry, Prince of Wales (1594–1612), who despite his youth had begun to collect on a serious basis. His mark is found on paintings by Dutch artists like Hendrick Goltzius of Haarlem, Michiel van Mierevelt of Delft – an internationally renowned 'famous master' who had been the subject of fruitless efforts to lure him to London – Jan Porcellis of Rotterdam and Hendrick Vroom of Haarlem.[9] The two paintings by Vroom came into the Prince of Wales's possession in 1610, as part of a gift from the Dutch States General, which was hoping for recognition of the still young Republic by the prince, 'whose friendship is needed by this country'.[10] Until 1672, the works by Porcellis and Vroom were the only seascapes in the royal collection, but in that year Willem van de Velde and his son came to London, an event that will be discussed in more detail later.[11] The Prince of Wales's entire collection of paintings was inherited by his brother, Charles I (1600–1649), who would emerge as one of the greatest patrons and collectors of art that England has ever known, acquiring many old and contemporary paintings of the highest quality.[12] Italian art unmistakably predominated in his collection, along with the peerless portraits of Charles and his family that the king commissioned from the brilliant Sir Anthony van Dyck from Antwerp, but he was certainly also interested in what Dutch painters had to offer. Among the king's most important advisors on Dutch art were George Villiers, Duke of Buckingham (1592–1628), who died young; Sir Dudley Carleton (1573–1632), the English ambassador to the Republic from 1616 to 1628 and a major intermediary between the English court and Dutch painters; and the courtier Thomas Howard, Earl of Arundel (1586–1646), who like Carleton had visited the Dutch Republic and himself amassed a huge art collection in which Dutch art was also represented.[13]

From the start of his reign in 1625, Dutch artists travelled to London to supply paintings to Charles I, among them Hendrick Pot of Haarlem, whose small portraits must have appealed to the king.[14] Large portraits were supplied by the talented Daniel Mijtens of The Hague, a pupil of Van Mierevelt's who had been a protégé of the Earl of Arundel and had worked for King James I (1566–1625) since 1618. Until the arrival of Van Dyck in 1632, Mijtens was the leading portraitist at the court of Charles I; he returned to The Hague in 1634.[15] Another portrait painter from The Hague, Adriaen Hanneman, probably worked as an assistant to both Mijtens and Van Dyck in London. When he returned to the Republic in 1638, he enjoyed great success with his international style.[16]

The work of architectural painters, such as Gerrit Houckgeest of The Hague, was remarkably popular at

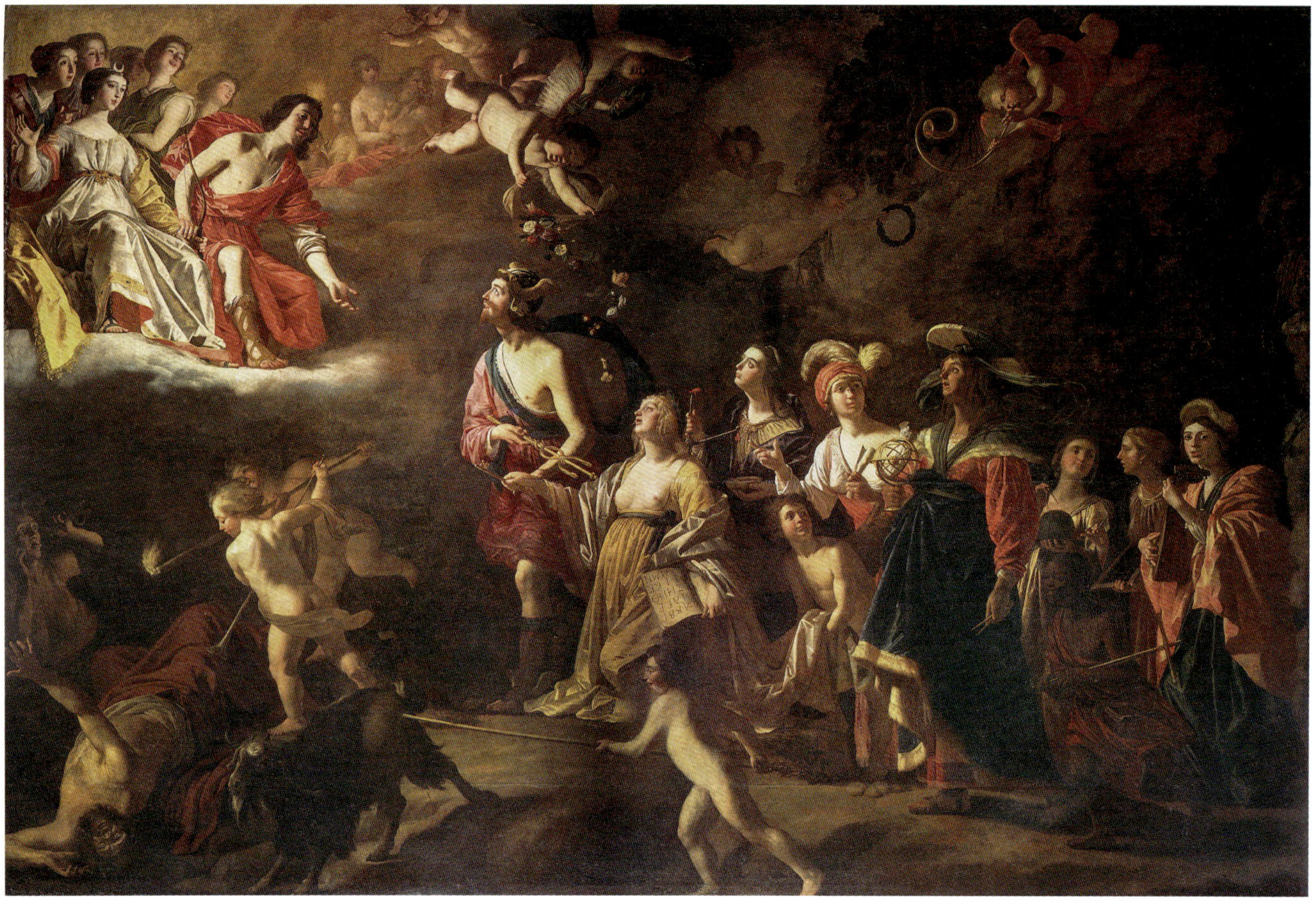

FIG. 11
Gerrit van Honthorst (1592–1656)
Apollo and Diana, 1628
Oil on canvas, 357 × 640 cm
Hampton Court Palace,
Royal Collection Trust (RCIN 405746)

the English court. If Houckgeest was ever in London, there is no record of his presence,[17] but the king owned at least four of his paintings, all described as 'Prosspective'.[18] One particularly interesting work is a perspective by Houckgeest to which Cornelius Johnson, who will be discussed later, added the portrait of Queen Henrietta Maria (1609–1669); this panel bears Charles I's mark.[19] Another panel by Houckgeest, probably dating from the 1630s, which also bears the king's mark, is still in the Royal Collection.[20] Hendrick van Steenwijck II also supplied the 'perspectives' of which the king was so fond. Although Steenwijck was born in Antwerp, after his time in London in the period 1617–37 he worked in The Hague and Leiden, on the basis of which he is also regarded as a Dutch artist.

The king was also fond of the work of artists from Utrecht. He bought work by the landscape painter Cornelis van Poelenburch, who with some interruptions lived and worked in London between 1637 and 1641, in a house for which the rent was paid by the king, who had personally invited the artist to come to England in 1637 (see p. 141).[21] Van Poelenburch's idyllic landscapes inspired by the Italian light were highly sought after in England, and their popularity

FIG. 12
Gerrit van Honthorst (1592–1656)
King Charles I with a Letter, 1628
Oil on canvas, 76 × 64 cm
London, National Portrait Gallery, acquired with help from the Art Fund, 1965 (NPG 4444)

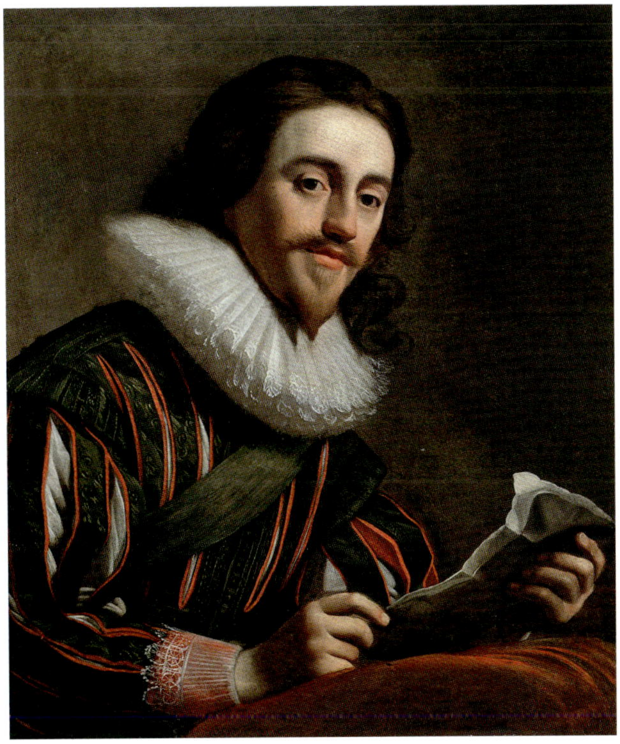

continued after he returned to the Republic for good in 1641 (cat. 16). It is perhaps difficult for us to imagine, but landscapes like these must have made a great impression in England. Earlier in the seventeenth century, probably in the late 1620s, the English artist and author Edward Norgate (1581–1650) had credited the Dutch with the invention of the landscape ('landskip'), 'an art soe new in England, and soe Lately come a shore, as all the language within our fower seas cannot find it a Name, but a borrowed one, and that from ... the Dutch'.[22] Through his agents and possibly on Carleton's advice, Charles I bought several paintings by Utrecht artists, including Hendrick ter Brugghen's 1625 *Laughing Bravo with a Bass Viol and a Glass* and Paulus Moreelse's *Shepherdess* of 1628.[23] And it was in that year, at the king's request, that the Utrecht-born artist Gerrit van Honthorst came to London, where he completed *Apollo and Diana*, an enormous history painting measuring nearly 3.6 × 6.4 m (12 by 21 feet) with *portraits historiés* of the king and queen. It is a sort of homage to the artistic patronage of Charles I, with the Duke of Buckingham in the guise of Mercury introducing the seven Liberal Arts to the royal couple (fig. 11).[24] Van Honthorst also made individual portraits of the English royals, among them a very informal and utterly charming portrait of the king himself, looking up at us from a letter in his hands (fig. 12).[25] Had he wished, it seems, Van Honthorst could have continued to work at court for a very generous salary, but he returned to the Republic, where he had an extremely successful career. He was awarded numerous commissions by Stadholder Frederick Henry of Orange (1584–1647) and his wife, Amalia of Solms-Braunfels (1602–1675), who introduced an international court style in The Hague in 1625 and built up a large art collection. In 1641 their son William II (1626–1650), then still Prince of Orange, married the Princess Royal, Mary Henrietta Stuart (1631–1660), the eldest daughter of Charles I, tightening the ties between England and the Republic still further, although the prince died young. Van Honthorst also worked for Elizabeth Stuart (1596–1662), Charles I's sister, who lived in exile in The Hague after her husband Frederick V, Elector Palatine (1596–1632), was deposed as King of Bohemia and banished in 1620 (see cat. 9).

The Amsterdam painter Johannes Torrentius was a particularly unusual case. In 1627, after a succession of prosecutions, this incorrigible womaniser was sentenced to twenty years' imprisonment in Haarlem for his godlessness and blasphemy, but a few years later he was granted a pardon after Charles I wrote a personal request to Stadholder Frederick Henry. Through the intermediary of former ambassador

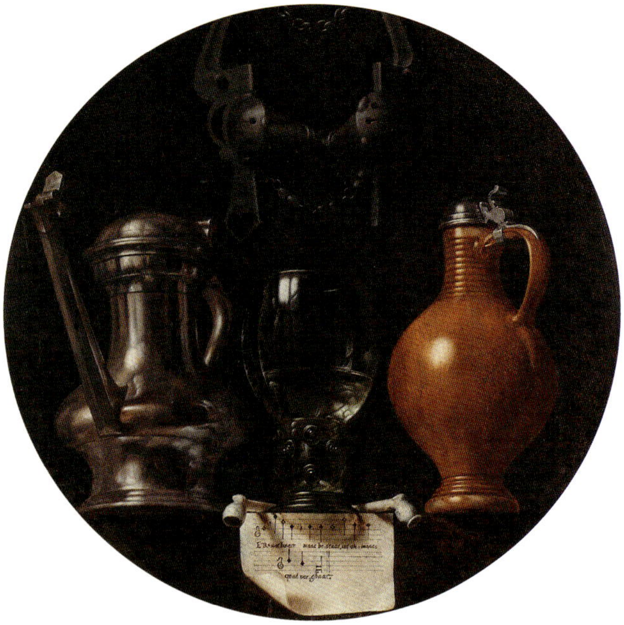

FIG. 13
Johannes Torrentius (1589–1644)
Emblematic Still Life with Flagon, Glass, Jug and Bridle, 1614
Oil on round panel, 51 cm diam.
Amsterdam, Rijksmuseum (SK-A-2813; originally in the collection of Charles I)

Carleton, in late 1630 Torrentius was permitted to travel to London, where he was appointed court painter and would work until 1642. There is documentary evidence that he painted still lifes and nude scenes, but none of these works is known today with the exception of a painting in the Rijksmuseum, *Emblematic Still Life with Flagon, Glass, Jug and Bridle*, signed and dated 1614 (fig. 13).[26] The highly illusionistic, true-to-life character of this extraordinary still life, an allegory of moderation, was much admired at court. The panel, described in the royal collection as 'a round peece w[i]th potts and glasses', still bears Charles I's mark.[27] We do not know when it entered the king's collection, in which there were at least two other works by the artist, one of them already acquired through Carleton before 1630.[28]

It is perhaps no coincidence that the first Surveyor of the King's Pictures was a Dutchman, Abraham van der Doort, whose leather-bound inventory of the royal collection of *c.*1639 (the first of its kind) remains a unique source of information in the study of the paintings owned by the king.[29] For instance, Van der Doort describes at length the first Rembrandts in England, paintings given to Charles I by a member of the royal household, Sir Robert Kerr (1578–1654), before he was made 1st Earl of Ancram in 1633.[30] Kerr had probably acquired the two paintings from Rembrandt after an introduction by Huygens, whom he had met in 1629 while he was on a diplomatic mission in the Republic. *Study of an Old Woman* (fig. 14) was sold during the Commonwealth – a fate that befell nearly all Charles I's paintings after his execution in 1649 – but it was returned to the collection during the Restoration.[31] A Rembrandt *Self-portrait* that was also sold during the Commonwealth and subsequently went missing can be identified as a painting in the Walker Art Gallery in Liverpool.[32] Rembrandt was a celebrated artist, but as far as we know he never left the Republic,[33] not even to cross the Channel, something Jan Lievens, who had shared a studio in Leiden with Rembrandt in his youth, did do (cat. nos. 13, 14). He was probably acting on the advice of Elizabeth Stuart, for whom he had worked, or Huygens, a pivotal figure on the Dutch art scene. Lievens was out of luck, however, for less than a month after his arrival in London Van Dyck established himself in the city as court painter to the king, and he had to revise his ambitions. Lievens nevertheless managed to gain admittance to court circles, for he made portraits of the king and his family, paintings that are no longer known. In 1635 the artist left England and went – of all places – to Antwerp, the birthplace of Van Dyck.[34]

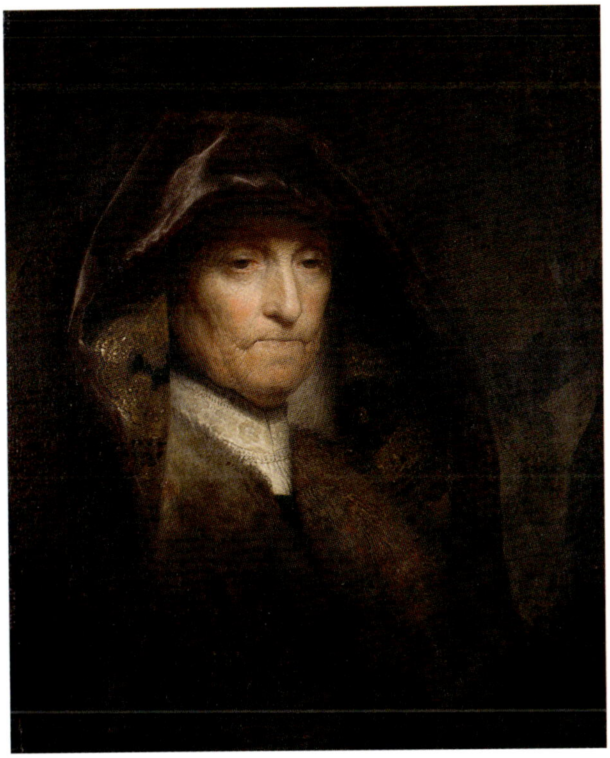

FIG. 14
Rembrandt van Rijn (1606–1669)
Study of an Old Woman, c.1629–30
Oil on panel, 61 × 48 cm
Royal Collection Trust
(RCIN 405000)

After the Restoration

At the outbreak of the Civil War in England in 1642, when many people fled the country, the royal collection was the largest group of Dutch paintings outside the Republic.[35] In 1660, after the interregnum, Charles II (1630–1685) was restored to the throne. During his nine years in exile on the Continent he had acquired paintings, among them 71 primarily Dutch and Flemish works in April 1660; two years later they were paid for and shipped to London.[36] They included the Mannerist *Marriage of Cupid and Psyche* by the Utrecht artist Abraham Bloemaert (see cat. 2), painted at the end of the sixteenth century at the dawn of the Dutch Golden Age.[37] During his stay in the Republic, many portraits of the prince and his entourage were painted by Dutch artists, but it seems that few of these went back with him to England.[38] The prince's return to England became a popular subject for a number of Dutch artists, who painted his departure from the Continent at Scheveningen (fig. 15).[39]

As soon as Charles II arrived in London, he appealed for the return of his father's paintings, including those by Dutch artists, and the response was broadly good.[40] Because the king was chiefly interested in French and Italian art, Dutch paintings were acquired only incidentally, although it is hard to establish this precisely in the absence of detailed inventories.[41] Where works were received as gifts to the king, however, they are well documented. In 1660, for instance, the States of Holland and West-Friesland made a gift to the English royal house to strengthen the bonds between the two countries. This 'Dutch Gift' had been preceded by a similar present to Crown Prince Henry in 1610 and one to Charles I of mostly sixteenth-century Dutch and Flemish paintings in 1636. As well as a very valuable bed, a tapestry, sculptures and twenty-four Italian paintings, the gift to Charles II included four 'modern' paintings.[42] Among them were two by the genre painter Gerrit Dou, including his 1658 *Young Mother*, which later, in a twist of fate, would leave London with William III (see cat. 1) and eventually find its way to the Mauritshuis in 1822 (fig. 16),[43] and an exceptionally large church interior of 1648 by Pieter Saenredam (now Scottish National Gallery, Edinburgh; for the artist, see cat. 19).[44] His preference for French and Italian paintings notwithstanding, the king was so impressed by Dou's work that he offered the painter a position at court – but in vain.[45] He had more success with the Leiden-born Willem van de Velde the Elder and his son, also Willem. In 1672, when the French invaded the Republic, these two generations of marine painters moved from Amsterdam to London, where father and son were given a studio in the Queen's House at Greenwich and,

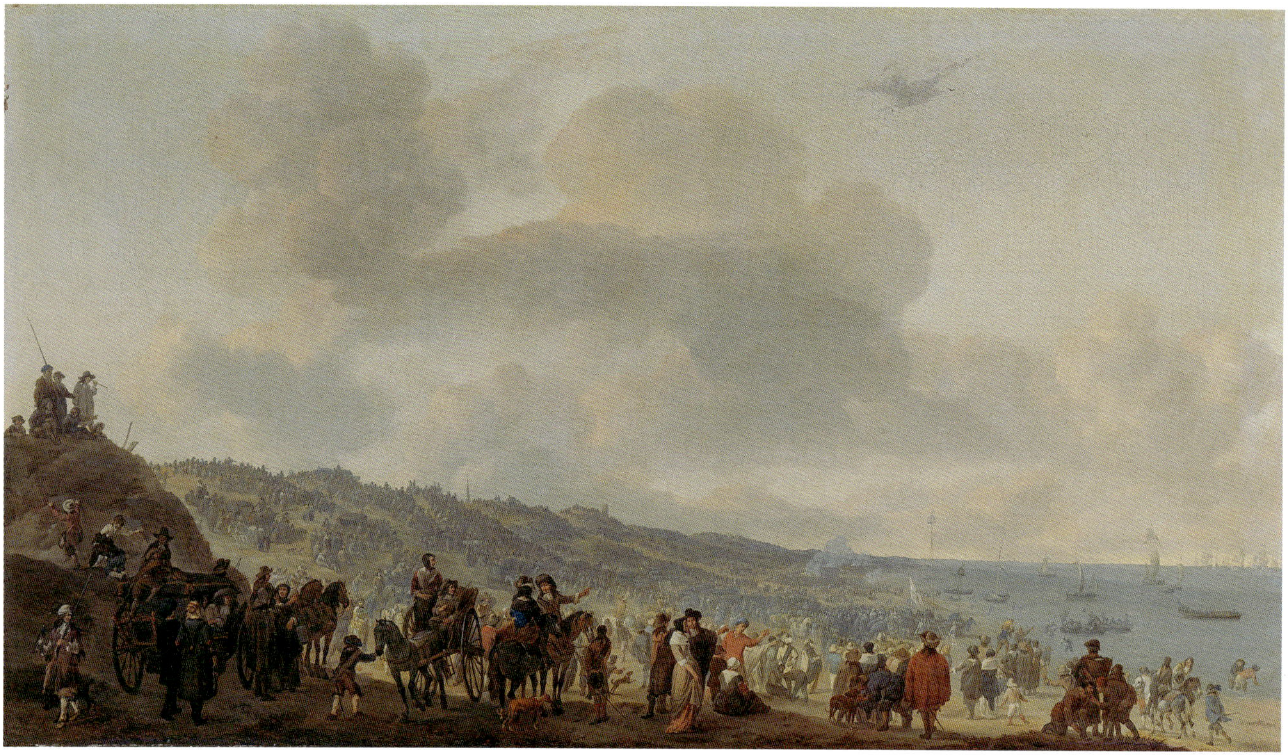

FIG. 15
Johannes Lingelbach (1622–1674)
The Departure of Charles II from Scheveningen, 2 June 1660, 1660s
Oil on canvas, 59 × 100 cm
Amsterdam, Rijksmuseum (on loan from the Mauritshuis, The Hague; SK-C-1224)

according to a surviving contract, an annual stipend of a hundred pounds each as 'draughtsmen of the British fleet'.[46] They sailed with the fleet to observe the action and make sketches on the spot (see cat. 21). Remarkably, they started this job just after the outbreak of the third Anglo-Dutch War in 1672; the conflict continued until 1674. One moment they were working as 'war reporters' on the Dutch side, soon afterwards they were accompanying the English fleet to depict the various naval engagements.[47] At the time, the English fleet was more successful than the Dutch and so the commissions came from the winning side (see fig. 18). In 1675 the king's brother, James, Duke of York, later King James II (1633–1701), commissioned paintings of English naval battles from the Van de Veldes, a series that is still in the Royal Collection.[48] It was not until the 1680s that the artists also started to paint seascapes for the open market. Willem van de Velde the Elder died in London in 1693, his son Willem van de Velde the Younger died there in 1707. Their work was emulated by countless artists of successive generations in England, where seascapes have always been popular.[49]

As well as genre works and seascapes, still lifes always found favour. An artist who must have worked for the king, although there is no firm evidence of this, is Pieter van Roestraeten of Haarlem.[50] This still-life specialist gradually adapted his paintings to suit English tastes by expanding his repertoire to include still lifes of silver objects, imported porcelain, lacquerware and china that was used in the preparation

FIG. 16
Gerrit Dou (1613–1675)
The Young Mother, 1658
Oil on panel (arched top), 74 × 56 cm
The Hague, Mauritshuis (32; originally part of the Dutch Gift to Charles II, 1660)

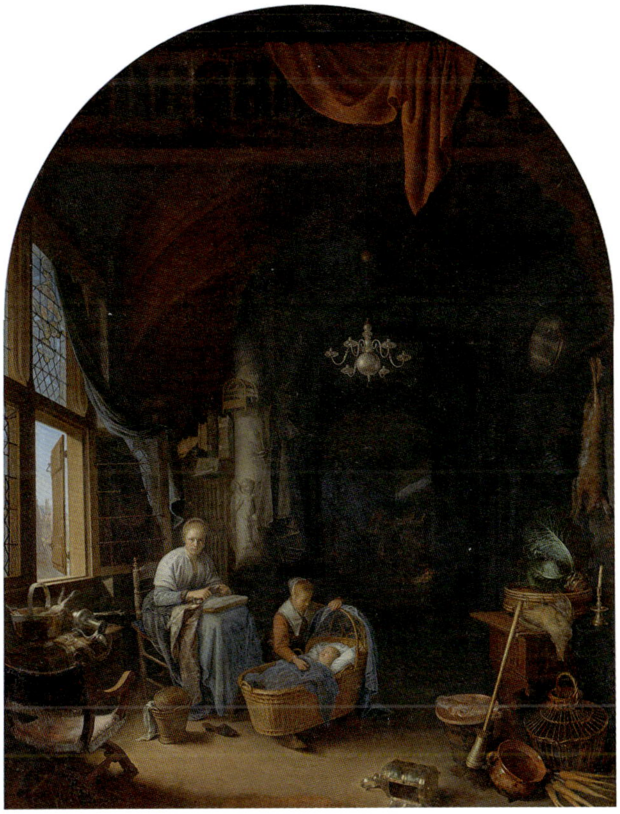

and drinking of tea.[51] Sources tell us that he was introduced to Charles II's court by the portraitist Sir Peter Lely (cat. 12), who had also trained in Haarlem. Lely was a very highly regarded artist, earning the same salary as his famous predecessor Van Dyck, in whose footsteps he followed, although his own style was less subtle.[52] Lely would later be succeeded by his most successful pupil Willem Wissing, who had trained in The Hague and came to London in 1676.

A still-life painter known to have worked for the king was Simon Verelst, born in The Hague, who went to London on his own initiative in or before 1669. Contemporaries like Samuel Pepys (1633–1703) were greatly impressed by Verelst's sophisticated, illusionist technique (see p. 175).[53] A painter of countless flower still lifes, Verelst was also a creditable portrait painter (cat. 22), working for the king and his successor, the future James II, as well as other highly placed individuals. Some of these works show the sitter life-size and full-length. Later in life Verelst fell on hard times and the quality of his work suffered.[54] In May 1693, another still-life painter, the Leiden artist Edwaert (Edward) Collier, went to London, where his *trompe l'oeils* of letter racks and still lifes of books, writing implements, globes and musical instruments proved hugely popular. He was back in the Republic from 1702 to 1706 but spent the last two years of his life in London, as the Dutch or English inscriptions and the precise signatures on his still lifes testify.[55]

There were also, of course, artists who took the reverse route. Perhaps the best known is the portraitist Cornelius Johnson (Jonson van Ceulen), who was initially very successful. Born in London to Flemish-German immigrants, following the outbreak of the Civil War in England he and his family moved to the Continent in 1643, where he painted portraits of Dutch burghers in various cities.[56] He continued to paint the portraits of English subjects in the Dutch Republic, among them William Hamilton and John Maitland (cat. 11) who, like the painter, had fled to the Republic because of the political situation. Sir Robert Kerr, discussed earlier in connection with Rembrandt, had his portrait painted in the Republic in 1654, the year of his death, by Jan Lievens, whom he knew very well (see fig. 71).[57] After the Restoration, English visitors continued to come to the Republic, some as real tourists who wanted to explore the country and recorded their travels in journals and letters.[58] The wealthier among them passed through on their way to Italy to see the legacy of Classical Antiquity and the Renaissance with their own eyes as part of their Grand Tour.

A Dutch colony

The year 1672 has gone down in Dutch history as the Year of Disaster because of the French invasion and the start of the Franco-Dutch war that would last until 1678, resulting in a severe economic downturn. In a proclamation issued on 10 June 1672, Charles II used this situation as an opportunity to invite Dutch people to settle in England. With the economic malaise in the Republic, it was an offer seized by many painters and members of their families, along with numerous craftsmen, engravers and cartographers.[59] In consequence, in the period up to around 1715, there was a veritable colony of Dutch artists in London, the heart of the country where some had already settled before this.[60] The talents of these artists were variable, to say the least, and it is not surprising that some of them are almost unknown today, judging by the poor quality of their work. What is striking is that Dutch artists were usually very productive in their new home country, making not only easel paintings for the open market but also many decorative compositions to be built into interiors as overdoors or above fireplaces. The best-known expatriates included the landscape painter Jan Griffier of Amsterdam (see fig. 63), the genre painter Egbert van Heemskerk of Haarlem, Abraham Hondius of Rotterdam and Jan Wyck of Haarlem, son of the famous Thomas Wijck, known as 'Old Wyck'.[61] Both Hondius and Jan Wyck (whose work had a considerable influence on later English painters) specialised in affordable hunting scenes for the middle segment of the market, paintings that were evidently much sought after, given the substantial output.

While the latter four artists all breathed their last in their new homeland,[62] some worked in the country for shorter periods. The renowned Samuel van Hoogstraten of Dordrecht was in London from May 1662 to around 1667, so he and his wife witnessed the Great Fire. Van Hoogstraten's *trompe l'oeils* had found a ready market among English collectors during his time in the city (see pp. 15–17 and fig. 3). The most famous and most talented Dutch artist in London at the end of the seventeenth century was the 'fine painter' Godfried Schalcken, also from Dordrecht, who lived and worked there from the spring of 1692 to the summer of 1696, painting chiefly portraits, but also genre works and history pieces and even some still lifes, a new departure for him.[63] His distinctive nocturnes, in which the effect of candlelight is always superbly conveyed, were much in demand in England.[64] Schalcken's paintings are of the highest quality and were clearly aimed at the top end of the market, and in this respect they cannot be compared with the works of artists like Hondius and Wyck, which were sold for relatively low prices and in large numbers.

The exceptional portrait Schalcken made of King-Stadholder William III with a lit candle (fig. 4, p. 18) is a reminder how, after the Glorious Revolution in 1688 that saw the Dutch Stadholder William III and his wife Mary become King and Queen of England, there was growing interest in Dutch art and collecting Dutch paintings, whether they were painted in England or the Republic. For a variety of reasons, the Stadholder's arrival in England did not bring about a new influx of Dutch artists through court appointments, however. William and Mary loved French court culture and gave employment to a very international group of artists, among them the highly versatile French designer and architect Daniel Marot, the renowned portrait painter Godfrey Kneller, who was originally from Germany but trained in Amsterdam, the still-life painter from Hungary Jakob Bogdány and the extremely popular Italian ceiling-painter Antonio Verrio, who had previously worked for Charles II.[65] The Dutch influence was essentially confined to garden design (see pp. 110–13)and decorative art.

Portraits of country houses

In their new home, some Dutch artists turned to a novel genre that was quite specific to England – bird's-eye-view 'portraits' of country houses with their surrounding estates and paintings of other notable buildings or palaces. One of these painters was Adriaen van Diest of The Hague, whose *Dunham Massey: Bird's-eye View from the South* of 1697 (cat. 6) is still in its original location. Other Dutch artists made similar works, among them Leendert Knyff of Haarlem (see fig. 64), Jan Griffier, mentioned above, and Jan Wyck (see fig. 45).[66] Prior to that, Hendrick Danckerts (see fig. 62), who was born in The Hague, had painted royal residences such as Greenwich, Windsor Castle and Hampton Court, for the king and for private clients, Samuel Pepys among them.[67] These very informative topographical scenes by Van Diest and others, not always executed with the greatest refinement, may not be the most important paintings produced in England,[68] but they do provide a unique insight into the way the English economy flourished in the last decades of the seventeenth century, fuelling an immense building boom. The strong economy attracted increasing numbers of people from within the kingdom and beyond to London, where new houses had to be built to accommodate them. This led to a growing demand for paintings to decorate prosperous Londoners' homes.[69] There was also much building outside the city, as the *nouveaux riches* bought their first country houses, or had them built, while the upper classes had their existing properties completely renovated or enlarged. The wall space available for paintings grew at an extraordinary rate.

There is a fine example of an existing country house that was greatly improved just outside London. At Ham House, now a National Trust property (fig. 17), the paintings in some of the rooms are arranged exactly as they were in the time of Elizabeth Murray, Countess of Dysart, later Duchess of Lauderdale, an important collector and patron who had had her portrait painted by Peter Lely in 1648 (cat. 12). She inherited the house from her father in 1655 and, after her second marriage to John Maitland, Duke of Lauderdale (see cat. 11) in 1672, it was radically redecorated and refurbished, with the house doubling in size. This renovation, largely completed by 1676, reflects the way Dutch artists were regarded at that time, for many were employed for paintings that were set into the walls of the house (fig. 18) – including Willem van de Velde the Younger (whose seascapes can be seen in Elizabeth's bedroom) and Thomas Wijck (whose painting of an alchemist was built in as a chimneypiece in the Duke's Closet), while countless overdoors with scenes of harbours and landscapes were supplied by Abraham Begeyn of Leiden and Dirck van Bergen of Haarlem, a pupil of

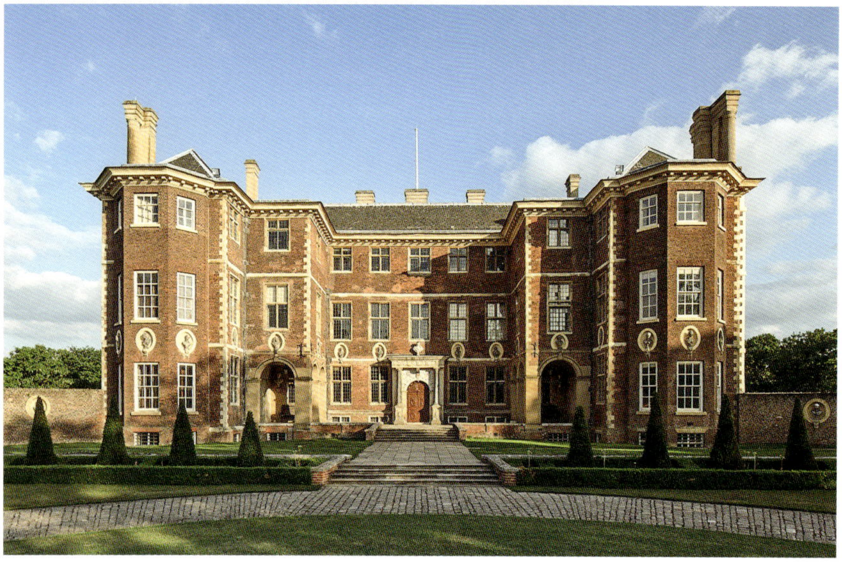

FIG. 17
Exterior of Ham House, Richmond, Surrey

the better-known landscape painter Adriaen van de Velde.[70] One of the most important decorations in the house, the ceiling of the White Closet, the private part of the house where the duchess received her friends, said her prayers and took tea, was commissioned not from a Dutch artist but an Italian, Antonio Verrio, who, like Willem van de Velde, Begeyn and Van Bergen, had settled in England in 1672 and was extremely successful.[71] It is clear that with their cleverly conceived history paintings the very talented Italians were without doubt regarded as the best painters; the Dutch and their detailed paintings of scenes from the everyday world played second fiddle.

As well as the integral works by Dutch immigrants, Ham House also has a group of Dutch paintings that must have been acquired on the art market and are described in inventories from the period (cat. nos. 2, 4), which list in total no fewer than 185 paintings by a variety of artists from different schools.[72] Some of the Dutch paintings may have been acquired during the artists' lifetime, such as the small Brazilian landscape by Frans Post (cat. 17), who died in 1680. Regrettably, we do not know exactly how the Dutch easel paintings in Ham House were acquired, but it was probably through an agent or the art trade. It should be noted that the auction system in England developed relatively late; the history of the great auction houses like Sotheby's (established in 1744) and Christie's (founded in 1766) dates to the eighteenth century, by which time England had produced its own outstanding artists. It was only in the 1680s and 1690s that auction sales really started to take off, particularly after the collection of paintings owned by the renowned Sir Peter Lely, which included Dutch and Flemish works, was sold at auction in London in 1682, attracting huge interest.[73] For a long time the import of paintings had been banned under the terms of a sixteenth-century law that protected the work of the members of the Painters-Stainers Company, the artists' guild, but by the end of the seventeenth century their power was waning.[74] London would eventually emerge as the capital of the international auction world.

New opportunities for collectors

Many top-flight seventeenth-century paintings made in the Republic were imported from the Continent in the eighteenth century and sold to English collectors, who hung them in their stately London mansions and later also in their country houses.[75] Little by little, owners began publishing printed catalogues of their

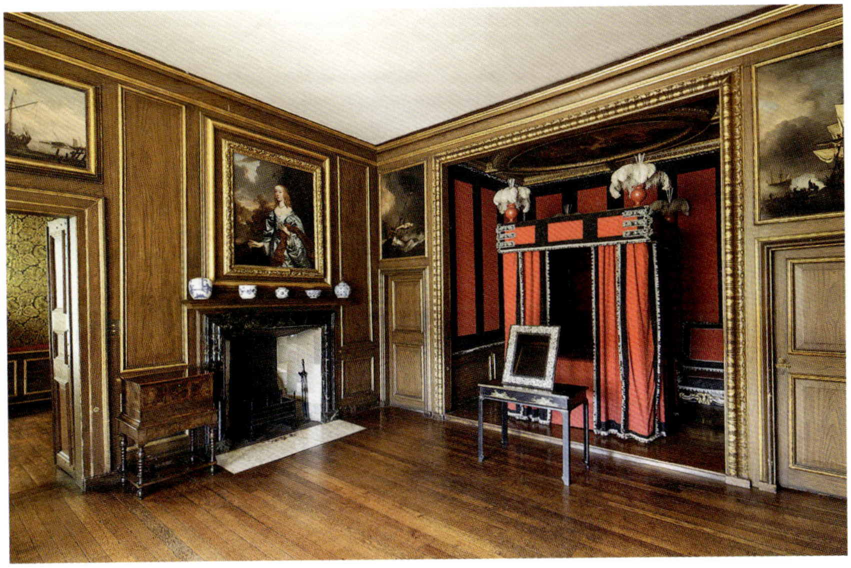

FIG. 18
Interior of Ham House, Richmond, showing the bedchamber of Elizabeth Murray, Countess of Dysart, later Duchess of Lauderdale, with her portrait by Lely above the fireplace (cat. 12) and seascapes by Willem van de Velde the Younger over the doors

collections, a process that was accelerated as country houses were increasingly viewed as tourist attractions and there was a growing need for guides.[76] At the end of the eighteenth century, collectors were presented with an opportunity that they did not hesitate to seize, when some of the finest collections of Old Masters came on to the market in Paris and London as a consequence of the start of the French Revolution in 1789, when heads rolled and aristocrats fled the country, and was compounded by the chaos in Europe after the outbreak of the Napoleonic Wars in 1792.[77] In 1793 Dutch and Flemish paintings belonging to Louis-Philippe-Joseph, duc d'Orléans (1747–1793), who had been declared bankrupt and sent to the guillotine, came on to the market in London. Francis Egerton, 3rd Duke of Bridgewater (1736–1803), was able to pick up some of the most important Italian and French paintings from the Orléans collection by artists like Raphael, Titian and Poussin.[78] In his notorious *Memoirs of Painting* of 1824, the Scottish art dealer William Buchanan (1777–1864) was very frank about the amount of money earned in the art trade during that period.[79] Huge numbers of Dutch paintings, formerly owned by French aristocrats, became available for the first time in many decades, and English collectors saw their chance, for there were still plenty of walls to be filled. Some paintings were a fitting decoration for English country houses, because many Dutch still lifes and landscapes involved motifs related to the ever popular hunt. Smaller Dutch paintings, so-called cabinet pieces, also sold well. They directly reflected the taste of eighteenth-century French collectors, who had filled their cabinets or art rooms with Dutch paintings of this kind, usually executed in a highly finished technique (e.g. cat. 15).[80] While large Dutch paintings were seen at their best in grand reception rooms or special galleries, cabinet pieces were lost in these vast spaces and could be better enjoyed in the rooms in which people lived and went about their day-to-day business. People liked to surround themselves with charming compositions by Leiden 'fine painters' like Dou and his pupil Frans van Mieris I, with landscapes by Potter, the extremely productive Philips Wouwerman or Adriaen van de Velde, the brother of Willem van de Velde the Younger, and with sun-drenched paintings by Italianates such as Jan Both, Claes Berchem and Karel du Jardin.

Before 1800 collectors had already developed a special interest in the work of painters of the monumental Dutch landscape after 1650: Aelbert Cuyp (cat. 5), Meindert Hobbema (cat. 8 and fig. 19),

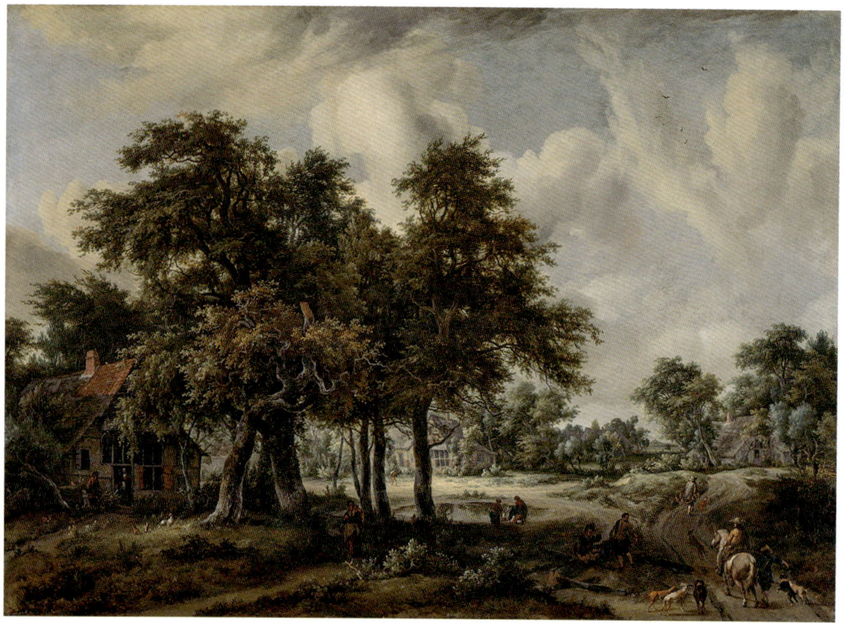

FIG. 19
Meindert Hobbema (1638–1709)
Wooded Landscape with Cottages, c.1665
Oil on canvas, 88 × 121 cm
The Hague, Mauritshuis (1105; from the collections of Henry, 2nd Viscount Clifden, Robert, 2nd Earl of Grosvenor and Hugh, 2nd Duke of Westminster)

Philips Koninck and Jacob van Ruisdael.[81] Cuyp was the great favourite and many of his works made the crossing from the Continent to England; such high prices were paid for his work that there were virtually no important Cuyp paintings left in the Netherlands, as a result of which England had the monopoly on his masterpieces for a long time (fig. 20).[82] Cuyp's elegant landscapes with distinguished looking horsemen in a setting populated by servants or peasants struck a chord with the status-conscious English nobility and there were (and still are) more Cuyps in England than in the rest of the world.[83] Countless English artists then looked for inspiration to the artist known in England as 'the Dutch Claude'. William Turner, for example, was captivated by the atmosphere of Cuyp's ships in calm water and in 1817 actually went to Dordrecht, the artist's birthplace; John Constable praised Cuyp's chiaroscuro contrasts. These and many other English landscape painters, of whom Richard Wilson was the first, followed by Thomas Gainsborough, were repeatedly and profoundly influenced by Cuyp, although other Dutch artists had a major impact too.[84] No one expressed it better than the author Anna Jameson (1794–1860), who wrote in 1844 that 'to come upon one of Cuyp's pictures after looking at Berghem or Both [Claes Berchem and Jan Both] is like opening a door and stepping out into the fresh air – into heaven's own light and earth's own verdure'.[85]

A canon of Dutch art

The nineteenth century saw the emergence of a new group of collectors of Dutch paintings – industrialists and City of London merchants and bankers (among them members of the famous Rothschild family; see cat. 5), who bought from the art trade and at auctions. Taste was set not only by the collectors themselves, but also by their agents. One of these was the famous art dealer John Smith (1781–1855), whose nine-volume *Catalogue Raisonné of the Works of the Most Eminent Dutch, Flemish and French Painters* (1829–42) would long serve as a bible for collectors and created and solidified a canon for seventeenth-century Dutch painting (fig. 21).[86] Smith catalogued the work of Bakhuysen, Berchem, Ter Borch (cat. 3), Andries and Jan Both, Cuyp (cat. 5), Dou, Hackaert, Van der Heyden, Hobbema (cat. 8), De Hooch (cat. 10), Van Huysum, du Jardin, Maes,

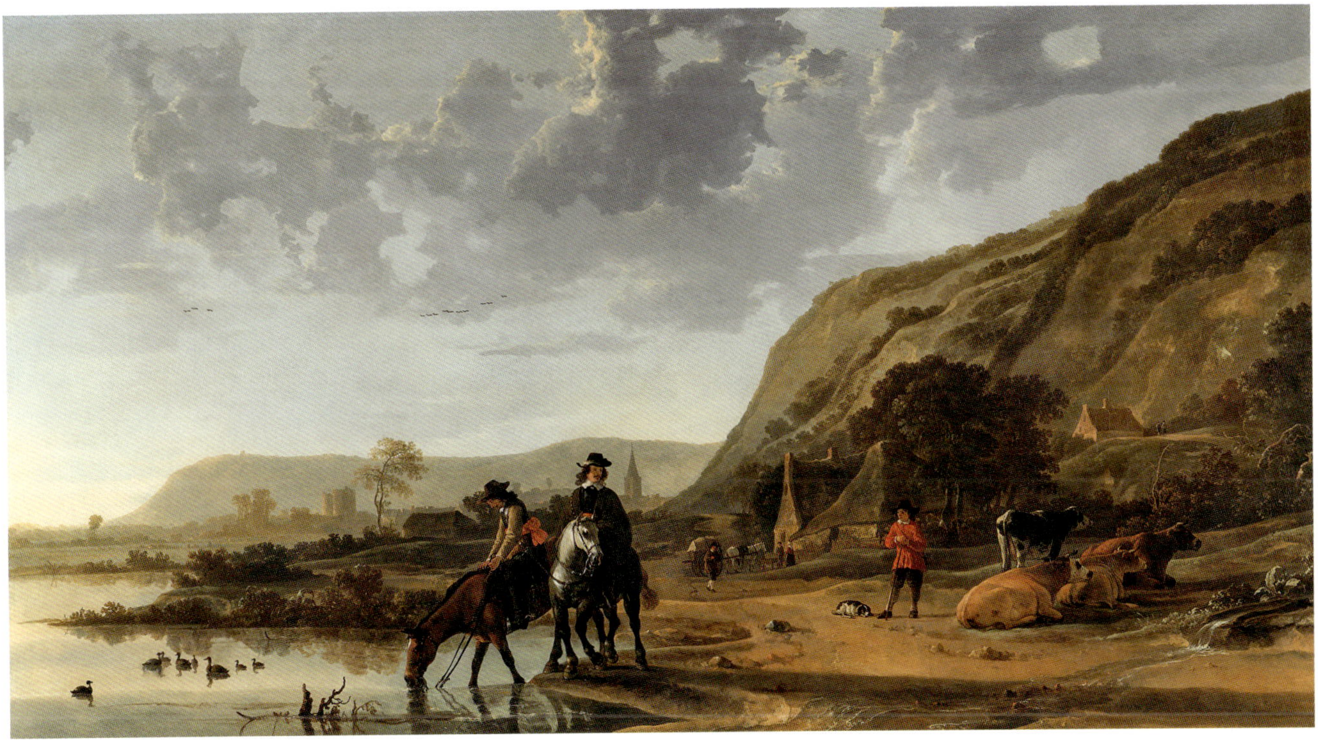

FIG. 20
Aelbert Cuyp (1620–1691)
River Landscape with Two Horsemen, late 1650s
Oil on canvas, 128 × 228 cm
Amsterdam, Rijksmuseum (SK-A-4118; from the collection of Baron Alfred de Rothschild)

Metsu (cat. 15), Frans I and Willem van Mieris, Eglon van der Neer, Adriaen and Isack van Ostade, Potter (fig. 24), Pynacker, Rembrandt (cat. 18), Van Ruisdael, Ruysch, Schalcken, Van Slingelandt, Steen (cat. 20), Adriaen van de Velde and Willem van de Velde the Younger, Van der Werff, Wouwerman and Wijnants – but early Dutch seventeenth-century painters were overlooked altogether. Smith chose Coques, Van Dyck, Rubens and Teniers as representatives of the Flemish school.[87] The artists listed by Smith were represented in many nineteenth-century public and private English collections, including the National Gallery in London, whose collection had been put together after a founding purchase by Parliament in 1824, not by members of a royal house as was the case with other major museums in Europe such as the Louvre in Paris

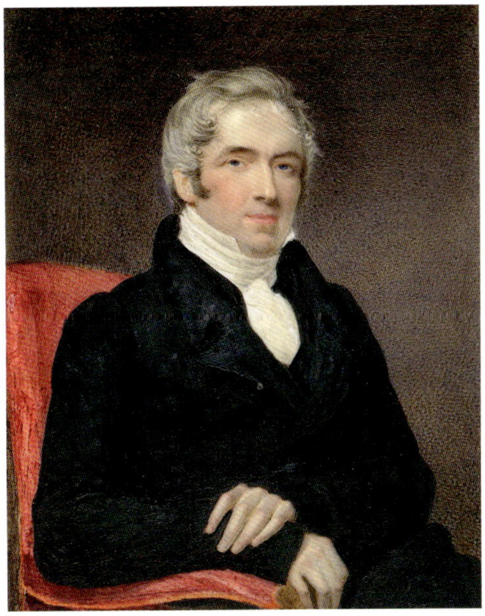

FIG. 21
Moses Haughton Jr (1772/74–after 1848)
John Smith, *c.*1830
Watercolour on ivory, 16 × 13 cm
London, British Museum (1881,0409.1)

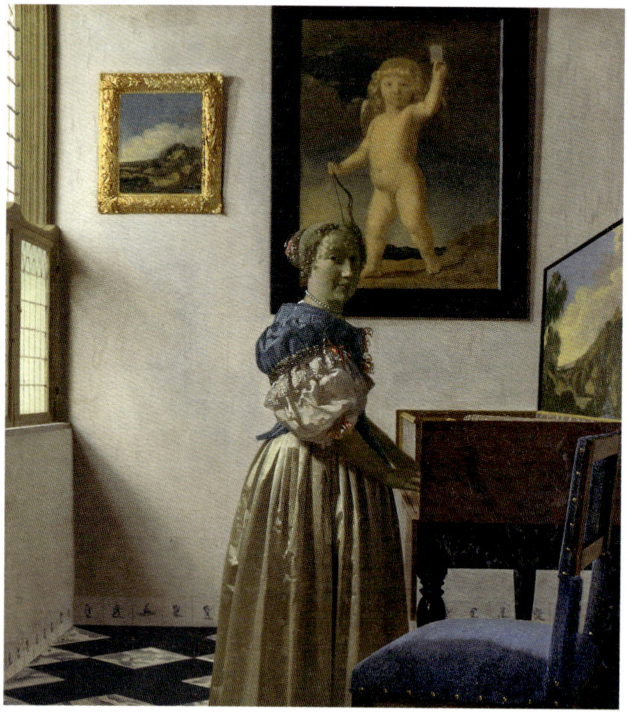

FIG. 22
Johannes Vermeer (1632–1675)
A Young Woman Standing by a Virginal, c.1670–72
Oil on canvas, 52 × 45 cm
London, The National Gallery (NG 1383; bought 1892 from the collection of Thoré)

or the Prado in Madrid.[88] In 1871 the National Gallery had acquired the collection of Robert Peel (1788–1850), twice Prime Minister of England, forming the nucleus of the National Gallery's Dutch and Flemish holdings, including Meindert Hobbema's famous *Avenue at Middelharnis*.[89] Peel had bought many of his paintings from Smith, and Smith had dedicated his major publication to the collector, his most important British client. Interestingly, Peel had not been the only Prime Minister to collect Dutch and Flemish art, as he had followed in the footsteps of Sir Robert Walpole (1676–1745), England's first Prime Minister, whose major collection of Old Master paintings including many Italian masterpieces was brought together between 1717 and 1742. In 1779 the collection was sold *en bloc* by Walpole's grandson to Catherine the Great (1729–1796), including Rembrandt's 1635 *Sacrifice of Isaac*, the finest Dutch painting in Sir Robert's collection. Most of these paintings ended up in the collection of the State Hermitage Museum in St Petersburg; some are now in other museums.[90]

The work of artists such as Hals and Vermeer, today regarded as celebrities of Dutch art, was not promoted by Smith and had yet to be rediscovered by their principal champion, the French art historian and critic Etienne-Joseph-Théophile Thoré (1807–1869), who published under the alias of William Bürger.[91] Following the sale of Thoré's art collection in 1892, two of his Vermeers went to the National Gallery. The museum purchased *A Young Woman Standing by a Virginal* in the art trade a month after the sale (fig. 22). *A Young Woman Seated at a Virginal* was acquired later, in 1910, as part of the George Salting (1835–1909) bequest.[92] By then, Vermeer's *Lady at the Virginals with a Gentleman* had long been hanging in one of the royal palaces, most of that time with an incorrect attribution, because King George III (1738–1820) had bought the painting in 1762 as a work by Frans van Mieris the Elder. It was not until 1929 that the painting, which Thoré had recognised as a Vermeer many years earlier, was finally transferred to the Picture Gallery in Buckingham Palace.[93]

Treasures of art in Great Britain

In the nineteenth century, English collectors had almost unimaginably large and wide-ranging collections that often included many seventeenth-century Dutch paintings. This is particularly well illustrated by the books written by the German art historian Gustav Waagen (1794–1868), who was greatly respected in England (fig. 23). From 1835 onwards, he had visited many public and private collections of paintings. When one leafs through his renowned *Treasures of Art in Great Britain: Being an Account of the Chief Collections of Paintings, Drawings, Sculptures* (3 vols.

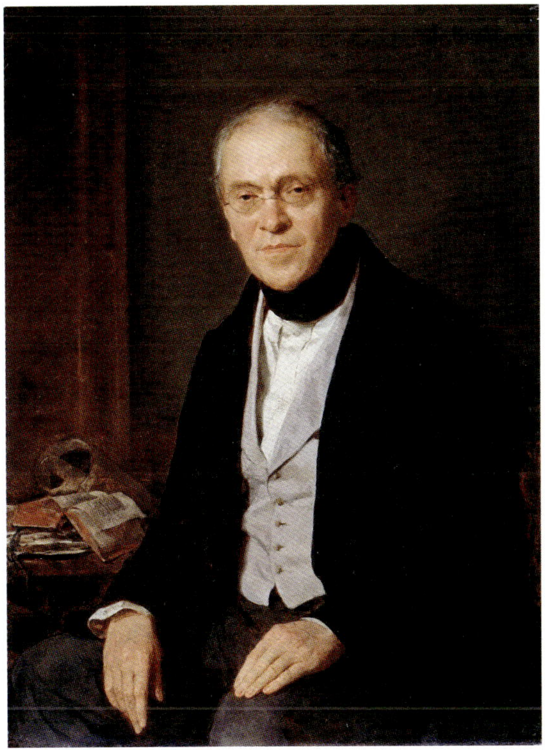

FIG. 23
Ludwig Knaus (1829–1910)
Gustav Waagen, 1855
Oil on canvas, 57 × 42 cm
Berlin, Staatliche Museen zu Berlin, Nationalgalerie (A1 1094)

and supplement, published in London, 1854 and 1857), translated from the German by Elizabeth Eastlake, wife of the first director of the National Gallery, Charles Eastlake, a personal friend of the author, one cannot help but be surprised by the large numbers of good-quality Dutch paintings that had been shipped to England. The book is an indispensable source for the study of Dutch art in England, then still largely in private hands – many famous names appear. We find Robert Staynor Holford (1808–1892), a central figure of the Victorian arts establishment, who brought together in Dorchester House, among the finest houses in London at the time, one of the best private collections of Old Masters. Many, like the exceptionally fine Cuyp now in Ascott House (cat. 5), or the Paulus Potter in the Otterloo collection (fig. 24), were by Dutch artists.[94] Waagen also visited Richard Seymour-Conway, 4th Marquess of Hertford (1800–1870), whose exquisite collection now forms the basis of the unsurpassed Wallace Collection, London, where visitors can imagine themselves in a French interior of the *ancien régime*.[95] The same was true of the interior of Carlton House in London, where in the early nineteenth century the Prince Regent, later King George IV (1762–1830), displayed his collection of Dutch and Flemish paintings in lavishly decorated rooms strongly influenced by French taste.[96] Interiors of the demolished Carlton House show eighteenth-century

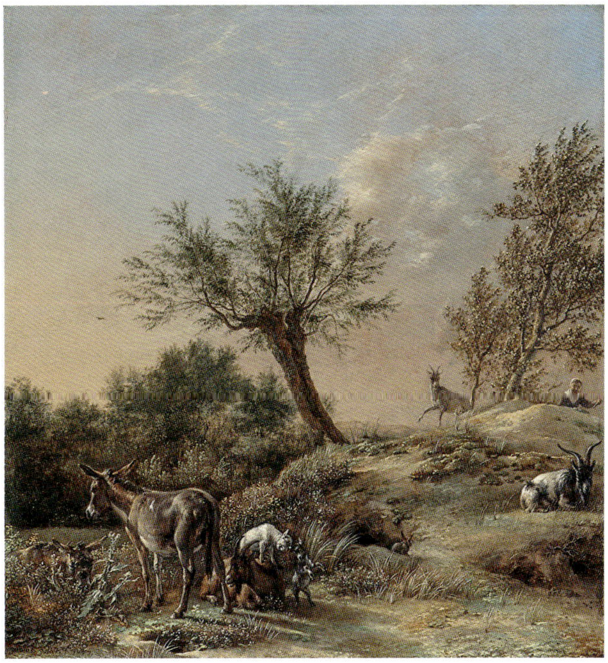

FIG. 24
Paulus Potter (1625–1654)
Spring Landscape with Donkeys and Goats (*'The Rabbit Warren'*), 1647
Oil on panel, 40 × 36 cm
Rose-Marie and Eijk van Otterloo collection

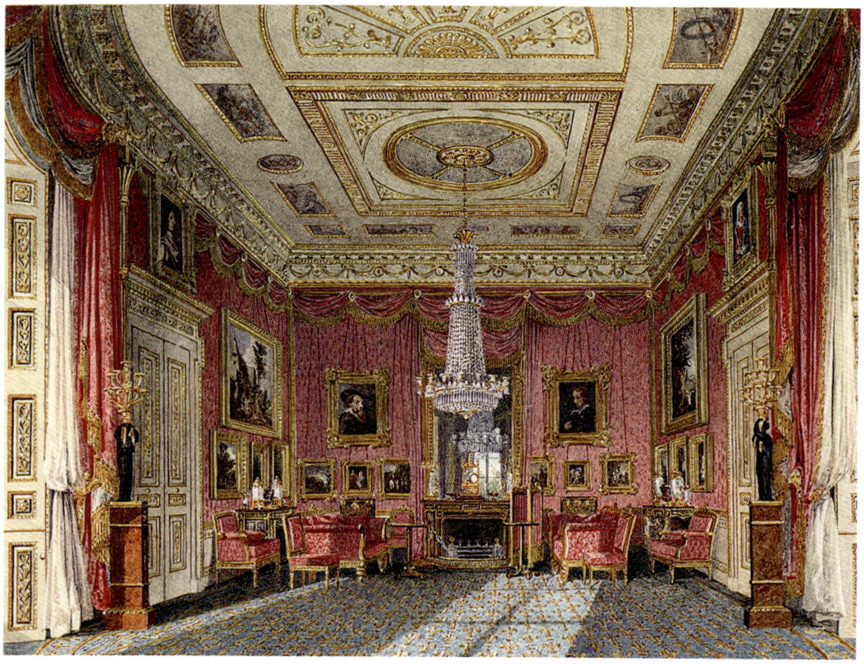

FIG. 25
Charles Wild (1781–1835)
The Rose Satin Drawing Room, Carlton House (looking North), 1815–19, for W.H. Pyne's *The History of the Royal Residences*, 3 vols., London 1819
Watercolour, 21 × 27 cm
London, Royal Collection Trust
(RCIN 922180)

French furniture and seventeenth-century paintings in gilded frames, hung in groups of four on silk-covered cords – three smaller works below one large painting, with a piece of furniture beneath (fig. 25).[97] The most iconic Dutch artists in the present Royal Collection, which contains more than three hundred works from the Dutch Golden Age, were largely acquired by George IV, save for the Vermeer acquired by his father.

Waagen also acted as a consultant for exhibitions, including the renowned *Art Treasures of the United Kingdom* in Manchester from 5 May to 17 October 1857. With sixteen thousand works on show, it was the largest exhibition ever staged in the United Kingdom. Among the more than eleven hundred Old Masters that were seen by one and a half million visitors were many Dutch paintings of the Golden Age.[98] The list of lenders in the catalogue reads like a *Who's Who* of collectors in England at that time. Almost a century later, in 1952–53, the Royal Academy in London staged *Dutch Pictures 1450–1750*, and the 644 catalogue numbers show yet again just how rich England was in seventeenth-century Dutch paintings, even if one subtracts the small group of loans from foreign collections from this number. Many of the works shown in London were in private ownership and the list provides an informative insight into the number of high-quality Dutch paintings acquired in England between 1700 and 1950.[99] Since the exhibition many of the paintings have changed hands. Important collections of Dutch paintings were also amassed in England after 1950, by collectors such as Harold, Baron Samuel of Wych Cross, founder of Land Securities Group, whose collection of Dutch paintings is now on view almost complete in the Mansion House, London (a few paintings left the collection, including cat. 18), or the Dutch-born businessman Willem, Baron van Dedem (1929–2015), who lived in London and gifted and bequeathed part of his collection to leading museums in England and the Netherlands (see fig. 85, p. 153).[100] Dutch paintings in English private ownership still change hands and leave their original locations, sometimes to go abroad, but it happens at a significantly slower pace than in the past.[101]

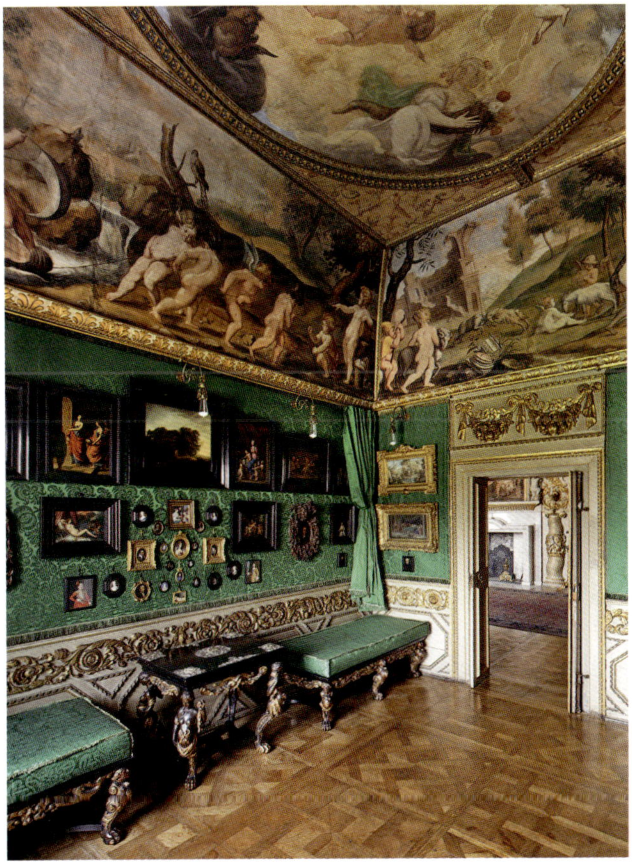

FIG. 26
The east wall and painted ceiling of the Green Closet at Ham House, Surrey

In a significant number of the houses managed by the National Trust, and in properties controlled by English Heritage, or by foundations, the collections have remained largely intact and are tied to the house in perpetuity. In cases where the collection has stayed together, the paintings can often be seen in their original location and configuration, as they can at Ham House, where some rooms have remained virtually intact (fig. 26). It is this aspect that makes the National Trust collection of paintings so special, for the houses managed by the Trust not only contain the family portraits collected through the ages,[102] but also the original overdoors, chimneypieces and other paintings incorporated in the walls or ceilings, as well as old and contemporary works acquired on the art market by successive generations. People who are sensitive to the *genius loci* (spirit of place) can enjoy the many houses preserved by the National Trust, which takes great care of the buildings and maintains their historic interiors with their extraordinary contents. When one looks at paintings by seventeenth-century Dutch artists in National Trust houses, one can only conclude that the English have always been impressed by these painters' observational powers and the astounding technical skills of their realistic compositions.

NOTES

1 Jackson-Stops 1985; Stourton and Sebag-Montefiore 2010. For the presence of Dutch paintings in Scotland, see Lloyd Williams 1992.
2 White 2015, p. 2.
3 Hearn 1995–96, pp. 104–05, 108–12; E.J. Sluijter, 'The English Venture: Dutch and Flemish Artists in Britain', in Roding *et al.* 2003, pp. 11–27, at p. 14; White 2015, pp. 2–3.
4 See Haak 2003.
5 Waterhouse 1994, p. 13.
6 See Sluijter 2003, p. 11.
7 Ekkart *et al.* 2007–08.
8 See Gerson 1983.
9 White 2015, pp. 5–6. For Van Mierevelt, see Birch 1760, pp. 485–99; A. Jansen in Jansen, Ekkart and Verhave 2011–12, p. 32.
10 White 2015, pp. 4–5. A painting by Vroom dating from soon after 1623 was acquired by Charles I (*ibid.*, no. 233).
11 Sluijter 2003, p. 15.
12 Shawe-Taylor and Rumberg 2018; for Charles I as a collector of Dutch pictures, see White 2015, pp. 7–23.
13 White 2015, p. 7.
14 Sluijter 2003, p. 17; White 2015, pp. 18–19.
15 Sluijter 2003, pp. 16–17; White 2015, p. 11.
16 R. Ekkart in Buijsen 1998, pp. 155–61, 312; Sluijter 2003, p. 18.
17 See Giltaij in Giltaij and Jansen 1991, p. 163.
18 Giltaij in Giltaij and Jansen 1991, p. 165; White 2015, p. 56, note 124.
19 White 2015, p. 19, fig. 11 and p. 56, note 125; Sluijter 2003, p. 17; Hearn 2015, p. 26, fig. 16.
20 White 2015, p. 204.
21 White 2015, p. 19; Sluijter-Seijffert 2016, pp. 34–35, 236.
22 See Millar 1964, p. 23; Muller and Murrell 1997, pp. 82, 158.
23 White 2015, p. 10, fig. 3 and no. 33; see R. Hill, 'Sir Dudley Carleton and his relations with Dutch artists 1616–1632', in Roding *et al.* 2003, pp. 255–74, at p. 265.
24 White 2015, no. 74.
25 Van der Ploeg in Ekkart and Buvelot 2007–08, pp. 144–45, no. 31. See also White 2015, nos. 75, 79, 80.
26 Y. Bruijnen in Bikker, Bruijnen and Wuestman 2007, I, pp. 367–69, no. 280 (with references).
27 Y. Bruijnen in Bikker, Bruijnen and Wuestman 2007, I, p. 368 and notes 3–4.
28 White 2015, pp. 16–17.
29 *Catalogue of the Collection of Pictures, Medals, Agates and The Like, of King Charles I*, Ms. (Royal Collection Trust, London, RCIN 1047433); Millar 1960. For versions of this inventory, see White 2015, pp. 524–25. Van der Doort was originally appointed by Henry, Prince of Wales.
30 White 2015, pp. 21–22.
31 White 2015, no. 158.
32 White 2015, p. 21 and fig. 15; E. Buijsen in White and Buvelot 1999–2000, no. 26.
33 Gerson 1983, pp. 395–96.
34 A. Wheelock in Wheelock 2008–09, pp. 12–13.
35 White 2015, p. 2.
36 White 2015, p. 25.
37 White 2015, no. 1.
38 White 2015, p. 25.
39 London 1964, no. 42; White 2015, p. 26.
40 White 2015, p. 23.
41 White 2015, p. 27.
42 White 2015, pp. 23–24.
43 Buvelot in Van Suchtelen and Buvelot 2016, no. 12.
44 Schwartz and Bok 1989, no. 58, fig. 216.
45 White 2015, pp. 24–25; See Sluijter 2003, p. 16.
46 White 2015, p. 28.
47 White 2015, pp. 28–31.
48 White 2015, nos. 218–29.
49 Gerson 1983, pp. 420–28.
50 White 2015, pp. 31, 330, 331, 333.
51 Shaw 1990, pp. 132–36; see also London 1964, no. 63.
52 Sluijter 2003, p. 20.
53 Karst 2013–14, p. 28.
54 Karst 2013–14, p. 47 and figs. 15–16.
55 Van der Willigen and Meijer 2003, p. 64.
56 K. Hearn, 'The English career of Cornelius Johnson', in Roding *et al.* 2003, pp. 113–28.
57 V. Treanor in Wheelock 2008–09, no. 51.
58 Van Strien 1998.
59 White 2015, p. 28; Karst 2013–14, p. 27; D. Shawe-Taylor, 'The "Broad-Bottomed Dutch School": Royal Taste and Netherlandish Painting', in Shawe-Taylor and Buvelot 2015–17, pp. 10–29, at p. 17.
60 Karst 2013–14; Roding 2003.
61 On Wyck, see O. Millar, 'Jan Wyck and the Battle and the Chase in late Stuart England', in Roding *et al.* 2013, pp. 153–76.
62 Thomas Wijck returned to Haarlem in 1669 where he died in 1677.
63 W. Franits, '"A Very Famous Dutch Painter": Schalcken in England, 1692–1696', in Sevcik 2015–16, pp. 36–49; G. Jansen *ibid.*, pp. 26–27. A book by Franits on Schalcken's London years is in preparation (Amsterdam University Press).
64 Franits 2015–16, pp. 45–46.
65 B. Brenninkmeyer-de Rooij and E. de Heer in Brenninkmeyer-de Rooij *et al.* 1988, pp. 17–32.
66 Laing 1995, pp. 52–53, no. 16 (Wyck); see also *ibid.*, pp. 82–83; see also D. Jacques, 'Netherlandish topographical artists and English gardens', in Roding *et al.* 2003, pp. 177–88.

67 Karst 2013–14, p. 29 and fig. 2; White 2015, pp. 27–28.
68 The views of country houses by the Antwerp-born Jan Siberechts (e.g. Karst 2013–14, p. 44, fig. 14) are of good quality.
69 Karst 2013–14, p. 43.
70 Rowell 2013; for the painting of an alchemist by Wijck, see Washington 1985, no. 101.
71 Rowell 2013, figs. 114, 116; Stourton and Sebag-Montefiore 2010, pp. 77–78.
72 A. Laing, 'Appendix 2: Fitting Pictures to Rooms: A Re-Examination of the Ham House 'Estimate of Pictures' (*c.*1683), and its Collation with the Inventories', in Rowell 2013, pp. 408–29.
73 Stourton and Sebag-Montefiore 2010, p. 77; Karst 2013–14, pp. 28, 30, 34–36.
74 Kollmann 2000, p. 88; Karst 2013–14, p. 35.
75 See Simpson 1953, pp. 39–42; the Getty Provenance Index covering the period 1650–1945 is a wonderful source of information for English art sales throughout the centuries; see http://piprod.getty.edu/starweb/pi/servlet.starweb.
76 Stourton and Sebag-Montefiore 2010, pp. 323–29.
77 See Peronnet *et al.* 1998; Fredericksen *et al.* 1988–96.
78 Stourton and Sebag-Montefiore 2010, pp. 153–57.
79 Buchanan 1824.
80 For cabinet pictures, see Laing 1995, especially pp. 155–57.
81 See Laing 1995, p. 112 (Hobbema).
82 See B. Broos in Broos *et al.* 1990–91, p. 215.
83 A. Chong in Wheelock 2001–02, pp. 47–48.
84 Bachrach, Thijssen and van Karnebeek-van Roijen 1970–71; A. Chong in Wheelock 2001–02, pp. 45–47; for the influence of Dutch artists on later English painting, see Gerson 1983, pp. 420–50.
85 Jameson 1844, pp. 17–18; A. Chong in Wheelock 2001–02, p. 45.
86 Smith 1829–42; on Smith and the nineteenth-century art market, see Sebag-Montefiore and Armstrong-Totten 2013. Another London art dealer, Christianus Johannes Nieuwenhuys (1799–1883) from Brussels, son of Dutch-born dealer Lambertus Johannes Nieuwenhuis (1777–1862), had been a business partner of Smith and published himself; see Nieuwenhuys 1834.
87 The famous Dutch art historian Hofstede de Groot would base his much-used volumes on Dutch painters on those of Smith; Hofstede de Groot 1907–28.
88 Stourton and Sebag-Montefiore 2010, pp. 235–43.
89 For a contemporary description of the Peel collection, see Jameson 1844, pp. 341–80.
90 Dukelskaya and Moore 2002; A. Moore, 'Sir Robert Walpole: A Prime Minister collects Dutch and Flemish art', in Roding *et al.* 2003, pp. 287–306.
91 Bürger 1858–60; Bürger 1866, pp. 297–330, 458–575; Haskell 1976, pp. 146–50; Jowell 1977. For the rediscovery of Hals, see Suzman Jowell in Slive *et al.* 1989, pp. 61–86. Sir Robert Walpole was among the early admirers of Hals in England: see Dukelskaya and Moore 2002, no. 149; Moore 2003, pp. 293–94, fig. 5.4.9.
92 MacLaren 1991, I, pp. 466–69, nos. 1383 and 2568. Vermeer's *Guitar Player* (English Heritage, Kenwood House, London) was part of the collection of Edward Cecil Guinness (1889–27), Earl of Iveagh, who bequeathed it in 1927.
93 White 2015, p. 418; Shawe-Taylor in Shawe-Taylor and Buvelot 2015–17, p. 29.
94 Waagen 1854–57, II, pp. 193–222; *Art Treasures* 1857, no. 1002 (the present fig. 24); for Holford, see Stourton and Sebag-Montefiore 2010, pp. 248–51.
95 Waagen 1854–57, II, pp. 154–61.
96 For Dutch paintings acquired by George IV, see White 2015, pp. 36–50.
97 Made for Pyne 1819; see Shawe-Taylor and Buvelot 2015–17, pp. 11–12, 22 and figs. 1–3.
98 See also the important publication by William Bürger, *Trésors d'art exposés à Manchester en 1857 et provenant des collections royales, des collections publiques et des collections particulières de la Grand Bretagne*, Paris 1857. The earliest exhibitions of Dutch art are those organised by the British Institution from 1815 onwards; see Smith 1860, p. 156, quoted in Shawe-Taylor and Buvelot 2015, pp. 26, 168, note 67.
99 Waterhouse *et al.* 1952–53; see also Van Gelder 1953(1), pp. 33–34.
100 Sutton 1992; Sutton 2002; Buvelot and Gordenker 2016.
101 See Q. Buvelot, 'Has the Great Age of Collecting Dutch Old Master Paintings Come to an End?', in Quodbach 2014, pp. 182–93, 210–11.
102 See Laing 1995, pp. 17–18.

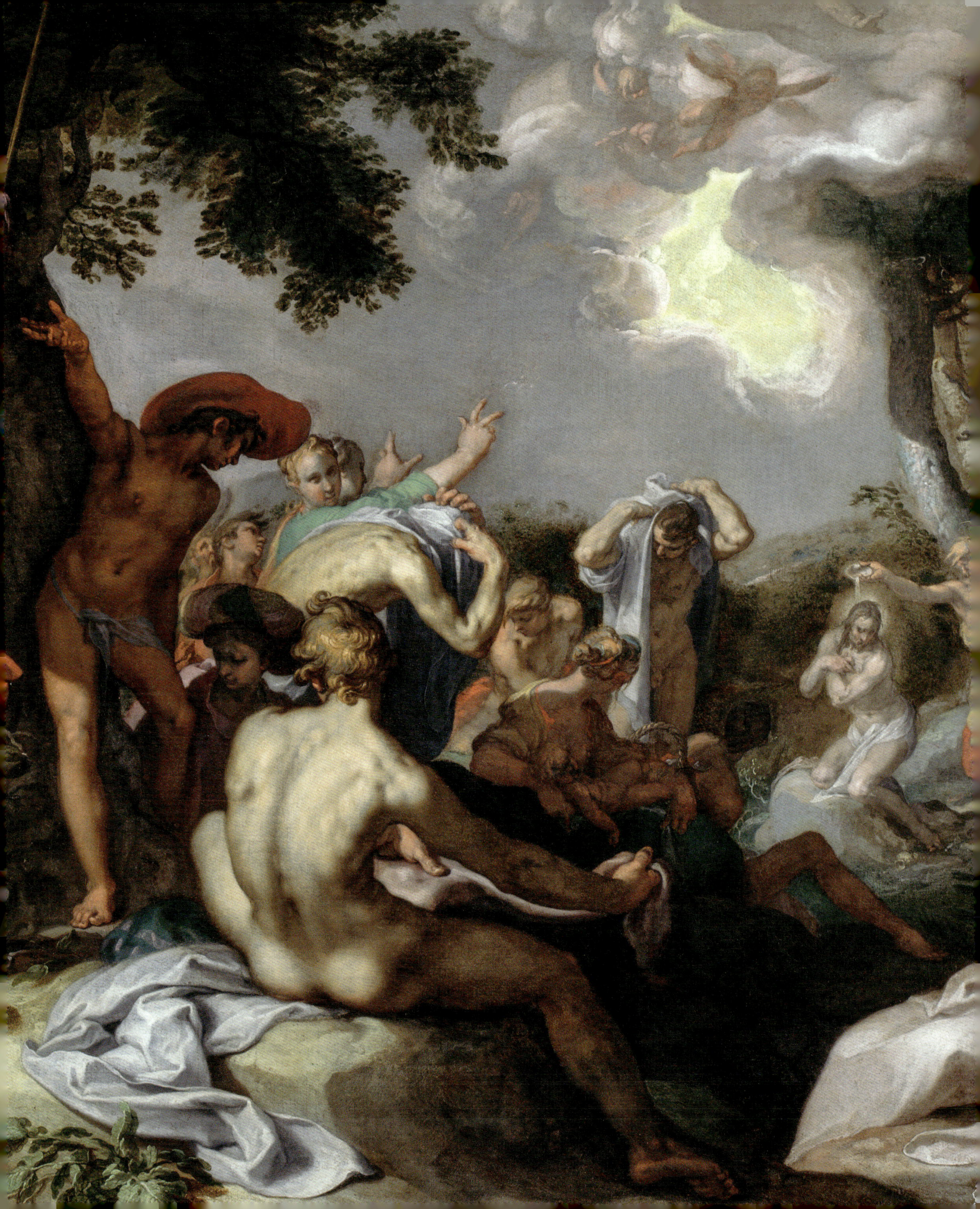

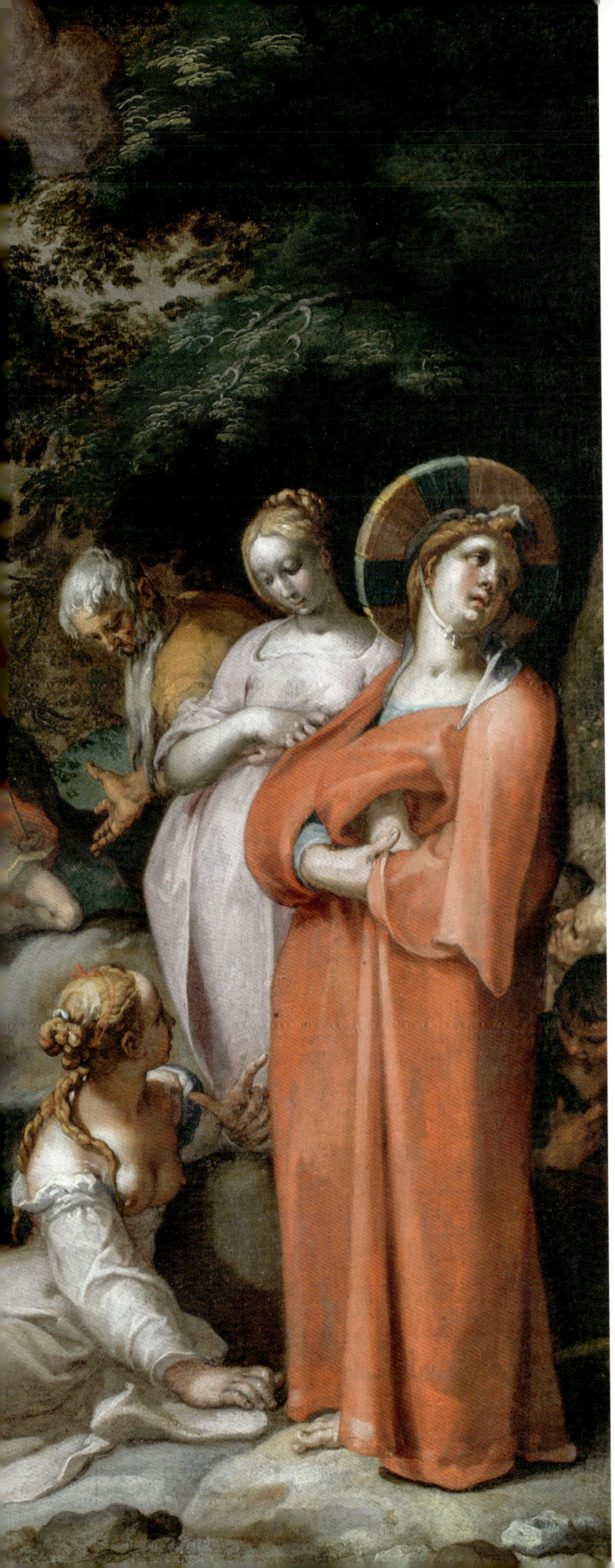

Catalogue

CONTRIBUTORS

QB Quentin Buvelot, Senior Curator, Mauritshuis
JC John Chu, National Trust Assistant Curator of Pictures and Sculpture
AG Allison Goudie, English Heritage Curator of Collections, The Iveagh Bequest, Kenwood
RG Rupert Goulding, National Trust Lead Curator (South West)
CR Charlotte Rulkens, Assistant Curator, Mauritshuis
CS Christine Sitwell, National Trust Picture Conservation Advisor
DT David A. H. B. Taylor, National Trust Curator of Pictures and Sculpture

1

ATTRIBUTED TO JAN DE BAEN (1633–1702)

William III, as Prince of Orange (1650–1702)

Oil on canvas, 61 × 51.5 cm
National Trust, Dyrham Park, Gloucestershire – The Blathwayt Collection (NT 453821)

PROVENANCE
Probably acquired by William Blathwayt; thence by descent; the J.R.W Blathwayt sale, Sotheby's, 29 February 1956, probably lot 22; bought by the National Trust at Christie's, 24 July 1987, lot 85

LITERATURE
Ingamells 2009, p. 329

William III (1650–1702) is shown, despite his long hair, as a modern interpretation of a Roman general, with his cloak draped, toga-like, across his shoulders. The portrait was intended to convey his suitability for strong leadership. He was the son of Mary Stuart, the British Princess Royal (1631–1660) and William II, Prince of Orange and Stadtholder of the United Provinces of the Netherlands (1626–1650). Born in The Hague, he became Prince of Orange at birth as his father died of smallpox just eight days beforehand. Through his mother he was an heir to the English, Scottish and Irish thrones and, in 1677, in a highly strategic and political match organised by the courts in London and The Hague, he married his cousin, Princess Mary (1662–1694). During the increasingly unpopular reign of his Catholic father-in-law James II (1633–1701), he was invited to invade England. Subsequently, in 1688, he led the so-called Glorious Revolution, which resulted in his father-in-law being deposed. William III and his wife succeeded as Britain's only joint monarchs, ruling as William III and Mary II.[1]

The portrait came to Dyrham Park in Gloucestershire through William Blathwayt (?1649–1717), who was a close associate of the king and worked in various posts in his government, including running the army. He also spoke Dutch, and at Dyrham the Dutch character of the house would have been

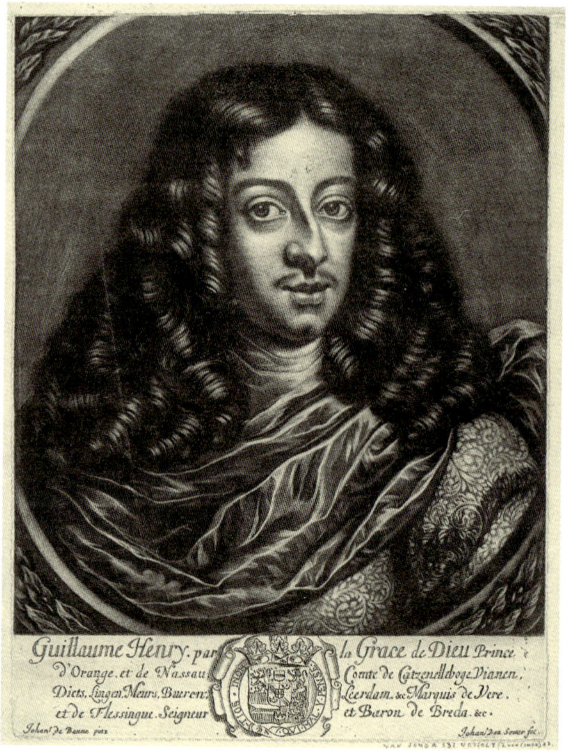

FIG. 27
Jan van Somer (1645–1699),
after Jan de Baen (1633–1702)
William III when Prince of Orange (1650–1702)
Mezzotint and engraving on paper,
350 × 257 mm
London, British Museum
(1927,1008.346)

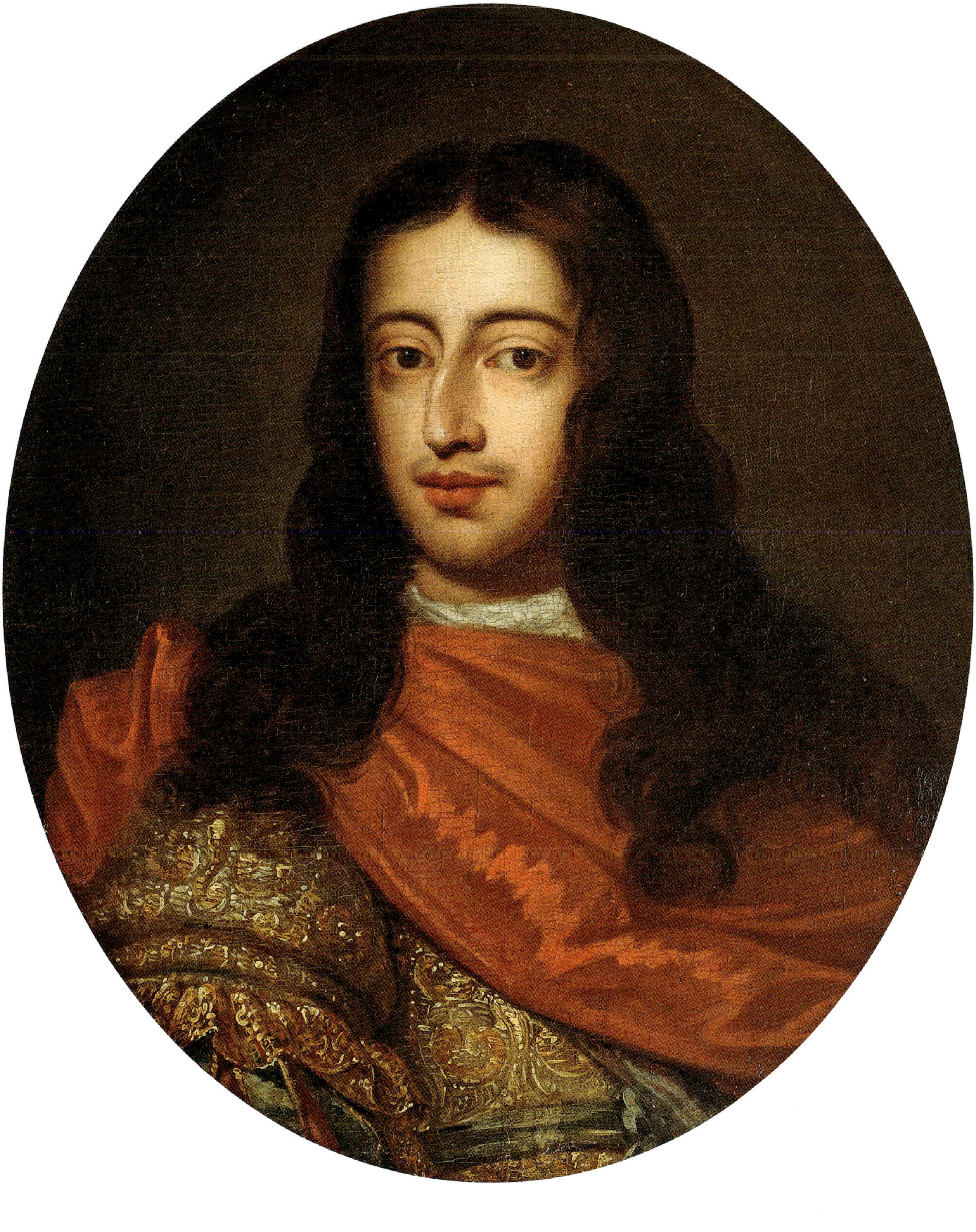

FIG. 28
Jan de Baen (1633–1702)
William III when Prince of Orange (1650–1702), *c.*1667
Oil on canvas, 180.3 × 133.1 cm
Royal Collection Trust (RCIN 404779)

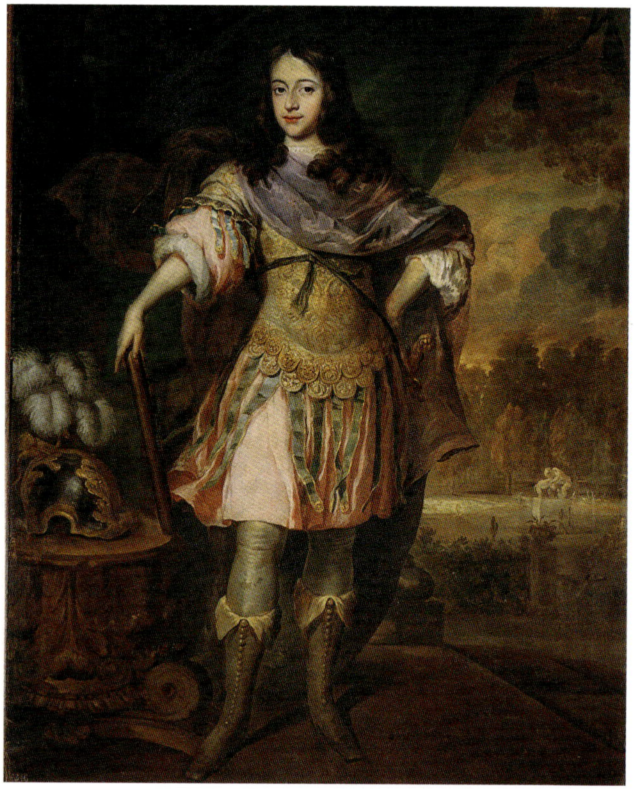

noticeable to the visitor as they arrived through parks and gardens influenced by Dutch examples, such as at Het Loo, despite the hilly Gloucestershire setting. Inside, the house was filled with Dutch pictures, furniture and porcelain. The visitor to Dyrham today will see portraits of the later Protestant Stuarts that Blathwayt was so loyal to – two of William and one each of Mary II and of Queen Anne (1665–1714) and her consort, George of Denmark (1653–1708).[2]

The present picture has been attributed to various artists, including Abraham Ragenau, to someone painting in the style of Pieter Nason, or to a copyist working after Caspar Netscher, all of whom who did paint William's portrait. But it is closer in style to portraits by Jan de Baen, and a mezzotint of the image (fig. 27), of which there are two impressions, states that the original painting was by De Baen, an artist who had trained in Amsterdam under Jacob Adriaensz Backer and then had moved to The Hague, where his patrons included the exiled Charles II.

Sets of portraits in country houses sometimes include works that were produced by an artist's studio assistants, or works that were copied later by painters who were outside the circle of the original artist, and these would be hung alongside autograph pictures by the same painters (for example, this is the case with the set of Honthorst portraits on the stairs at Ashdown House – see cat. 9 – or the set of Lely portraits in the Long Gallery at Ham House – see cat. 12). Versions and copies of such portraits were acquired for a number of reasons, such as availability of an autograph work, the desire for a copy of a specific image, or sometimes expense. It appears that the aesthetic look of a room as a whole would often take precedence over the quality of individual pictures. The National Trust has many key collections with such images, among them the present portrait of William, which may have been painted by studio assistants. It is clear, however, that Blathwayt wanted a painted version of his royal friend and master in this particular youthful, optimistic image of him. One of the reasons for that may have been that it reminded him of when he first met William, during the three years that he worked as a young man in the embassy in The Hague, which was around the time the future king sat to De Baen.

Two versions exist of a full-length portrait of William by De Baen (in the Royal Collection and the National Portrait Gallery, London),[3] a picture that relates to the Dyrham image and again shows the sitter in a fanciful version of a classical costume (fig. 28).[4] It was highly fashionable to show a contemporary ruler in such a Roman costume, as it alluded to their suitability to rule and command, but William here is also linked to specific classical figures. The background of the composition includes a landscape with a statue of Hercules fighting the Nemean Lion, with the allusion that William himself is a Hercules, a figure of fortitude and virtue with whom he particularly associated himself.

Visual references to the king as Hercules continued after he became king in 1688, most notably in the decorative scheme at Hampton Court. He was also associated with other classical figures, for instance dancing in the role of the god Mercury in a ballet in 1668 at the Binnenhof in The Hague, performed to celebrate the signing of the Treaty of Breda. In 1697 he was presented as the Trojan hero Aeneas, the eponymous subject of Virgil's *Aeneid*. Jacob Tonson had acquired the engraving plates for the 1654 *Aeneid* published by John Ogilvy, which was illustrated with what appeared to be depictions of a young Charles II as the hero. When Tonson was preparing to publish John's Dryden's translation of Virgil, he had the images reworked to show Aeneas with William's recognisable features, as he needed royal patronage to help finance the publication and he wanted to avoid the king's displeasure at Dryden's refusal to swear allegiance to William and Mary after the revolution. DT

NOTES

1 William ruled Scotland as William II.
2 *Mary II*, studio of Willem Wissing, NT 453782; *Queen Anne*, after Sir Godfrey Kneller, NT 453783; *George of Denmark*, studio of Michael Dahl, NT 453784.
3 RCIN 404779 and NPG 6269.
4 White 1982, no. 12, pl. 11; Ingamells 2009, p. 323.

2

ABRAHAM BLOEMAERT (1566–1651)

*The Baptism of Christ, c.*1598–1600

Oil on canvas, 77 × 115 cm
National Trust, Ham House, Surrey – The Dysart Collection (NT 1140058)

PROVENANCE
At Ham House by 1679; thence by descent; acquired by HM Government when Sir Lyonel Tollemache, 4th Baronet and Sir Cecil Tollemache, 5th Baronet gave Ham House to the National Trust in 1948; entrusted to the care of the Victoria and Albert Museum until 1990, when returned to the National Trust; ownership transferred to the National Trust in 2002

SELECTED LITERATURE
Lowenthal 1986, pp. 88 and 145; Roethlisberger and Bok 1993, I, pp. 108–09, no. 61, and II, fig. 110; Luijten, Van Suchtelen, Baarsen and Kloek 1993, pp. 554–55, no. 225

This painting by Abraham Bloemaert shows a number of colourfully dressed converts preparing to be baptised in a luxuriant forest. In the foreground, a soldier clad in red bends over to take off his shoe. Next to him sits a man who removes his last article of clothing, a stocking, while the youth leaning against the tree only has to remove his hat. More people undress behind the tree, at left and right; perhaps the figures in the right foreground have already participated in the ritual.[1] Christ, visible in the background, kneels on a rock in the River Jordan as he undergoes baptism by John the Baptist. Above them, the sky opens up, as recounted in the Gospel according to St Luke, 3: 21–22: 'Now when all the people were baptised, it came to pass, that Jesus also being baptised, and praying, the heaven was opened, and the Holy Ghost descended in a bodily shape like a dove upon him, and a voice came from heaven, which said, "Thou art my beloved Son; in thee I am well pleased".' No dove is visible here, but there are angels in the sky. A number of those receiving baptism look or point heavenwards, moved by the parting of the clouds and the voice speaking to Christ.

This episode from the Bible was a rewarding subject for Mannerist painters, since the figures disrobing in preparation for baptism provided opportunities to depict many different poses.[2] This aspect must have appealed to the Utrecht painter Abraham Bloemaert as well. Bloemaert was born on 25 December 1566 into a Catholic family in Gorinchem.[3] After receiving his first drawing lessons from his father, the sculptor and architect Cornelis Bloemaert, he went on to study with no fewer than six other painters, including Gerrit Splinter and Joost de Beer in Utrecht and Jean Bassot and Hieronymus Franken in Paris. Around 1585 he returned to Utrecht, where he spent the rest of his life, apart from a stay in Amsterdam between 1591 and 1593. His very long and highly successful career led him to be called the 'father of the Utrecht school of painting'.[4] Bloemaert operated internationally, coming into contact with such highly placed persons as Elizabeth Stuart, the 'Winter Queen', and Christian IV, King of Denmark.[5] Many of his numerous pupils developed into renowned painters, among them Cornelis van Poelenburch (cat. 16), Hendrick ter Brugghen and Gerrit van Honthorst (cat. 9).[6]

Various elements in the work discussed here can be traced to Bloemaert's *Tekenboek*, a drawing 'manual' or series of examples of draughtsmanship published several times as engravings from around 1650.[7] The

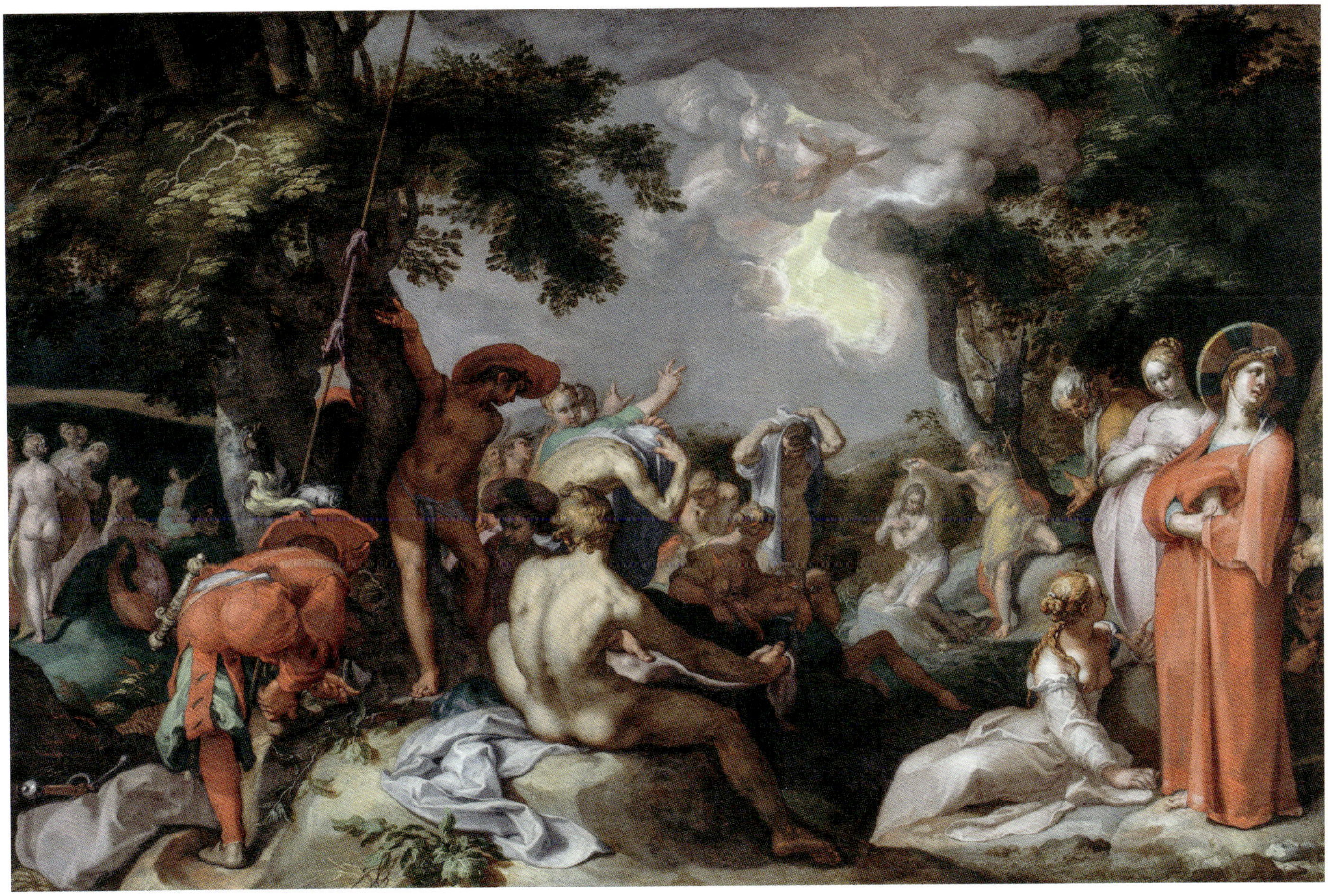

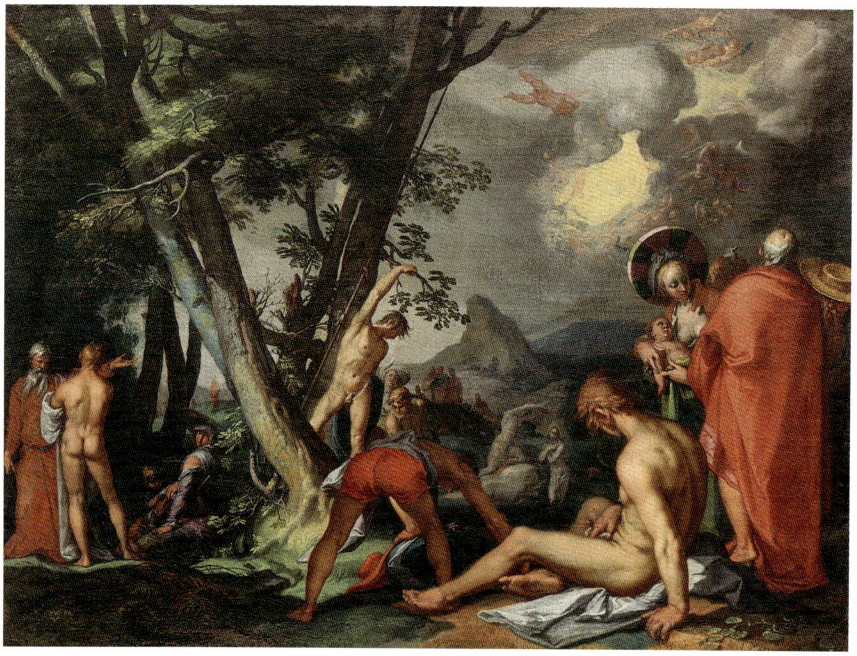

FIG. 29
Abraham Bloemaert (1566–1651)
The Baptism of Christ, 1602
Oil on canvas, 60 × 77 cm
Ottawa, National Gallery of Canada
(inv. 3340)

pose of the soldier preparing to undo his shoelace corresponds to the *Tekenboek* drawing of a man tying on his skates,[8] and the right leg of the man removing his stocking can also be seen in one of the set.[9] The woman on the right displays close similarities to a study of a man that is in the State Hermitage Museum in St Petersburg.[10] By placing these and other groups of figures at the front and back of the scene and by varying their size, Bloemaert created layers of planes, whereby Christ and John the Baptist appear at the back of the stage, between the coulisses formed, as it were, by supporting actors.

Bloemaert deployed this theatrical style to a slightly lesser extent twice more in paintings of the same subject, in which he recycled and rearranged motifs from earlier works. In a second version, painted in 1602, some years after the present work, dated *c.*1598–1600, the composition is less crowded (fig. 29). This painting includes the same cloudburst of angels, as well as the spear leaning against the tree. The protagonists, Christ and John the Baptist, are somewhat smaller and placed in the background.

Bloemaert painted the Baptism of Christ a third time in 1646, at a much older age (present location unknown). This time he portrayed the subject in a more classicist manner. Despite the difference in style and the fact that the painting originated more than four decades later, we see once again the nude man seated in the foreground of the 1602 work, and a man undressing at right who displays similarities to the figure in the background of the painting at Ham House.[11]

Given Bloemaert's fame, which extended well beyond the borders of the Dutch Republic, it is hardly surprising that his work had made its way into the collection of Ham House by the last quarter of the seventeenth century. The painting is first mentioned in a 1679 inventory of the house and subsequently in the 'Estimate of Pictures' compiled around 1683, when Elizabeth Murray, Countess of Dysart (see pp. 14 and 39 and cat. 2 and 12), was living in the house with her second husband, John Maitland (1616–1682), 1st Duke of Lauderdale. In the estimate the painting is described as 'St. John baptizing of Abra: Bloomhart',

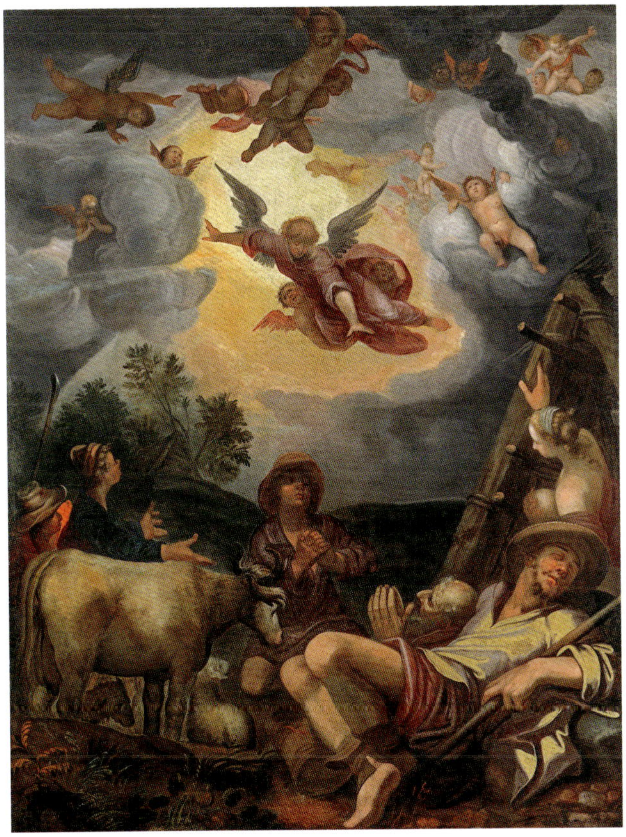

FIG. 30
After Abraham Bloemaert (1566–1651)
The Angel Appearing to the Shepherds, before 1677
Oil on canvas, 203 × 150 cm
National Trust, Ham House, Surrey
(NT 1139663)

and valued at fifteen pounds and listed as hanging in the Duchess's White Closet.[12] An early copy after a lost painting by Bloemaert, *The Angel Appearing to the Shepherds*, had already been recorded in the 1677 inventory of the collection at Ham House (fig. 30).[13] Together with Bloemaert's *Wedding of Cupid and Psyche*, which became part of the collection of Charles II in the seventeenth century, these works are among the earliest documented paintings by or after Bloemaert in England.[14] The present painting has been at Ham House for almost three-and-a-half centuries. CR

NOTES

1 Roethlisberger and Bok 1993, p. 108.
2 W. Kloek in Luijten, Van Suchtelen, Baarsen and Kloek 1993, p. 554.
3 On Abraham Bloemaert, see Roethlisberger and Bok 1993; Wegener 1995, pp. 547–48; Bolten 2007; https://rkd.nl/explore/artists/9120 (with bibliographical references).
4 Wegener 1995, pp. 547–48.
5 M.J. Bok in Luijten, Van Suchtelen, Baarsen and Kloek 1993, p. 301.
6 Wegener 1995, pp. 547–48.
7 M.J. Bok in Roethlisberger and Bok 1993, p. 585; M.J. Bok in Luijten, Van Suchtelen, Baarsen and Kloek 1993, p. 301. Original model drawings for the *Tekenboek* were compiled in the second half of the seventeenth century in the so-called Cambridge Album, which is kept at the Fitzwilliam Museum, Cambridge (PD 166.1963). The first edition of this book of engravings appeared around 1650; an edition by Bernard Picart followed in 1723, and in 1740 an edition by Reinier and Josua Ottens: see Roethlisberger and Bok 1993, pp. 389–94, and Bolten 2007, p. 362, note 22.
8 Roethlisberger and Bok 1993, p. 108.
9 Abraham Bloemaert, *Six Legs*, Cambridge, The Fitzwilliam Museum (Bolten 2007, I, p. 389, no. 1275).
10 Abraham Bloemaert, *A Standing Man in a Wide Cloak, seen from his Left Side*, c.1620–30, St Petersburg, State Hermitage Museum (Bolten 2007, I, p. 302, no. 907).
11 Roethlisberger and Bok 1993, pp. 108–10, nos. 61, 62, and 350, no. 561.
12 Quoted from A. Laing, 'Appendix 2: Fitting Pictures to Rooms: A Re-Examination of the Ham House 'Estimate of Pictures' (c.1683), and its Collation with the Inventories', in Rowell 2013, pp. 410–11, no. 29.
13 Laing in Rowell 2013, pp. 414–15, citing the 1677, 1679 and c.1683 inventories.
14 Roethlisberger and Bok 1993, p. 109.

Architecture

RUPERT GOULDING, NATIONAL TRUST LEAD CURATOR (SOUTH WEST)

THE ARCHITECTURAL RELATIONSHIP between the Netherlands and Britain in the seventeenth century – and this is also the case with gardens – is hard to quantify on detailed examination. So-called 'dolls' houses' like Uppark or Ashdown and gables like those at Blickling are popularly taken to be Dutch, yet rarely are the influences on their design straightforward or direct. This was nevertheless a period of cultural exchange between the two countries: there were British resident in the Netherlands and British travellers were impressed with what they encountered there; Dutch architectural treatises and prints were published and bought, and some Dutch designers found work in Britain.[1]

Two National Trust houses are attributed to designers with clear Dutch associations. Lodge Park in Sherborne, Gloucestershire (fig. 32) is a kind of grandstand from which to watch coursing, first described as 'lately built' in 1634, with specific reference being made to Inigo Jones's Banqueting House. The basis of the design in fact derives from the Italian theorist Sebastiano Serlio and his principles of harmonic proportion, and the attribution to Jones himself is unlikely; but a plausible candidate is Jones's master-mason Nicholas Stone, who worked locally. Stone introduces a Dutch connection, because Stone, through Jones, met the Dutch sculptor and architect Hendrick de Keyser and subsequently moved to study under him in Amsterdam and to marry his daughter Mayken. It may never be known who designed the compact, classically inspired building at Sherborne, but its spirited, though also mathematical, design perhaps stems from a close Anglo-Dutch relationship.

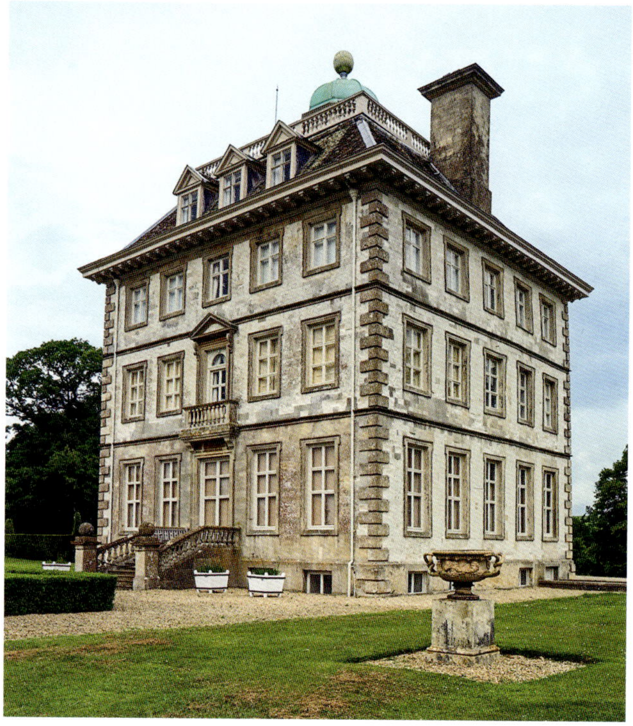

FIG. 31
The exterior of Ashdown House, Oxfordshire

Ashdown House, Oxfordshire, was built as a hunting lodge in the 1660s by William, 1st Earl of Craven for Elizabeth Stuart, the 'Winter Queen' of Bohemia (fig. 31). The design is attributed to the Dutch émigré Sir Balthazar Gerbier, who at the time was working on Lord Craven's house Hampstead Marshall, Berkshire. Gerbier was assisted by Captain William Winde, who is credited with completing both projects after his death. Born in the Netherlands to exiled British royalists, Winde served with English troops

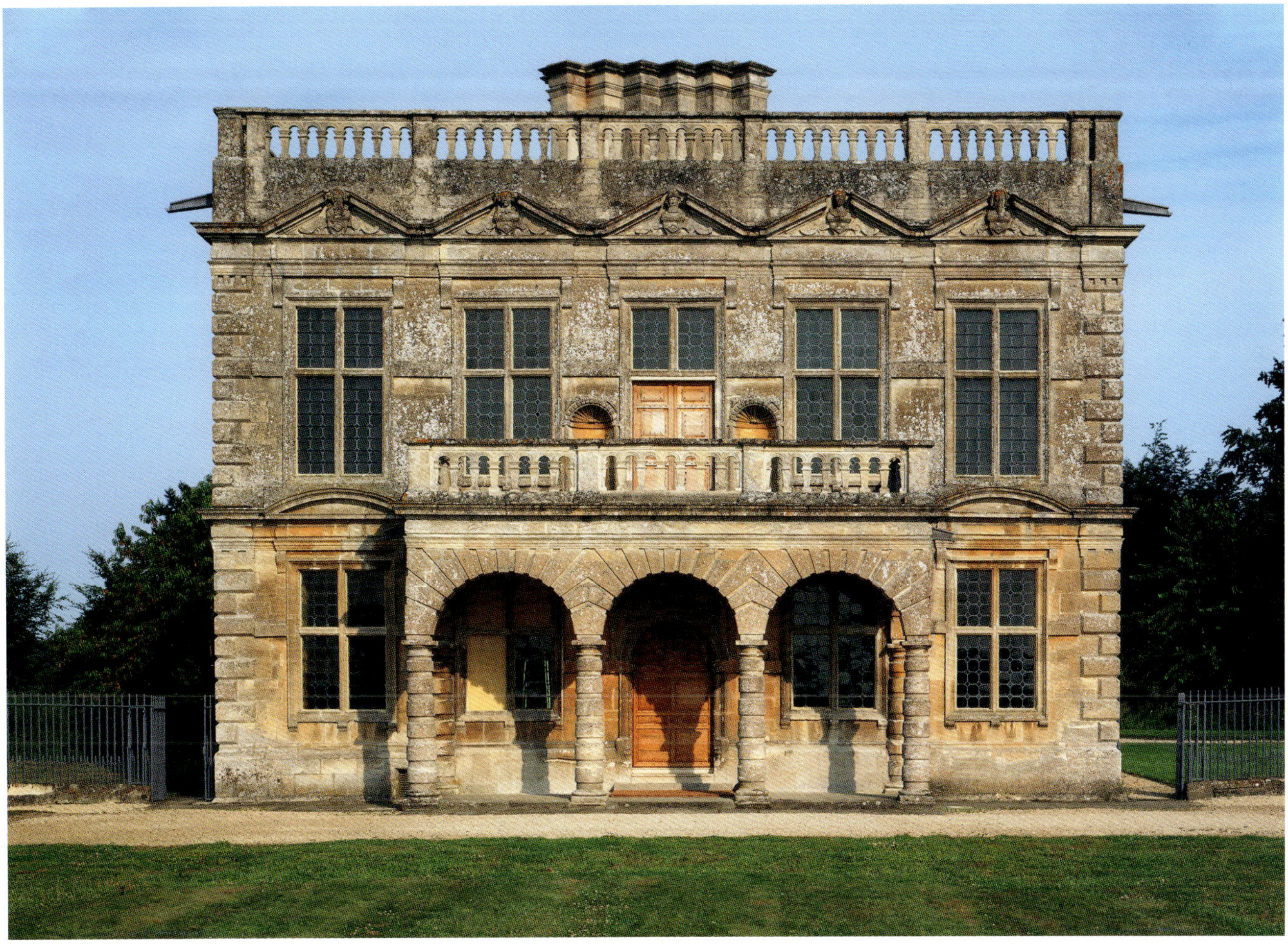

FIG. 32
The East Front of Lodge Park, Gloucestershire

based there and was appointed Gentleman Usher to Elizabeth (in exile in Holland) before coming to England with the Restoration of Charles II. Winde worked on other National Trust properties – an earlier house at Cliveden, Berkshire (destroyed 1795); apartments and gardens at Powis Castle, Powys, and an initial design at Belton House, Derbyshire. But only in Ashdown can we identify a confluence of Dutch designers and patronage.[2]

The first house in Britain credited with drawing directly on Dutch rather than from Italian sources of classicism is Eltham Lodge in Kent (private; 1663–64), where gentleman-architect Hugh May based his design on the Mauritshuis in The Hague. Eltham is sometimes grouped with Coleshill, Oxfordshire (*c*.1658–62, destroyed by fire in 1952). The clean classical style and the involvement of Sir Roger Pratt, who travelled in the Netherlands during the Civil War, had encouraged this association, but recent scholarship suggests a more significant role for Inigo Jones instead. However, when Pratt came to design Kingston Lacy (1663–65, remodelled by Sir Charles Barry in 1835) we know that

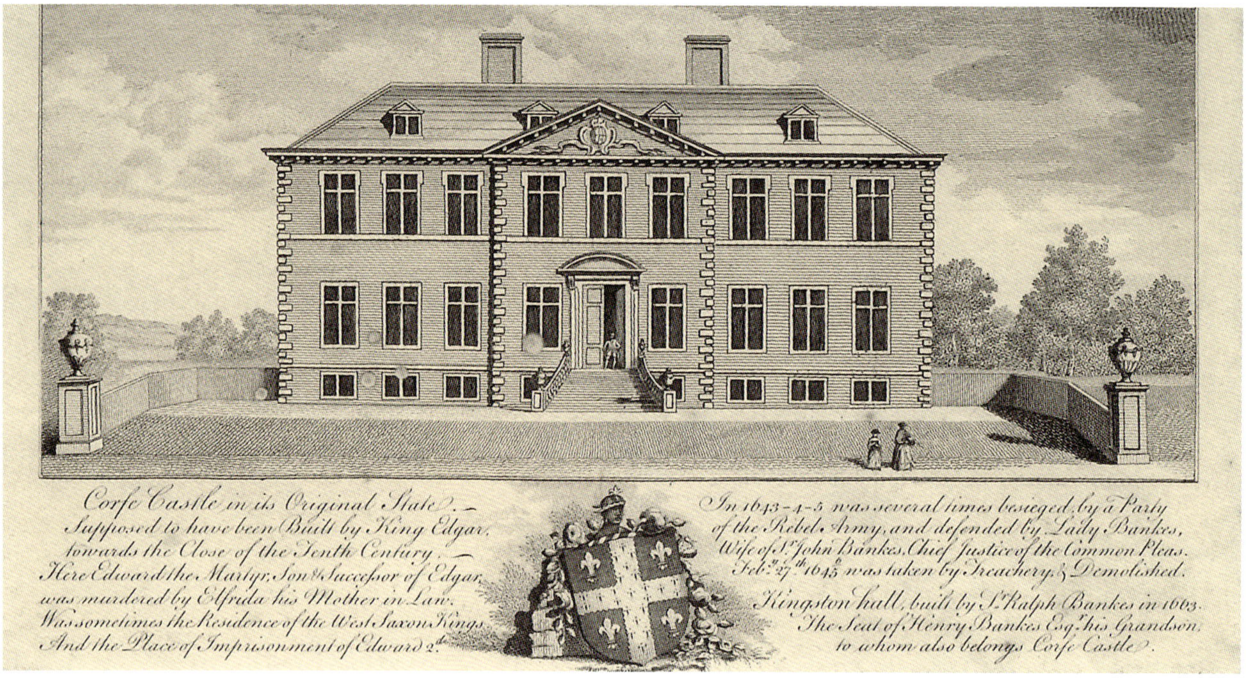

FIG. 33
Kingston Hall after the roof had been rebuilt without a cupola and balustrade, engraving (detail) from Rev. John Hutchins, *The History and Antiquity of the County iof Dorset*, 1774
National Trust, Kingston Lacy, Dorset
(NT 1251346)

he purchased the classicising Dutch architect Jacob van Campen's *Stadt huys van Amsterdam* (1661), and the house he built here (fig. 33) has greater similarity to the Dutch 'astylar' (non-columnar) classicism he would have witnessed on his travels.

Anglo-Dutch cultural exchange encompassed architectural technology and building materials. British stone was exported to the Netherlands, perhaps in less quantity and variety than may be expected given the geological range available, and bricks returned from Holland in great and increasing volumes as the seventeenth century progressed.[4] The British bought decorative tiles, notably from Delft, though similar tiles were also available in other towns, such as those ordered for chimneypieces in Ham House in the 1670s, and to line a *bagnio* (bathroom) at Dyrham Park in the 1690s. Also at Ham, between 1673–74, over fifty 'sash' windows – featuring the new English innovation involving weights, pulleys and ropes – were installed, and similar windows were subsequently adopted in the Netherlands at William III's houses of Het Loo and Honselaarsdijk during the following decade.[5]

Dutch craftsmen came to work in England, but none are still as well known as Grinling Gibbons. Born in Rotterdam to English parents, he emigrated to England aged nineteen, but spoke the language with a pronounced Dutch accent. At Dunham Massey, Cheshire, Gibbons's panel of *The Crucifixion*, based on a painting by Tintoretto, remains above the Library fireplace – the very piece Gibbons was working on when the diarist John Evelyn discovered the young artist in Deptford and enthusiastically began promoting his talent. His exuberantly carved wooden festoons of fruit, flowers, trophies and game form the most extraordinary architectural moments in many houses; they can be found at Sudbury, Derbyshire (1678), Belton, Lincolnshire, and, most famously, in the Carved Room at Petworth (*c.*1692; fig. 34).

On examination, the joint monarchs William III and Mary II did not stimulate the development of a distinctly Dutch aesthetic in Britain; instead their court style embraced a broader medley of English, French, Italian, Dutch and classical forms. A critical figure was the Dutch-French émigré Daniel Marot, who designed (and published) unified architectural interiors, fixtures, furnishings and gardens for William III and his courtiers. His first English commission is supposed to be the remodelling of Petworth for the 6th Duke of Somerset in a grand French Baroque style, featuring a central squared dome. Marot worked at the royal palaces under William Talman, Comptroller of the King's Works, who is considered the leading proponent of the court style in country house architecture.[6] Talman designed the east front and greenhouse at Dyrham Park (*c.*1700), while Uppark, West Sussex, is attributed to him. He himself never travelled to the Netherlands, but his son John studied in Leiden University from 1697 and made purchases for Talman's famously extensive and valuable collection of architectural prints, books and drawings while there.

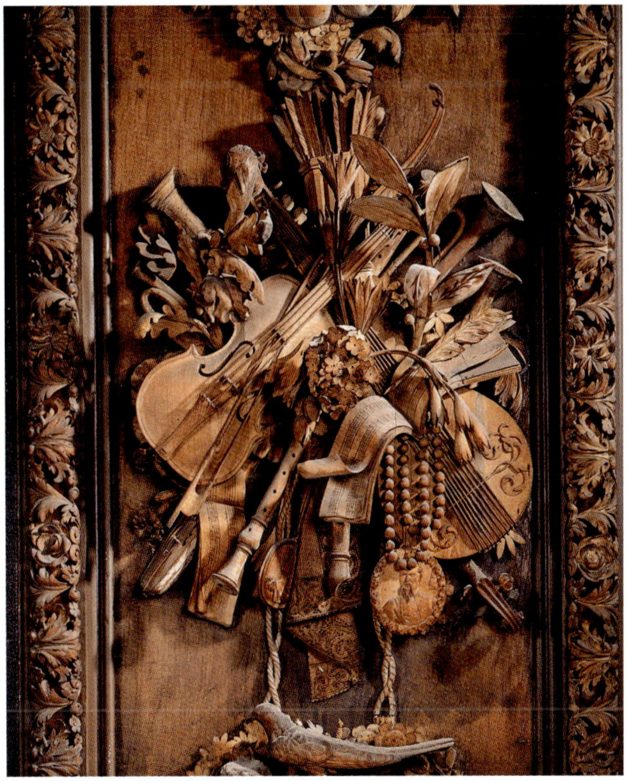

FIG. 34
The lime-wood carving of musical instruments by Grinling Gibbons, situated on the east wall of the Carved Room at Petworth House, West Sussex (*c.*1692)

NOTES

1 See Jardine 2008.
2 Colvin 1984, pp. 248–309.
3 Mowl and Earnshaw 1995, p. 55; Stoesser-Johnston 2002, pp. 121–37.
4 Louw 2009, pp. 83–120.
5 See D. Adshead, 'Altered with Skill and Dexterity: The Caroline House', in Rowell 2013, pp. 107–08.
6 See Jackson-Stops 1988.

3

GERARD TER BORCH (1617–1681)

The Introduction, *c*.1662

Oil on canvas, 76 × 68 cm
National Trust, Polesden Lacey, Surrey – The McEwan Collection (NT 1246491)

PROVENANCE
The Johan Aegidiusz van der Marck sale, Amsterdam, 25 August 1773, lot 326, to De Bruijn; the Jan Jacob de Bruijn sale, Amsterdam, 12 September 1798, lot 8, to Philippus van der Schley, dealer; George Craufurd, Rotterdam; bought by George Granville, 2nd Marquess of Stafford at his sale, Christie's, 26 April 1806, lot 11; at Stafford House in and after 1833; bought by Adrian Lesser at the Yolande Stephens sale, Christie's, 11 May 1895, lot 347; from whom bought by Sir William McEwan in 1896; by descent to Dame Margaret Greville; bequeathed by her to the National Trust in 1942

EXHIBITED
Dutch Pictures 1450–1750, Royal Academy of Arts, London, 1952–53, no. 398; *The Treasure Houses of Britain*, National Gallery of Art, Washington, 1985–86, no. 293; *In Trust for the Nation*, National Gallery, London, 1995–96, no. 64

SELECTED LITERATURE
Gudlaugsson 1959–60, I, pp. 132–33; II, pp. 183–84, no. 187; Langemeyer *et al.* 1974, pp. 168–69, no. 49; Laing 1995, no. 64; A. McNeil Kettering in Wheelock *et al.* 2004, pp. 141–43, no. 36

Gerard ter Borch, a native of Zwolle, was one of the most widely travelled Dutch artists of his time. His apprenticeship to the landscape painter Pieter de Molijn in Haarlem was followed by an international career. Ter Borch spent at least a year training in London with his uncle, the engraver Robert van Voerst, whose collaboration with the celebrated Anthony van Dyck and other portraitists active in England no doubt strongly influenced the young artist. After that, Ter Borch spent time in a succession of cities in the Low Countries, Germany, France, Italy and possibly Spain, acquiring a reputation as a talented portraitist before turning to genre painting in around 1650. Four years later Ter Borch married in Deventer, the provincial town where he would live and work for almost the rest of his life, and it was there that he painted *The Introduction*.

With its subtle lighting and unequalled rendering of fabrics, this ambiguous painting – datable to about 1662 – is one of Ter Borch's masterpieces. The viewer's eye is instantly drawn to the young woman in her beautifully rendered dress of satin. This was the painter's trademark, though he never depicted more than one satin dress per painting, as is the case here. In an otherwise dark interior, the woman is bathed in light, which allowed Ter Borch to make the most of painting the effects of light on the satin folds. The woman's dress perfectly reflects the fashions of the 1660s, with its round, low shoulder line, puffed lower sleeves, and bodice cut horizontally at the top, with a shawl draped at the front.[1] Her hand is held by an officer who bows deeply to her, by way of formal introduction. This is undoubtedly their first meeting. That he is a professional soldier is evident from his metal breast-plate and the sword hanging from his coat; like the spurs on his boots, these elements were executed with great feeling for detail. The man still holds his hat in his hand and has obviously just come into the room, for his entrance has interrupted the music-making of the couple sitting at the table. The man seated there plays the lute – in those days, this string instrument was inevitably associated with

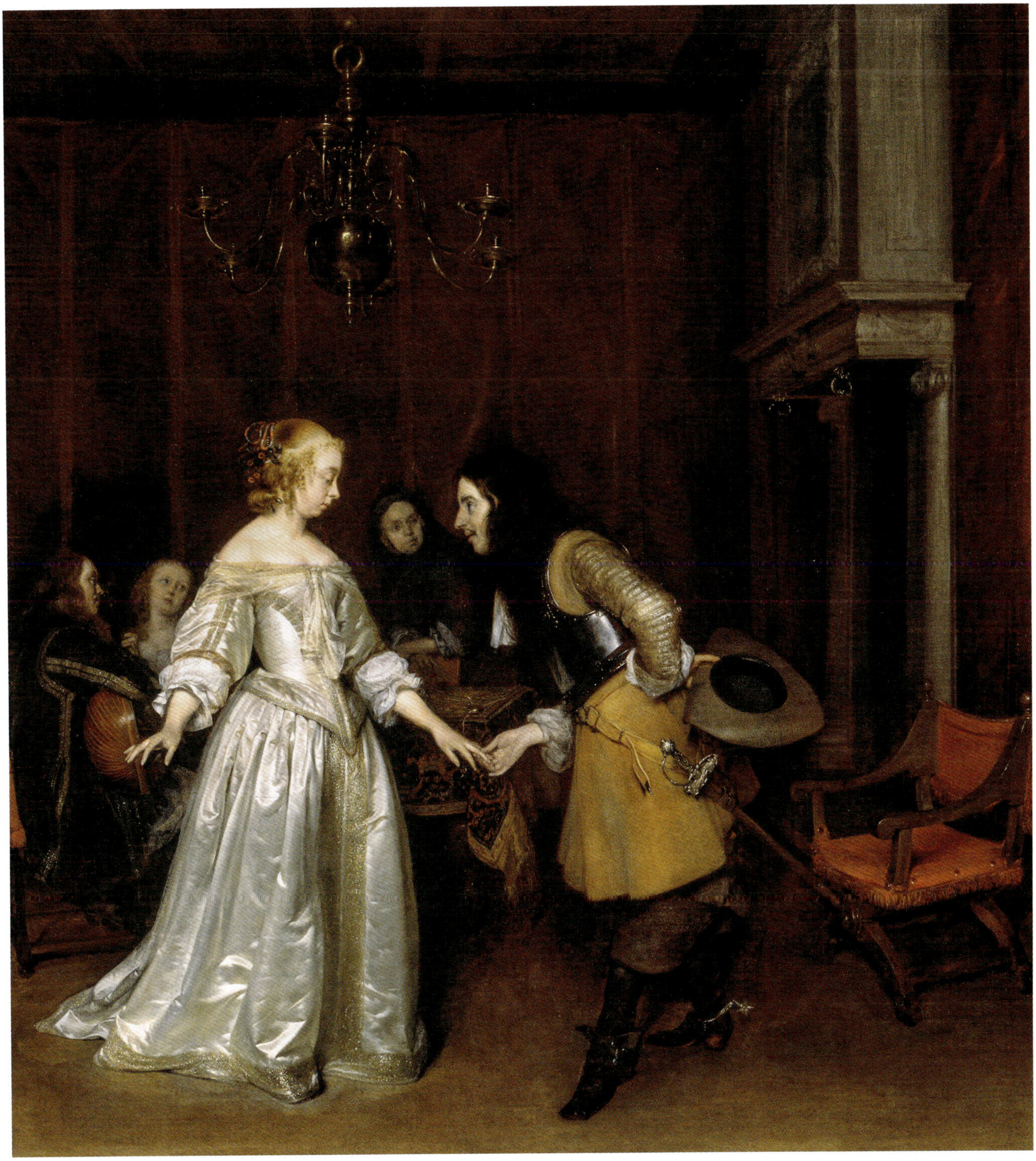

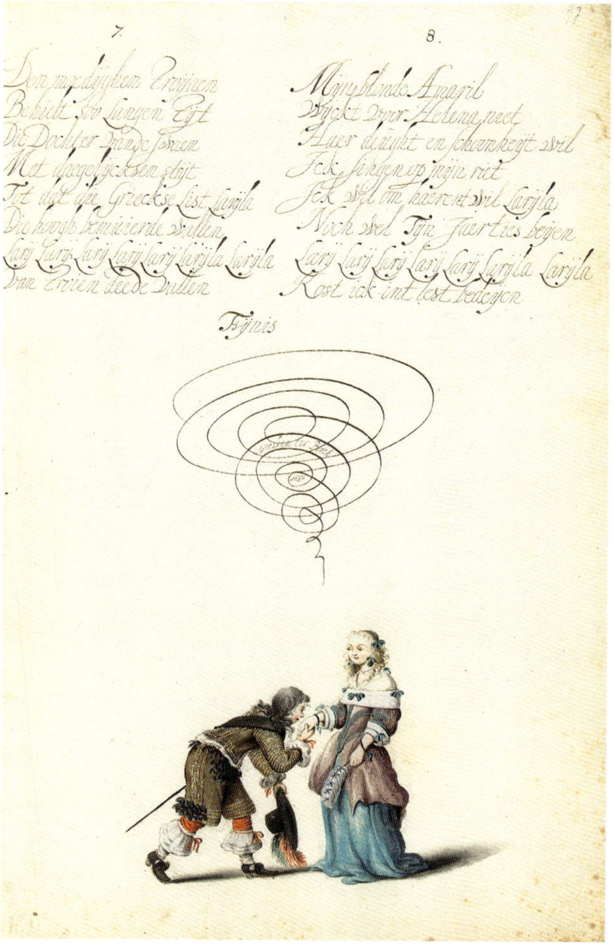

FIG. 35
Gesina ter Borch (1617–1681)
Gentleman Bowing to Kiss a Lady's Hand, 1656
Brush and black ink and various colours,
318 cm × 210 mm (entire sheet with text,
part of Gesina's poetry album, fol. 97 *recto*)
Amsterdam, Rijksmuseum, acquired with the
support of the Rembrandt Association, 1887
(BI–1890–1952–97)

love (see cat. 15) – and accompanies the song sung by the woman next to him. She has turned to scrutinise the officer, whose armour and spurs are at odds with the refined world of satin and music that he has just entered. The singer is not the only one to train her eyes on the soldier. Strategically placed between the protagonists in the foreground is an older woman wearing a veil, who seems to be assessing the couple's meeting with her piercing gaze. We can only speculate about what will happen next, for, even though the officer gives the young woman a highly expectant look, with his mouth slightly open and his body bending forwards, her back is ramrod straight and unyielding, and her look extremely reserved, as if she is still considering her reaction. Perhaps the old woman is a procuress, who has brought the officer and the woman together, in which case the setting must be a brothel.[2] Procuresses of this type occur frequently in genre paintings of the Dutch Golden Age. Ordinary soldiers and higher-ranking officers alike were notorious for their loose morals,[3] and the painting would therefore conform to an old tradition in Dutch painting. Whereas brothels in older paintings are generally furnished as fairly simple rooms (according to contemporary descriptions, they could be rather foul places),[4] it is possible that Ter Borch wished to obscure the setting of this and similar scenes by giving the room quite splendid furnishings, so that a painting of this kind could also hang in the homes of well-to-do clients without causing too much offence.[5] The costly carpet on the table, the impressive stone mantelpiece, the brass chandelier hanging from the ceiling and the wall hangings combine to make this a richly appointed interior. On closer inspection, one notices a timepiece lying on the table: its glass cover is open, and the key used to wind it up is attached to a chain, which hangs in front of the carpet, exactly where the hands of the man and woman come together – a detail not previously observed. Should this be interpreted as a reference to the man's search for the key to the woman's heart?

Whatever the exact nature of this setting, Ter Borch's portrayal of the poses and facial expressions of the man and woman in the foreground testifies to profound psychological insight and a subtle approach. It is striking that the woman's face is worked out smoothly and in great detail, certainly in comparison to the man's, which catches less light. The painter's refined technique is characterised by soft brushwork, with which he succeeds in rendering all the surfaces very convincingly, not only the dazzling satin of the dress but also the officer's beautifully finished sleeve, where Ter Borch took great pains to render the effects of light on the gleaming fabric. He placed similar white highlights on the handle of the man's sword, making it just as eye-catching as his sleeve.

The woman is a type that Ter Borch painted with some regularity. Her features recall those of his younger sister, Gesina ter Borch (1631–1690).[6] In this context it is interesting that Gesina, herself a gifted artist, depicted in a poetry album a similar scene portraying a gentleman bowing to a lady, this time to kiss her hand (fig. 35).[7] Just as in the painting discussed here, we see a lady with a rather guarded look who is approached by a very eager man. The text accompanying this illustration makes clear that 'it's dogged that does it', and the lady happily accepts the gentleman's offer of love.[8] Gesina's illustration also reveals that the description of her brother's painting as the performance of a dance is definitely incorrect, as is also clearly shown by comparison with dancing figures in contemporary Dutch painting.[9]

Since the beginning of the twentieth century, *The Introduction* has been at Polesden Lacey, where it was no doubt seen by countless members of high society: weekend guests taking part in the sensational *diners dansants* hosted from 1906 by Margaret McEwan (1863–1942) and her husband Ronald Greville (1864–1908), who died at a relatively young age.[10] Upon her death in 1942, McEwan bequeathed Polesden Lacey and its precious contents to the National Trust, in which collection this canvas is among the highlights of seventeenth-century Dutch genre painting. QB

NOTES

1 Langemeyer *et al.* 1974, p. 168. On Ter Borch's painting technique, see Wallert in Wheelock *et al.* 2004, pp. 32–41.
2 Laing 1995, p. 176; McNeil Kettering in Wheelock *et al.* 2004, p. 143.
3 McNeil Kettering in ibid., pp. 143–44.
4 Schama 1987, pp. 467–80.
5 Laing 1995, p. 176.
6 Laing 1995, p. 176; McNeil Kettering in Wheelock *et al.* 2004, p. 143.
7 McNeil Kettering in Wheelock *et al.* 2004, p. 141.
8 McNeil Kettering 1988, II, p. 469.
9 Gudlaugsson 1959–60, I, pp. 132–33, and II, p. 183; see the critical remarks in Langemeyer *et al.* 1974, p. 168; Laing 1995, p. 219, note 1; McNeil Kettering in Wheelock *et al.* 2004, p. 141.
10 Jackson-Stops 1985, p. 364.

4

AMBROSIUS BOSSCHAERT THE YOUNGER (1609–1645)

Blackbird, Butterfly and Cherries, c.1635

Oil on panel, 27 × 41 cm
Signed lower right, on side of ledge: *A. Bos[sc]ha[er]t*
National Trust, Ham House, Surrey – The Dysart Collection (NT 1140187)

PROVENANCE
At Ham House by 1683; thence by descent; acquired by HM Government when Sir Lyonel Tollemache, 4th Baronet and Sir Cecil Tollemache, 5th Baronet gave Ham House to the National Trust in 1948; entrusted to the care of the Victoria and Albert Museum until 1990, when returned to the National Trust; ownership transferred to the National Trust in 2002

SELECTED LITERATURE
Thornton and Tomlin 1980, p. 96; *Public Catalogue Foundation*, V, 2013, p. 93 (as Abraham Bosschaert or Ambrosius Bosschaert the Younger)

A blackbird perches on a stone table-top. In its beak is some pulp from one of the bright red cherries lying in front of it on the table. The bird stands with its left foot on a cherry stem; to its right lies a sprig of cherries, with leaves, which extends along the entire length of the table. The fruit's sweet fragrance has also attracted the peacock butterfly that hovers at left above the table. This simple still life was painted by Ambrosius Bosschaert the Younger, son of the renowned flower painter Ambrosius Bosschaert the Elder.[1] Ambrosius the Younger was baptised in 1609 in Arnemuiden, near the city of Middelburg, where many still-life painters were then active. He had two brothers, Johannes and Abraham, who also became painters. Ambrosius was first trained by his father, who died in 1621, after which his artistic development was influenced by the flower painter Balthasar van der Ast, his maternal uncle.[2] Bosschaert mainly painted flower still lifes, but he also made paintings of fruit and several *vanitas* still lifes. It is apparent from the documentation of his marriage to Maria Struys in 1634 that Roelant Savery acted as one of the witnesses, which demonstrates his ties to this internationally celebrated painter, in addition to the family connections mentioned above. Bosschaert was buried in Utrecht on 19 May 1645.[3]

In the past, doubt has been cast on the authorship of some of the paintings attributed to Ambrosius the Younger, because of the confusion caused by his having the same initials as his father and his brother Abraham. In 1960, Laurens Bol clarified the situation by studying the dated works.[4] At the beginning of his career, Ambrosius the Younger signed his work – just as his father had done – with a square monogram composed of the interlaced capital letters A and B; paintings with a signature written in full are known from 1631 onwards. In these complete signatures, the letters A and B are still square in shape. In a painting of 1635, the letters are no longer square but curly, as also seen in the work discussed here. It is unlikely that his brother Abraham made this painting, because he signed his work with an A and a B in ligature.[5]

Not only the manner of signing but also the metallic appearance of the leaves and the fly are characteristic of Ambrosius Bosschaert the Younger.[6] In fact, the frequency of flies in Bosschaert the Younger's paintings led Bol to nickname him 'master of the flies'.[7] His *Dead Frog with Flies* in the Frits Lugt Collection in Paris even

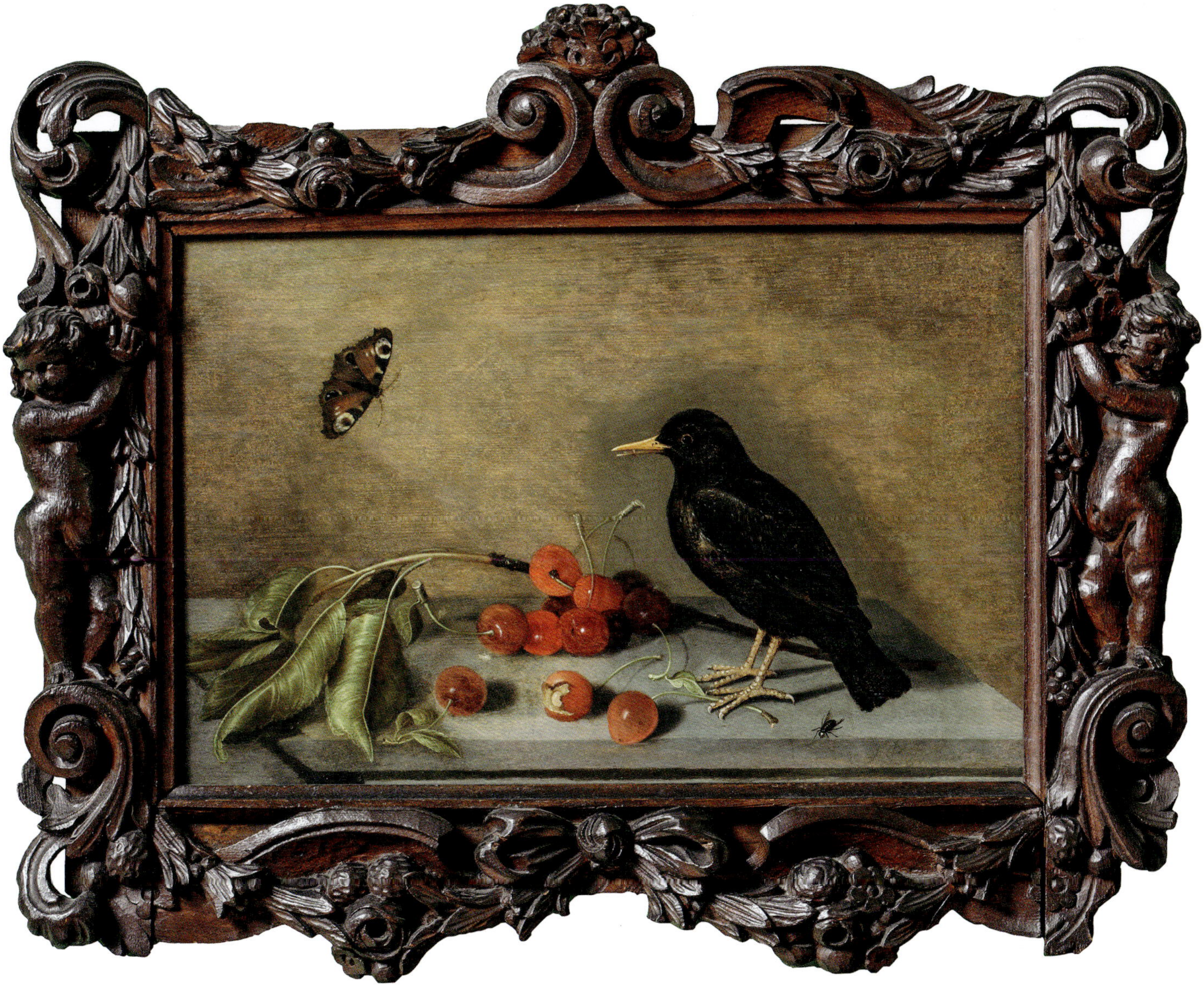

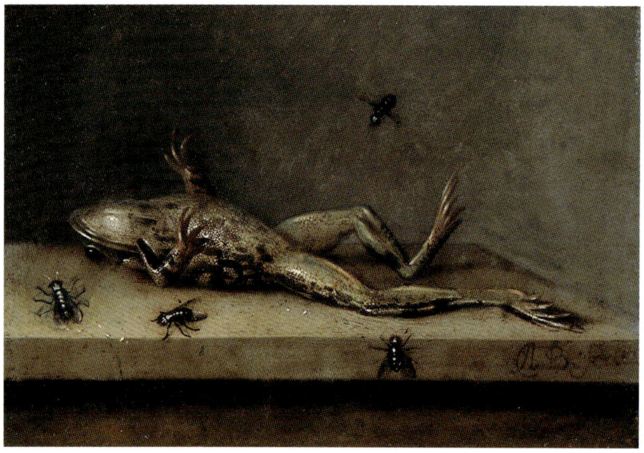

FIG. 36
Ambrosius Bosschaert the Younger (1609–1645)
Dead Frog with Flies, *c.*1635–39
Oil on copper, 12.5 × 17.5 cm
Paris, Frits Lugt Collection, Fondation Custodia (182)

contains four of these insects (fig. 36).[8] Like the present painting, that work is based on a standard composition that Bosschaert often used, consisting of a table top and a light grey background.[9] Most of his tables display flowers and insects, which makes *Blackbird, Butterfly and Cherries* – and indeed the Paris painting – something of an oddity in Bosschaert's oeuvre. Live (song)birds seldom appear prominently in still lifes, and, when they do occur, they usually play a minor role in the composition or are included in a presentation of hunting spoils.[10] Bosschaert did not often depict live birds either, though a still life he painted in 1635 does display two parrots and also features a peacock butterfly and cherries (fig. 37). These similarities, combined with the comparable, curling signature, means that Bosschaert probably made the present painting in the same period, around 1635.[11]

The painting has belonged to the collection of Ham House, near London, since the seventeenth century, and its long residence there probably explains why it has gone largely unnoticed in the literature. Ham House was built between 1608 and 1610 for the knight marshal Sir Thomas Vavasour (1560–1620). After 1625, William Murray (*c.*1600–1655), childhood 'whipping boy' to Charles I and later 1st Earl of Dysart, moved into the house. He must have acquired a number of paintings, but it is not known if the present painting was among them.[12] It is first recorded in an inventory drawn up in 1683, when the eldest daughter of the 1st Earl, Elizabeth Murray, Countess of Dysart, was living in the house. Various paintings, possibly even this still life, had been brought to Ham House by her second husband, John Maitland, 1st Duke of Lauderdale. The numbering in the 1683 inventory suggests that the work was probably then hanging in the Inner Hall by the Great Staircase.[13] This is consistent with the fact that the panel is surrounded by a splendid seventeenth-century oak frame, carved – possibly by one of the German or Dutch cabinetmakers working at Ham House – in the same style as the other picture frames in the staircase.[14] The Great Staircase was rebuilt in 1637 or 1638 at the behest of William Murray, and the frames of some of the paintings in this space were also made in that period.[15] In 1670, long after Murray's death, four large paintings in the Great Staircase were given new frames. These later frames are in the style of the frames from the 1630s, but are somewhat more naturalistic and three-dimensional.[16] The similarity in style of the frames made in 1670 to the frame surrounding the present painting suggests that this frame also dates from the third quarter of the seventeenth century.[17] After being moved from one room to another for hundreds of years, this simple still life with its elaborate frame can now be admired in the Green Closet of Ham House. CR

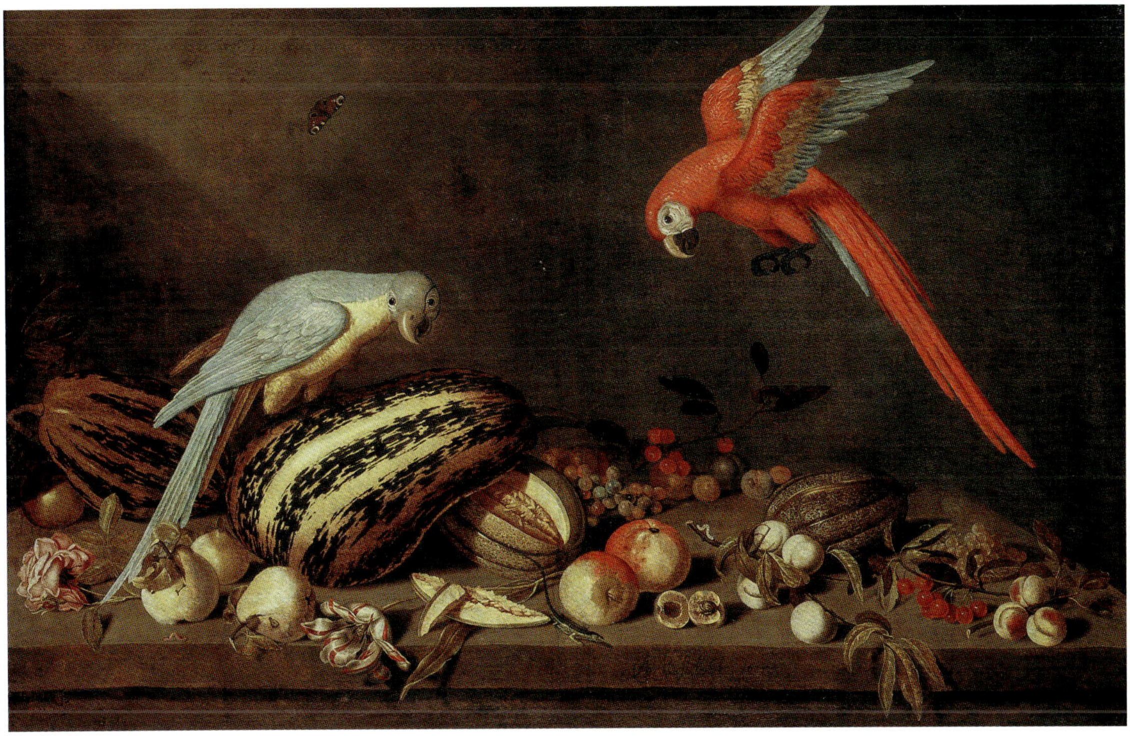

FIG. 37
Ambrosius Bosschaert the Younger (1609–1645)
Still Life with Fruit, Flowers and Two Cockatoos, 1635
Oil on canvas, 109 × 163 cm
Utrecht, Centraal Museum (on loan from the Cultural Heritage Agency of the Netherlands, Amersfoort; 26358)

NOTES

1 Communicated by Fred G. Meijer in an e-mail of 13 December 2017; Meijer states with certainty that the painting was made by Ambrosius Bosschaert the Younger. On this painter, see Bol 1960, pp. 44–48; Bol 1982, pp. 64–65; Gemar-Koeltzsch, Ertz and Nitze-Ertz 1995, pp. 170–77; Meijer 1996, p. 201; Briels 1997, p. 304; Van der Willigen and Meijer 2003, pp. 45–46; https://rkd.nl/explore/artists/11148 (with bibliographic references).
2 Van der Willigen and Meijer 2003, pp. 45–46.
3 Gemar-Koeltzsch, Ertz and Nitze-Ertz 1995, II, p. 170.
4 Bol 1960, p. 44.
5 Van der Willigen and Meijer 2003, pp. 45–46.
6 Communicated by Fred G. Meijer in an e-mail of 13 December 2017.
7 Bol 1960, p. 140.
8 Nihom-Bijstad 1983, pp. 21–22.
9 See, for example, Ambrosius Bosschaert the Younger, *Tulip and Rose and Some Insects on a Stone Plinth*, 1630–39, present location unknown (Segal and Roding 1994, p. 67, no. S12, fig. 36) and Ambrosius Bosschaert the Younger, *Flowers on a Wooden Table*, *c.*1634, present location unknown (Bol 1960, p. 95, no. 18).
10 See, for instance, Roelant Savery, *Flower Still Life with Imperial Crown, Cockatoo and Kingfisher*, 1624, Centraal Museum, Utrecht (De Meyere 2006, p. 360, no. 84) and Clara Peeters, *Hunting Still Life with Fowl*, 1611, Museo Nacional del Prado, Madrid (Buvelot *et al.* 2017, pp. 162–65, no. 17).
11 Communicated by Fred G. Meijer in an e-mail of 13 December 2017; Meijer dates the painting slightly earlier, to around 1633.
12 *Public Catalogue Foundation*, V, 2013, p. 86.
13 Thornton and Tomlin 1980, p. 96.
14 J. Simon, 'Picture Framing at Ham in the Seventeenth Century', in Rowell 2013, pp. 153.
15 *Public Catalogue Foundation*, V, 2013, p. 86.
16 J. Simon in Rowell 2013, p. 153.
17 See, for example, J. Simon in Rowell 2013, p. 153, fig. 134.

Clocks

SIMON CHESTERS-THOMPSON, NATIONAL TRUST CURATOR (MIDLANDS)

THE NATIONAL TRUST'S CANONS ASHBY IN Northamptonshire is soon to receive the forensic attentions of a buildings archaeologist, who will be seeking to make greater sense of its broad palette of ochre stones, its concealed voids and puzzling floor-levels. Those who spend time in the house's sepia world of creaking boards can for now, of course, only speculate as to what may be discovered. But they are nonetheless quietly confident of significant findings, as even the emergency building works of the early 1980s revealed several lost sixteenth-century wall paintings.

Two of the most extraordinary are detailed grisaille depictions of Old Testament scenes that warn of the dangers of worshipping false gods. These were discovered behind panelling in a bedroom, and are believed to have been commissioned around 1590 by Canons Ashby's devout puritan owner, Sir Erasmus Dryden. Such discoveries would have delighted the house's nineteenth-century owner, Sir Henry Dryden the Antiquary, who spent a lifetime investigating the history of his estate and the surrounding county. He would, however, have been familiar with another of his antecedent's commissions, the much-faded mural in a sitting room in the donor family's flat (fig. 38) – almost discreetly sited, immediately left of the door from the long gallery. It is still just possible to make out within it Sir Erasmus and Lady Dryden – plus household – beneath their arms, but overwhelmingly surmounted by a Hebrew Christian symbol within a sunburst. But perhaps puzzlingly secular-looking is the clearly shown wall-mounted clock high up to their right.[1]

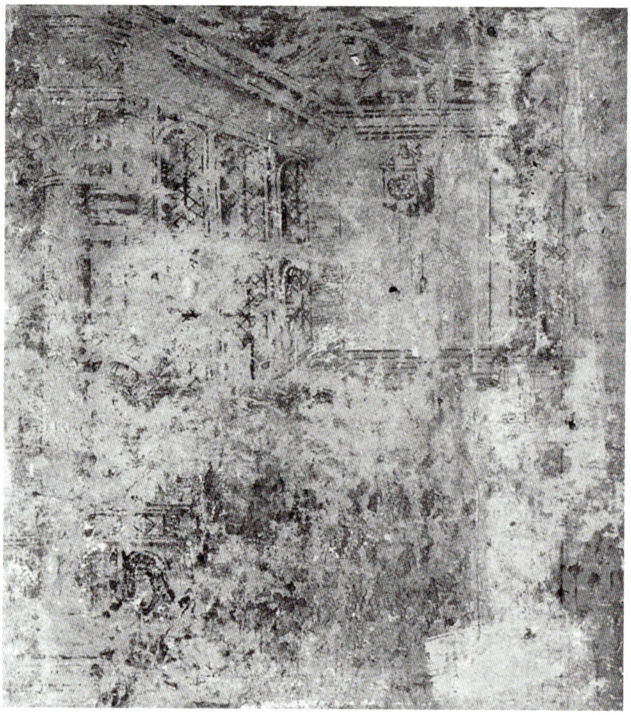

FIG. 38
The much faded 16th-century mural at Canons Ashby, Northamptonshire

Sir Erasmus's very name is illustrative of the strength of the Drydens' northern European Protestant leanings – probably taken from the great Dutch Christian humanist who spent time in England from the end of the fifteenth century and formed lasting friendships with religious thinkers of the time such as Thomas More.

Although remaining within the Catholic Church and occupying the religious centre ground, Erasmus of Rotterdam strongly promoted the importance of the believer's direct relationship with God over splendour and ritual, and thus opposed what he felt was the excessive mystery and abstruseness of the Catholic faith. These were clearly religious ideas that strongly appealed to the Drydens.

But why is there a large clock so prominently displayed in this devoutly sombre mural of a puritan Northamptonshire family? The answer lies beyond its being a simple display of their wealth, and involves some more subtle iconography – something Sir Erasmus also showed an enthusiasm for in his other murals. Here, perhaps, is an analogy of the 'divine watchmaker' as creator of the Earth – a God whose natural laws were beginning to seem more comprehensible through the application of the Renaissance's scientific advances, especially in geometry and astronomy.

There is, too, a sense of the clock's imposed regularity of virtuous habit on the god-fearing household, who would have viewed time itself as sacred. It was a sort of literal and metaphorical regulator for the Protestant life, and therefore essential to post-Reformation thought. After all, time would have seemed in short supply with such low life-expectancy and evidence of mortality all around. Time must, consequently, be used wisely and not wasted on sinful, frivolous or material things, but spent diligently and prayerfully.

Theology aside, it is also possible to say a little about the clock itself in this mural. Domestic clocks – then known as Gothic or chamber clocks – were exceedingly rare and expensive in the sixteenth century, and none were in fact made in Britain until quite near the end of that century, so the Drydens' one would have been imported. They were made of iron, and, although most came from the area stretching between the south of Germany and north of Italy, the bell on this one suggests it might actually be Flemish.

While there may be this uncertainty as to its origins, it is possible to say definitely that its strike would have been very loud and its time telling woefully inaccurate – perhaps plus or minus half-an-hour a day. Given sufficient sunshine to reset it from a sundial, the lack of precision of clocks at this time might just about be acceptable for domestic use, but was quite useless for any scientific purpose, such as astronomy. A most significant breakthrough – also scientific – would be required for that, and it is one that can in fact be inspected at the National Trust's Lyme Park in Cheshire.

Although it was unarguably a major breakthrough when it did come, the advent of the pendulum clock was really the application of something already known, but for horological use – the properties of the pendulum's swing having, famously, been observed by Galileo when he had watched the swinging of a chandelier in Pisa Cathedral.

Three-quarters of a century, however, passed before Dutch polymath Christiaan Huygens (fig. 39) succeeded on Christmas Day 1656 in inventing the first proper pendulum clock. This advance was to initiate what is widely known as the 'Golden Age' of clockmaking, when so many beautiful and accurate clocks were made for both domestic and scientific use by famous makers such as Thomas Tompion.

Huygens, though, was not a practising clockmaker, and thus unable fully to exploit his own invention.

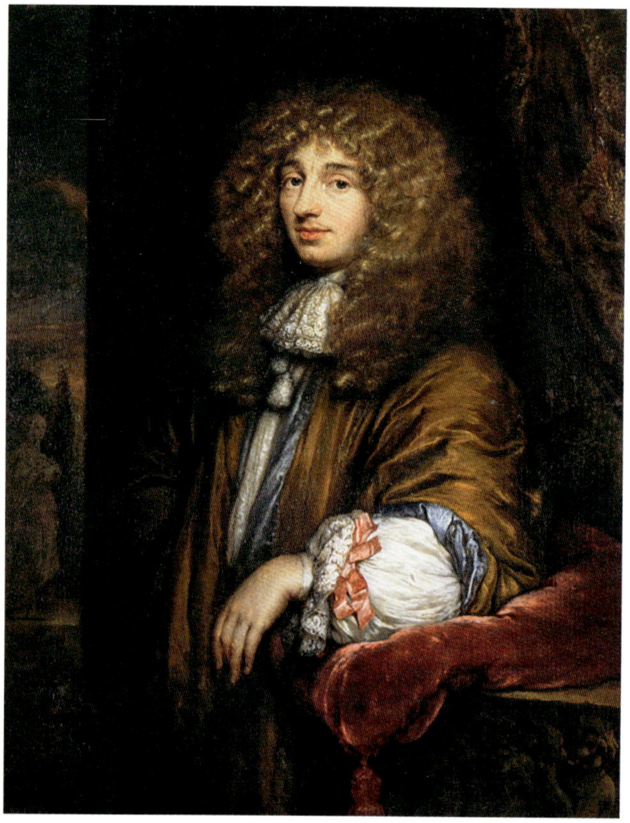

FIG. 39
Caspar Netscher (1639–1684)
Christiaan Huygens, 1671
Oil on paper mounted on panel, 30 × 24 cm
Haags Historisch Museum, The Hague,
on loan to the Boerhaave Museum, Leiden

Consequently, six months later he granted a twenty-one-year license – or *privilege* – to a clockmaker in the Hague called Salomon Coster to allow him to manufacture and sell these new pendulum clocks with their unprecedented accuracy and usefulness.

Interestingly, there was nothing apparently nationalistic or protectionist in either Huygen's ambitions for his invention or Coster's for his business, as a clockmaker from Paris and an English journeyman clockmaker of Dutch extraction called John Fromanteel soon started visiting Coster to learn how to make these clocks, too.

Wonderfully, there survives in the Museum Boerhaave at Leiden – the city, in fact, where Huygens attended university – a pendulum clock signed *Salomon Coster mit privilege 1657*. This is the world's earliest extant pendulum clock, and thus something of extraordinary significance to the history of both horology and science more broadly; but the trail then leads to England, with the return home to his father's workshop of the journeyman, John Fromanteel.

With all that John had learnt in the Hague, his father, Ahasuerus Fromanteel, was able in October 1658 to advertise in a London newspaper, *Mercurius Politicus*, that:

> *There is lately a way found out for making of Clocks that go exact and keep equaller time than any now made without this Regulator* [i.e. the pendulum] *(examined and proved before his Highness the Lord Protector by such Doctors whose knowledge is without exception .... Made by Ahasuerus Fromanteel, who made the first that were made in England. You may have them at his house on Bank-side in Moses Alley, Southwark, or at the sign of the Mermaid in Lothbury, near Bartholomew Lane end, London.*

Many of the National Trust's visitors to Lyme Park enjoy its marvellous clock collection, the bulk of which was put together by Lyme's last owner, the late Sir Francis Legh. This collection includes the black table clock engraved *A. Fromanteel London Fecit 1658* on its backplate, which was discovered in about 1940 as a few remains in a box (figs. 40 and 41). It will never be known, of course, if its original owner had read the advert in *Mercurius Politicus*, but the few surviving original parts are unquestionably very similar to the Coster clock in Leiden, confirming Fromanteel as its maker as well as its importance as England's earliest surviving pendulum clock.[2]

The discoverer and disseminator of the pendulum's adaptation for horology, Christiaan Huygens, worked

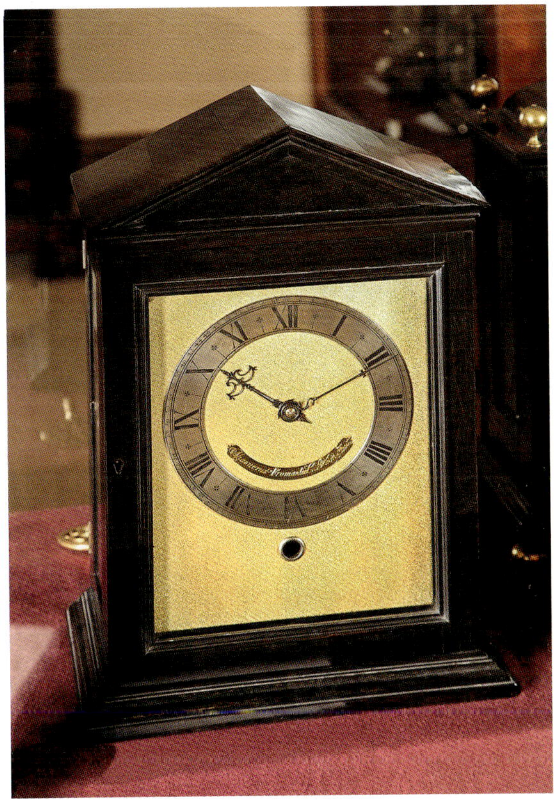

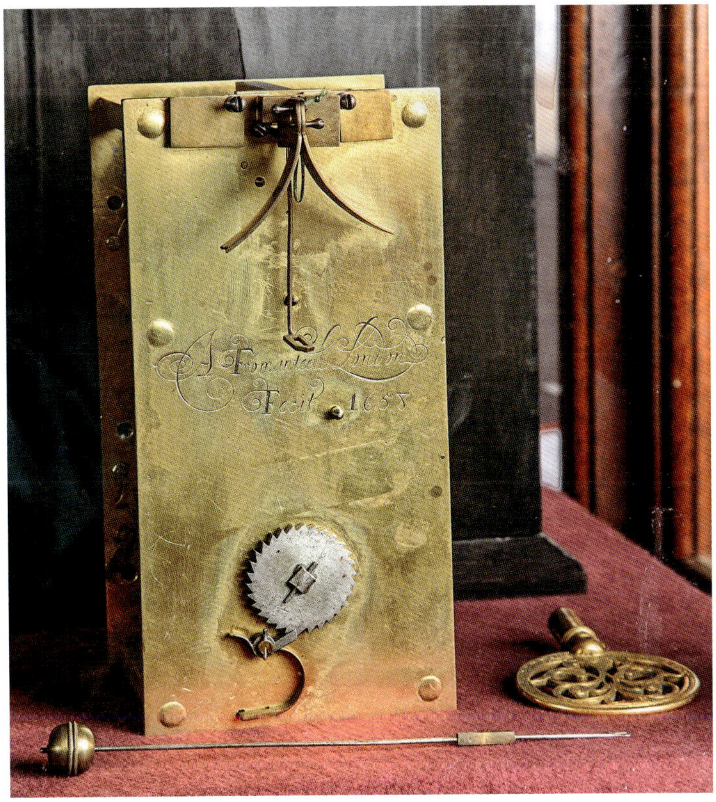

FIGS. 40, 41
Ahasuerus Fromanteel (1606–1693)
Ebony spring-driven table timepiece with pendulum (front and back views)
National Trust, Lyme Park, Cheshire (NT 499761)

on many other projects, too, some also horological, such as accurate timekeepers for use at sea and the balance spring that is still found in mechanical watches. But an especially appealing aspect of his work was the way it crossed national boundaries to further scientific understanding in this early stage of the Enlightenment. He was, for instance, both a member of the Royal Society in London and a founder of the Academie des Sciences in Paris – and remained actively involved with both even during the regular bouts of hostility between England, France and the Netherlands of his time – and so truly embodied the timeless international spirit of scientific advancement.

NOTES

1 The sadly faded grisaille mural is believed to date from the late sixteenth century ownership of Canons Ashby's extremely puritan Sir Erasmus Dryden. The wall clock, hung high up in the top left corner, symbolically regulates the devout family beneath.
2 Fromanteel's table timepiece, in an ebony architectural case, was acquired by Sir Francis Legh *c.*1940.

5

AELBERT CUYP (1620–1691)

View of Dordrecht from the North, c.1655

Oil on canvas, 68.6 × 193 cm
National Trust, Ascott House, Buckinghamshire – The Anthony de Rothschild Collection (NT 1535110)

PROVENANCE
Reputedly owned and cut in two by Captain William Baillie; bought as two pictures by C. Bathall at the Sir George Colebrooke sale, at Christie's, 23 April 1774, lots 22–23; possibly in the collection of John Stuart, 3rd Earl of Bute; in the collection of his daughter-in-law, Louisa Bertie, Lady Stuart by 1815; bought by Thomas B. Brown as two pictures at her sale, Christie's, 15 May 1841, lots 74–75; united by him and sold to Robert Stayner Holford; by descent; bought by Agnew's on behalf of Anthony de Rothschild at the Sir George Lindsay Holford sale, Christie's, 17 May 1928, lot 10; given by him to the National Trust in 1949

EXHIBITED
In Trust for the Nation, National Gallery, London, 1995–96, no. 29; *Aelbert Cuyp*, National Gallery of Art, Washington; National Gallery, London; and Rijksmuseum, Amsterdam, 2001–02, no. 35 (exhibited Washington and London only)

SELECTED LITERATURE
Marijnissen *et al.* 1992, pp. 132–36, no. 22; Laing 1995, no. 29

Exhibited in Bath and The Hague only

Views of Dordrecht were a speciality of Aelbert Cuyp, who lived and worked his entire life in this prosperous Dutch city. It was here too that he took his first steps as a painter under the supervision of his father, the portraitist Jacob Gerritsz Cuyp. Although Aelbert practised other genres as well, he was primarily a landscape painter. His work betrays the influence of various artists: in painting sunlight, for example, he drew inspiration from the work of Italianate painters such as Jan Both, who around 1641 returned to his native city of Utrecht from Italy, a country Cuyp never visited. In about 1650 Cuyp found his own style in his landscapes, in which light is the binding and dominant element. The present *View of Dordrecht from the North* is traditionally dated to around 1655. Undoubtedly it is the most spectacular manifestation of this talent and without precedent in Dutch painting of the Golden Age.[1] Cuyp made at least twenty-five paintings of Dordrecht and its surroundings, but none has such beautiful light effects as this masterpiece, not even the somewhat smaller variant of the composition in Kenwood House, a fine painting that presumably originated slightly earlier (fig. 42).[2] The painter's ability to render extraordinary effects of light soon became one of his trademarks, as emerges from the biography of him written at the beginning of the eighteenth century by Arnold Houbraken: 'Moreover he is particularly adept at conveying the time of day at which his subjects are depicted, so that it is possible in his paintings to distinguish the misty early morning from bright midday, and bright midday from saffron eventide'.[3]

Cuyp was not the first artist to immortalise Dordrecht in paintings. His forerunner was an artist of Utrecht, Adam Willaerts, whose large panoramic view of the city, painted in 1629, hung in the council chamber of the Dordrecht town hall, where Cuyp undoubtedly saw it and subsequently took it as the

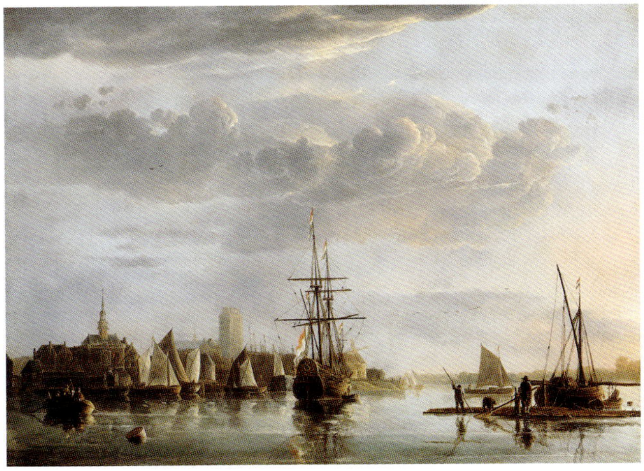

FIG. 42
Aelbert Cuyp (1620–1691)
View of Dordrecht from the North, *c.*1655
Oil on canvas, 98 × 138 cm
English Heritage, Kenwood House,
The Iveagh Bequest (46)

point of departure for the work discussed here.[4] Like Willaerts's work, Cuyp's *View of Dordrecht* depicts the city skyline seen from Papendrecht, to the north-east of Dordrecht, where the Old Maas flows into the Lower Merwede, at that time a very busy waterway. Thanks to its favourable location, from which it was easy to reach Antwerp, Rotterdam and the North Sea, or else steer a course for Arnhem and Nijmegen, Dordrecht – the oldest city in Holland – developed into an important centre of trade. The importance of these waterways to the city's economy should not be underestimated, particularly because most goods were shipped by water in those days.

Among the many buildings depicted in this painting, two towers stand out. At left, we see the tower of the Groothoofdspoort, the main entrance to the city from the waterfront. This monumental gate, situated next to the grain exchange, had the spire of its tower replaced in 1692. At right, we see the unfinished, truncated tower of the Grote Kerk, next to it a drawbridge, and at far right a windmill, its sails standing out against the blue sky.[5] Here Cuyp painted the profile of the waterside city as it looked after the reconstruction of the harbour in 1647, which had caused the disappearance of old walls and towers. Like the version in Kenwood House, this painting appears to have been carefully prepared with drawings. For example, Cuyp made a preparatory study in chalk, the details of which correspond closely to those in the painting, including the so-called *kaagschepen*, or flat-bottomed boats, moored by the city (fig. 43).[6] What is missing in the drawing but present in the painting is the large trading vessel flying the flags of Holland and the small sloop next to it, between the church tower and the windmill. To intensify the feeling of depth, Cuyp added to the foreground some vegetation and old wooden poles, *repoussoirs* such as those often seen in his paintings. Another drawing served as the starting point for the raft, the freighter and the sloop on the water at right (fig. 44).[7] In the painting, Cuyp omitted the sails that he drew here behind the freighter (where he initially intended to draw a ship seen from the side), but he incorporated the two workers on the raft, exactly as they appear in the drawing. He added a steersman to the raft in the painting. Such rafts occur only in the views of Dordrecht painted by Willaerts and Cuyp, and that is no accident, because in those days the city played a leading role in the timber trade, despite increasing competition from other Dutch cities.[8] Dordrecht had various *houtplaetsen* (timber yards), where imported wood was trans-shipped. In 1639, Cuyp had made a painting of the timber yards to the south of the Grote Kerk.[9] The peace and tranquillity that pervades the Ascott painting is a reminder of the economic prosperity that prevailed in the Dutch Republic after the ratification of the Treaty of Münster in 1648. Indeed, some of Cuyp's earlier views of Dordrecht include warships.[10]

The constant adjustments Cuyp made to his brushwork – in strokes that remained visible on the

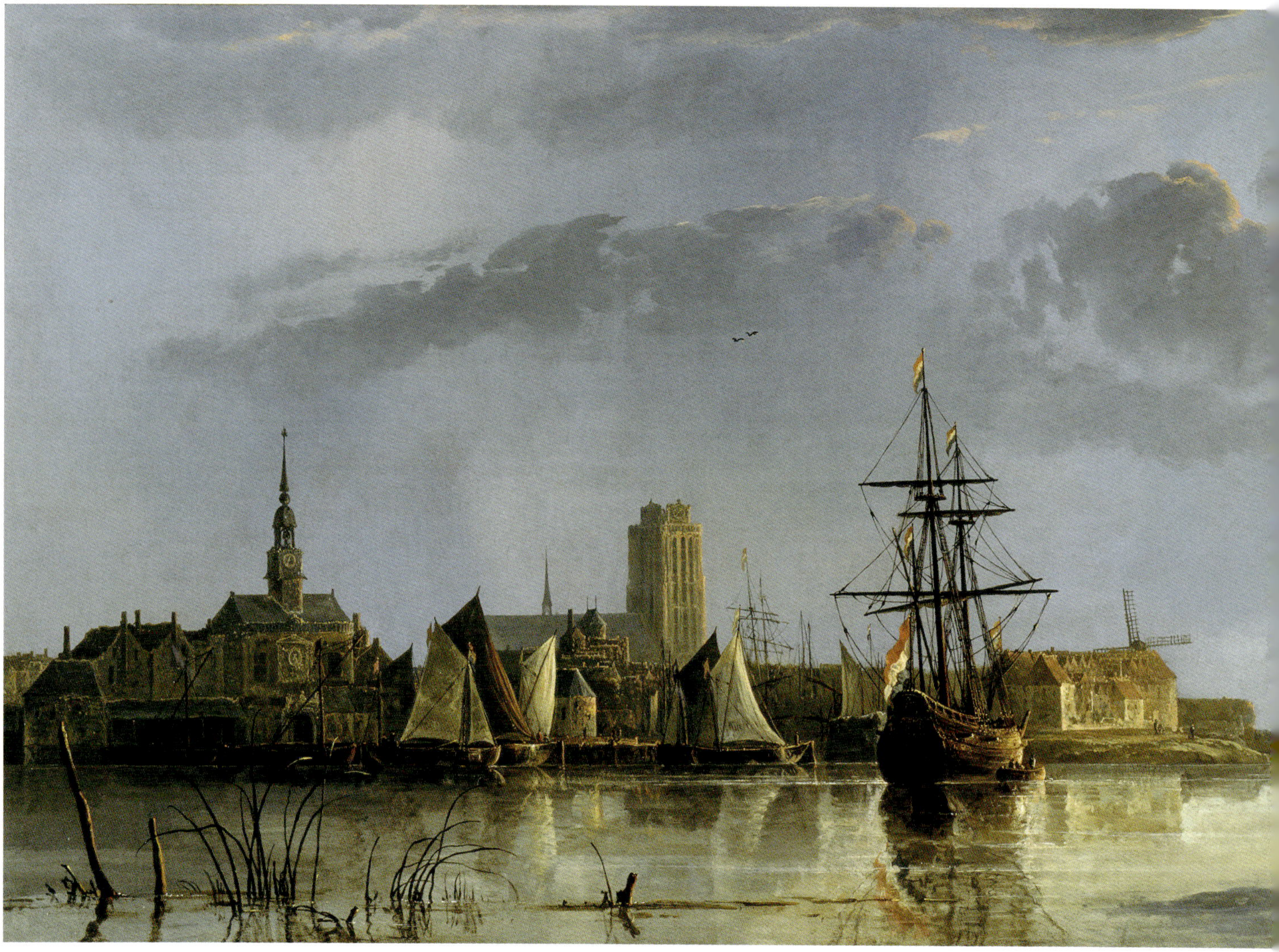

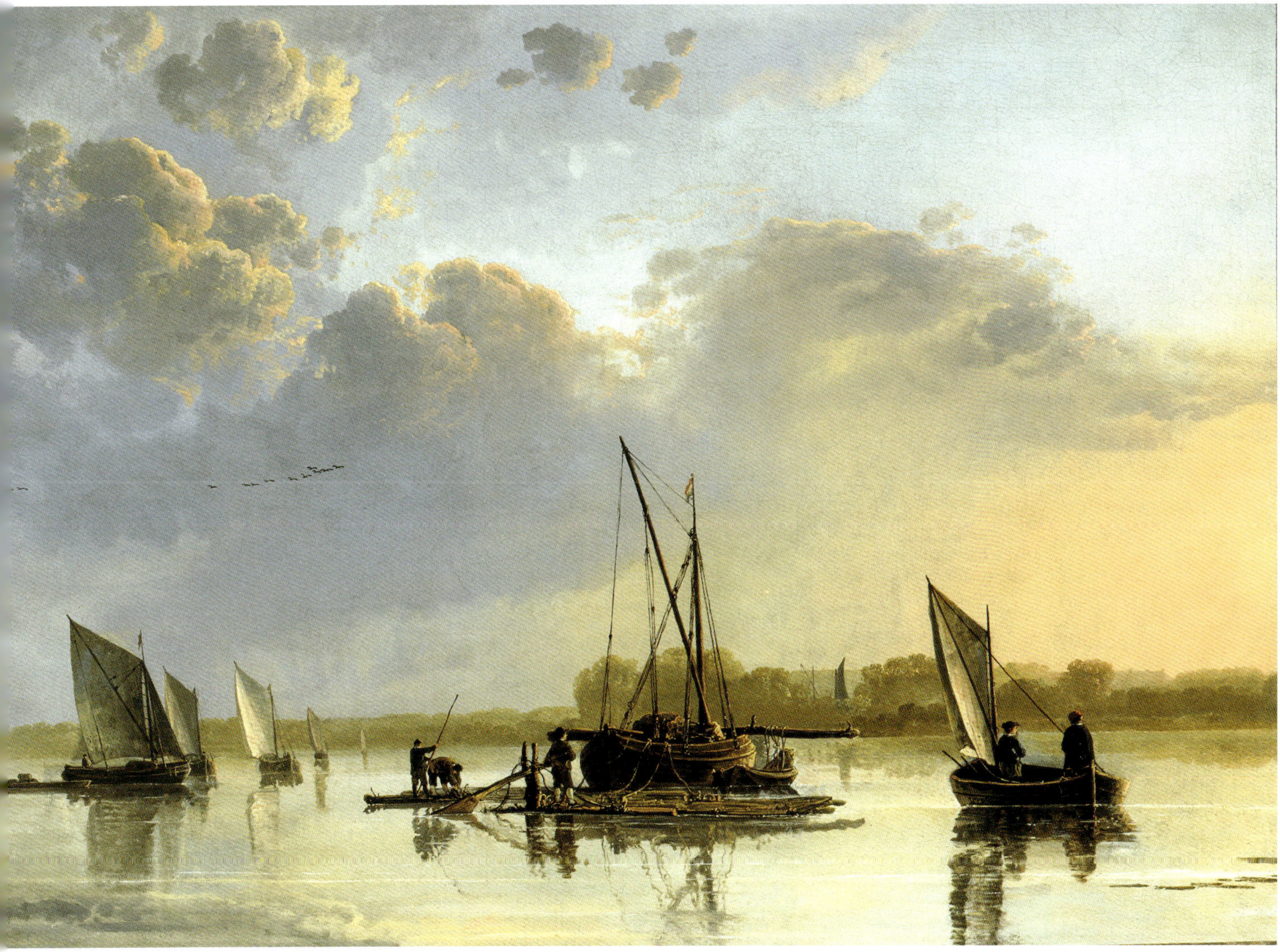

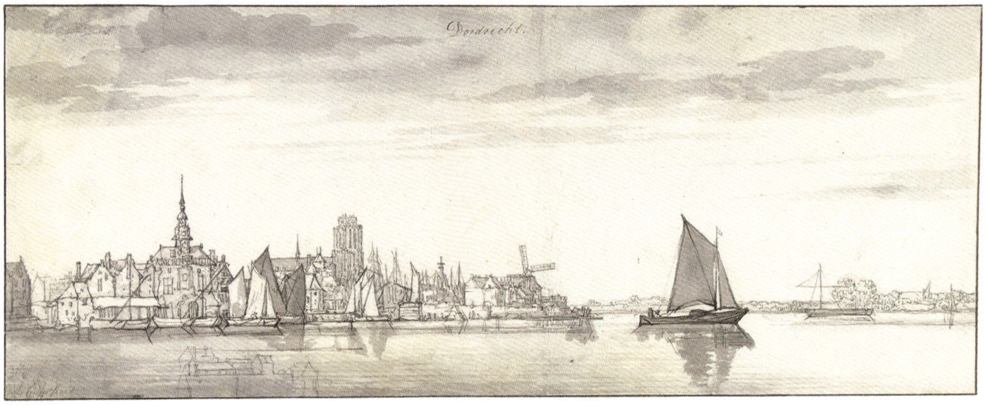

FIG. 43
Aelbert Cuyp (1620–1691)
View of Dordrecht from the North, c.1647
Black chalk, grey wash 187 × 460 mm
Amsterdam, Rijksmuseum
(RP-T-1900-A-4376)

surface – proved to be an extremely effective means of rendering the desired atmosphere and effects of light. His unerring placement of accents that catch the play of light – seen clearly by the Groothoofdspoort or in the buildings in front of the tower of the Grote Kerk – also served to define the shape of various elements in the painting. Cuyp lavished attention on such details, for he even placed these highlights on the tips of the reed stems and along the sides of the poles in the foreground. The subtle transition of the leaden sky above the city to more pronounced cloud formations – the edges of which are tinged a pinkish yellow by the setting sun, an effect typical of the late afternoon or early evening[11] – was executed with inimitable skill, as was the reflection of those coloured clouds in the silvery water, in which the buildings and vessels are also mirrored very convincingly.

It is almost impossible for us to imagine that Cuyp, now considered one of the foremost Dutch landscape painters, was scarcely known outside Dordrecht in his day. The unusual format of this painting – it is nearly two metres wide – is exceptional for Cuyp, and one would assume that such an ambitious painting was made to commission rather than for the free market.[12] Although in general we are reasonably well informed about the earliest owners of Cuyp's paintings, the early provenance of this exceptional canvas is still a mystery, in spite of attempts to unearth more information.[13] Worse still, it was even cut in two at some point, perhaps to make it easier to sell – a fate that has befallen other canvases in the past.[14] The division of the present painting happened some time before 1774, in which year the two parts were offered at auction as pendants – 'A view of Dort, with a variety of shipping' and 'Boats with a raft floating, its companion' – from the collection of the London banker Sir George Colebrooke (1729–1809), the earliest known owner.[15] An eighteenth-century copy of the left-hand side of the depiction, now in the Rijksmuseum, Amsterdam, documents this phase and also clearly shows that the spatial coherence of this impressive painting was completely destroyed by cutting the canvas in two.[16] Only in 1842 were the two parts re-joined by the art dealer and restorer Thomas B. Brown.[17] Technical research has shown that the painting was in fact conceived as a single canvas and that it was divided in two and joined together again so carefully that there was almost no paint loss.[18] In 1928 it was acquired at

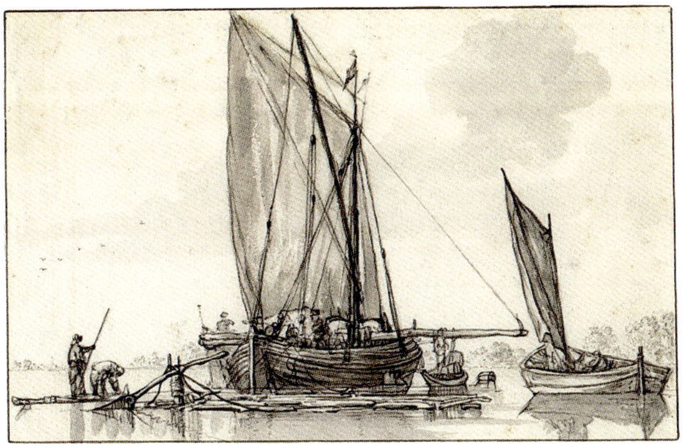

FIG. 44
Aelbert Cuyp (1620–1691)
A Freight Boat and a Timber Raft on Calm Water, early 1650s
Black chalk, grey wash, 168 × 254 mm
London, British Museum (1895,0915.1142)

auction, through Thomas Agnew & Sons, London, by Anthony de Rothschild, who bequeathed it to the National Trust, along with Ascott House, its grounds and the remainder of the ground-floor collections, in 1949.

It is widely known that since the eighteenth century Cuyp's best works have been in England, where his landscapes found particular favour among the elite.[19] In the Netherlands, landscapes by Cuyp are still extremely rare. In 1965, the Rijksmuseum managed to acquire a monumental landscape of around 1655–60 which had long been part of the collection of the Rothschild family in England (see fig. 20).[20] It is still the most important work by Cuyp in a Dutch collection. The Mauritshuis, though it succeeded in 1820 in buying the interesting *Equestrian Portrait of Pieter de Roovere* of around 1650 from a descendant of the sitter, can only dream of acquiring such a first-rate piece by the artist. For many years, therefore, it has exhibited a painting on loan from the National Gallery, London, which boasts an impressive collection of paintings by Cuyp. QB

NOTES

1 See Van Suchtelen and Wheelock 2008–09.
2 A. Rüger in Wheelock *et al.* 2001, pp. 164–65, no. 36, p. 205, note 5; for Kloek's important observations about the pentimenti in the Ascott Cuyp see ibid., p. 286, note 1, and Kloek 1977, pp. 117–18.
3 Translated from the Dutch: Houbraken 1718–21, I, p. 249.
4 A. Wheelock in Wheelock *et al.* 2001, p. 23, fig. 8; A. Rüger, ibid., p. 162. Jan van Goyen also painted views of Dordrecht.
5 Of the three sails that are visible, one was mistakenly painted the wrong way round.
6 W. Kloek in Wheelock *et al.* 2001, no. 84.
7 Wheelock *et al.* 2001, no. 85. This sloop is not depicted in the painting at Kenwood House, though this does display the freighter and the wooden raft that appear in the drawing.
8 A. Rüger in Wheelock *et al.* 2001, p. 162.
9 George and Ilone Kremer Collection; see Q. Buvelot in Buvelot *et al.* 2011–12, pp. 136–37, no. 27.
10 Laing 1995, p. 84.
11 The clocks on the towers of the Groothoofdspoort and the Grote Kerk seem to show that the time was just after seven in the evening.
12 Laing 1995, pp. 84–85; A. Rüger in Wheelock *et al.* 2001, p. 204, note 10.
13 Laing 1995, p. 202, note 2.
14 This happened, for example, to Rembrandt's *Saul and David* and Jan van Goyen's *View of the Rhine near Hoog-Elten* before these paintings entered the Mauritshuis collection (see Buvelot 2004, p. 132, no. 838, and 262, no. 621).
15 Quoted from A. Chong in Marijnissen *et al.* 1992, p. 132; Sir George Colebrooke sale, London, Christie's, 22 April 1774, lots 22 and 23.
16 Bequest of Adriaan van der Hoop to the City of Amsterdam, 1854 (on loan to the Rijksmuseum since 1885, SK-C-123); see A. Chong in Marijnissen *et al.* 1992, p. 136, and A. Pollmer in Bergvelt *et al.* 2004, pp. 144–45, no. 37.
17 See Smith 1829–42, IX, pp. 665–66, no. 52; A. Chong in Marijnissen *et al.* 1992, p. 132; A. Rüger in Wheelock *et al.* 2001, p. 204, note 12.
18 Carried out by the Conservation Department of the National Gallery, London, 1993; see Laing 1995, p. 85.
19 See A. Chong in Wheelock *et al.* 2001, pp. 35–51.
20 Wheelock *et al.* 2001, no. 42.

6

ADRIAEN VAN DIEST (1655–1704)

Dunham Massey: Bird's-eye View from the South, c.1697

Oil on canvas, 99 × 124 cm
Inscribed left from centre: *A...Diest f*; right lower corner: *Dunham/in 1697*
National Trust, Dunham Massey, Cheshire – The Stamford Collection (NT 932334)

PROVENANCE
Presumably painted for George Booth, 2nd Earl of Warrington; thence by descent; bequeathed by Roger Grey, 10th Earl of Stamford to the National Trust in 1976

SELECTED LITERATURE
Harris 1978, pp. 4–11, p. 6, fig. 5; Harris 1979, p. 146, no. 157; Sambrook 2003, pp. 24–25 (repr.); *Public Catalogue Foundation*, III, 2013, p. 11

This exceptional painting by Adriaen van Diest depicts Dunham Massey, a country estate near Manchester, seen from a fairly high perspective. The house, surrounded by a green, rolling landscape, is bathed in the sunlight that has found its way between the clouds blowing past in the bright blue sky. The foreground lies in shadow, which focuses the viewer's attention all the more on the large house. This painting is one of the few sources to document the appearance of Dunham Massey shortly after George Booth, 2nd Earl of Warrington (1675–1758), inherited it from his father, Henry Booth, 1st Earl of Warrington (1652–1694), in 1694. After years of financial decline, resulting from the political turmoil in seventeenth-century England, the young heir managed to save the estate from ruin by marrying an extremely rich woman, Lady Mary Oldbury (d. 1740), in 1702.[1]

It must have been George Booth who asked Van Diest to immortalise his recently acquired estate.[2] Van Diest's topographical approach became increasingly popular in England in the seventeenth century. Painting 'portraits' of country houses was a genre practised in England mostly by Dutch and Flemish artists, among them Leendert Knyff of Haarlem and Jan Siberechts of Antwerp.[3] Van Diest, a native of The Hague, worked in England from the age of seventeen until his death in 1704. Like his father and grandfather before him, he was known as a painter of seascapes, but he also produced portraits and landscapes.[4] In addition to Dunham Massey, Van Diest painted Sprotborough Hall.[5] Work by Van Diest can be found in various English collections.[6]

Country houses like Dunham Massey were pleasant refuges from the bustling cities; they were places where one could receive guests and enjoy fresh fruit and vegetables in the summer. But such estates, which often included extensive tracts of land, were also an investment intended to yield a profit. The 'portrait' of Dunham Massey therefore includes not only the country house, but also the rural activities taking place around it. Since the addition of the south façade in 1650, the main building had been a closed structure with an inner courtyard.[7] The south façade also appears in a painting commissioned by George Booth in 1700 from the Dutch painter Jan Wyck of Booth's favourite pet, a Dutch mastiff (fig. 45).[8] The garden was flanked on the north and west by a wide lake with water from the River Bollin, which also fed the narrow moat on the south and east side. This moat was described as early as 1411, but is possibly older, and served as both a means of defence and a source of fishing. Fruit and vegetables were cultivated in the enclosed gardens. On the west side there was an ornamental garden with adjoining orangery. The conical hill behind it was

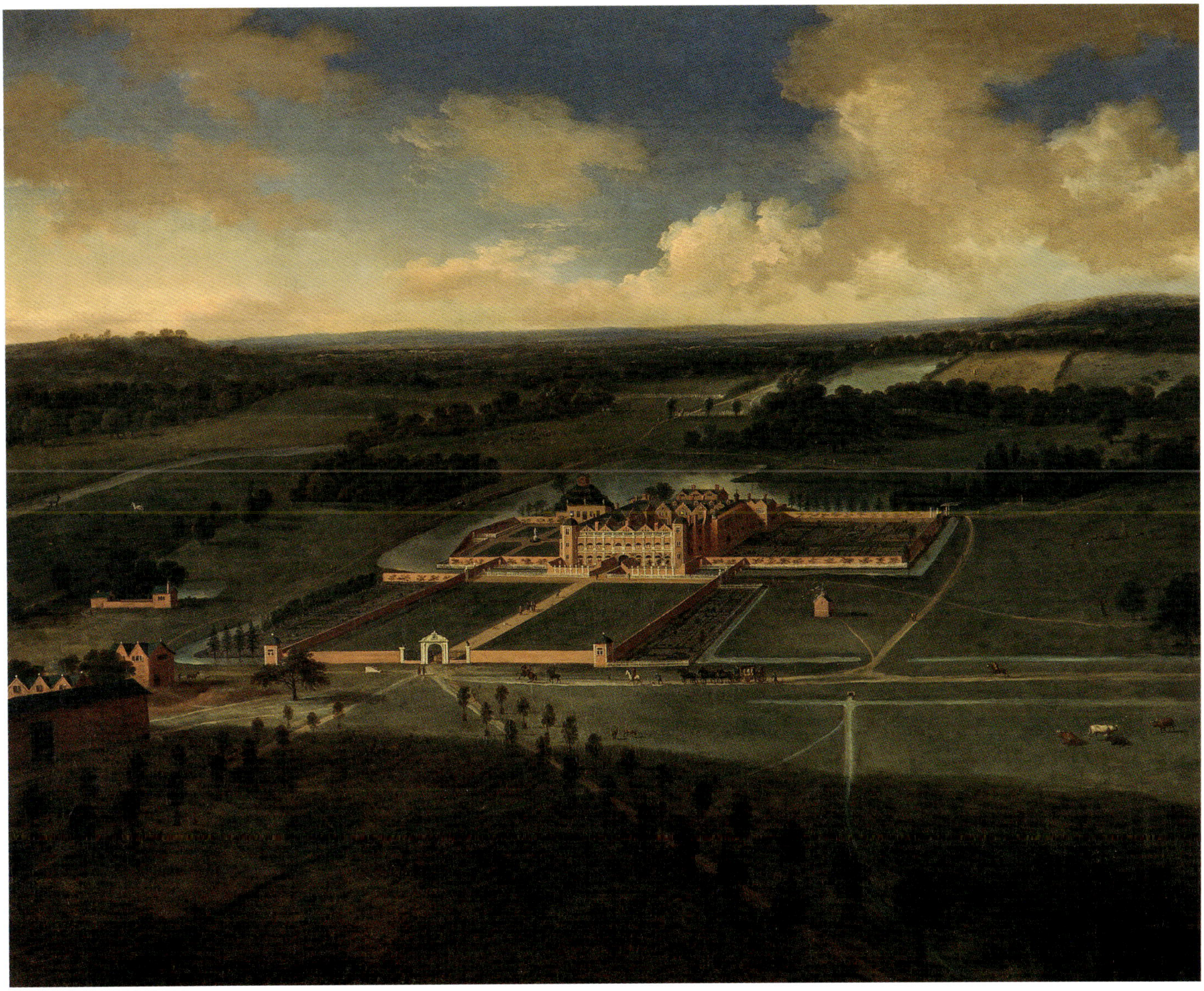

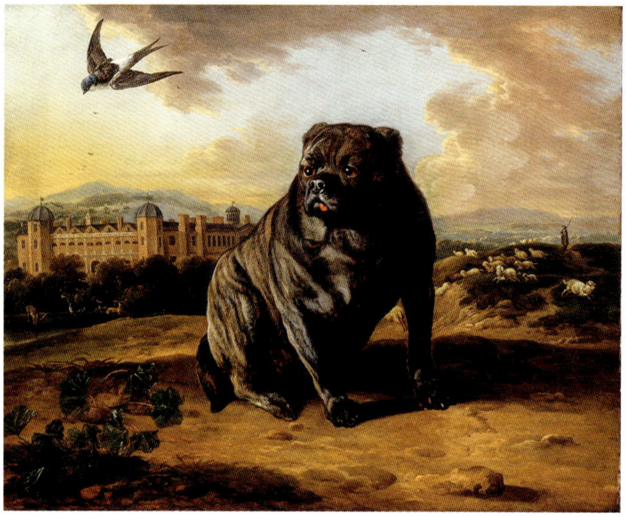

FIG. 45
Jan Wyck (1645–1700)
A Dutch Mastiff ('Old Vertue'?) with Dunham Massey in the Background, 1700
Oil on canvas, 89.5 × 69 cm
National Trust, Dunham Massey, Cheshire
(NT 932341)

possibly the remains of an earlier fortress.[9] The estate generated revenues through such activities as raising livestock, hunting and farming. The fruits of the harvest have been gathered in the two meadows in the right background. At left front, outside the enclosure, is the watermill, built in 1616 for processing grain. Oats and barley were used not only for baking bread and brewing beer, but also as fodder for the cattle. Fallow deer, which could be hunted to stock up the kitchen, graze in the field in the foreground.[10] At right centre, a carriage decorated with a coat of arms – unfortunately unidentified – and drawn by six black horses signals the arrival of important guests or the earl himself.[11] Anyone who compares the painting to the present-day situation at Dunham Massey will find, in addition to the main house, only the moat, the mill and a herd of fallow deer.

This view of Dunham Massey bears Van Diest's signature, but the date, 1697, was presumably added by a later hand. The painting displays many similarities to an engraving showing the estate from the south-west which was made the same year by Johannes Kip after a drawing by the previously mentioned Leendert Knyff (fig. 47).[12] However, the entrance gate in Kip's engraving differs from the one seen in Van Diest's painting, and the painting lacks the tree-lined avenue running north from the back of the house recorded in the engraving. This strengthens the suspicion that the date on the painting is not autograph; indeed, the work probably originated before 1697, given that the avenue on the north side had not yet been planted with trees. The saplings in the foreground, however, appear in both the painting and the engraving, which means that the painting must have been made in or shortly after 1694, considering that George Booth started planting the trees after the death of his father that year. He did this with a view to future profits from felling the trees and selling the timber. He showed great foresight in this respect, for a century later the sale of timber made up twenty per cent of the estate's revenues.[13] To speed up the processing of the wood, the grain mill was converted into a sawmill in the 1860s.[14]

In addition to redesigning the park and extending the water system, George Booth had the main house rebuilt, starting in 1732, by the architect John Norris. To mark the completion of this huge project in the 1740s, Booth commissioned the painter John Harris II to document the result from four viewpoints. In 1751 Harris finished the series *Dunham Massey from the South, South-east, South-west and North*, in the style of Van Diest (fig. 46).[15] The four paintings show the rebuilt main house and the new plantings, including the trees lining the north avenue. These works crowned George Booth's successful development of the domain. Together with the earlier depictions, they make Dunham Massey one of the most frequently portrayed country estates. The paintings by Van Diest and Harris still hang in the Great Gallery of the house and have been given eighteenth-century black-and-gold frames, which are

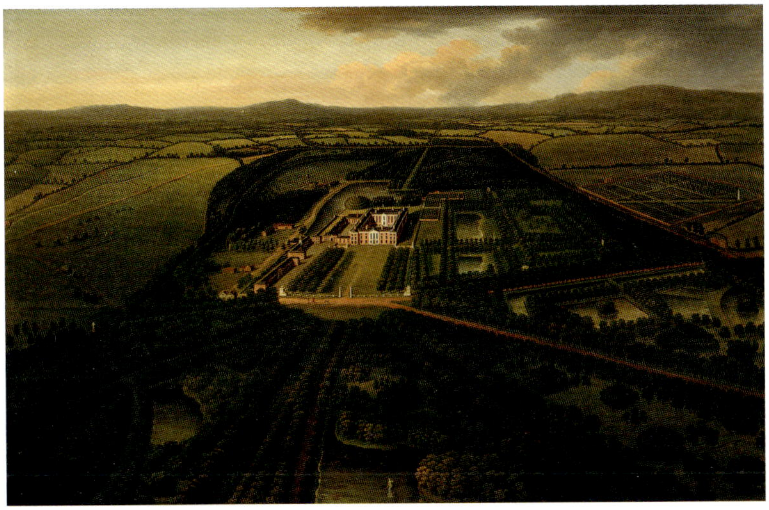

FIG. 46
John Harris II (1715–1755)
A Bird's-Eye View of Dunham Massey from the South, 1751
Oil on canvas, 132 × 200.7 cm
National Trust, Dunham Massey, Cheshire (NT 932335)

FIG. 47
Johannes Kip (*c.*1653–1722)
after Leendert Knyff (1650–1721)
Dunham Massey, Cheshire in 1697, 1697
Engraving on paper in black wood and gilt frame, 61.2 × 71.5 cm
National Trust, Dunham Massey, Cheshire (NT 930116)

typical of the paintings that entered the collection during the life of the 2nd Earl of Warrington.[16] The engraving hangs on the Crimson Staircase. In 1736 the earl's only daughter, Lady Mary Booth (1704–1772), married Harry, Lord Grey of Groby, later 4th Earl of Stamford (1715–1768). His descendant, Roger Grey, 10th Earl of Stamford (1896–1976), bequeathed the estate, the house and the collection to The National Trust – one of the most generous bequests in the Trust's history.[17] CR

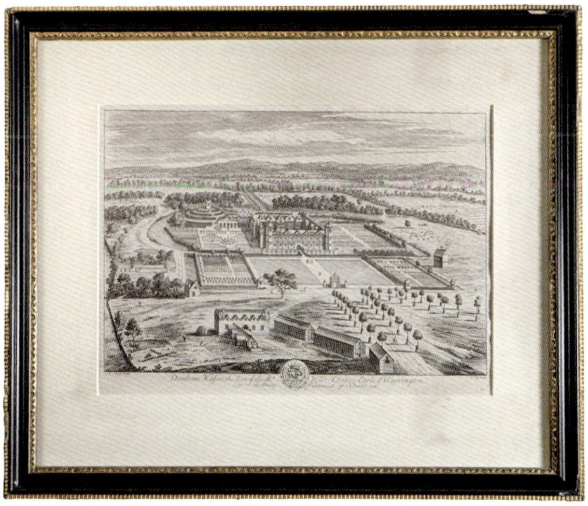

NOTES

1 Rothwell 2000, p. 56.
2 On Van Diest, see Van der Willigen and Kinkelder 1993–98; Buijsen 1998, pp. 118–22, 299; Ekkart in Saur, part 27 (2000), p. 276; Kollmann 2000, pp. 181–82; https://rkd.nl/explore/artists/22725 (with references).
3 Hearn 2004, p. 85. The first examples of topographical portraits of estates can be found in J. A. du Cerceau's *Des plus excellents Bastiments de France*, 1576 (later edition 1579).
4 Buijsen 1998, pp. 118–22.
5 Adriaen van Diest, *Prospect of Sprotborough Hall*, undated (Sotheby's, London, 12 July 1989, lot 72) and https://rkd.nl/explore/images/30624.
6 Ekkart 2000, p. 276. Works by Van Diest appear 256 times in the sale catalogues, now in the British Library, of public auctions held between May 1689 and March 1692. This makes him one of the five best represented painters in those auctions. See Karst 2013–14, pp. 30–33, fig. 5, and notes 38–39.
7 Sambrook 2003, p. 10.
8 Laing 1995, pp. 52–53, no. 16.
9 Harris 1978, pp. 4–11, at p. 5; Rothwell 2000, p. 42.
10 Sambrook 2003, pp. 10, 132; Rothwell 2000, p. 51.
11 Topographical portraits of country houses often include the arrival of carriages. See, for example, Jan Siberechts, *View of a House and its Estate in Belsize, Middlesex*, 1696, Tate (Karst 2013–14, p. 44, fig. 14).
12 Harris 1979, p. 146, no. 157. The engraving was published in 1707–08 as part of *Britannia Illustrata*.
13 Rothwell 2000, p. 49.
14 Sambrook 2003, p. 11.
15 Harris 1978, pp. 4, 6.
16 Laing 1995, p. 227.
17 Rothwell 2000, pp. 4–5, 58, 65.

East Asian Luxury Goods

EMILE DE BRUIJN, NATIONAL TRUST LEAD REGISTRAR (COLLECTIONS DEVELOPMENT)

ONE OF THE FASCINATING PHENOMENA developing alongside the British taste for Dutch paintings in the seventeenth century was the shared Anglo-Dutch interest in East Asian luxury goods. Although the English and Dutch East India Companies, founded in 1600 and 1602 respectively, were commercial rivals, some elements of the British taste for things Asian seem to have been shared with or derived from the Dutch. One of these is the appropriation and creative reuse of East Asian lacquer. Shortly after 1654 Amalia of Solms-Braunfels, Princess of Orange (1602–1675) decorated the walls of a small room at Huis ten Bosch, on the outskirts of The Hague, with lacquer taken from Japanese screens, cabinets and coffers.[1] The origin of the lacquer reflected the Dutch East India Company's access to Japan.

The taste for adapting Asian lacquer spread to Britain as well. A number of examples of this practice can be identified at Ham House, which was being redecorated by John Maitland, 1st Duke of Lauderdale and his wife Elizabeth Murray in the 1670s (see pp. 39–40). A cabinet dated around 1675, in the Queen's Antechamber at Ham (fig. 48), appears at first sight to be a purpose-made Chinese cabinet made of incised (or *kuan cai*) lacquer, a type which was being exported to Europe in increasing volumes towards the end of the seventeenth century. However, on closer inspection it becomes clear that the sides and the front are made up of sections of what was originally an elongated lacquer panel decorated with scenes of hunters in a landscape.[2]

The practice of panelling whole rooms with lacquer seems to have been disseminated at least in part along the political and family networks

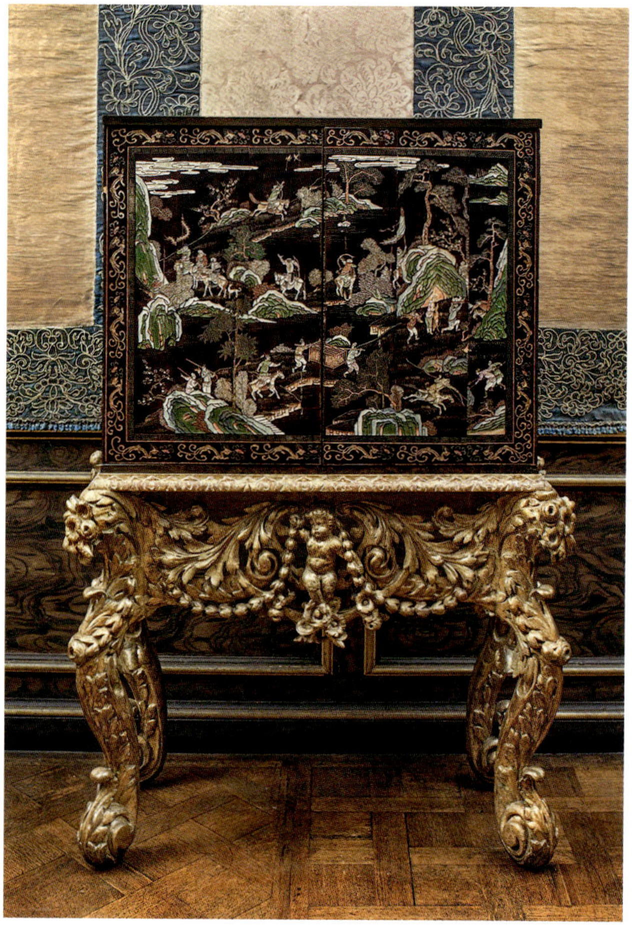

FIG. 48
Cabinet made up of sections of a Chinese incised (*kuan cai*) lacquer panel, *c.* 1675; the vertical break in the scenery near the right edge of the right-hand door shows where two sections of the original panel were combined
National Trust, Ham House, Surrey (NT 1140111)

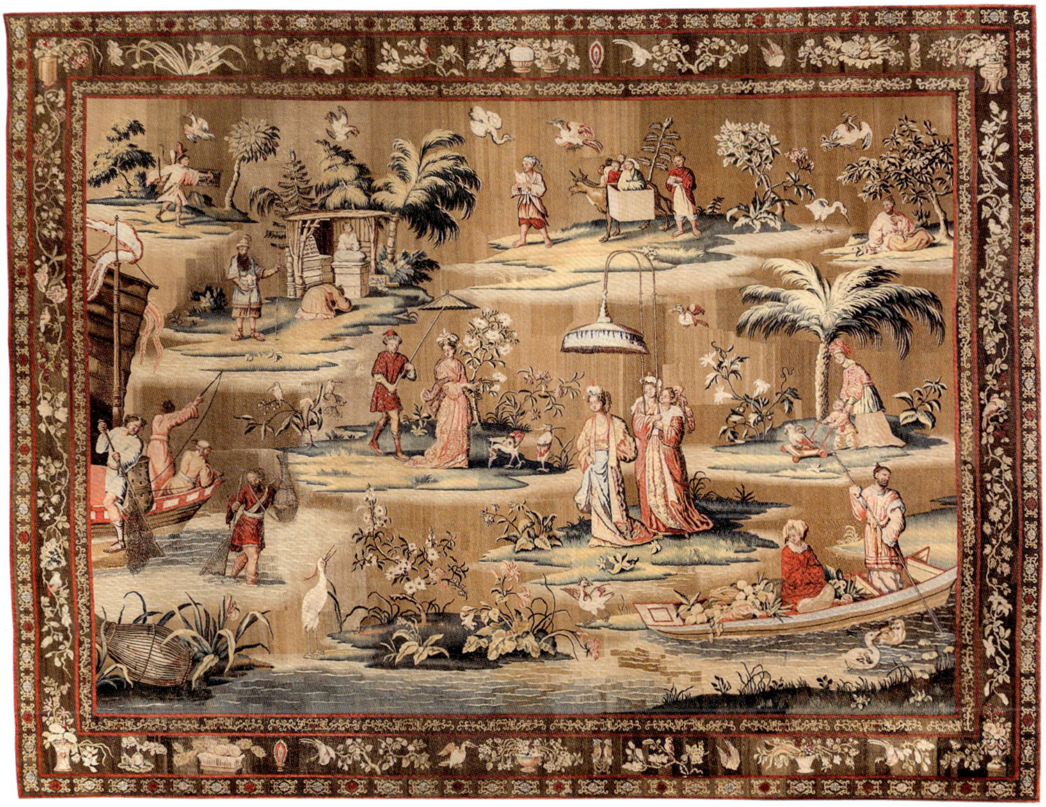

FIG. 49
Tapestry by John Vanderbank the Elder, partly inspired by the appearance of Chinese *kuan cai* lacquer, 1691–92
National Trust, Belton House, Lincolnshire (NT 436999.1)

of the House of Orange, eastwards to Friesland and Brandenburg[3] and westwards to England. King James II's daughter Mary, who had married her cousin Prince William of Orange (one of Amalia's grandchildren), commissioned the designer and architect Daniel Marot (see p. 63) to create a lacquer room in her residence Huis Honselaarsdijk near The Hague in 1687.[4] After William and Mary had jointly assumed the British throne in 1688, another lacquer-panelled room was created for Queen Mary II (as she had now become) at Hampton Court Palace, south-west of London, in about 1690. Similar lacquer rooms were created at Chatsworth, Derbyshire, in 1692, at Burghley House, Lincolnshire, in 1697, and at Dyrham Park, Gloucestershire, in about 1700.[5] The owner of Chatsworth, William Cavendish, 4th Earl (soon to become 1st Duke) of Devonshire (1640–1707) had been one of the power brokers behind William and Mary's takeover of the British throne. His sister Lady Anne, née Cavendish, Countess of Exeter (*c.* 1650–1703) was the chatelaine of Burghley, and William Blathwayt, who rebuilt Dyrham in the 1690s (see p. 90), was Secretary of State at War to William III, so in all of these cases the taste for lacquer seems to have had connotations of personal and political allegiance.

The contemporary taste for Asian lacquer also inspired the design of the two orientalist tapestries

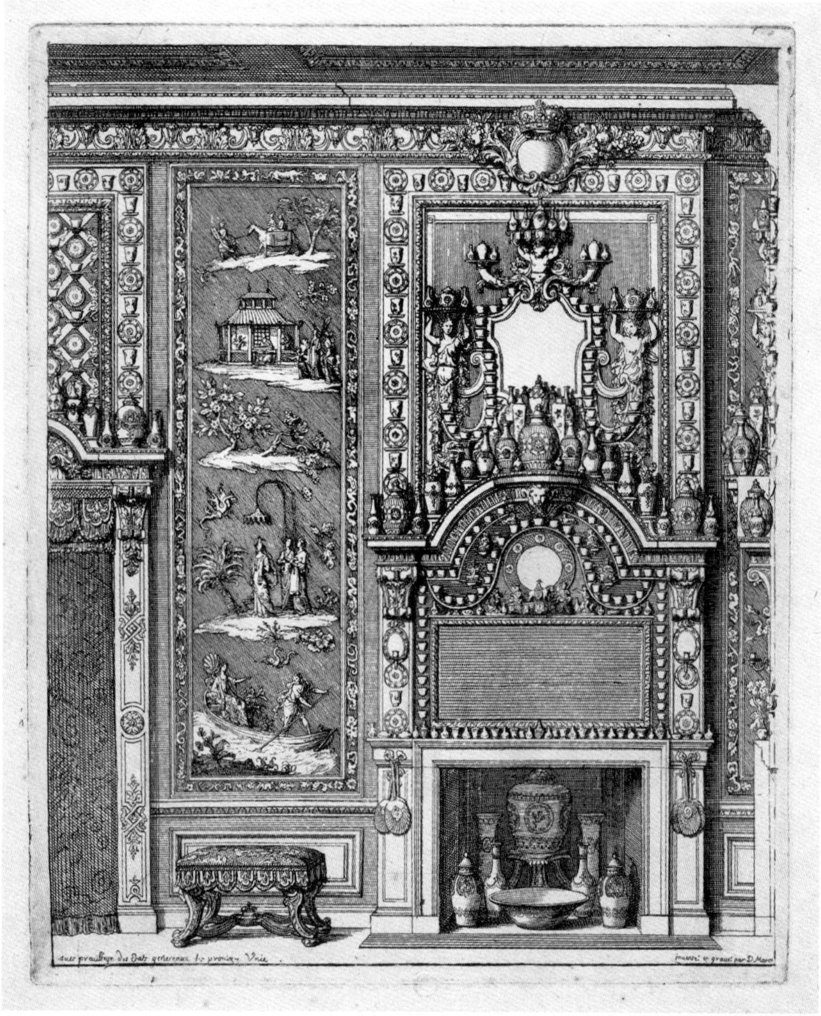

FIG. 50
Print by Daniel Marot of a grand Dutch interior, one of a set of six entitled *Nouvelles Chiminees Faittes en Plusieur en Droits de la Hollande et Autres Provinces du Dessin de D. Marot*, published in The Hague in 1703. The vertical section of wall decoration to the left of the chimneypiece is either panelling painted in imitation of *kuan cai* lacquer or a Vanderbank 'Indian manner' tapestry

hanging at Belton House, Lincolnshire, made by the London workshop of John Vanderbank the Elder in 1692 (fig. 49).[6] They show various groups of figures and landscape elements against what would originally have been a dark brown or black background (other surviving tapestries of this type are darker) and surrounded by a decorative border, reminiscent of the appearance of *kuan cai* lacquer panels like the one used on the Ham cabinet, but rendered in a Baroque style. It has been demonstrated that some of the motifs are Turkish, Indian and Chinese in origin, while others were taken from an illustrated book by Arnoldus Montanus, *Atlas Japannensis*, describing a Dutch trade mission to the Japanese court and published in Dutch in 1669 and in English in 1670.[7] This promiscuous mixture of various Asian styles and motifs was referred to as the 'Indian manner'.

When the owner of Belton, Sir John Brownlow, 3rd Bt (1659–1697) commissioned these tapestries, he stipulated that they were to be based on the designs of the four tapestries Vanderbank had supplied to Queen Mary II's apartments at Kensington Palace, on the outskirts of London, in 1690.[8] These tapestries, and additional ones also supplied by Vanderbank to

Kensington Palace in 1691 and 1696, have not survived. But a very similar 'Indian manner' wall decoration, possibly associated with Mary II, can be seen in one of a set of six prints after Daniel Marot entitled *Nouvelles Chiminees Faittes en Plusieur en Droits de la Hollande et Autres Provinces* (New chimneypieces made in several places in Holland and other provinces; fig. 50), probably created between 1696 and 1703.[9] One of the 'Indian' motifs visible in the print, of a lady accompanied by two servants sheltering her with a parasol, based on an illustration in Montanus, can also be seen in the Belton tapestry illustrated here (fig. 49).[10]

Does the print show an 'Indian' tapestry, or does the narrow width of the decoration indicate that it is in fact a section of panelling painted in imitation of *kuan cai* lacquer?[11] If it is indeed meant to represent imitation lacquer, then could this print be an evocation of the 'lacquer' room at Honselaarsdijk, originally designed by Marot in 1687? Does the recurrence of the motif of the lady with attendants and parasol in the Belton 'Indian' tapestry mean that Marot was connected, directly or indirectly, with the design of those tapestries? In view of the lack of corroborating evidence, we may never find conclusive answers to these questions. But, whatever the case may be, these examples do demonstrate the interconnectedness of Asian lacquer, European imitation lacquer, book illustrations and tapestry design, and of the Dutch and British taste for Asian objects and imagery in the late seventeenth century.

NOTES

The author is grateful to Wolf Burchard, Furniture Research Curator at the National Trust, for commenting on the text of this article.

1 Kisluk-Grosheide 2000, p. 27.

2 I am grateful to Kate Hay, curator in the Department of Furniture, Textiles and Fashion at the Victoria and Albert Museum, London, for sharing her insights into this cabinet and other adapted lacquer objects at Ham.

3 For the lacquer room in the Stadhouderlijk Hof in Leeuwarden (created before 1695, now in the Rijksmuseum, Amsterdam, BK–16709), see J. Dorscheid, P. van Duin and H. van Keulen, 'The Late 17th Century Lacquer Room from the Palace of the Stadtholder in Leeuwarden, Preserved in the Rijksmuseum, Amsterdam', in Krist and Iby 2015, pp. 239–59. For the lacquer room in the Berlin Stadtschloss (1690s), see M. Kopplin, "es ist vielleicht ein indianer ...' – Daglys Stilassimilation an ostasiatischen Vorbilder', in Kopplin 2015, pp. 30–65, at pp. 31–39; see also there no. 1 (pp. 136–39).

4 C. Willemijn Fock, 'Frederik Hendrik en Amalia's appartementen: Vorstelijk vertoon naast de triomf van het porselein', in Van der Ploeg and Vermeeren 1997–98, pp. 76–86, at p. 84.

5 For the lacquer rooms at Chatsworth and Burghley see Kisluk-Grosheide 2000, p. 33. The author is grateful to Dr Rupert Goulding for alerting him to the previous existence of a Japan Room at Dyrham Park.

6 NT 436999.1 and NT 436999.2.

7 Standen 1980, pp. 119–42.

8 See the catalogue entry by Helen Wyld on tapestry NT 436999.1 in the National Trust Collections database, http://www.nationaltrustcollections.org.uk/object/436999.1, accessed 22 November 2017.

9 Bowett 2007, pp. 86 and 95–96.

10 Standen 1980, pp. 137–38, where the similarity between the Belton tapestry and the wall decoration in the Marot print is noted, but not the derivation of the lady and attendants with parasol from Montanus's *Atlas Japannensis*. The illustration, of a Japanese aristocratic lady and her entourage, is on p. 338 of the Dutch edition and on p. 367 of the English edition. I am grateful to Adeline van Roon for suggesting I check Montanus, available via the Internet Archive (https://archive.org/stream/ned-kbn-all–00004499–001#page/n428/mode/2up, accessed 25 November 2017).

11 Kisluk-Grosheide 2000, pp. 30–33. Similar baroque-style 'Indian' figures were painted on the panelling of a London house by Robert Robinson in about 1696, see inv. nos. P.6–1954 to P.16–1954 in the collection of the Victoria and Albert Museum, London.

7

CORNELIS DE HEEM (1631–1695)

A Still Life of Flowers and Fruit Arranged on a Stone Plinth in a Garden, c.1685

Oil on canvas, 92.1 × 77.5 cm
Signed middle right, on the edge of the stone ledge: *C. DE HEEM*
National Trust, Dyrham Park, Gloucestershire – The Blathwayt Collection (NT 2900107)

PROVENANCE
Probably acquired by William Blathwayt; thence by descent; bought by Leonard Koetser at the J. R. W. Blathwayt sale, Sotheby's, 29 February 1956, lot 44; acquired from him by an English private collector in 1965; acquired from this collector by Johnny Van Haeften Ltd in 2013; bought from Van Haeften by the National Trust with funds from the National Heritage Memorial Fund, the Mr and Mrs Kenneth Levy bequest, the Art Fund, a fund set up by the late Hon. Simon Sainsbury, the Royal Oak Foundation's Ervin-DesChamps Fund, and a private donation in 2015

EXHIBITED
On Land and Water, Leonard Koetser Gallery, London, March 1965

SELECTED LITERATURE
'Acquisitions' in 'National Trust Historic Houses & Collections Annual', *Apollo*, 2015, pp. 60–61

This exuberant and colourful still life displays a profusion of cultivated flowers and fruit, as well as wild plants and creatures, set centrally around a stone bench. The scene is in a shady corner of a garden. Snails and slugs encircle a dark pond edge alongside overripe peach and melon. Above is a flamboyant arrangement of technically detailed flowers shown at their peak, such as blowsy peonies and viburnum. Interrupting this display are the sinuous tendrils of wild plants, including thistle and oak sapling. The scene continues to rise towards the bright blue and clouded sky with a tortoiseshell butterfly. Cornelis de Heem probably produced this unusually large and extravagant work in the mid-1680s, and it was likely to have been purchased by William Blathwayt (see p. 16 and cat. 1) for Dyrham Park in the 1690s.[1]

In 1668 William Blathwayt started his first job, as a clerk in the embassy of Sir William Temple at The Hague. This was a formative experience, where the studious young man honed skills and developed interests and enthusiasms that continued throughout his life. Significantly, this included knowledge of Dutch language and culture; he was the only member of the embassy staff capable of translation. Blathwayt spent three years in the Netherlands, and beyond his clerical duties he travelled and bought books for private study, all encouraged by his *virtuoso* uncle Thomas Povey (see p. 16).[2]

Some years earlier, in 1662, Samuel van Hoogstraten had arrived in London and produced the famous *View through a House* for Thomas Povey (see fig. 3, p. 17). The painting enraptured the diarist Samuel Pepys, who recorded his appreciation after several visits. An equally enthralled Van Hoogstraten recounted attending a dinner with Royal Society members where Povey, 'the very great art lover', provided a ten-course meal with twenty-four wines.[3] The young Blathwayt was evidently familiar with the artist for Povey wrote in August 1671 requesting that he help The Hague-bound Sir Joseph Williamson 'find Hoogstratens house, my Perspective Painter'.[4] These formative influences of Dutch aesthetic culture on Blathwayt were later

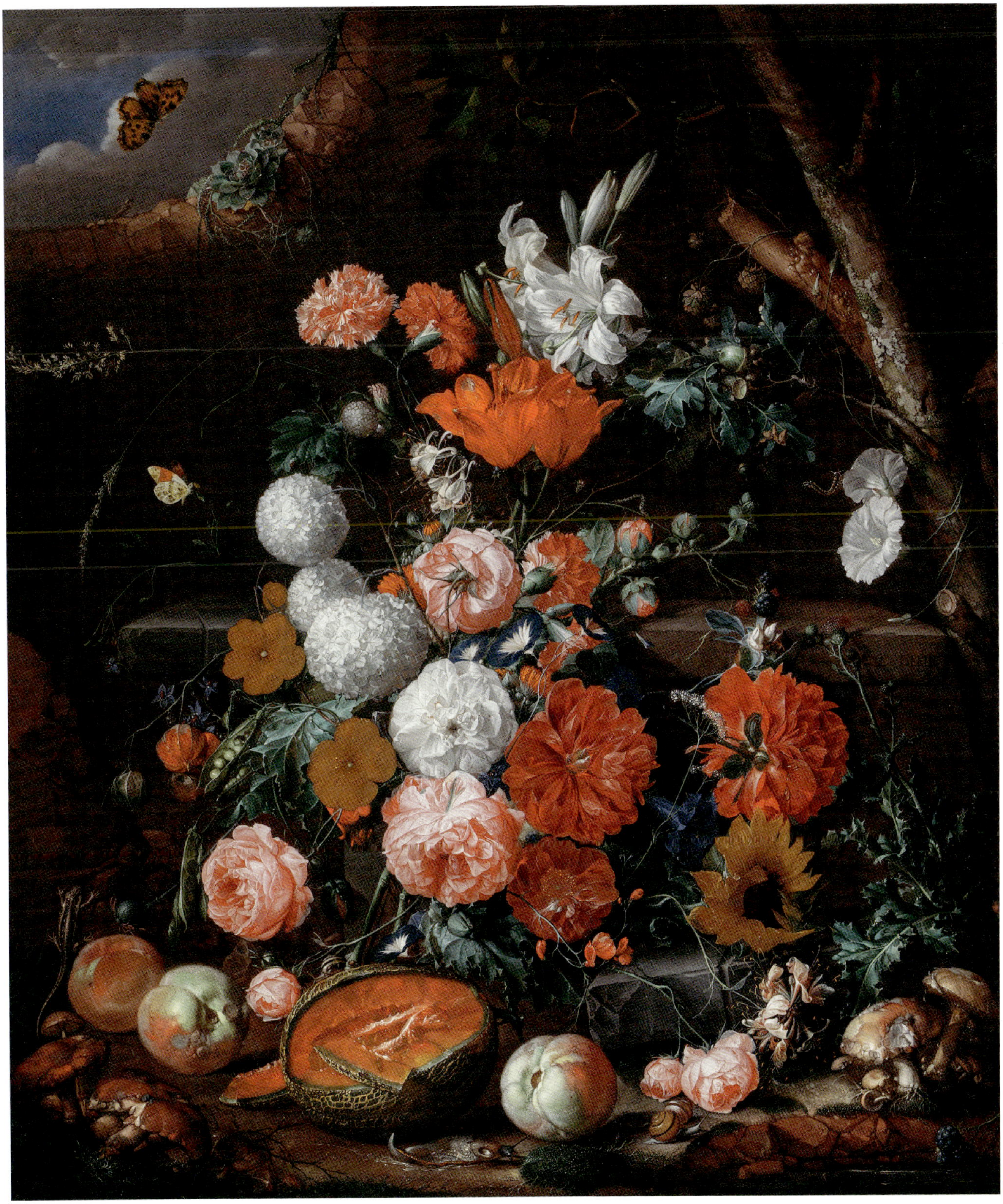

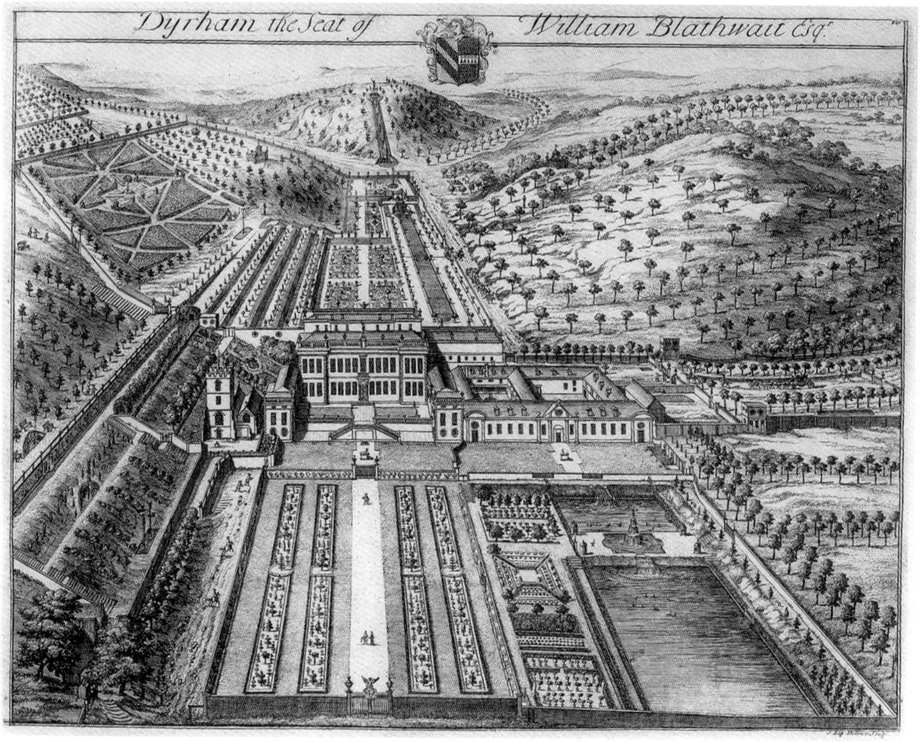

FIG. 51
Johannes Kip (*c.*1653–1722)
*Dyrham the Seat of William Blathwayt Esq*r, published in Sir Robert Atkyns, *The Ancient and Present State of Gloucestershire*, 1712, engraving, 465 × 380 mm
National Trust, Dyrham Park, Gloucestershire (NT 452643)

reflected and became a defining characteristic of Dyrham Park, the house and garden he constructed and furnished between 1691 and 1704.

By the time William III acquired the British throne Blathwayt's career had ascended to include the offices of Secretary at War and Clerk of the Council. These roles brought Blathwayt into close proximity with the new Dutch king, where his mastery of the language and proven administrative skills sustained his continued royal favour. Every year from 1692 to 1701 Blathwayt attended William III in the Netherlands during his conflict against Louis XIV. Before and after each military campaign Blathwayt accompanied the king to his great houses and hunting estates such as Het Loo. The construction and furnishing of Dyrham coincided with this extended period of Dutch travel, gave him exposure to architectural and garden designs, and offered direct access to merchants, suppliers and artists. Dyrham reflects a specific Anglo-Dutch milieu facilitated by close proximity to William III. Surviving at Dyrham today are a significant collection of Delft ceramics by a royal supplier, the 'Greek A' factory, Amsterdam-manufactured gilt-leather wall-hangings, Dutch books including designs by Daniel Marot, and many Dutch paintings, quite apart from what is now lost.[5]

That Blathwayt's taste was influenced by the court of William and Mary, and perhaps more specifically William III, is suggested by the cumulative similarities and associations between Dyrham and the king's creations. Blathwayt built exuberant water-gardens with fountains, cascades and intricate parterres reflecting the influence of the many Dutch gardens he knew and visited (fig. 51). He built a greenhouse for the cultivation of delicate plants and especially orange trees, but included a Latin motto – an instruction for princely living – as quoted by Sir William Temple, who was always the king's most respected confidant and

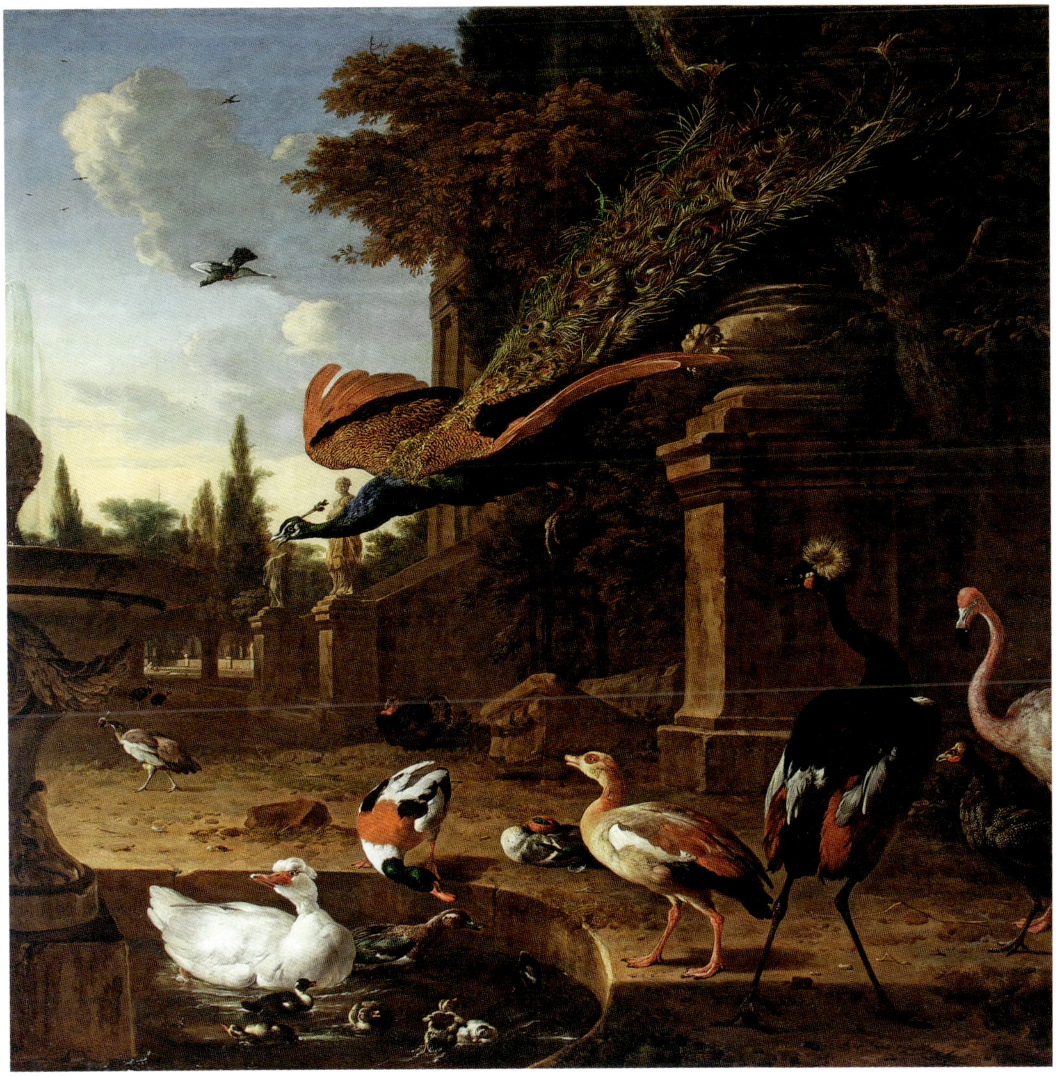

FIG. 52
Melchior d'Hondecoeter (1636–1695)
Ornamental Fowl in and beside a Pond in a Park, with a Peacock in Flight, 1679
Oil on canvas, 241.2 × 215.9 cm
National Trust, Dyrham Park, Gloucestershire (NT 453772)

statesman. The house interior with its profusion of Delft ceramics, extravagant tulip vases and substantial flower tubs echoed royal taste, but there was also an overt declaration of loyalty on small Delft trophies with royal cyphers. Perhaps it is the six surviving pictures by Melchior d'Hondecoeter (see fig. 52) which truly fix the Williamite style: Hondecoeter was court painter and royal favourite, and the presence of these works by him at Dyrham affirms Blathwayt's aesthetic convergence with his master.

In 1693 Blathwayt purchased pictures through Jan Siebrechts in Antwerp. Seven identifiable works remain in the Dyrham collection, including 'ye peacoke' that could be Hondecoeter's extravagant and large bird in flight in fig. 52.[6] Within the same purchase were '2 pieces of flowers' – though unidentifiable from such a description it is tempting to wonder if they were those by Cornelis de Heem and his father Jan Davidsz.[7] These two flowerpieces were always favoured and given prominent locations within the house when identifiable in household inventories.

Cornelis de Heem's flowerpiece has a clear pictorial quality and brings obvious colour and energy – the large scale, artistic flair and skill as enjoyable now as then. For Blathwayt, who built a career handling and remembering factual detail, this work surely satisfied an aspect of his personality, and so too the botanical range depicted. The *vanitas* composition of fragile floral beauty set against overripe and decaying fruit, consuming creatures and encroaching weeds, presents the established teaching on the futility and brevity of life. But perhaps here lies a specific resonance. During the 1690s Blathwayt was a military secretary attending war, away from home and young family, living in actual danger. But it was a lifestyle of contrast: the annual routine juxtaposed palatial luxury with the hardships of campaign, the pleasures of court life with the hazards of war. For Blathwayt it was a period of significant accumulation, a large salary to invest in building a new country house and garden, furnishing, decorating and collecting – but as a recent widower he knew these material gains were only for this life. Thus the flowerpiece captures deeper truths about William Blathwayt's own life, personality and the significant impact his Dutch experiences had on his career and ultimately the creation of Dyrham Park. RG

NOTES

1 With thanks to Pippa Mason, Johnny Van Haeften Ltd.
2 Jacobsen 1932, pp. 66–76.
3 *Inleyding tot de Hooge Schoole der Schilderkonst: Anders de Zichtbaere Werelt* (1678).
4 Gloucestershire Archives D1799/C3.
5 Blathwayt purchased silks, imported Indian textiles, porcelain and tea from the Netherlands in 1695: *Calendar of Treasury Books*, vol. 10, pp. 1225–26.
6 Signed and dated: *1679*; British Library S.C. 1360.
7 Sold from Dyrham in 1956.

8

MEINDERT HOBBEMA (1638–1709) and ADRIAEN VAN DE VELDE (1636–72)

*A Landscape with a Common and Coppice, c.*1663

Oil on canvas, 87 × 113.5 cm
National Trust, Petworth House, West Sussex – The Egremont Collcction (NT 486134)

PROVENANCE
Possibly inherited by the 3rd Earl of Egremont from the Earl of Thomond in 1774; at Petworth by 1822; thence by descent; accepted by HM Treasury from John Wyndham, 6th Lord Leconfield and 1st Lord Egremont in lieu of inheritance tax in 1956; transferred to the National Trust in 1982

EXHIBITED
Remastered: Bosch to Bellotto, National Trust, Petworth House, West Sussex, 9 January–6 March 2016

LITERATURE
Loukes 2016, no. 43

This wooded scene with a pond and scattered cottages is exemplary of the imposing works of art which Dutch landscape painters were able to create out of even the most humble subjects. Set somewhere in the flat rural regions of the United Provinces, it shows a village common planted with trees as a source of fuel and shelter known as a *brink*.[1]

Considerable forces of art have been deployed to create an image of deceptive simplicity. Organised around dual perspectives, the picture invites the eye to roam in two alternative directions, either directly to the horizon across the brighter side of the view or over the pond and deep into the shadowy wood. Nothing of greater note is happening than a cow coming to water, yet the composition entertains the eye with innumerable pictorial incidents – wheel tracks almost literally carved out of a painted road; delicate flicks of the brush describing the fall of light on leaves; patches of sun and shadow alternating to the far distance; and above everything a majestic, changeable sky setting off the delicate tracery of the treetops.

Paintings of rustic subjects were just one manifestation of the pleasure that citizens of the Dutch Republic derived from their native countryside, which also took the form of country strolls and pastoral verse descriptions. Peaceful, sparsely populated and somewhat ramshackle, this scenery was celebrated as a refreshing contrast to the emphatically urban and mercantile character of Dutch society.[2] Given the extraordinary military aggression which this landscape repeatedly repelled over the course of the seventeenth century, it has been suggested that its very modesty and ordinariness was a source of immense patriotic pride.[3]

The picture is the creation of two emerging talents working in Amsterdam in the early 1660s, Meindert Hobbema, who painted the landscape, and Adriaen van de Velde, who was responsible for adding the human and animal elements. Both, in fact, were skilled landscape practitioners, although Van der Velde's abilities as a figure painter led to many similar collaborations, which enhanced the value of the final product.[4] Such an edge was crucial in the market in landscape painting where high demand was equalled and even surpassed by the quality and volume of supply.[5] In these conditions few managed to make a living from their chosen speciality alone. Van de Velde rapidly established a strong following but his wife had to keep a linen shop to help makes ends meet and he was heavily in debt when he died at the age of thirty-five. Hobbema fared even less well, largely

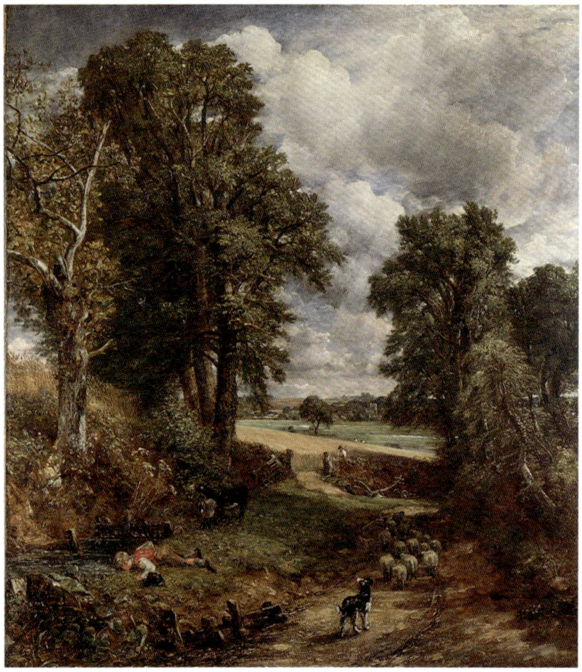

FIG. 53
John Constable (1776–1837)
The Cornfield, 1826
Oil on canvas, 143 × 122 cm
London, The National Gallery (NG130)

giving up his painting career after securing a salaried job measuring wine consignments in the Amsterdam customs in 1668. He died a pauper four decades later.

The difficulties of this situation contrast vividly with the great premium that the works of seventeenth-century landscape painters commanded on the international art market in subsequent centuries. Artists whose names had barely been known in their own lifetimes became celebrated masters in the galleries of connoisseurs, rulers and aristocrats, where they were associated with favourite subjects. A work by Hobbema, for example, was all the more prized when it depicted woodland scenery, as here. The present work probably entered the possession of the Earls of Egremont at Petworth House just as Hobbema's name was in the ascendant in the second half of the eighteenth century. It was certainly in the collection by 1822, when the 3rd Earl lent it to an exhibition of Old Master paintings in the British Institution, Pall Mall, London.

The increasing visibility of Dutch rustic landscapes in commercial showrooms, aristocratic collections and, from the early nineteenth century, public museums and exhibitions made a deep impact on British picturesque and Romantic artists, from Thomas Gainsborough to the Norwich painter John Crome, whose last recorded words were 'Oh! Hobbima, my dear Hobbima, how I have loved you!'[6] When John Constable exhibited *The Cornfield* (fig. 53) at the Royal Academy of Arts it was felt to be 'singularly beautiful, and not inferior to some of Hobbema's finest works' – presumably on account of the Hobbema-like prominence it gives to large irregular trees.[7] Constable may well have seen *A Landscape with a Common and Coppice* when it was lent to the British Institution and must have got to know it well when he was invited by the 3rd Earl of Egremont to stay at Petworth and study the collection in 1834. He drew inspiration for his own ideal of art from the steady way in which Dutch landscape painters had achieved greatness through sensitive repetitions of a limited repertoire of natural subjects, writing:

> *I do not enter into that notion of varying one's plans to keep the Publick in good humour – subject and change of weather & effect will always afford variety. What if* [Willem] *Van de Velde had quitted his sea pieces – or* [Jacob] *Ruysdael his waterfalls – or Hobbema his native woods – would not the world have lost so many features in art?*[8] JC

NOTES

1 Lambert 1985, p. 67.
2 Shawe-Taylor 2010, pp. 33–37.
3 Schama 1987–88, pp. 64–83.
4 Cornelis and Schapelhouman 2016, pp. 34–36. The picture formerly bore the signatures of both artists although only Hobbema's is now visible.
5 Chong 1987–88, pp. 104–20.
6 Sharpin 1842, p. 361.
7 *The Times*, 29 April 1826, transcribed in Crosby Ivy 1991, p. 117.
8 Beckett 1968, p. 181.

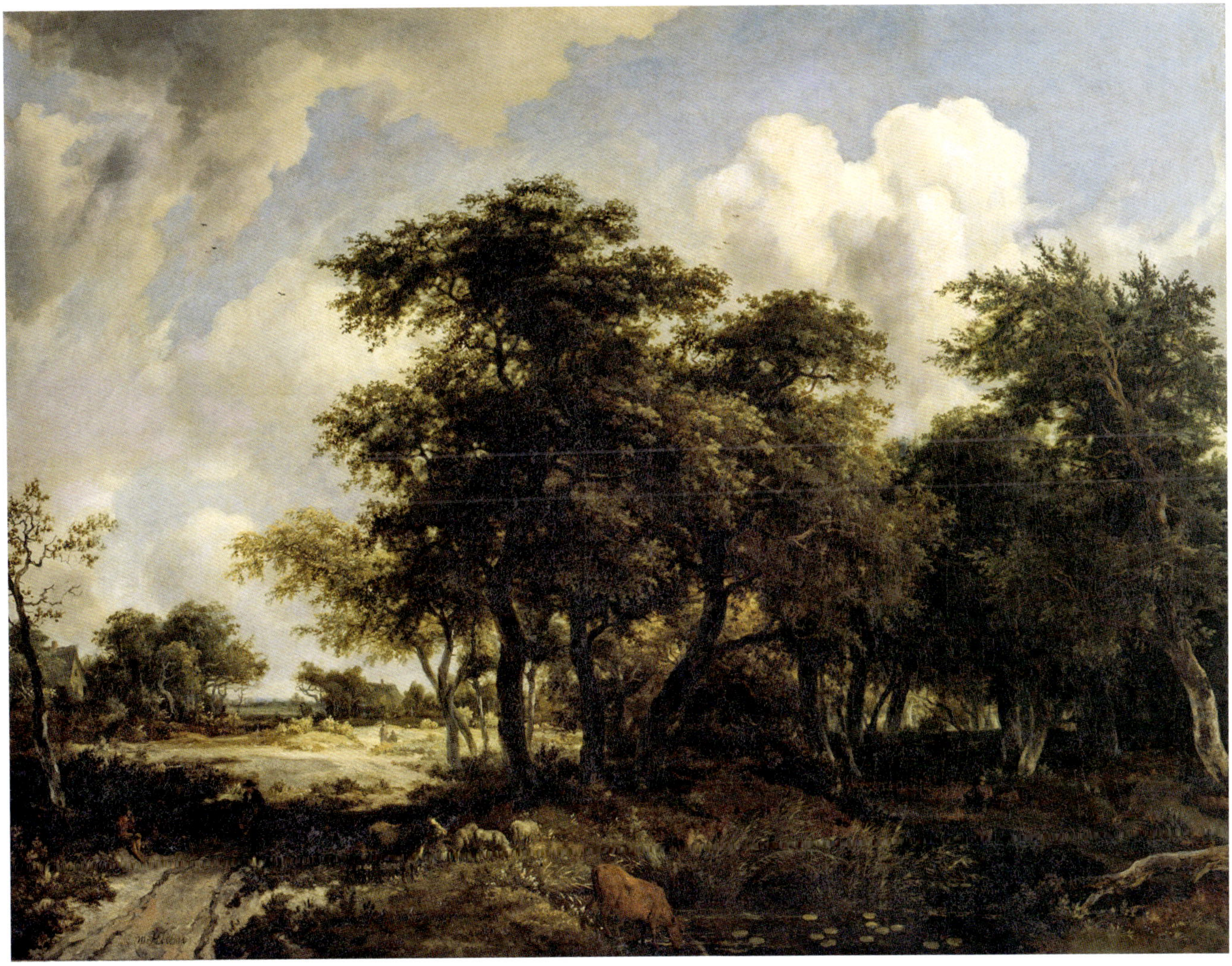

Books

TIM PYE, NATIONAL TRUST LIBRARIES CURATOR

AT SHUGBOROUGH, THE ANSON FAMILY'S Neoclassical mansion in Staffordshire, there is a clue as to the importance of Dutch Golden Age books in the country house library. In the former Smoking Room, with banks of book-shelving across the length of the north wall, one small shelf has the distinction of a simple brass label on which is written *Elzevir Press*. The shelf is small, just big enough to house a run of the duodecimo-sized classical texts that are synonymous with the Elzevier name, and is prominently positioned directly above a doorway, unmissable by anyone passing through the room. The shelf is now empty, owing to the devastating 1842 sale of the contents of Shugborough (including the library) but the sale catalogue gives some indication as to how the 42 Elzevier books would have looked in situ, describing the collection as 'a beautiful set bound in old red Morocco, and richly tooled on the sides, with gilt leaves'.[1] In a library as vast and grand as the one at Shugborough it may at first seem odd to single out one publisher, but it reflects the standing of the Elzevier name, particularly in eighteenth century England. Long prized for their typographical, textual and aesthetic precision, it was in this period that Elzevier books began receiving special mention on the title-page of book auction catalogues. Perhaps most telling is the pride evident in the correspondence of Horace Walpole, collector of Dutch books and founder of the Strawberry Hill Press, when recalling 'Elzevir Horace' as one of his nicknames.[2]

The interest in seventeenth-century Dutch books shown by Walpole and the Ansons came some years after the last publication was issued by Abraham Elzevier in Leiden in 1702. But it is in the eighteenth century that Golden Age books from the Dutch Republic began to be venerated in England, spurred on by great book collectors such as the Duke of Devonshire and the Earls of Oxford and Sunderland. Dutch booksellers, resident in London, imported vast numbers of old books from the Continent, often at the behest of these collectors, and prices for the choicest publications soon rocketed. This vigorous trade could only flourish because of the large number of Golden Age books available. The Dutch Republic's role as a centre of international trade in the eighteenth century, and the fact that there was no church or state censorship, allowed publishers to situate the Netherlands as the centre of Western book production. By some counts the printed output of the Republic in this period is said to have been greater in number than the combined output of all other countries.[3]

The majority of the *c.* 5,000 Dutch Golden Age books found on the shelves in National Trust libraries, like those at Shugborough, were collected after 1701. However, there is a substantial number that can be tied directly to contemporary acquisition and, critically, use by country-house residents. The copy-specific aspects of these books provide clues as to the significance of Dutch books in private library collections, and in England more generally, during the eighteenth century.

In a discussion of Dutch books in National Trust libraries Dyrham Park (fig. 54) must be front and centre as it contains the largest collection of seventeenth-century Dutch books acquired by a country house owner of the period, William Blathwayt (for whom see

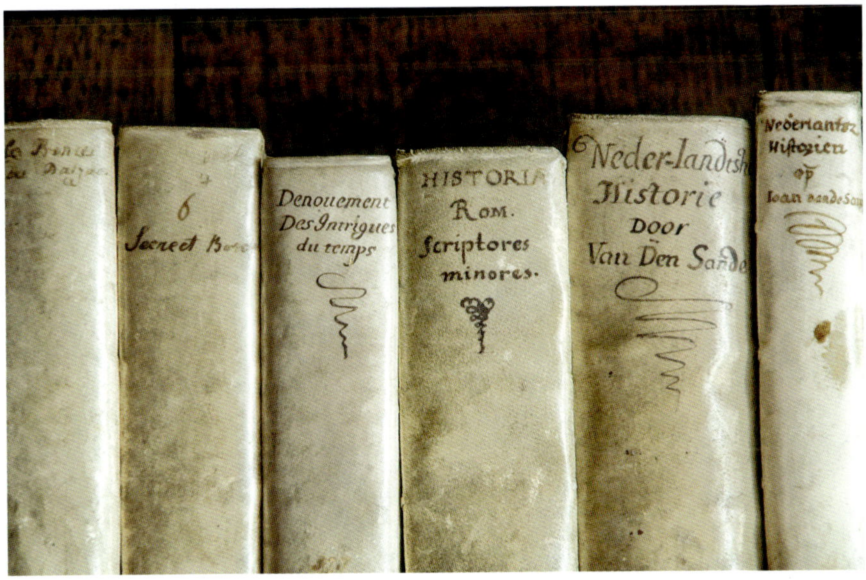

FIG. 54
Vellum-bound Dutch books at Dyrham Park, Gloucestershire

also p. 16 and cat. nos. 1 and 7). All of the collections within his house at Dyrham have a strong Dutch flavour, a direct consequence of his career as a civil servant in the Low Countries. In 1668 he was appointed as clerk in the embassy at The Hague – apparently the only Dutch speaker on the staff – and his association with the Netherlands carried on into the final decade of the eighteenth century, when he accompanied William III on visits to the Low Countries. Blathwayt's collection is similar to those formed by other contemporary civil servants (like Samuel Pepys and John Evelyn) but in a greater variety of modern languages. Blathwayt was proficient in Danish, German and Polish as well as Dutch, and all these languages are represented on the Dyrham shelves. His Dutch books include the kind of titles essential for everyday diplomatic work – legal texts, such as the first three volumes of the *Groot Placaet-Boeck* (The Hague, 1658–83),[1] Dutch histories by Pieter Schrijver and others, and a first edition of Willem Sewel's important *A New Dictionary English and Dutch* (Amsterdam, 1691).[2] A further item of note, Louis Cappel's *Commentarii et Notæ Criticæ in Vetus Testamentum* (Amsterdam, 1689),[3] is inscribed to Blathwayt by the editor and author's son, Jacques Cappel (1639–1722). A French Protestant exile in London, Cappel had his father's writings published in Amsterdam by the third generation of the famous printing firm Blaeu, a multinational approach to publishing that highlights the central position of the Dutch book trade in this period.

Other books arrived in country house libraries as a direct result of the close relationship between the Netherlands and Royalist England during the Civil War and Interregnum. Droves of young men found themselves exiled on the Continent and many used the opportunity for education and betterment. The scholarly European journeys of some of these men can be traced through the notes left in books acquired during exile. One such man, John Bankes (1626–1656; fig. 55) of Kingston Lacy, Dorset, the son of Sir John Bankes, Charles I's Chief Justice, spent much of the 1640s travelling across Europe. He kept notes of his travels in France and Italy in late 1646 but there is evidence that he was on the Continent at least eighteen months earlier.[4] It is inconceivable that some of these months were not spent in the Low Countries; at the very least there is evidence of his buying Dutch books on his travels between 1645 and 1648. Whether acquired in the place of publication, or in France or Italy, we find numerous Dutch publications providing him

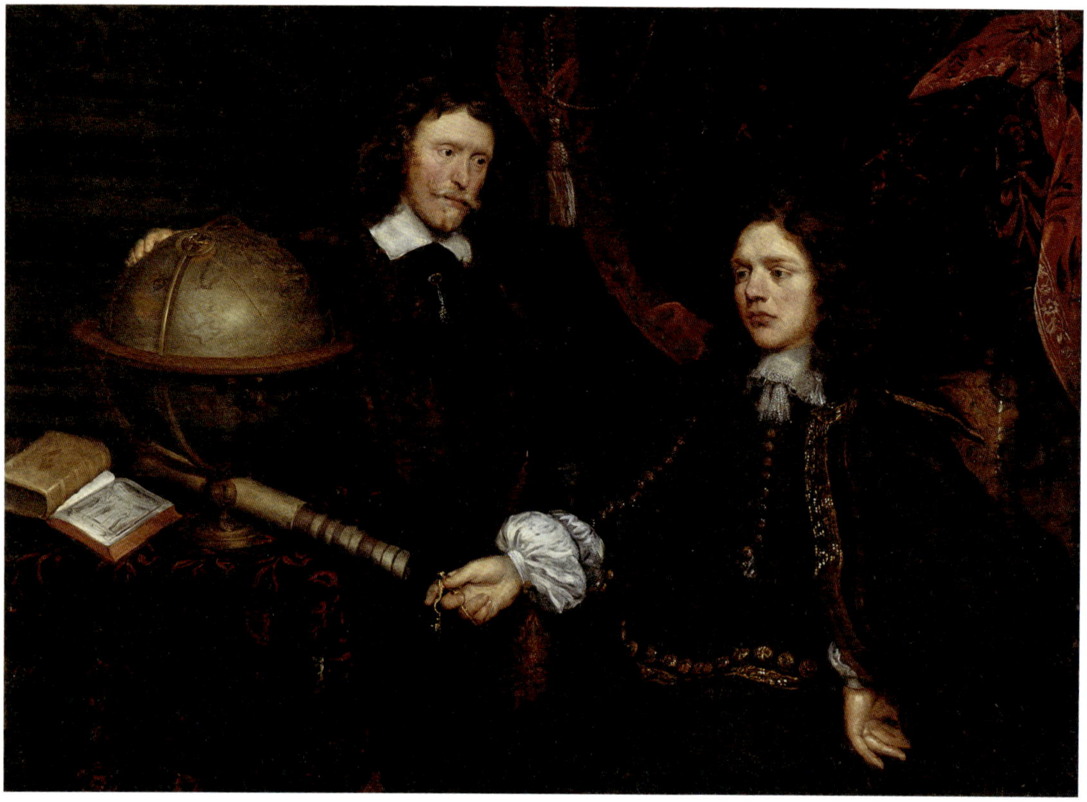

FIG. 55
Francis Cleyn (1582–1658)
John Bankes and his Tutor Sir Maurice Williams, 1643
Oil on canvas, 130 × 174.6 cm
National Trust, Kingston Lacy, Dorset
(NT 1257174)

with a foundation of European literature and culture. There is no better example of this than the Kingston Lacy copy of Thomas Erpenius's treatise on European travel, *De Peregrinatione Gallica Utiliter Instituenda Tractatus* (Amsterdam, 1631),[4] inscribed *J. Bankes 1645*, highlighting its acquisition near the beginning of his European tour.

Similar examples can be found on the shelves of other Royalist houses. At Nostell Priory, West Yorkshire, there are several books that were acquired by a young Edmund Winn (1644–1694), later 2nd Baronet, during the period 1656–59. Perhaps the most interesting of these is a copy of the charmingly titled *The English Schole-master; or, Certaine Rules and Helpes, Whereby the Natives of the Netherlandes, May Bee, in a Short Time, Taught to Read, Understand, and Speake, the English tongue. By the Helpe Whereof, the English Also May be Better Instructed in the Knowledge of the Dutch Tongue* (Amsterdam, 1658),[5] which includes an inscription recording the book's purchase in Haarlem for fourteen *stuivers* on 2 May 1659.

No story of Dutch Golden Age books in country house libraries is complete without mention of Blickling Hall and the remarkable collection amassed by Sir Richard Ellys (1682–1742). Although primarily formed in the first half of the eighteenth century, and including the kind of Dutch treasures that one might expect to find in a fine collector's library – incunabula

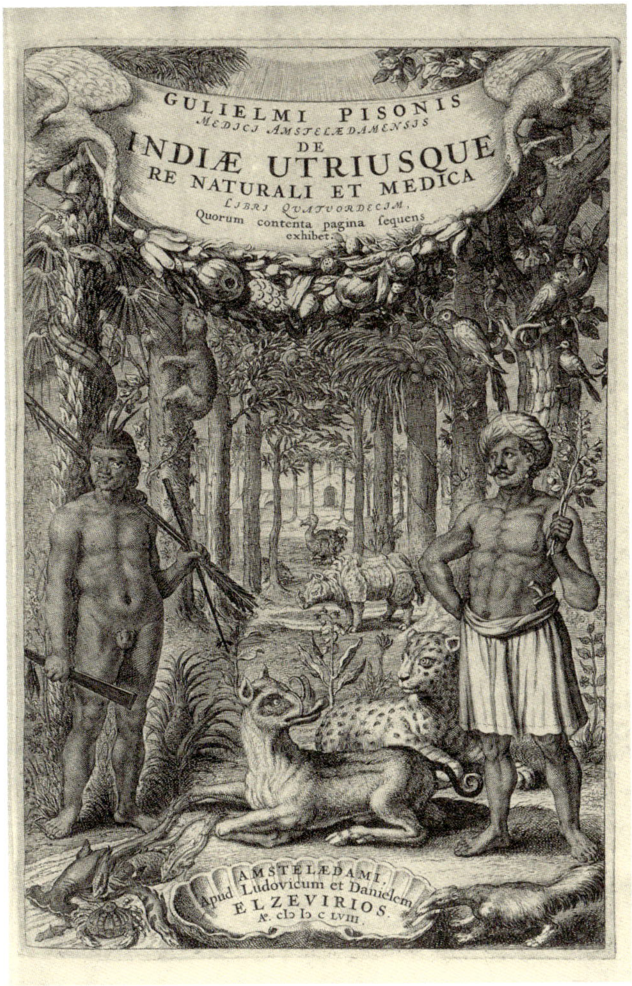

FIG. 56
Ornately engraved title page of Willem Piso's monumental work on South America and tropical medicine, *De Indiae utriusque re naturali et medica*, published in Amsterdam by Elzevier, 1658 (from the copy at Blickling Hall, Norfolk, NT 3199983)

from Schiedam and Deventer, great atlases of Ortelier, Blaeu and Doncker, exceptional copies of Elzevier publications (fig. 56) – Ellys's collection exhibits a sophisticated approach to the acquisition of Golden Age books. This can undoubtedly be attributed to his time spent as young man in Holland in the 1690s, acquiring his love of learning and honing his linguistic skills.[5] It is likely that he attended lectures at Leiden University and met intellectuals of the calibre of Ludolf Küster (said to have been Ellys's tutor). As an adult he retained close associations with Dutch scholars and was very active at Dutch book auctions, all of which explains the wealth of items at Blickling with interesting Dutch provenance – Pieter Pauw (1564–1617), the Leiden University anatomist and botanist; Gijsbert Voet (1589–1676), theologian, to name but two – the numerous seventeenth-century Dutch bindings and the provincially printed items still in their original wrappers. It is not an overstatement to suggest that the collection of Dutch Golden Age books at Blickling, as at Nostell, Kingston Lacy, Dyrham and countless other country houses, is one of the cornerstones of the library.

NOTES

1 Robins 1842, p. 11.
2 Walpole 1937–83, XL, p. 104.
3 Hellinga 1962, p. 29.
4 Lewis 2014, p. 10.
5 Mandlebrote and Lewis 2004, pp. 9–10.

9

GERRIT VAN HONTHORST (1592–1656)

Elizabeth Stuart, Queen of Bohemia (1596–1662), 1650

Oil on canvas, 72.4 × 59.1 cm
Signed and dated middle left: *GHonthorst 1650*
National Trust, Ashdown House, Oxfordshire – The Craven Collection (NT 493054)

PROVENANCE
The Craven Family by descent; at Coombe Abbey by 1866; accepted by HM Government in lieu of inheritance tax and allocated to the National Trust in 1968

LITERATURE
Judson and Ekkart 1999, p. 264, no. 340 (4)

Elizabeth Stuart was the daughter of James VI and I (1566–1625) and Anne of Denmark (1574–1619). Raised in Scotland until her father succeeded to the English throne in 1603, the well-educated and popular Elizabeth was the focus of various potential dynastic marriages until 1613, when she married the Protestant prince Frederick V, Count Palatine of the Rhine (1596–1632). They lived at Heidelberg until Frederick was offered the Bohemian throne in 1619. The marriage was a rare royal love-match, and the couple had thirteen children, including Prince Rupert (see cat. 22). At the death of Queen Anne in 1714, Elizabeth's grandson, through her daughter Sophia, Electress of Hanover (1630–1714), became George I (1660–1727), the first monarch of the House of Hanover, whose descendant is the current British monarch, Queen Elizabeth II (b. 1926).

Elizabeth and Frederick's brief tenure as monarchs in Bohemia, which they ruled until the Protestant defeat at the 1620 Battle of the White Mountain, gave them their 'Winter' King and Queen soubriquets. They moved, in exile, to the Dutch Republic, where Elizabeth stayed, following her husband's death in 1632, until the last year of her life, when she returned to London following her nephew Charles II's restoration to the throne.

During Elizabeth's long exile in the Dutch Republic, where she lived in The Hague, she commissioned the Utrecht painter Gerrit van Honthorst to paint her with her family as well as employing him as a painting teacher to her children. Honthorst had been taught by Abraham Bloemaert (see cat. 2) before spending ten years in Rome, where he was one of the best-known followers of Caravaggio. He began working for the king and queen of Bohemia soon after he returned to Utrecht in 1620. It was through Elizabeth's patronage that Honthorst travelled to England, where he was commissioned by her brother, Charles I, to make paintings such as the huge *Apollo and Diana* (1628) still in the Royal Collection (fig. 11, p. 32).[1] After he returned from London, he moved to The Hague, where he worked on decorations in the Bohemians' palaces. Owing to the large demand for portraits of these Protestant heroes and their heirs, many of them were copied in his studio.

In the Ashdown House portrait, Honthorst has depicted the Winter Queen in mourning, wearing a plain black dress, albeit discreetly adorned with huge pearls, both on her dress and as earrings and a necklace.[2] This is closely related, in terms of costume and hairstyle, to another version by Honthorst in the collection of the Prince of Hanover. Both relate to the artist's magnificent full-length portrait of her in mourning, now in the National Gallery, London.[3] Painted in 1642, it is thought to have been

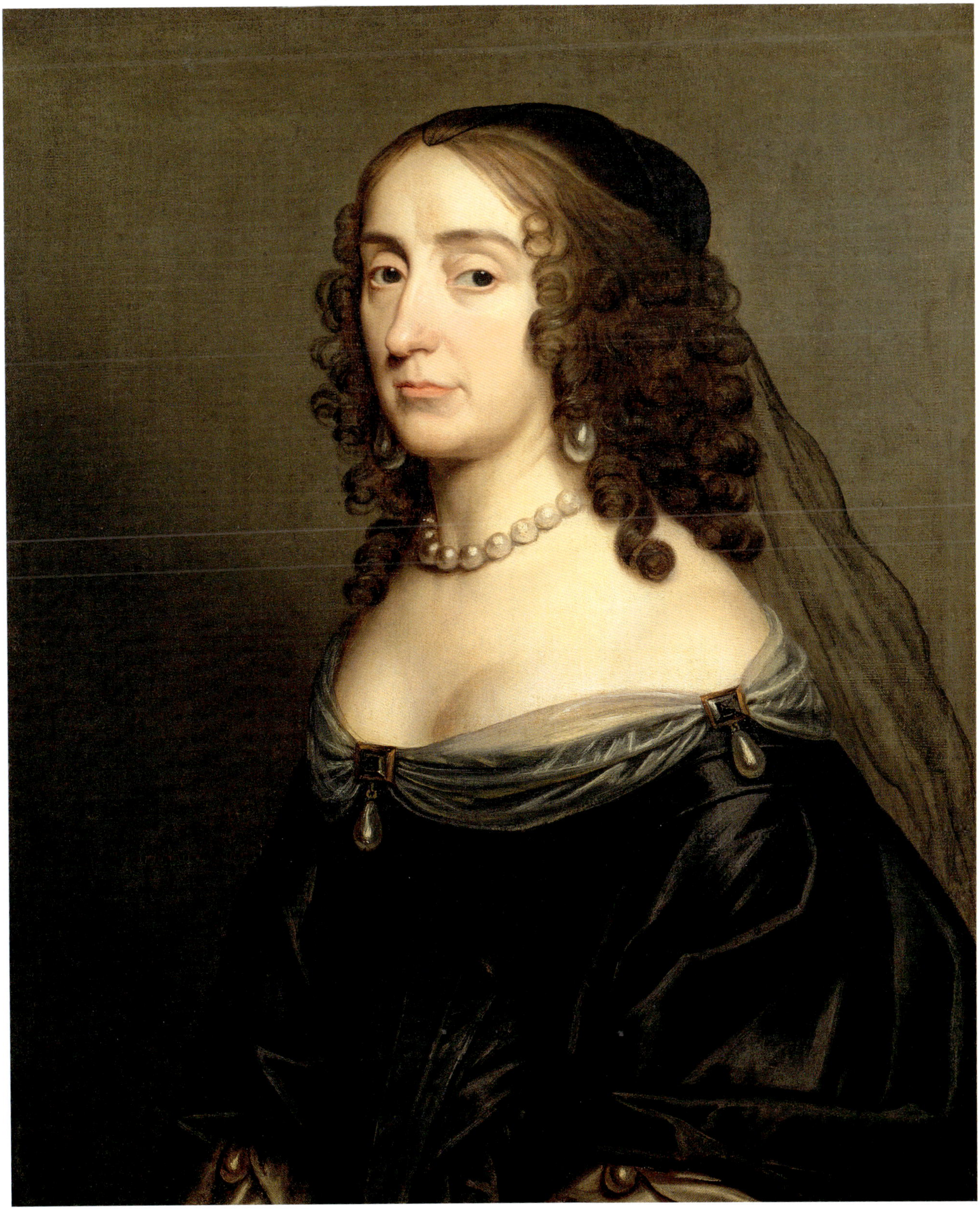

commissioned to commemorate the sitter's decade-long widowhood. In the picture she stands under an oak tree, on a terrace, before a brooding, dark grey sky, while a dog, representing marital fidelity, paws at her skirts. She holds up a rose, on the stem of which is a second flower that appears to have died.

Signed and dated 1650, the Ashdown House portrait was created during a period when the artist was receiving fewer commissions from both Elizabeth and from Amalia van Solms, the widowed Princess of Orange, who had employed him as one of the contributing artists to decorate the Oranjezaal in Huis ten Bosch.[4] The portrait was previously owned by William Craven, 1st Earl of Craven (see p. 104), Elizabeth's most prominent English supporter, who had fallen in love with her before her exile in the Netherlands. His military background is referred to in the full-length portrait of him wearing armour that Honthorst painted in 1642, the same year as his full-length of Elizabeth in the National Gallery (fig. 57). Craven offered his London house to Elizabeth following her return to the city after the restoration of the Stuart monarchy in 1660. He was the builder of Ashdown House, which he had hoped to present to her as a hunting lodge, although she died before it was built. His full-length portrait was kept at his home, Coombe Abbey, which was, coincidentally, the house where Elizabeth was raised as a child by the Harington family. Elizabeth left her portraits to Craven and the present portrait of her was also at Coombe Abbey, where it stayed, by descent, until it was acquired by the National Trust in 1968 from the sale of Cornelia, Countess of Craven's pictures.[5] Ashdown House was given to the National Trust by Lady Craven in 1956. DT

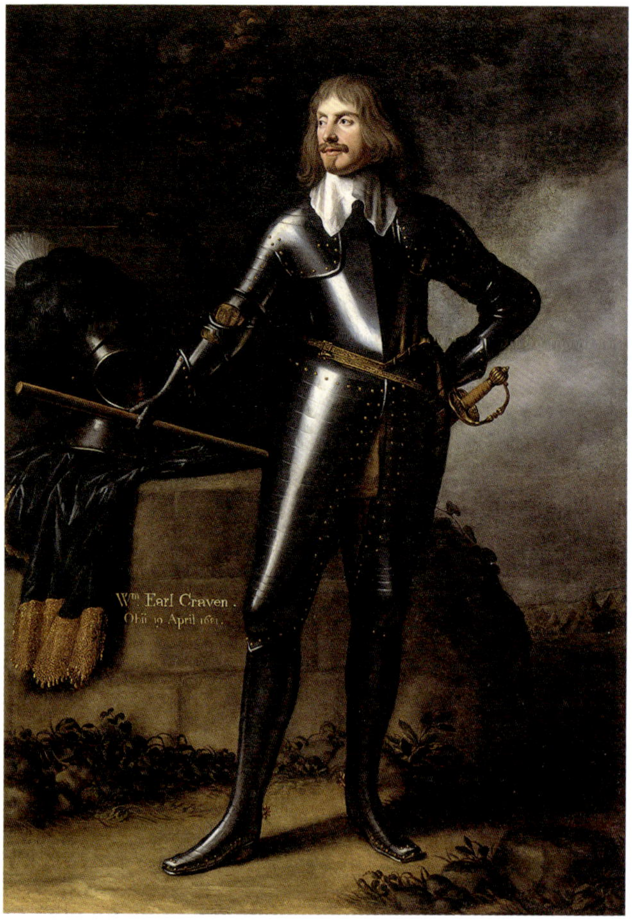

FIG. 57
Gerrit van Honthorst (1590–1656)
William Craven, 1st Earl of Craven (1608–1697), 1642
Oil on canvas, 209.6 × 144.8 cm
Cambridge, Fitzwilliam Museum
(PD.117–1992)

NOTES

1 RCIN 405746.
2 Judson and Ekkart 1999, pp. 264–65, no. 340 (4).
3 London, National Gallery, NG6362.
4 See Frijhoff and Spies 2004, p. 494.
5 *Catalogue of the Pictures at Combe Abbey, Warwickshire, the Seat of William Earl of Craven*, 1866, p. 6, no. 27.

10

PIETER DE HOOCH (1629–1684)

The Colf Players, *c.*1658–60

Oil on panel, 64 × 46 cm
Signed lower left, on the door: *P d Hooch*
National Trust, Polesden Lacey, Surrey – The McEwan Collection (NT 1246485)

PROVENANCE
Said by Hofstede de Groot to have belonged to Count von Fries, but not included in his sales in 1824 and 1826 in London and Vienna; the H. Héris sale, Brussels, 19 June 1846, lot 27, to Piérard; the Piérard sale, Paris, 20 March 1860, lot 29; bought in at the Sir H. Hume Campbell sale, Christie's, 25 May 1867, lot 77; bought by Adrian Lesser at the sale of the same owner, Christie's, 16 June 1894, lot 37; from whom acquired by William McEwan; by descent to Dame Margaret Greville; bequeathed by her to the National Trust in 1943

EXHIBITED
The Art of Upbringing, Dordrechts Museum, Dordrecht, 2013, no. 3

SELECTED LITERATURE
P. Sutton in Sutton 1980, pp. 47, 88, no. 41; B. Broos in Broos *et al.* 1990–91, p. 303; P. Sutton in Sutton 1998, pp. 130, 132, 136–37, no. 23

Second only to Johannes Vermeer (1632–1675), Pieter de Hooch is considered the leading exponent of the Delft school of painting, even though he spent less than ten years of his life in the city.[1] He must have lived in Delft from *c.*1652 until some time in 1654 (the year of his move to Rotterdam) and from 1655 to 1660, when he moved for good to Amsterdam. It was precisely in the period before 1660 that there seems to have been artistic rivalry between De Hooch and Vermeer, his junior by three years, and this rivalry apparently continued even after De Hooch's move to Amsterdam.[2] Among De Hooch's earliest paintings are simple domestic interiors with soldiers and serving girls. The rooms in these scenes are plain, with little detail. From around 1657, at which time Vermeer too was beginning to paint genre scenes, De Hooch began to produce (in addition to several outdoor scenes with figures in inner courtyards or public gardens) indoor scenes with one or more figures from the upper classes, in which the interior constitutes an essential part of the composition. The figures are usually engaged in household work of some kind, or else they are portrayed reading letters, making music, or eating and drinking. In this exceptionally attractive painting from Polesden Lacey, all attention is focused on the young child standing in the doorway between two rooms, holding the door handle in one hand and a *colf* stick in the other. The custom of dressing young children of both sexes in dresses makes it practically impossible to say whether this child is a boy or a girl. A white smock was a standard article of boys' clothing in those days,[3] and it was also quite usual for boys to have shoulder-length curls. In the seventeenth century it was thought practical to dress children in skirts, so skirts were worn by both boys and girls until about the age of six. This particular child also wears a dark apron to protect the clothes, but aprons that left this much of the skirt visible were typically worn by girls.[4]

The child in the foreground seems to have been playing a game of *colf* with a slightly older boy (a brother?), who stands outside and is visible through the open 'Dutch door'. This boy is about to hit a ball, although his gaze is fixed on the child in the house. It must be late autumn or winter, judging by the bare

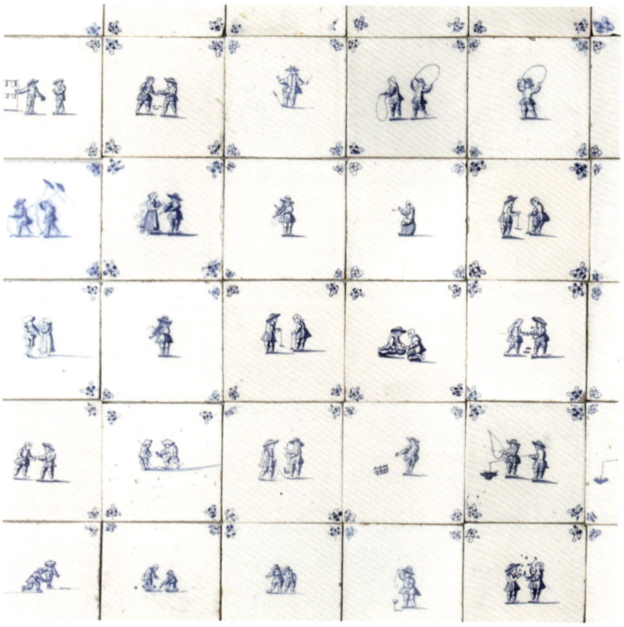

FIG. 58
Sixty-four Delftware tiles decorated with children's games, *c.*1670–1750 (detail)
Each tile *c.*13 × 13 cm; set in a frame
Philadelphia, Philadelphia Museum of Art, Gift of Anthony N. B. Garvan, 1983 (1983-101-32-95)

trees, between which we see the low houses that De Hooch typically depicted.[5] The game of *colf*, which was extraordinarily popular in the seventeenth century, was the forerunner of the game of *kolf* that was all the rage in the eighteenth century and of the game of golf played today. The object is to hit, in as few turns as possible, a hard ball over a long distance to a predetermined goal.[6] This sport was practised the whole year round by people of all ages, and, because flying *colf* balls were a nuisance and could cause damage, attempts were made to prohibit the sport in cities. Outside the town walls, special *colf* courses were laid out, such as the Maliebaan in Utrecht, which still exists. In the winter, this game was played on the ice. De Hooch's painting shows us the wooden sticks with iron (or lead) heads that were used in those days. The handle of the stick held by the child in the foreground seems to be wrapped in leather. *Colf* balls were generally made of soft sheepskin filled with cows' hair, but wooden balls such as the one depicted here were also used.

Lovely views from one room to another are characteristic of De Hooch's interiors. Here the open inside door affords a view of the adjoining hall, and the view continues from interior to exterior through the 'Dutch door', both halves of which stand open. These receding perspectives strengthen the illusion of depth, as do the lines in the grouting of the tile floor, which lead the viewer's gaze into the picture.[7] The first rows of tiles, on which the child stands – a tile at lower right is cracked – are interrupted by a very narrow threshold, after which the square tiles in the hall are no longer exactly in line with those in the foreground. This three-dimensional effect is magnified by the play of light, which is sublimely rendered and binds together all the elements of the interior. Daylight streams in through the outside door and from a window beyond our field of vision, lighting up some of the hand-painted, blue-and-white wall tiles to the left of the inside door opening. These tiles are characteristic of Dutch houses of the time, but here they also serve to underscore the central theme of the painting, because they contain depictions of playing children (see also fig. 58).[8]

In this painting De Hooch demonstrates his great skill at describing the various materials and surfaces by manipulating the play of light. The child's hair seems almost tangible, and the luminous effect of the sunlight on the curls creates the impression of an aureole. The contours of the child also catch the enchanting light. De Hooch's bravura is evident in the highlights which he applied to the grain of the wooden planks that form the inside door and to the earthenware floor tiles with their irregular surface. These lifelike passages are undoubtedly the result of De Hooch's close observation of reality. This is also apparent from small details, such as his unerring placement of highlights on the door handle, the metal

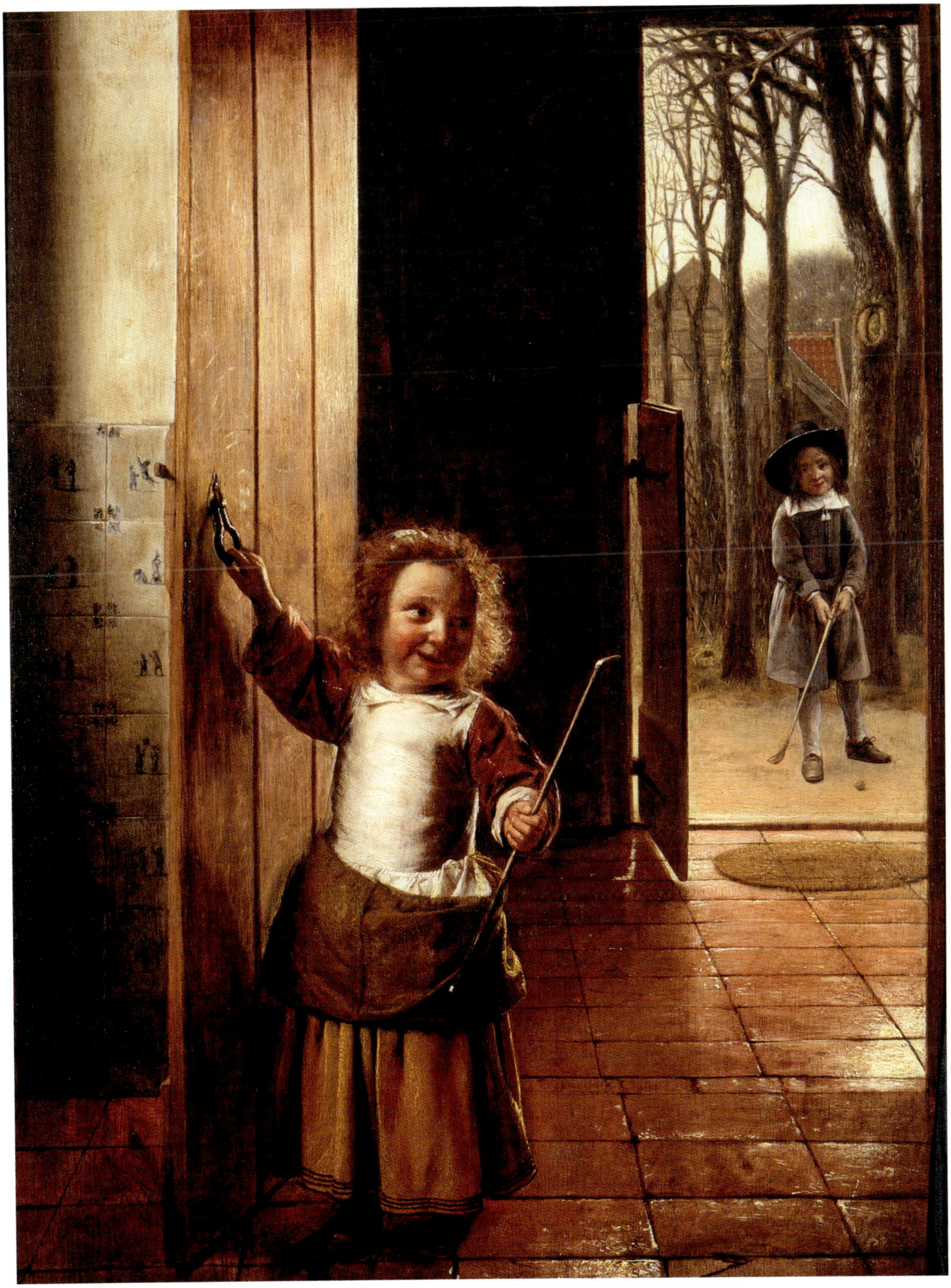

head of the child's *colf* stick in the foreground, and the streak of light on the tile floor, coming through the crack at the hinges of the outside door. All things considered, De Hooch's subtle and refined use of colour and his feeling for light, space and atmosphere make this painting a veritable *tour de force*. *The Colf Players* is usually dated to *c*.1658–60, De Hooch's last years in Delft. It is a masterpiece produced by an artist whose later works fail to match the high quality of the paintings he made in this earlier period.

The motif of a child holding the handle of an open door evidently appealed to De Hooch. In the same period he made at least two more paintings with this motif, which display small changes to such elements as the clothing.[9] For example, a child appears prominently in *The Bedroom*, a canvas of *c*.1658–60 that is now in Washington (fig. 59), of which at least one autograph variant is known.[10] As in the present work, the child in the Washington painting has just come into a room, where a woman (the child's mother?) is busy making the bed. Here too the child grips the door handle with one hand, this time holding a *colf* ball in the other. Again, there is a subtle play of light on the child's curls. The dimensions of the paintings in Washington and Polesden Lacey are similar, as are the floor plans of the houses depicted, but instead of the horizontal format on canvas which he chose for *The Bedroom*, De Hooch decided to paint *The Colf Players* in a vertical format on panel and to present the child as the principal figure.[11] On the basis of its resemblance to the painting in Washington (and the autograph variant of this composition in Karlsruhe), it has been suggested that the work discussed here is a fragment of a larger painting.[12] This is certainly not the case, however, if only because of the panel's impressive size.

It is not easy to establish a convincing chronology of these closely related compositions, but it is likely that De Hooch was so taken with the motif of a child by a door that he decided to use it as the main subject of a painting. Such repetitions of specific motifs or even of whole scenes are not uncommon in De Hooch's work, although taking a child from a genre scene and recasting the figure as a picture-filling protagonist is certainly unique in his oeuvre.[13] The child in the foreground of this painting is one of the largest figures De Hooch ever painted, and it has been hypothesised that this is one of his own offspring – his son Pieter perhaps, born in 1655, or his daughter Anna, born in 1656 – but there is no evidence to support this, as tempting as the idea may be.[14] This touching work is one of the most appealing examples of the many paintings of the Dutch Golden Age that feature children in prominent roles.[15] QB

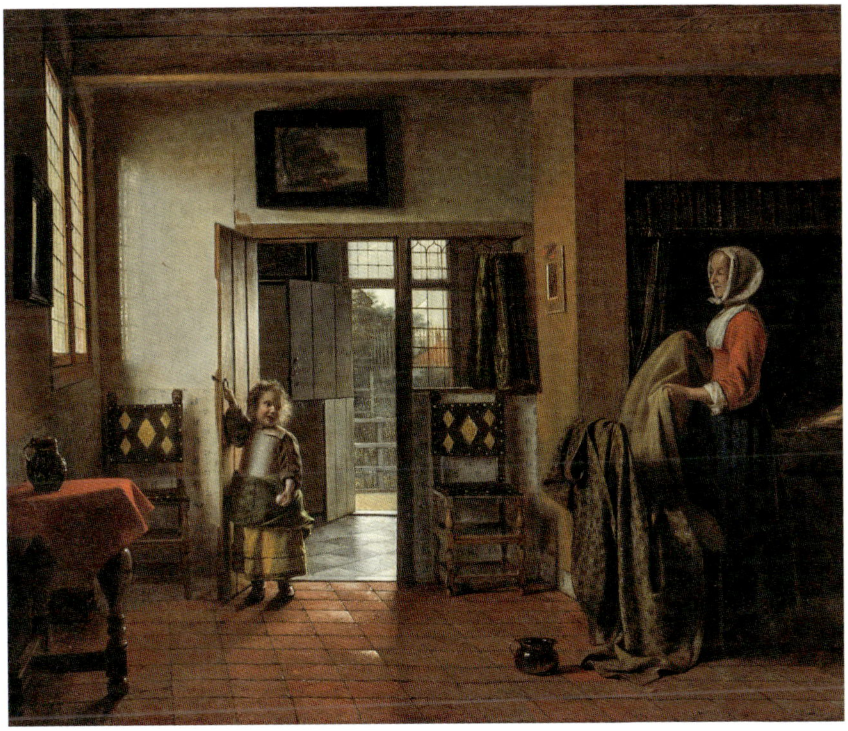

FIG. 59
Pieter de Hooch (1629–1684)
The Bedroom, *c.*1658–60
Oil on canvas, 51 × 60 cm
Washington, D.C., National Gallery of Art, Widener Collection (1942.9.33)

NOTES

1 Sutton 1980; Sutton 1998. Museum Het Prinsenhof in Delft is preparing an exhibition on the artist (2019–20).
2 On the rivalry between genre painters in the Dutch Golden Age, see Waiboer *et al.* 2017.
3 Van der Vinde 2007, p. 38.
4 See S. Kuus in Bedaux and Ekkart 2000, pp. 79–81.
5 For example, Sutton 1980, no. 38.
6 R. Ekkart in Bedaux and Ekkart 2000, p. 126; Van Suchtelen 2001, p. 26; Sutton in Sutton 1998, p. 136.
7 De Hooch added the round, woven doormat at a later stage in the painting process, and the lines of the grouting now shine through it.
8 See Westermann 2001, pp. 67–68, 187, no. 99.
9 Sutton 1980, p. 88; M. Kersten in Kersten, Lokin and Plomp 1996, pp. 150–52.
10 Sutton 1980, no. 40b; Wheelock 1995, pp. 133–36; A.K. Wheelock, 'Pieter de Hooch/The Bedroom/1658/1660', *Dutch Paintings of the Seventeenth Century*, NGA Online Editions, https://purl.org/nga/collection/artobject/1172 (accessed 31 January 2018). In addition to the possibly earlier variant in Karlsruhe, Staatliche Kunsthalle, inv. 259 (Sutton 1980, no. 40a), Sutton mentions another variant, which has not been seen since 1956 and whose authenticity is uncertain (ibid., no. 40c).
11 These works also display striking differences in the hall floors (which are tiled in marble in the Washington and Karlsruhe paintings) and the outdoor surroundings.
12 As suggested by J.G. van Gelder after the painting was exhibited at the Royal Academy, London: Van Gelder 1953 [1], no. 443: 'Fragment of larger picture'.
13 Sutton in London and Hartford 1998–99, p. 136.
14 B. Broos in Broos *et al.* 1990–91, p. 303 (as a portrait of Pieter); alternatively, the child in the foreground has been identified as the artist's daughter Anna (b. 1656) and the boy in the background as Pieter (see *Portrait Groups* 1960, p. 16, no. 13, and Wheelock 1995, p. 134).
15 See Bedaux and Ekkart 2000; Van der Vinde 2007.

Gardens

RUPERT GOULDING, NATIONAL TRUST LEAD CURATOR (SOUTH WEST)

THE CONCEPT OF 'DUTCH' GARDENING IN Britain is contested by modern scholarship, questioning whether tree-lined avenues, canals, pavilions, small compartments, raised bastions, topiary, and other hallmarks of these formal and often intricate gardens were specifically Dutch or more properly French, Italian, local or a combination of innovations. The greater emphasis now is placed upon the individual agency of garden owners, their specific contexts, rather than any trans-national influence and wholescale stylistic adoption or rejection.[1]

But one thing is certain, in the eighteenth century the proponents of what became known as the 'English Landscape Garden' railed against recent formality and regularity and put the blame squarely on the Dutch, who 'for more than half a century deformed the face of nature in this country'.[2] They particularly decried topiary associated with William III as a 'Mournful family of Yews' and dismissed box-lined parterres for 'the plain but nobler Embellishments of Grass'.[3] This convenient and hyperbolic Dutch backlash obscured the very real interaction with British gardens during the seventeenth century.

In 1698 William III wrote to his favourite Hans Willem Bentinck declaring that hunting and 'garden art' were two of his greatest passions.[4] Perhaps more than most monarchs William was a gardener, enhancing or commissioning new designs at his houses in the Netherlands and palaces in Britain. He shared these enthusiasms with courtiers who developed their own gardens in the prevailing Williamite style. Helping promulgate a design grammar if not a proscribed look was the hand of George London (d. 1714), Deputy Superintendent of Gardens, and proprietor with Henry Wise (1653–1738) of the Brompton Park Nursery – purveyors of garden design, construction and plant supply to the Crown and leading country estates. Canons Ashby, Clandon Park, Dyrham Park, Hanbury Hall and Petworth are just some of the scores of gardens the pair were involved with (see fig. 60). George London was first apprenticed to Charles II's gardener, but his career blossomed working for the botanist Bishop of London, Henry Compton, who sent him to the Netherlands to visit the Leiden botanic garden, Bentinck's Sorgvliet and Magdelena Poulle's famous collection of exotics at Gunterstein with its heated greenhouse.[5]

Gardens were not William's sole preserve, as the Princess of Orange, Mary, spent her time in the Netherlands absorbed in collecting Delft ceramics and exotic plants. Once returned to England Mary sent for the substantial botanical collection at Honselaarsdijk, The Hague, and transplanted them to Hampton Court along with gardener Hendrik Quellenburg. Mary had fresh flowers weekly in her apartments, and many filled her extravagant Delft flowerpots and vases, like those now at Dyrham Park, Lytes Cary Manor and Erddig.[6]

Dutch pre-eminence in horticulture spurred a strong seventeenth-century industry in plant nurseries, notably in a supply of exotics sourced from across the world through extensive trading networks. The British nursery trade was small for much of the century, and particularly dependent on French and Dutch plants and seeds supply. Specifically Dutch variants of vegetables and fruits were increasingly available and desired, as seen in household accounts such as Sir

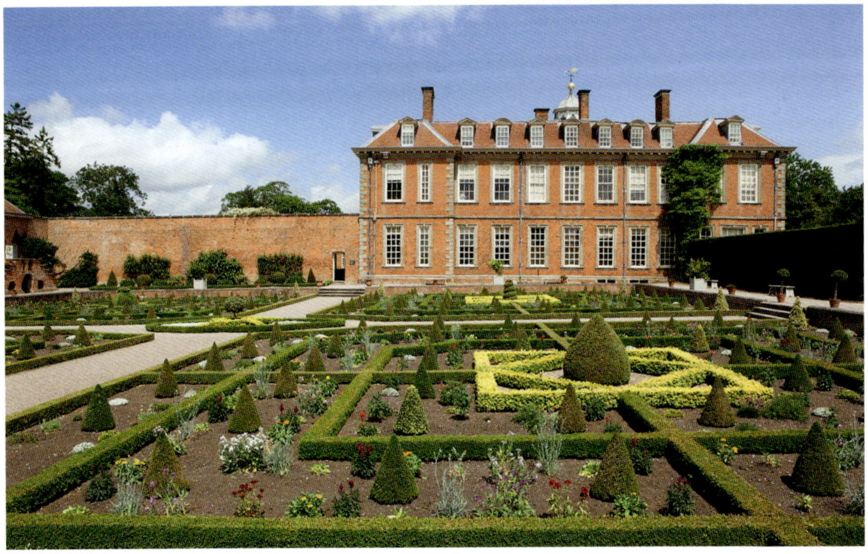

FIG. 60
The reconstructed George London garden at Hanbury Hall, Worcestershire

Ralph Verney's 1650s purchase of tulips, asparagus and carnations from the Netherlands for Claydon House. Dutch horticulturists developed new cultivars and hybrids, such as the 'fully double' hyacinth by Pieter Voorhelm of Haarlem in the 1680s – fifty of which Maynard Colchester had ordered for Westbury Court Garden, Gloucestershire, by 1702. The Kip engraving suggests how such plants were arranged in a regular series of geometric beds surrounded by low hedging (fig. 61).[7] This and other instructions as to how to arrange and manage a garden were published in several Dutch manuals, such as the popular *Den Nederlandsten Hovenier* (1669), once in the collection at Dyrham Park.

Perhaps the most lasting impact was not the ephemeral gardens themselves, but their record through paintings and prints. By 1674 Jan Siberechts had arrived in England and set in motion an enduring enthusiasm for topographical house and garden views. The first proponents were often Dutch artists, draughtsmen and engravers.[8]

These views now decorate many a British country house. The formal gardens and landscapes they capture have disappeared, but their pictures have become a quintessential decorative trope. The canon of artists includes Hendrick Danckerts, perhaps best known for

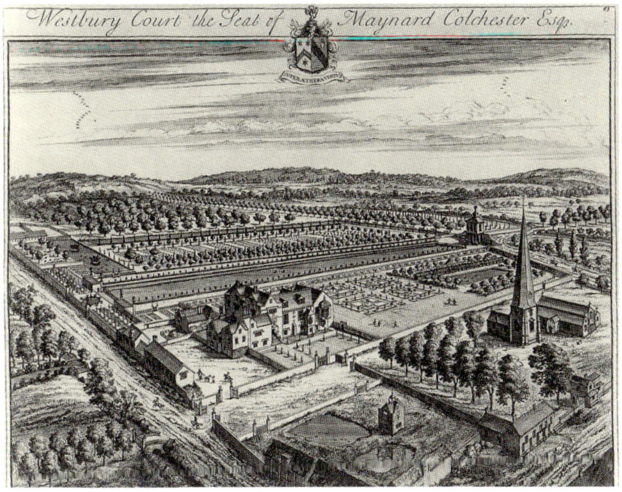

FIG. 61
Johannes Kip (*c.*1653–1722)
Westbury Court, the Seat of Maynard Colchester Esq, published in Sir Robert Atkyns, *The Ancient and Present State of Gloucestershire*, 1712, engraving, 465 × 380 mm
National Trust, Dyrham Park (NT 452663)

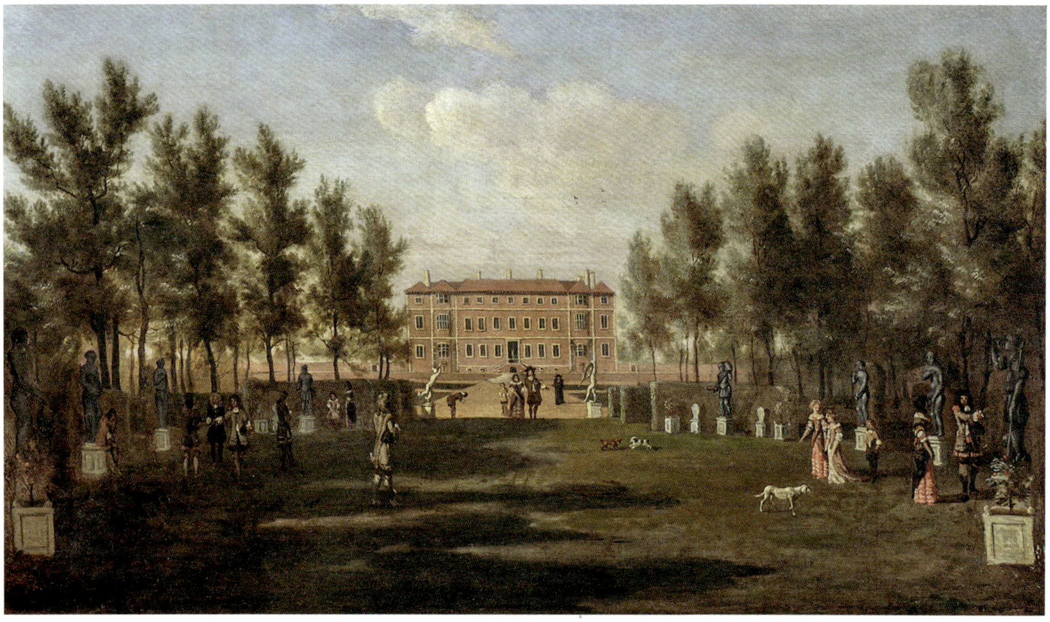

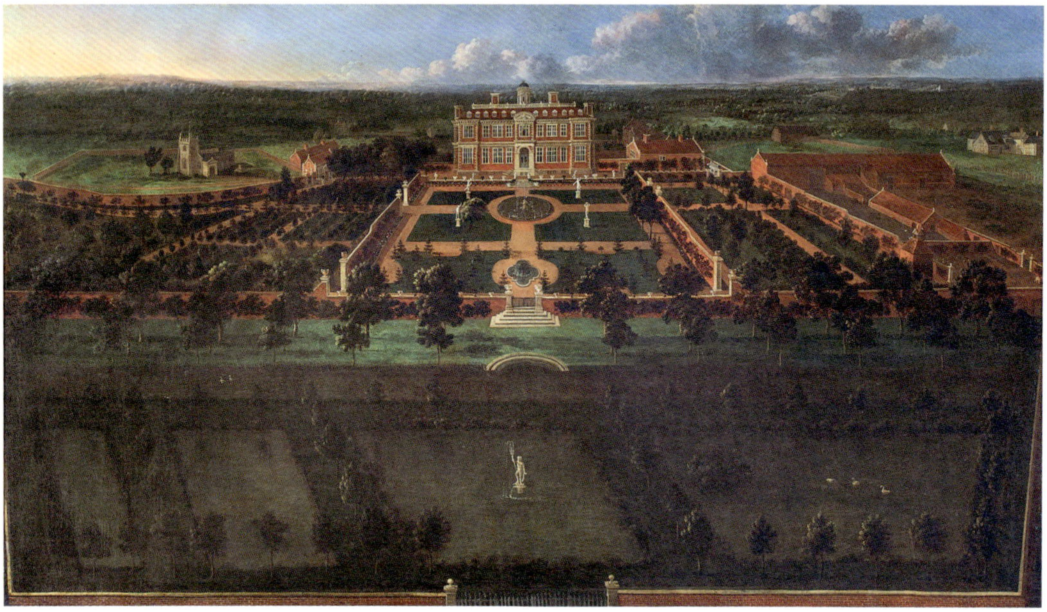

FIG. 62
Attrib. Hendrick Danckerts (1625–1680)
Ham House from the South, c.1675–79
Oil on canvas, 99.4 × 65.2 cm
National Trust, Ham House, Surrey
(NT 1139878)

FIG. 63
Jan Griffier the Elder (*c.*1645–1718)
Bird's-eye View of Sudbury Hall: South Front, c.1680–90
Oil on canvas, 105.4 × 175.3 cm
National Trust, Sudbury Hall, Derbyshire
(NT 653135)

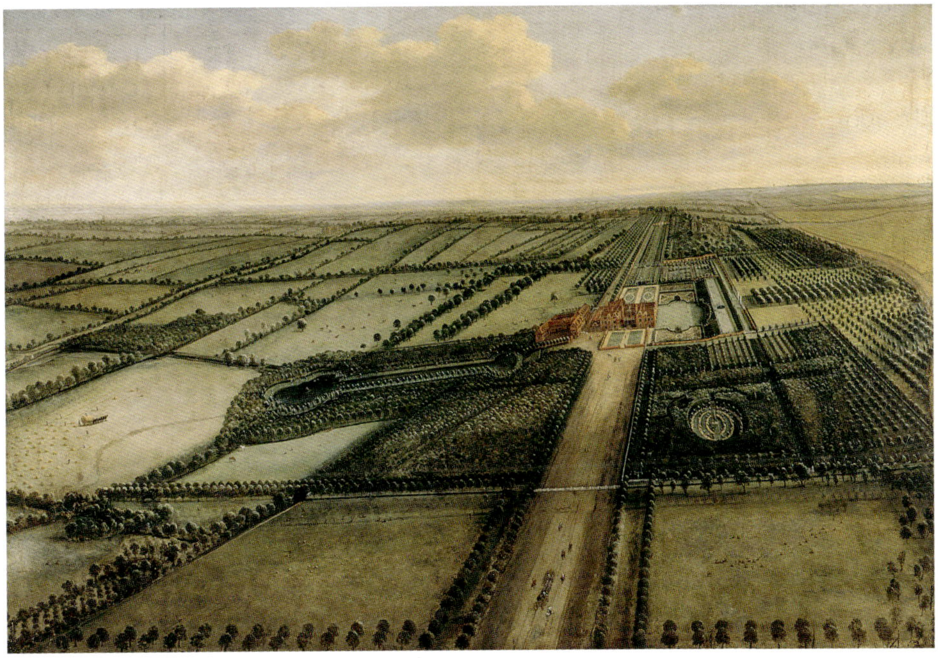

FIG. 64
Leendert Knyff (1650–1721)
A Bird's-eye View of Clandon, 1708
Oil on canvas, 149.9 × 215.9 cm
National Trust, Clandon Park, Surrey (NT 1441485)

his views of royal palaces and ports commissioned by Charles II and Samuel Pepys, but also credited with an important view of Ham House from the south (fig. 62). The Duke and Duchess of Lauderdale are shown in an apsidal clearing, decorated with lead statuary and painted wooden seats and planters containing orange trees. The bird's-eye view of Sudbury Hall attributed to Jan Griffier the Elder (*c.*1645–1718) depicts a formal garden with separate compartments and statuary (fig. 63), a style that is often associated with the partnership of artist Leendert Knyff and draughtsman/engraver Johannes Kip. The pair created scores of topographical views of houses for publication, notably in *Britannia Illustrata* (1707), which features many now National Trust properties including Ashdown House, Uppark and Wimpole. These views of once fashionable gardens are significant sources of evidence for what is lost, with few more poignant than Knyff's view of Clandon Park (1708), which succumbed to the devastating fire of 2015 (fig. 64).

NOTES

1 See Dixon Hunt 1990; Jacques 2002, pp. 114–30.
2 Jacques 2017.
3 S. Switzer, quoted in Jacques and Van der Horst 1988, p. 98.
4 Quoted in E. De Jong, 'For Profit and Ornament: The Function and Meaning of Dutch Garden Art in the Period of William and Mary, 1650–1702', in Dixon Hunt 1990, p. 37.
5 Sikkens-De Zwaan 2002, pp. 206–20.
6 Jacques 2017, pp. 161–63; Jacques and Van der Horst 1988, pp. 40–41.
7 Jacques and Van der Horst 1988, pp. 186–89.
8 Strong 2000, p. 132.

11

CORNELIUS JOHNSON (1593–1661)

William Hamilton, 2nd Duke of Hamilton and John Maitland, Earl (later Duke) of Lauderdale, 1649

Oil on canvas, 147 × 199.5 cm
Signed and dated lower right: *Cornelius Jonson/ fecit 1649*
National Trust, Ham House, Surrey – The Dysart Collection (NT 1139787)

PROVENANCE
At Ham House by 1677; thence by descent; acquired by HM Government when Sir Lyonel Tollemache, 4th Baronet and Sir Cecil Tollemache, 5th Baronet gave Ham House to the National Trust in 1948; entrusted to the care of the Victoria and Albert Museum until 1990, when returned to the National Trust; ownership transferred to the National Trust in 2002

LITERATURE
Hearn 2015, pp. 55–56, fig. 43

In this double portrait two men dressed in sombre black, passing a rolled scroll between them, stand in front of a curtain and a view towards a distant hilly landscape. At first sight, the image looks like a traditional depiction of a master and his amanuensis, in which someone in a position of importance dictates or passes a letter to a second figure. This could be a secretary, such as in Van Dyck's much-copied double portrait of Thomas Wentworth, 1st Earl of Strafford dictating to Sir Philip Mainwaring, painted a decade before the current picture, or Titian's *Georges d'Armagnac with Guillaume Philandrier* (Alnwick Castle). However, the sitters are the Duke of Hamilton, on the left, and the future Duke of Lauderdale, on the right, Scottish aristocrats and Covenanters (supporters of the Presbyterian Reformed Church in Scotland and England). The picture is instead an example of a friendship portrait, a commemorative depiction of two men united here in their politics and religion.[1]

It was painted by Cornelius Johnson (Cornelis Jonson van Ceulen) in The Hague in 1649, where the sitters had fled early that year after their failed negotiations with Charles I following his defeat in the English Civil War. Hamilton and Maitland were Scottish Covenanting commissioners sent to England in the mid-1640s to negotiate peace with the king and the Royalists. They would later try and persuade the king to support a Scottish invasion of England to defeat the New Model Army in return for concessions establishing Presbyterianism in England, Ireland and Scotland.

Both sitters had gone to The Hague for discussions with the exiled Charles II, now the new *de jure* king, following his father's execution. The city was the home of his sister Mary and her husband, William II, Prince of Orange, and it was a centre for Royalist activities; it was there that they persuaded Charles to support the Covenanting clause. After the signing of the 1650 Treaty of Breda, both men accompanied the king to Scotland, and both fought in the king's army at the Battle of Worcester, on 3 September 1651, which was defeated by the Parliamentarians. Hamilton died of his wounds after the battle and Maitland was captured and imprisoned for the next nine years, for some time in the Tower of London. Afterwards, he travelled back to The Hague and accompanied the king at the restoration of the monarchy in 1660. He was a member of Charles II's inner 'Cabal' ministry and he effectively ruled Scotland as secretary of state, where he had a reputation as a brutal and corrupt leader.

Cornelius Johnson was one of the great portrait painters in seventeenth-century England. Born in

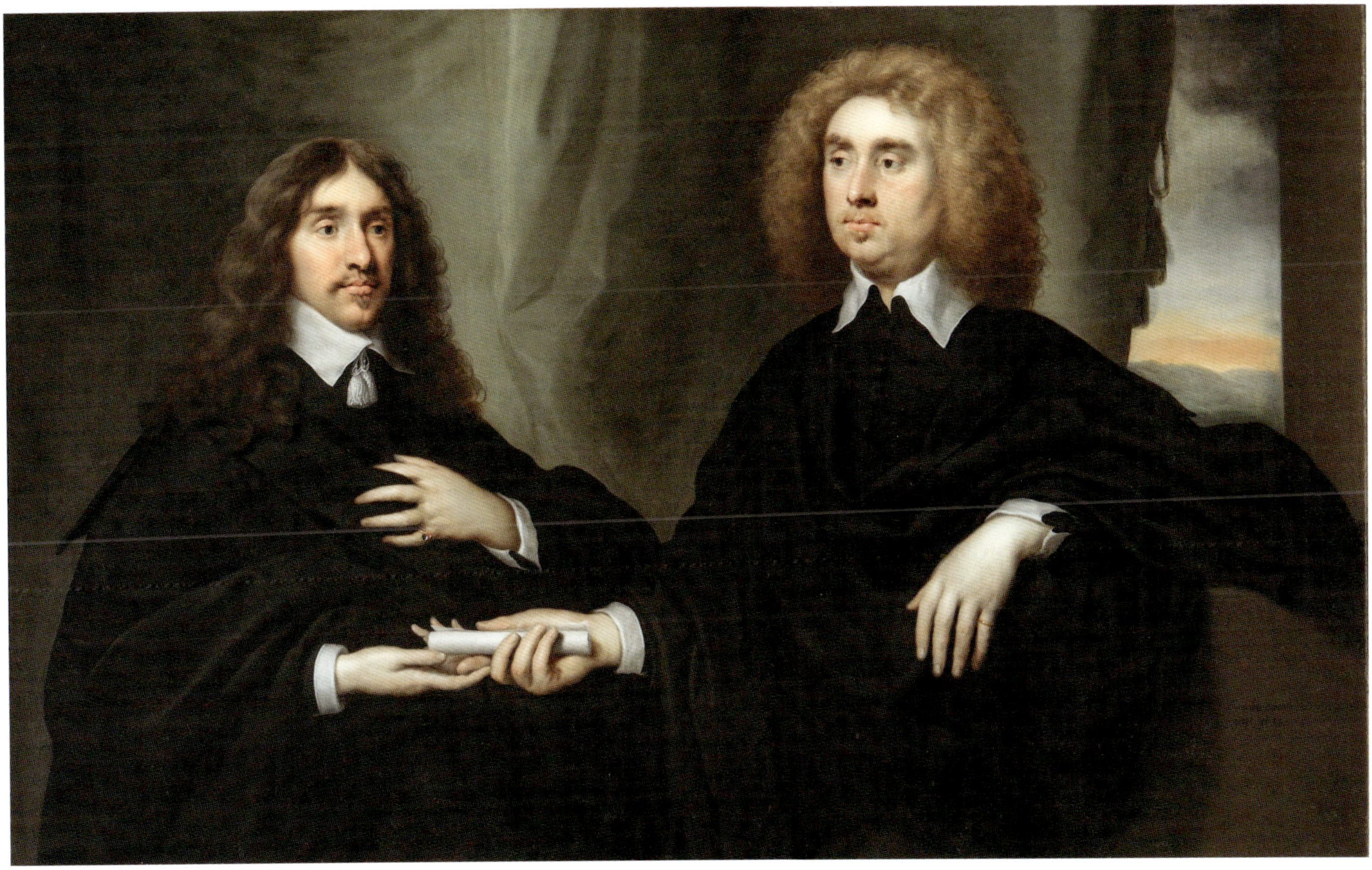

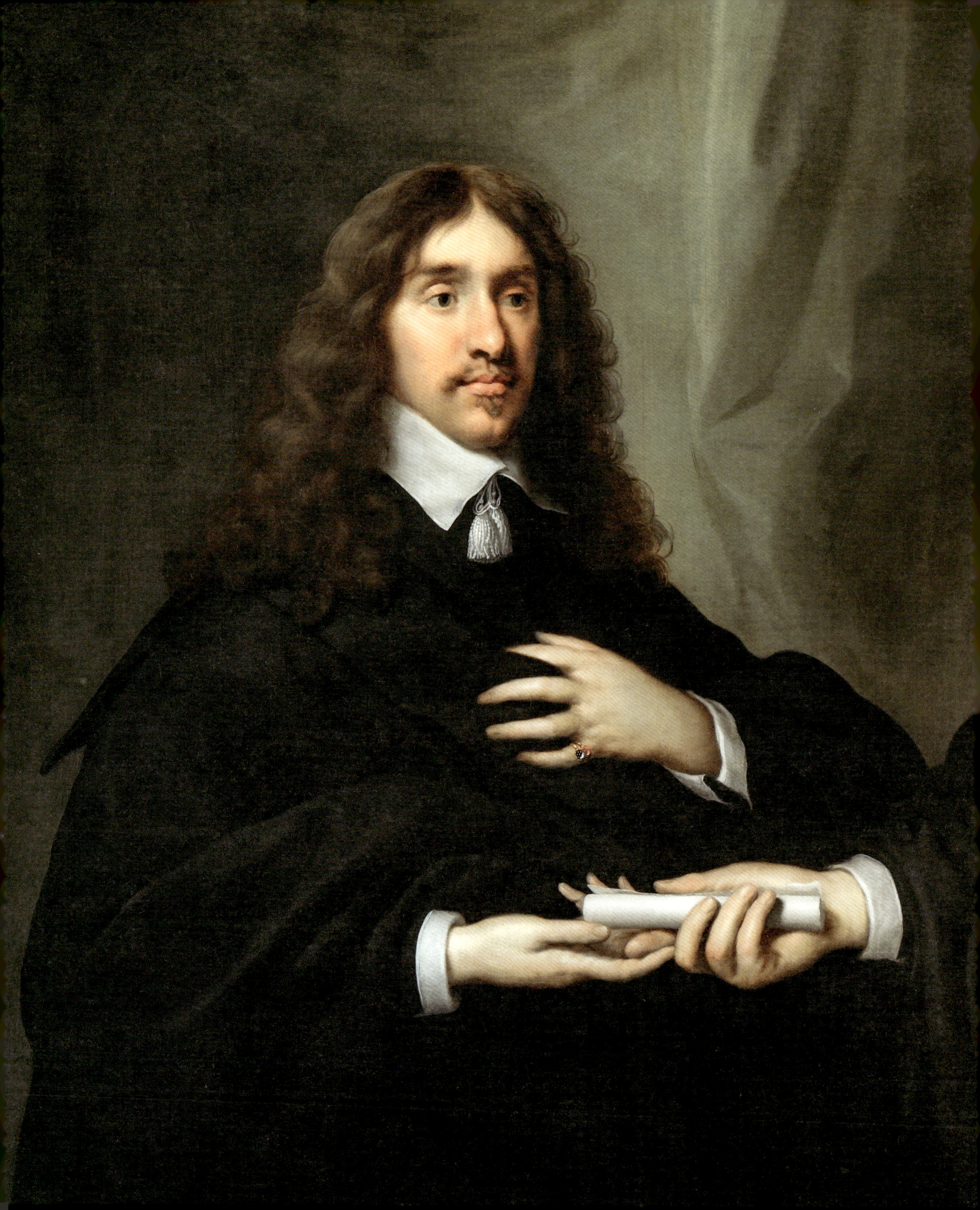

London to a Flemish/German family, he is presumed to have trained in the northern Netherlands before returning to London, where he was appointed Charles I's 'Picture Drawer' in 1632, the same year that Van Dyck was created the king's principal painter. Johnson had a successful and lucrative career, painting sitters from the professional classes, the gentry, the aristocracy and the royal family. In October 1643, following the outbreak of the English Civil War, Johnson and his family moved to Middelburg in the Northern Netherlands, and then briefly to Amsterdam, two years later. Johnson already painted miniatures as well as large-scale pictures, and during this second Dutch period he also painted grand group portraits of multiple sitters of The Hague magistrates and the Middelburg Archers' Guild. In 1652 he moved to Utrecht, where he died in 1661. A testament to his popularity in England is the large number of portraits by him in the nation's country houses and museums.

Johnson painted two versions of the portrait, both signed and dated 1649. Both sitters had a copy, and the second version remains in the Hamilton collection. The only obvious difference between the two versions is that Hamilton looks out at the viewer in the picture owned by his descendants, instead of looking at Maitland, as he does in the present picture. The commission seems to have come from Hamilton, as he paid three guilders 'to Mr Johnson, picture drawer ... for three pictures' on 24 October 1649. Another single portrait of Hamilton by Johnson is at Ham House. It is similar to his depiction in the current portrait, although he is shown wearing the sash of the Order of the Garter, which he was nominally awarded by the exiled Charles II on 12 January 1650.

Hamilton was painted the following year in The Hague by another Dutch artist, Adriaen Hanneman, also commemorating his being created a Knight of the Garter (fig. 65). Several versions of the portrait exist.[2] Hanneman had worked in London from 1626 to 1638 and he was influenced by Johnson as well as by Van Dyck. His familiar, Van Dyckian style meant that he was patronised by the exiled royal family and various Stuart courtiers, and his portrait of Hamilton was based on the 1637 Van Dyck composition of Charles I's (Gemäldegalerie Alte Meister, Dresden).

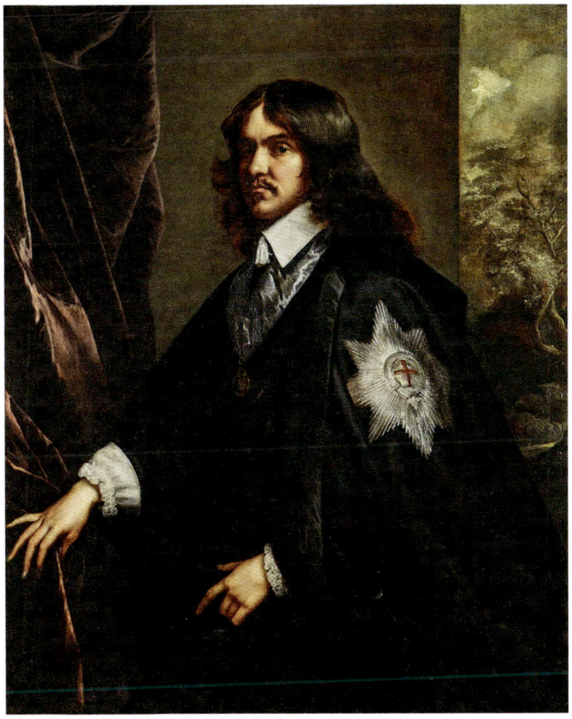

FIG. 65
Adriaen Hanneman (1604–1671)
William Hamilton, 2nd Duke of Hamilton, 1650
Oil on canvas, 133.7 × 105.7cm
Royal Collection Trust (RCIN 401251)

Maitland brought several of his own pictures to Ham House following his marriage to Elizabeth Murray, Countess of Dysart in her own right, in 1672 (see cat. nos. 2 and 12), the year he was created Duke of Lauderdale. These included the current picture, which is listed in the duke's 1677 inventory as 'one picture of his Grace with the Duke of Hamilton w^{t} a carved guilt frame', when it was displayed above the Great Staircase.

DT

NOTES

1 See Hearn 2015, pp. 55–56, fig. 43.
2 Millar 1963, I, p. 116, no. 213.

12

PETER LELY (1618–1680)

Elizabeth Murray, Countess of Dysart, later Duchess of Lauderdale (1626–1698), 1648

Oil on canvas, 121.9 × 97.8 cm
National Trust, Ham House, Surrey – The Dysart Collection (NT 1139764)

PROVENANCE
At Ham House by 1683; thence by descent; acquired by HM Government when Sir Lyonel Tollemache, 4th Baronet and Sir Cecil Tollemache, 5th Baronet gave Ham House to the National Trust in 1948; entrusted to the care of the Victoria and Albert Museum until 1990, when returned to the National Trust; ownership transferred to the National Trust in 2002

LITERATURE
Taylor 2002, p. 30

A young woman walking in a wooded landscape gestures behind her, past the silhouetted rocky outcrop that emphasises her pale skin, towards a waterfall and a darkening sky, the gathering clouds lit by a distant sunset. She is Elizabeth Murray, one of the most intriguing women in seventeenth-century Britain, Countess of Dysart in her own right and later Duchess of Lauderdale (see also pp. 14 and 39 and cat. 2). A powerful and, at times, unscrupulous player in the politics of the Commonwealth and at the Restoration court, she was also an important patron of the arts. She played a key role in supporting the Dutch émigré painter Peter Lely (Pieter van der Faes), who would become Charles II's principal painter, and the chief image maker of later seventeenth-century England.

Lely was a hugely successful and influential artist. His success resulted in having to employ a large number of studio assistants to help meet the demand for his portraits; the country houses of Britain have many portraits by him or from his studio, or by artists painting in his style. His success also meant that he had the financial means to purchase art and he had one of the largest and most important collections in England. Samuel Pepys sometimes visited the artist's studio and, in his diary entry for 25 March 1667, wrote '… called at Mr. Lillys', who was working; and indeed his pictures are without doubt much beyond Mr. Hales's, I think I may say I am convinced: but a mighty proud man he is, and full of state'.

Lely was born Pieter van der Faes, in 1618, to Dutch parents in the garrison town of Soest in Westphalia. He trained under Frans Pietersz de Grebber in Haarlem, where he was enrolled at the Guild of St Luke there in 1637. He travelled to England in the 1640s, where he initially painted subject pictures (possibly to set himself up as a picture dealer) of mythological, pastoral, musical and religious scenes,[1] but 'finding the practice of *Painting after the Life* generally more encourag'd, he apply'd himself to *Portraits*'.[2] He soon came to be considered the finest portraitist in England, painting prominent members of the Commonwealth regime during the interregnum, including Oliver Cromwell (1599–1658),[3] and soon after the Restoration, in 1660, being created Charles II's principal painter.

Elizabeth Murray was one of Lely's most important patrons, and he painted various portraits of her and her family members, fellow Scottish courtiers and political allies, with which she furnished the Long Gallery at Ham House, her Thames-side home near Richmond in Surrey, where it 'as a whole demonstrated most vividly how such portraits were assembled and displayed by Lely's patrons'.[4] One such friend and compatriot, the

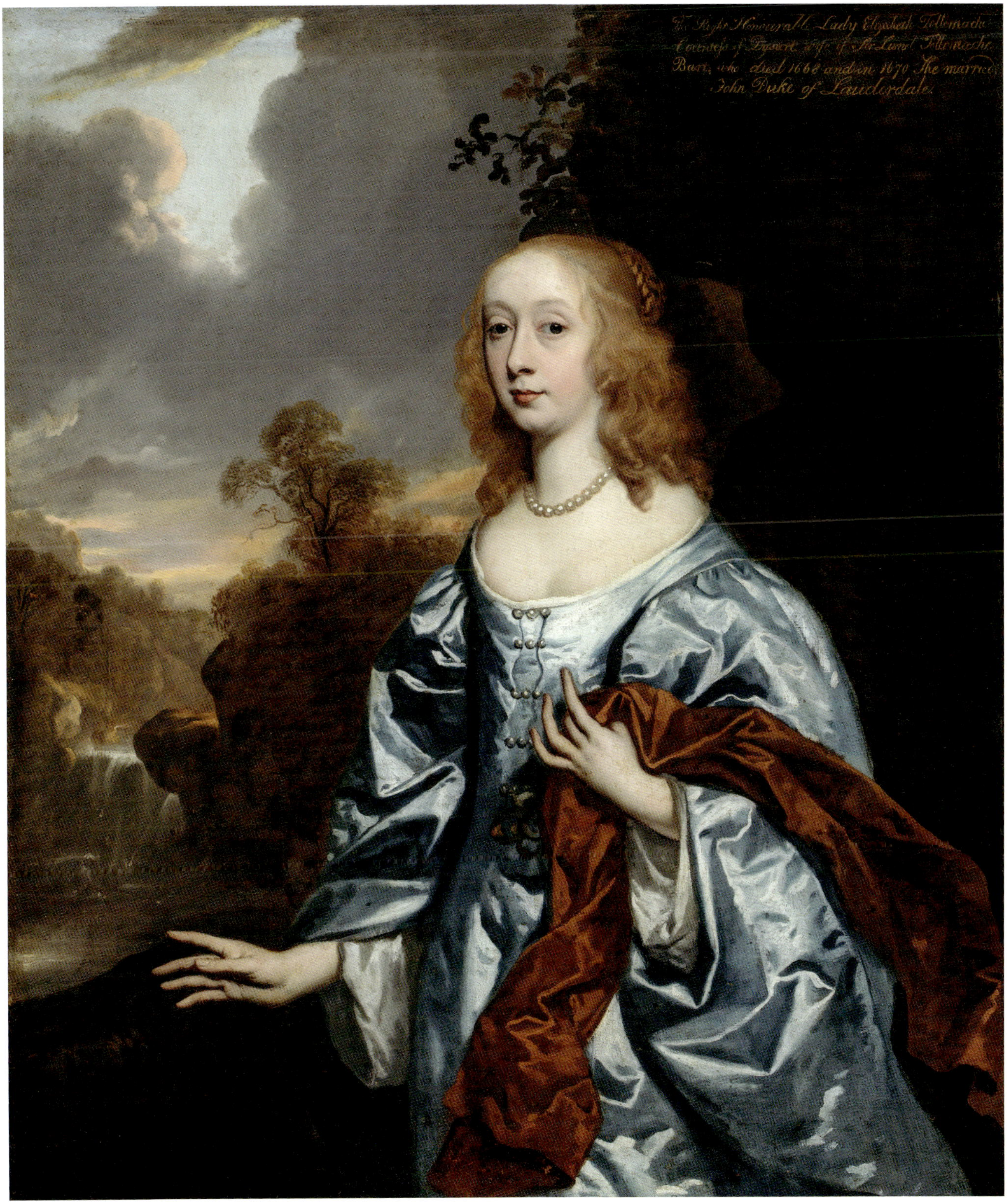
Lady Elizabeth Tollemache
Bart. who died 1668 and in 1670 She married
John Duke of Lauderdale

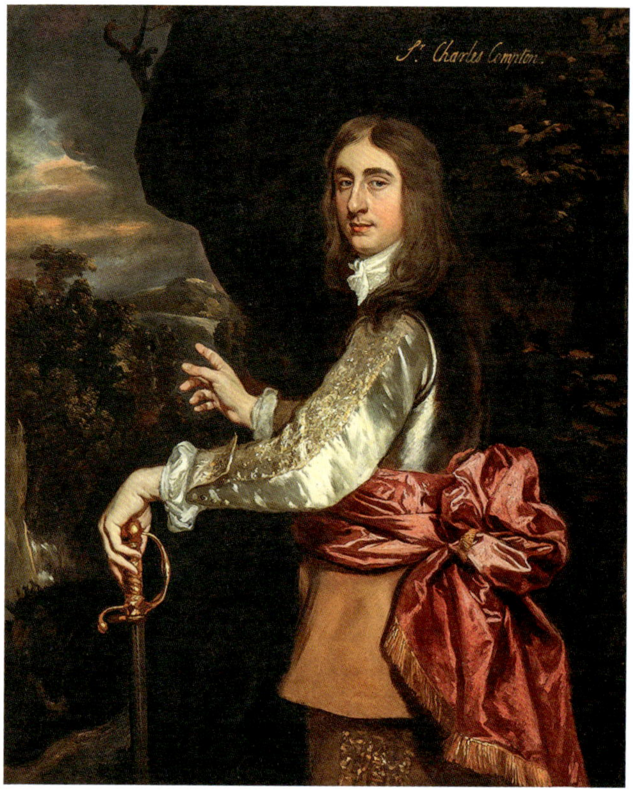

FIG. 66
Sir Peter Lely (1618–1680)
*John Leslie, Duke of Rothes (c.1630–1681), c.*1650–60
Oil on canvas, 122 × 105 cm
National Trust, Ham House, Surrey
(NT 1139951)

sitter in a recently re-identified Lely portrait at Ham, was John Leslie, Duke of Rothes (*c.*1630–1681; fig. 66).[5] A fellow Scot, fighting for the restoration of the monarchy after Charles I's execution, he is depicted as a Royalist soldier with a huge red sash over his cuirass and buff coat. He was captured following the Royalist defeat at the Battle of Worcester in 1651, the last battle of the English Civil War, as was the duchess's second husband, John Maitland, then Earl of Lauderdale, and both of them were imprisoned in the Tower of London.

Being a prominent courtier, especially after her marriage to Maitland, soon, in 1672, to be created Duke of Lauderdale, one of Charles II's most trusted ministers and secretary of state for Scotland, meant that Ham would have been a highly visible location for other courtiers and visitors, who would have marvelled at her display of Lely portraits. It was also at Ham that she would have displayed her other pictures by Dutch artists, such as works in this exhibition by Abraham Bloemaert, Ambrosius Bosschaert and Frans Post (cat. nos. 2, 4 and 17).

Of the four Lely portraits of Elizabeth Murray that are still at Ham the present picture is the earliest, painted in 1648, around the time of her first marriage, to Sir Lionel Tollemache (1624–1669). It was painted only a few years after an early description of her as 'a pretty one but for her deep coullerd hayer ... such a pretty witty Lass, with such a brave house & 'state as she is like to have, m'thinks might make a young fellowe think' her hayer very beautifull .... She seems to be a very good harmless vertuouse witty little bable.'[6] In her later years, she and her second husband were famous for their greed and political corruption, and a friend turned enemy, Gilbert Burnet, Bishop of Salisbury (1643–1715), noted she was 'a violent friend, but a much more violent enemy. She had a restless ambition, lived at a vast expense and was ravenously covetous, and would have stuck at nothing by which she might compass her ends'.[7]

Despite the bucolic tone of the portrait the sitter is not shown playing an Arcadian role; instead the depiction concentrates on her social status. She is shown wearing a fashionable, jewelled and waistless 'night-gown', with dressed hair and posing elegantly, set against the untamed natural world behind her, complete with a turbulent waterfall. The pastoral setting is reminiscent of those in Lely's subject pictures, painted not long before the present portrait. During the Commonwealth Elizabeth entertained Cromwell at Ham (her friendship with him led to rumours of a sexual relationship), developing a

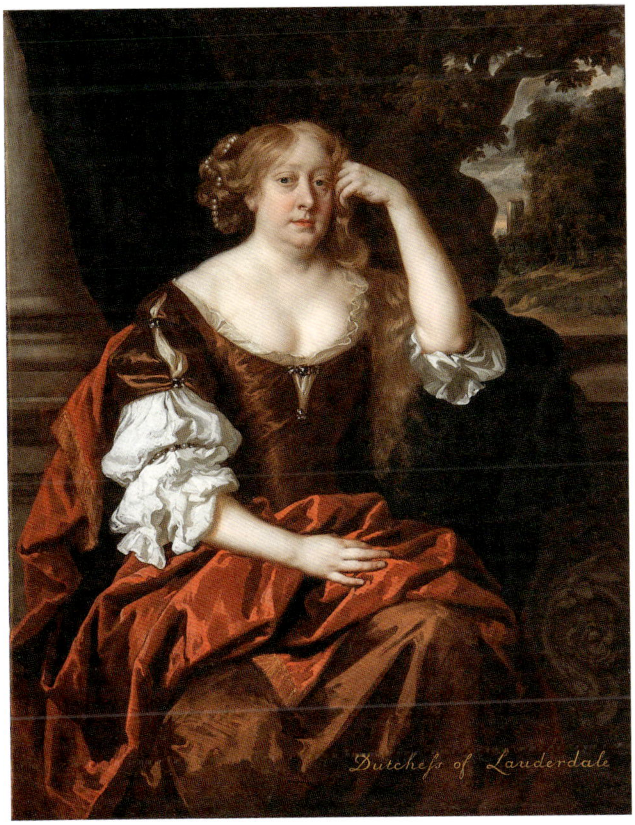

FIG. 67
Sir Peter Lely (1618–1680)
Elizabeth Murray, Countess of Dysart and Duchess of Lauderdale (1626–1698), c.1680
Oil on canvas, 155 × 133.5 cm
National Trust, Ham House, Surrey
(NT 1139783)

strategic relationship that meant the house stayed in her family ownership, rather than being sequestered by Parliament. At the same time Elizabeth was dealing with the secret, Royalist Sealed Knot society, raising funds for Charles II's restoration (in her coded correspondence with the king, she was 'Mrs Grey' or 'Mrs Legge').

Elizabeth continued to patronise Lely throughout his career, commissioning works from the 1640s until possibly 1680, the year of his death. There are three other Lely portraits of Elizabeth at Ham, comprising a double portrait of her *c.*1651 with an unidentified, enslaved servant,[8] referencing Van Dyck's 1634 portrait of *Henrietta of Lorraine, attended by a Page*;[9] a double portrait with the duke, painted around 1675;[10] and the last single portrait of her, painted *c.*1675–80[11] (fig. 67), where she is shown with a fashionable head-on-hand pose, with her hair worn modishly loose down one side, like an ageing Venus at her toilet. DT

NOTES

1 See D. Dethloff, 'Reception and Rejection: Lely's subject pictures in an "un-understanding land"', in Campbell 2012, pp. 41–61.
2 Graham 1716, p. 384.
3 Birmingham Museum and Art Gallery, 1949P27.
4 Millar 1978, pp. 47–48, no. 23.
5 The portrait is inscribed *Sr. Charles Compton*, but comparison to other portraits by Lely, Samuel Cooper and L. Schunemann confirm that it represents Rothes. The 'Estimate' of pictures at Ham House, dated *c.*1683, includes 'The Duke of Rothes, of Sr Peter Lely'.
6 B. Schofield (ed.), *The Knyvett Letters*, London, 1949, p. 152, quoted in MacLeod, Marciari Alexander *et al.* 2001, p. 192, no. 89, note 1.
7 Clarke and Foxcroft 1907, p. 101.
8 NT 1139940.
9 Kenwood (English Heritage), 88022826.
10 NT 1139789.
11 NT 1139783. The portrait was previously in the collection of the Duke of Buccleuch, where it had been displayed at two of his Scottish houses – Dalkeith Palace in Midlothian and Drumlanrig in Dumfriesshire.

Silver

JAMES ROTHWELL, NATIONAL TRUST LEAD CURATOR (LONDON AND SOUTH EAST) AND ADVISOR ON SILVER

As a consequence of the general tendency up to the early nineteenth century for silver to be melted down and exchanged for pieces in the latest fashion, the National Trust's overall collections from the late sixteenth and the seventeenth centuries are, in comparison with the number of paintings from the same period, remarkably slim. This is, inevitably, reflected in its holdings of Dutch silver also and is especially disappointing given the exceptional sophistication of goldsmithing in the northern provinces of the Low Countries from the founding of the Dutch Republic around 1580 to the early decades of the eighteenth century. Fortunately, however, there is sufficient evidence from the smattering that does survive – including one piece in particular of the very greatest significance – together with what is known of dispersed collections from archival sources, to get some sense of Dutch silver in the houses of the National Trust.

In the decades up to 1600 there was little to differentiate Dutch silver of the highest quality from comparable pieces being produced in Germany, and some examples at least would have been found in houses now cared for by the National Trust of the numerous cups and covers, *tazze*, basins and ewers, mounted nautilus shells and other such display pieces that were either bought contemporaneously or were subsumed into British collections following the French Revolution. Sadly not a single pre-1600 Dutch example now survives in a Trust house but the renewed fashion in the early nineteenth century for such highly decorative Northern European Renaissance wares, as led by the Prince Regent and his brothers, was best represented historically at Uppark in West Sussex.[1] There Sir Harry Fetherstonhaugh, 2nd Bt, who was prominent in the Prince Regent's circle, bedecked his new dining room, designed by Humphry Repton, with a formidable assemblage of German and Netherlandish Renaissance tankards, *tazze* and standing cups, including a magnificent nautilus cup which is probably that now in the Schroder Collection, made in Delft in 1595. It has exuberantly sculpted mythical sea creatures for its base and mounts and has been aptly described by the silver scholar Timothy Schroder, as 'one of the most dramatic examples of Netherlandish Mannerism'.[2]

As the new century got under way Dutch makers increasingly showed their skills at producing engraved and chased scenes of the highest quality. The National Trust has examples of both types in its collections and, though there is only one engraved piece, a *tazza* of *c.* 1610 showing *The Wedding at Cana* at Osterley Park,[3] it is exceptional. The engraver is not known but it is possible that he was Abraham van den Hecken (active 1608–34),[4] who produced comparable pieces such as a *tazza* in the Musées Royaux des Arts Décoratifs at Brussels.[5] Foremost amongst the goldsmiths who produced high-relief chased figural groups at this time were Ernst van Vianen of Utrecht and his better known cousins Adam and Paulus van Vianen. The densely packed scene attributed to Ernst on a *tazza* of 1602 in the Rijksmuseum[6] is not dissimilar in style to two oval plaques at Anglesey Abbey, Cambridgeshire, which were probably originally made for a pair of dishes but are now detached from their rims and bases. They form part of the finest grouping of Dutch silver in any National Trust house, brought together as part

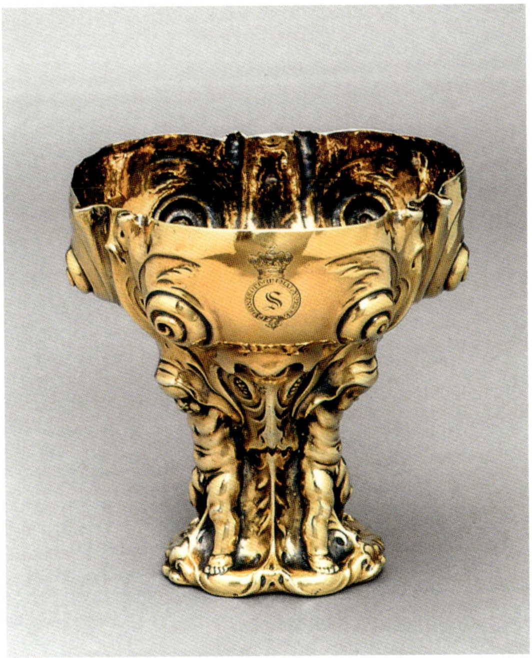

FIG. 68
Christiaen van Vianen (d. 1667)
Standing cup, 1640–41
Silver-gilt, 15.5 cm high, 14.5 cm diameter
Waddesdon, The Rothschild Collection (Rothschild Family Trust), on loan since 1997 (acc. no. 39.1997)

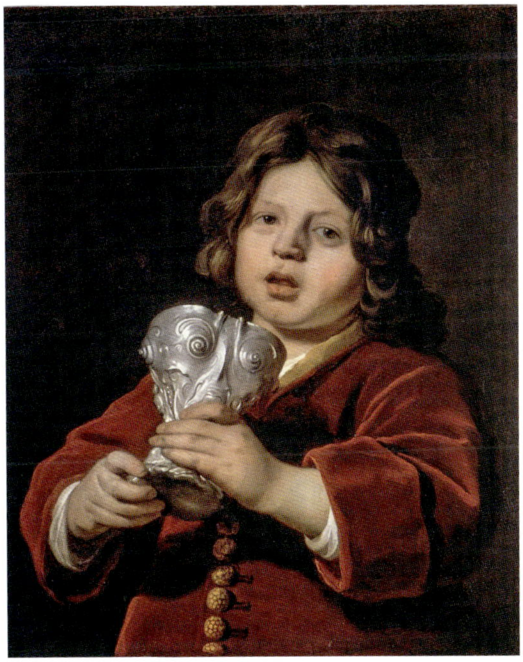

FIG. 69
Bartholomeus van der Helst (1613–1670)
A Boy with a Silver Cup, 1657
Oil on canvas, 63 × 51 cm
Waddesdon, The Rothschild Foundation, on loan since 2005 (acc. no. 12.2005)

of a wider collection of English and Continental pieces in the mid-twentieth century by Urban Huttleston Broughton, 1st Lord Fairhaven (1896–1966). His taste for richly decorated silver must have attracted him to the Anglesey Abbey pair of plaques, which depict *The Fall of the Giants from Mount Olympus* and *The Court of Venus* in a glade with a fountain.[7]

The style for which Dutch silver of the early seventeenth century is best known is the auricular, thus named because of the ear-like forms which distinguish it. The wildly flowing lines and amorphousness of this style are in striking contrast to the controlled and tight compositions that still represented the norm across Europe, and it is closest in spirit to the Rococo as yet a hundred years away, in particular the designs of Juste-Aurèle Meissonier. The masters of the Dutch auricular were Paulus and Adam van Vianen, Adam's son Christiaen and Johannes Lutma, and it was Christiaen van Vianen, under the patronage of Charles I, who brought the style directly to England. What is certainly the most significant piece of silver by a Dutch goldsmith in a National Trust house is Christiaen's standing cup of 1640 (fig. 68) at Waddesdon Manor,[8] made from a single sheet of silver (it was not originally gilded) and chased to give the effect of three *putti* plunging their arms and heads into molten and swirling metal. This is the only one of his surviving pieces known to bear a full set of London hallmarks and has the further distinction of having been depicted in a Dutch painting, Bartholomeus van der Helst's 1657 portrait of a boy, possibly van Vianen's son, holding a silver cup (fig. 69). This too is now at Waddesdon.[9]

Richly decorated surfaces employing both chasing and engraving continued to feature on Dutch silver

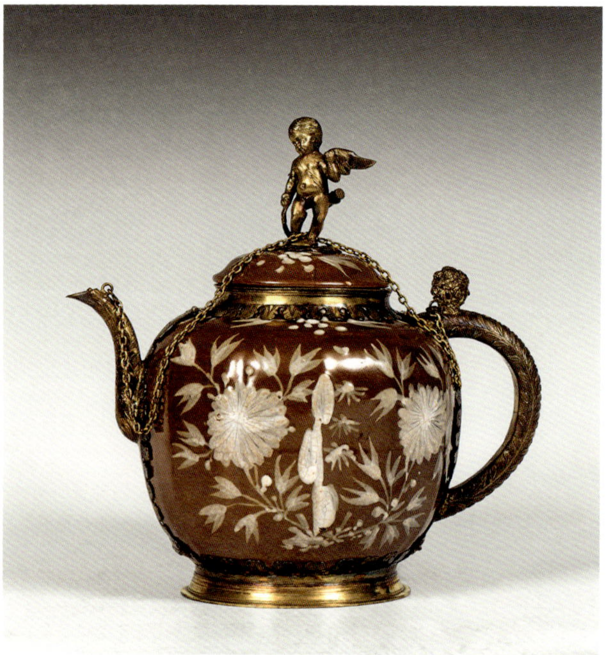

FIG. 70
The Burghley Teapot, adapted from a porcelain covered jar made in Jingdezhen, China, *c*.1600–40, with silver-gilt mounts added in Amsterdam *c*.1660–88, 21.8 × 19.2 × 13.5 cm
National Trust, Anglesey Abbey, Cambridgeshire (NT 513426)

throughout the seventeenth century, though the National Trust has little to show from this period of any distinction except in the form of mounts added to Chinese and Japanese ceramics. The prime example of these is to be found at Anglesey Abbey, a teapot (fig. 70) adapted from a Chinese porcelain covered jar of *c*.1600–40 by the addition of finely cast, chased and engraved silver-gilt mounts made in Amsterdam in the late seventeenth century.[10] This represents one of the earliest examples of the burgeoning fashion for mounted porcelain, and the silver-gilt chain which keeps the cover with the body may well have been inspired by early Yixing teapots as depicted in paintings attributed to Pieter Gerritsz van Roestraten.[11]

Though no longer as renowned or sought after, Dutch silver of the eighteenth and nineteenth centuries remained of good quality, and there are representative pieces in National Trust collections with, once again, Anglesey Abbey having the best accumulation, including several examples of rectangular tobacco boxes with distinctively Dutch towering covers. Though a visitor would have to work hard and travel far to get a sense of the history of Dutch silver of the Golden Age and beyond from National Trust collections, it would be possible, and amongst what they would see would be some exceptionally important pieces.

NOTES

1 I am grateful to Sophie Chessum for sharing her researches on the Uppark silver with me.
2 See Schroder 2007, pp. 191–93, no. 63, repr. This cup bears hallmarks for Delft, 1595, and its bowl, now silver, would originally have been a nautilus shell.
3 On loan from Heston church, to which it was given by Samuel Child of Osterley in 1742. The foot and stem are later and bear rubbed London hallmarks, perhaps for 1686.
4 Unpublished report by Timothy Schroder, 2011.
5 Frederiks 1958, p. 43.
6 Ter Molen 1984, II, p. 9, no. 1. I am grateful to Jet Pijzel-Dommisse for this reference.
7 NT 516393–94.
8 Acc. no. 39–1997; on loan to the National Trust. Catalogue information by Pippa Shirley. Another piece by Van Vianen that was almost certainly made in London but was not hallmarked is the stunningly bold, almost surreal dolphin basin in the Victoria and Albert Museum (M.1–1918).
9 Acc. no. 12.2005; on loan to the National Trust. Catalogue information by Philippa Plock.
10 NT 513426. This piece is known as the 'Burghley Teapot', having come from the collection at Burghley House.
11 Ferguson 2016, pp. 24–25.

13

JAN LIEVENS (1607–1674)

An Unknown Woman in a Green Velvet Hood, c.1622–32

Oil on panel, 75.6 × 62.9 cm
National Trust, Castle Ward, County Down – The Bangor Collection (NT 836187)

PROVENANCE
Purchased by the National Trust from Edward Ward, 7th Viscount Bangor with a grant from the Ulster Land Fund in 1967

LITERATURE
Sumowski 1983–90, III, p. 1802, no. 1266, repr. p. 1905

A young woman wrapped in velvet sits quietly, staring out into the distance, wide-eyed and lost in contemplation. It is not known who the sitter is, or indeed if Jan Lievens painted the picture as a *tronie*, depicting the woman as a character study or type rather than as a true portrait. The fact that the women is enveloped in her clothes, to the extent that we have little idea of her appearance underneath, has the effect of giving the picture an air of timelessness and in turn it is hard to decipher whether or not it is actually a depiction of a contemporary sitter. The picture is reminiscent of a number of figurative paintings by Lievens in which a single person is shown in a plain interior, lit from the top left. The artist seems to capture the essence of the woman portrayed, even though her quiet, reflective expression means she remains enigmatic.

The sitter was painted before Lievens visited London in 1632, where he stayed for three years and where he was influenced by the great Flemish painter Anthony Van Dyck. Lievens was known in England before then, primarily through the intervention of the Royalist statesman and poet Robert Kerr, 1st Earl of Ancram (1578–1654). Ancram, as well as being an influential courtier, was known for his cultural interests: his poetry was influenced by his friends the poets John Donne and William Drummond of Hawthornden, and he had a keen interest in collecting paintings. When he was in The Hague in 1629, where he served as Charles I's emissary, Ancram sent the king two pictures by Rembrandt (which were gifts from Frederick Henry of Orange) which, famously, were the first works by the artist seen in Britain. It was at this same time that Ancram met Lievens, who shared a studio with Rembrandt, and when he returned to London he presented the king with two of Lievens's paintings, *A Capuchin Monk Praying* and *Young Man Studying by a Peat Fire*. After the king's execution in 1649, Ancram fled to the Low Countries, remaining in exile there until his death. Despite his relative poverty he sat to several artists for his portrait, including Lievens – in 1654, some twenty-five years after they had first met. When he prepared to have his portrait (fig. 71) collected from Amsterdam to be taken to his native Scotland, he wrote to his son that the picture could be retrieved 'out of the hands of Mr. Lievens, the Duke of Brandenburg's painter. He lives at the sign of the fleur-de-luce and you may be sure of a good one. He is the better because he has so high conceit of himself that he thinks there is none to be compared with him in all of Germany, Holland, nor the rest of the seventeen provinces.'

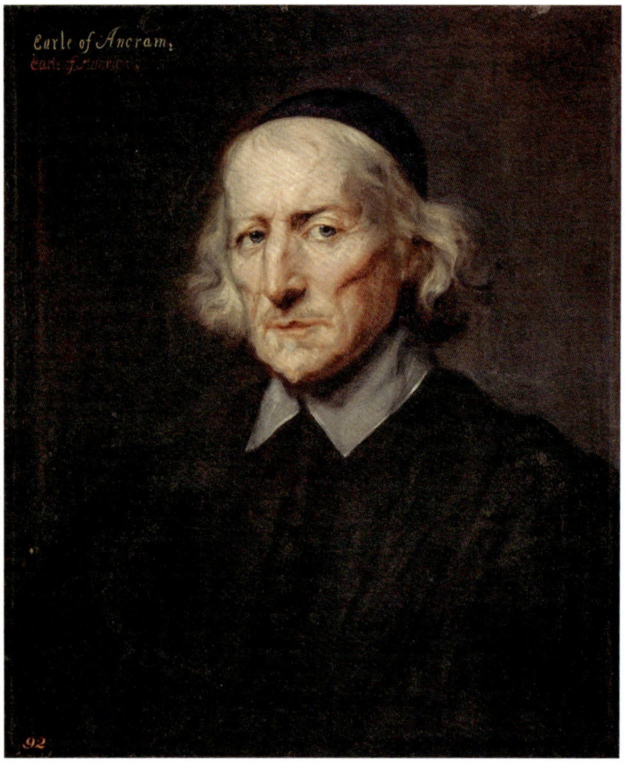

FIG. 71
Jan Lievens (1607–1674)
Robert Kerr, 1st Earl of Ancram (1578–1654), 1654
Oil on canvas, 62.20 × 51.40 cm
Scottish National Portrait Gallery,
Edinburgh (PG 3663)

The painting of the unknown woman has previously been catalogued as being after Willem Drost, who was one of Rembrandt's pupils. A label on the frame names *Cornelius Droost* as the artist – 'Cornelis Drost' is one of the many names given to Willem Drost during a period of confusion over his biography and work in the nineteenth century. However, the picture is now considered to be 'an excellent early work' by Lievens.[2] It came to the National Trust in 1967; Castle Ward, in County Down, Northern Ireland, was accepted in lieu of tax by Her Majesty's Treasury following the death of Maxwell Ward, 6th Viscount Bangor (1868–1950), and was transferred to the National Trust in 1952. The picture was purchased from Edward Ward, 7th Viscount Bangor (1905–1993) fifteen years later, with a grant from the Ulster Land Fund. DT

NOTES

1 Quoted in Wheelock 2008–09, p. 178, no. 51.
2 Sumowski 1983–90, III, p. 1802, no. 1266, repr. p. 1905.

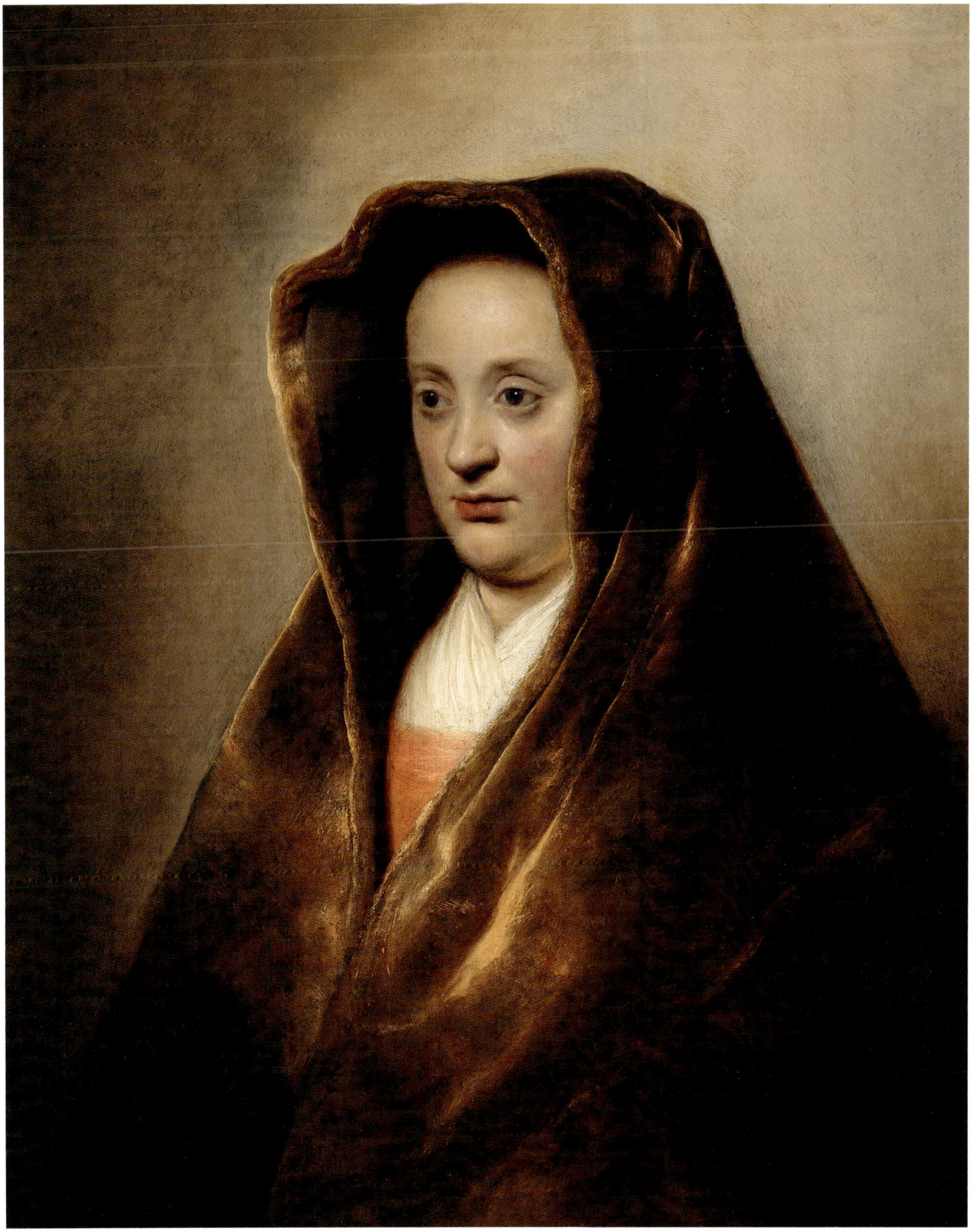

CAT. 13

14

JAN LIEVENS (1607–1674)

A Magus at a Table, *c.*1631

Oil on oak panel, 55.9 × 48.6 cm
National Trust, Upton House, Warwickshire – The Bearstead Collection (NT 446728)

PROVENANCE
The Schmidt sale, Amsterdam, 7 September 1803, lot 139; probably the Van Roothaan sale, Amsterdam, 29 March 1826, lot 52; possibly bought by 'Yates' at the William Seguier sale, Christie's, 4 May 1844 , lot 93; bought by Nicholson at the Maria Chippindall sale, Christie's, 28 May 1903, lot 154; bought by 'Nicholson'; John Walter by 1916; bought by 'Barnes' (probably acting for Walter Samuel, 2nd Viscount Bearsted) at the Arthur Walter sale, Christie's, 18 June 1937, lot 84; given by Lord Bearstead to the National Trust in 1948

EXHIBITED
New Light on Old Masters, Upton House – Squash Court Gallery, 2013

LITERATURE
De Groot 1911–12, p. 177; De Groot 1907–28, VI, no. 71; Valentier 1921, p. xvi, no. 18; Schneider 1932, p. 97; Van Gelder 1953 (2); Bauch 1960, p. 266, no. 186; Gore 1964, p. 36, no. 123; Bauch 1967, p. 166 and fig. 8; Sumowski 1983–90, III (1983), p. 1796, no. 1241

This contemplative image was painted during the time when the young Jan Lievens shared a studio in his native Leiden with his friend and collaborator Rembrandt van Rijn, and when their respective painterly styles were so close that their pictures from this period can be difficult to tell apart. In the past the picture was thought to have been painted by Rembrandt, and at some point a false signature was added in the bottom left of the panel, reading *Rembrandt f.*[*ecit*] *16..* (last two numerals indistinct). In the picture an old man stands by a table, writing in a book propped up on his arm. A second book falls open across the edge of the table, revealing an image of a figure with what appears to be a halo of light around its head. In an otherwise gloomy interior, the figure is illuminated by a pool of light that he stands at the edge of. Although he appears as some sort of venerable scholar with his skullcap and books, a different role is suggested by the gold robe he wears and the elaborate gold-embroidered table covering. He is instead thought to be a magus, a priest or magician of eastern origins, who followed the ancient religion of Zoroastrianism, and of a kind often depicted in paintings holding or reading from a book. Magi that appear in the bible include Simon Magus (Simon the Sorcerer) in the Book of Acts, and the three Magi who visited the infant Christ after his birth, albeit in the role of wise men rather than magicians.

An upholstered chair and large curtain behind the old man, as well as the leafy branch above his head, help to add a theatrical element to the composition. The dramatic lighting is reminiscent of another Lievens picture, *The Raising of Lazarus* (Royal Pavilion and Museums, Brighton and Hove), dated 1631, around the time the present Magus picture is thought to have been painted, and the composition is similar to his etching *A Scholar in his Study*, which shows a man wearing a cap and standing at a candlelit table, looking at an open tome.

At least ten copied versions of the present picture are known, and Rembrandt himself had a version in his collection, described in a 1656 inventory of his

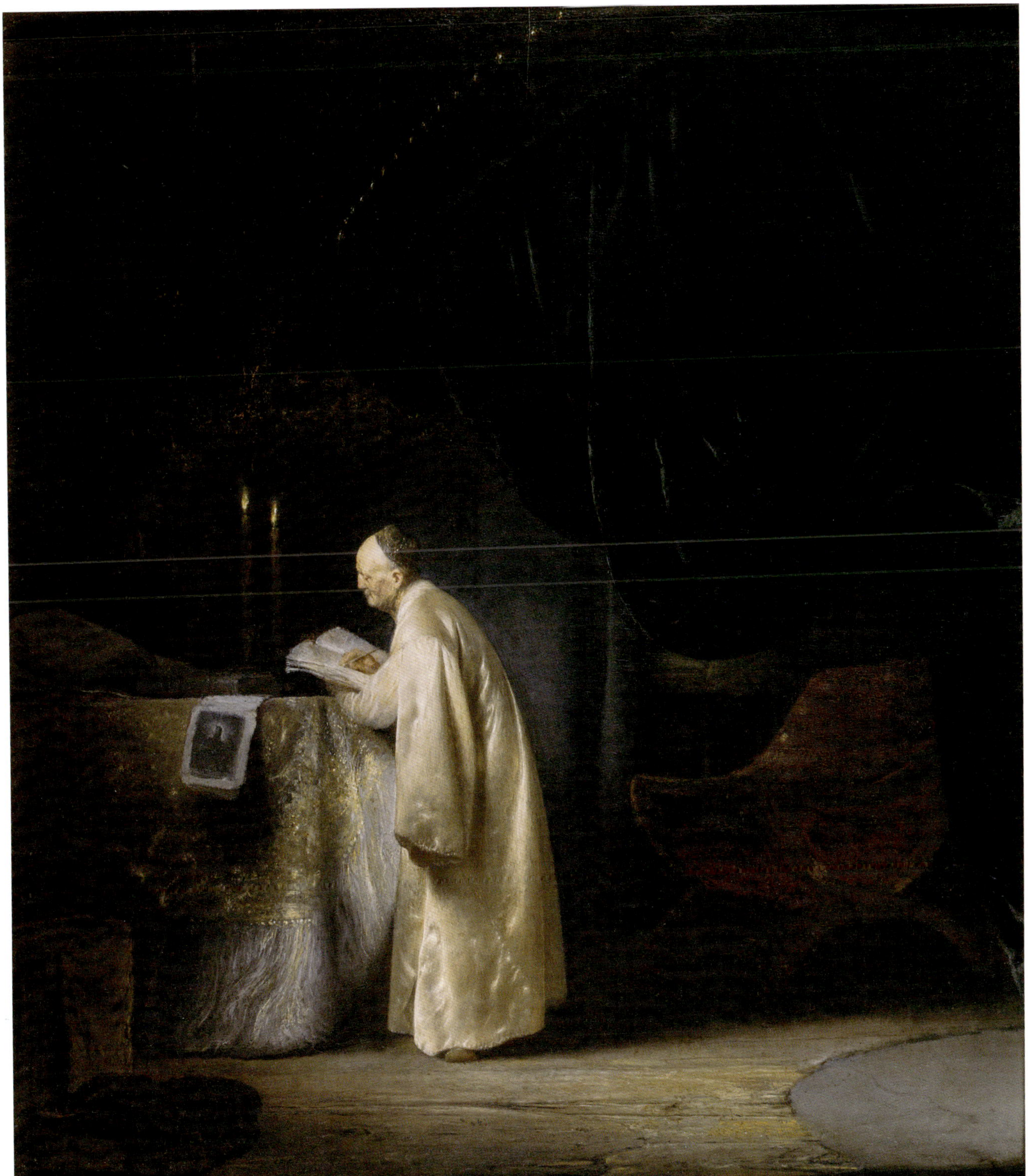

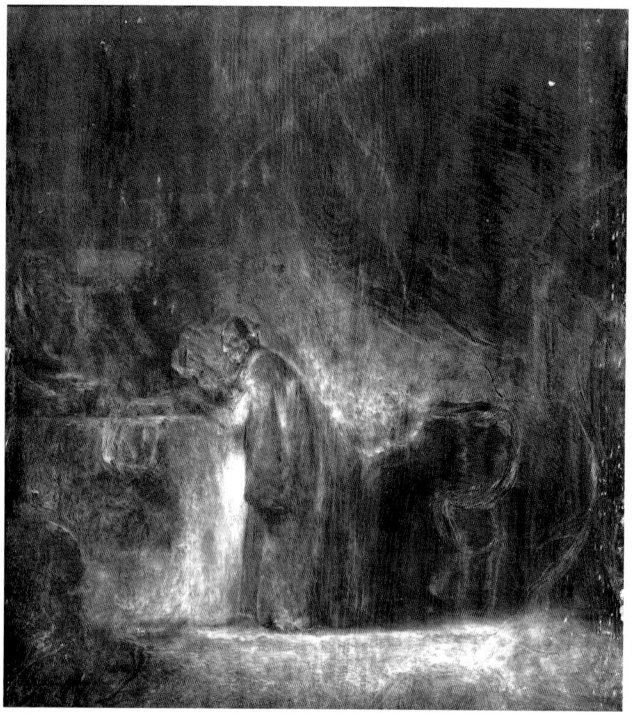

X-ray of cat. 14

possessions as 'One priest after Jan Lievens'. A version in Wavel Royal Castle, Krakow, is called *The Prophet Zachariah in the Temple* (engraved by Jean-Pierre Norblin de la Gourdaine in 1781),[2] and another, called *Zachariah Writes Down the Name of his Son*, was attributed to the school of Rembrandt when it was recently sold at auction (Lempertz, Cologne, 12 May 2012, lot 1235). Differing views over the authorship of the picture go back to at least to the early nineteenth century. For example, the current picture was sold in 1826 in Amsterdam as by Lievens, and then in 1844 as by Rembrandt, as 'A Jewish Priest in his robes, standing before a table'.[3] Once thought to be one of the copies, it is now believed to be an autograph work by Lievens and the prime version of the type.[4]

The picture was bought by Walter Samuel, 2nd Viscount Bearsted (1882–1948) in 1937 from Christie's, and added to his collection at Upton House in Warwickshire, which he had bought ten years earlier. Lord Bearsted, the son of Sir Marcus Samuel, 1st Viscount Bearsted (1853–1927), the founder and chairman of Shell Transport & Trading Co. Ltd and a collector in his own right, had bought Upton in 1927 from the Earl of Jersey. Bearsted was an avid and eclectic collector of Old Master pictures and he transformed Upton into one of the finest private art collections in Britain in the twentieth century. A particular strength at Upton is his collection of Dutch pictures, others of which are included in this exhibition (see cat. nos. 15, 19 and 21). As well as serving as a trustee of the National Gallery and the Tate Gallery, and as chairman of the Whitechapel Gallery, he gave money to the National Art Collections Fund and donated works to national collections. Upton was given to the National Trust by Lord Bearsted in 1948, shortly before his death. As a collector his attention was attracted to beautiful and unusual paintings, and this, as well as his sympathetic interest in the human condition, must have played no small part in the purchase of Lievens's pensive, mysterious picture.

TECHNICAL ANALYSIS

In order firmly to establish the painting's attribution to Jan Lievens and verify that it was the prime version, full technical analysis was undertaken at the Hamilton Kerr Institute (University of Cambridge).[5] Initial examination revealed the presence of various pentimenti, changes in the pigment layers and the mild wrinkling of the paint layers in certain areas, which were all indicative of compositional changes. X-rays revealed that the original compositional sketch was modified as the artist reworked the painting. The chair and the figure were originally placed closer to each other, suggesting that the figure has just risen from the chair, the curtain folds and hands were repositioned and a small candle held by the figure was painted out.

Paint analysis showed the complex layering of thin glazes to create depth in the background, and changes in the paint layers, most noticeable in the tablecloth, which was initially green, then altered to red with light purple detailing and finally silver with gold embroidery. The individual pigments and pigment combinations, particular azurite and yellow earth to create the green passages, as well as the presence of smalt, were typical of both Rembrandt and Lievens. Macro x-ray fluorescence, a non-invasive analytical technique which maps specific elements, clearly showed (through the presence of copper) the leafy branch on the table, which had become less visible due to thinning of the paint layer during previous restorations, and revealed (through the presence of copper and iron) what appeared to be a niche or monument positioned behind the table that had been subsequently painted out.

Overall the results of the technical analysis show that the materials and techniques appear to be consistent with Lievens's practice in Leiden, while the numerous compositional changes are also consistent with his working methods, thus confirming that the painting is the prime version and not a copy. DT & CS

NOTES

1 Sumowski 1983–90, III, p. 1796, no. 1241.
2 For the Krakow version, see Schneider and Ekkart 1973, p. 320, and Winiewicz-Wolska 2001, pp. 124–25, no. 44.
3 Van Roothaan sale, Amsterdam, 29 March 1826, lot 52, and Christie's, 4 May 1844, lot 93.
4 See Bauch 1960, p. 266, no. 186 and Sitwell 2015, p. 9.
5 Sitwell 2015, pp. 9 and 10; Kempski and Kuang 2015.

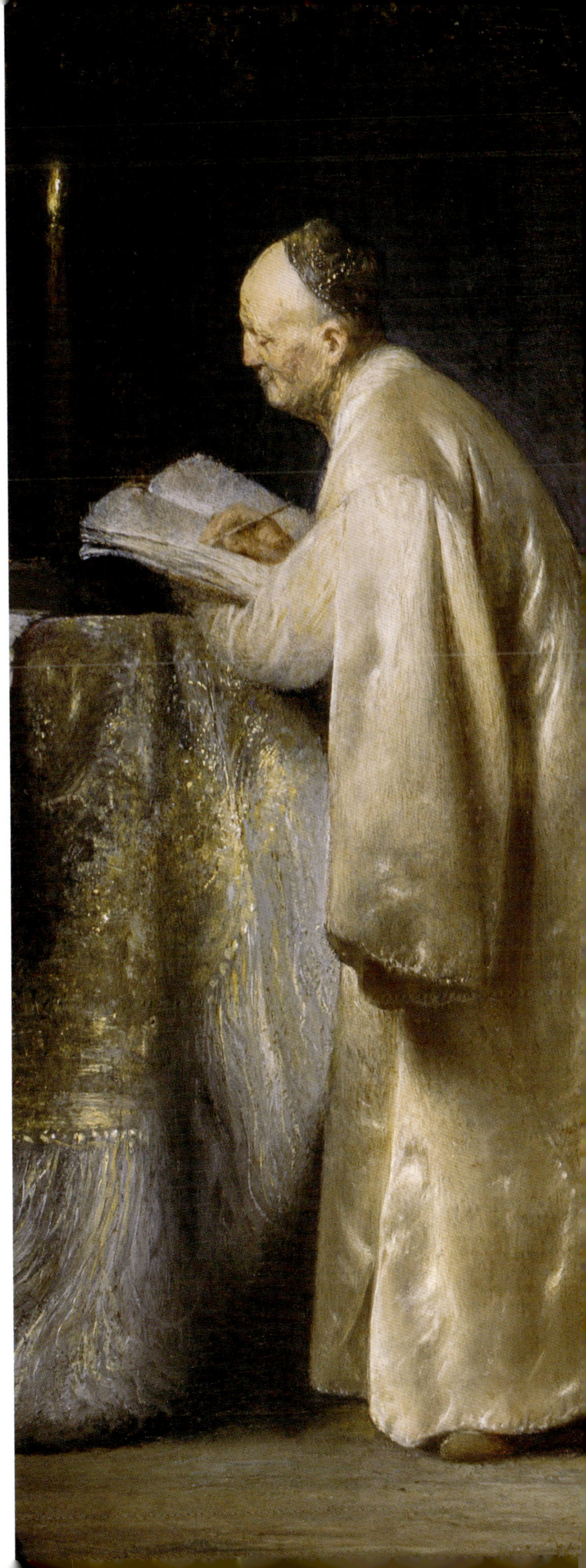

Dutch Delftware

PATRICIA F. FERGUSON, NATIONAL TRUST ADVISOR ON CERAMICS
AND CURATORIAL RESEARCHER AT THE VICTORIA AND ALBERT MUSEUM

THE GOLDEN AGE OF DUTCH DELFTWARE emerged in the last quarter of the seventeenth century under the influence of Queen Mary II of England and her Dutch husband, the King-Stadholder William III. It had been a conspicuous imported luxury ware in England throughout the seventeenth century, but escalated with the arrival of the Dutch sovereigns in 1689. Kensington Palace and Hampton Court Palace were spectacularly redecorated to display their blue and white ceramics 'in the Custom or Humour' they had perfected in furnishing their Dutch palaces under the French Huguenot designer Daniel Marot. Ambitious English aristocrats, recently rewarded with titles following the 'Glorious Revolution', quickly adopted their taste and acquired the most extravagant examples to furnish their Baroque palaces as visual evidence of their loyalty. Many remain in situ in country houses now owned by the National Trust and taken as a whole form the most important collection of Dutch Delftware in Britain.[1]

The blue-and-white ceramics included Chinese porcelain and its Dutch imitation, *hollants porceleyn*.[2] The latter was tin-glazed earthenware (or faience), popularly known in England as 'Delftware', as many of the finest examples were made in the town of Delft, but it was also made in Rotterdam and Amsterdam. The opaque white surface resembling porcelain was brought about by adding Cornish tin to the clear lead-glaze. This technique was developed by potters in Iraq in AD 800 and spread to Spain, Italy, France, the Netherlands and England. When imports of Chinese porcelain under the Dutch East India Company temporarily ceased during civil wars in China in the 1650s, Dutch potters seized the opportunity to expand their markets. They improved their materials and hired skilled painters to copy Chinese porcelain closely.

When the Chinese porcelain trade resumed in the 1680s, the Dutch had the immediate advantage, responding instantly to European fashions, especially for vessels to display flowers. Cavernous Baroque interiors were soon filled, both visually and olfactorily, with large blue-and-white vases designed to display costly, scented flowers, while outside parterres were edged with garden pots with growing plants. Examples of each are included in the important Delftware collection at Dyrham Park in Gloucestershire, home of William Blathwayt (for whom see pp. 16 and 98–99 and cat. 1 and 7). Between 1692 and 1701, acting as Secretary of State, Blathwayt accompanied the King on annual visits to the Low Countries, affording him numerous opportunities to acquire works of art. Inventories of Dyrham, dated 1703 and 1710, record over 85 items of Delftware, of which thirty-three survive.[3]

Many were made at the prestigious 'Greek A' (*De Grieksche A*) factory in Delft, marked with the proprietors initials 'AK' for Adrianus Kocx (d. 1701). They frequently resemble wares designed by Marot for Queen Mary II at the palace of Het Loo in Apeldoorn, where Blathwayt also had an apartment. A pair of seven-tiered Delftware flower pyramids, *c.* 1690–95, made at the factory were prominently displayed according to the 1710 inventory (see fig. 72). One, listed as a 'pyramid Delf flowerpot in ye chimney', was on the ground floor in the main entrance room lined with Dutch gilt-leather hangings, while the other was on the first floor in the Best Bed Chamber hung with *verdure*

FIG. 72
One of a pair of seven-tiered flower pyramids, tin-glazed earthenware, 'Greek A' factory, Adrianus Kocx proprietor, Delft, The Netherlands (one marked) *c.* 1690–95
Height 130 cm
National Trust, Dyrham Park, Gloucestershire (NT 452205)

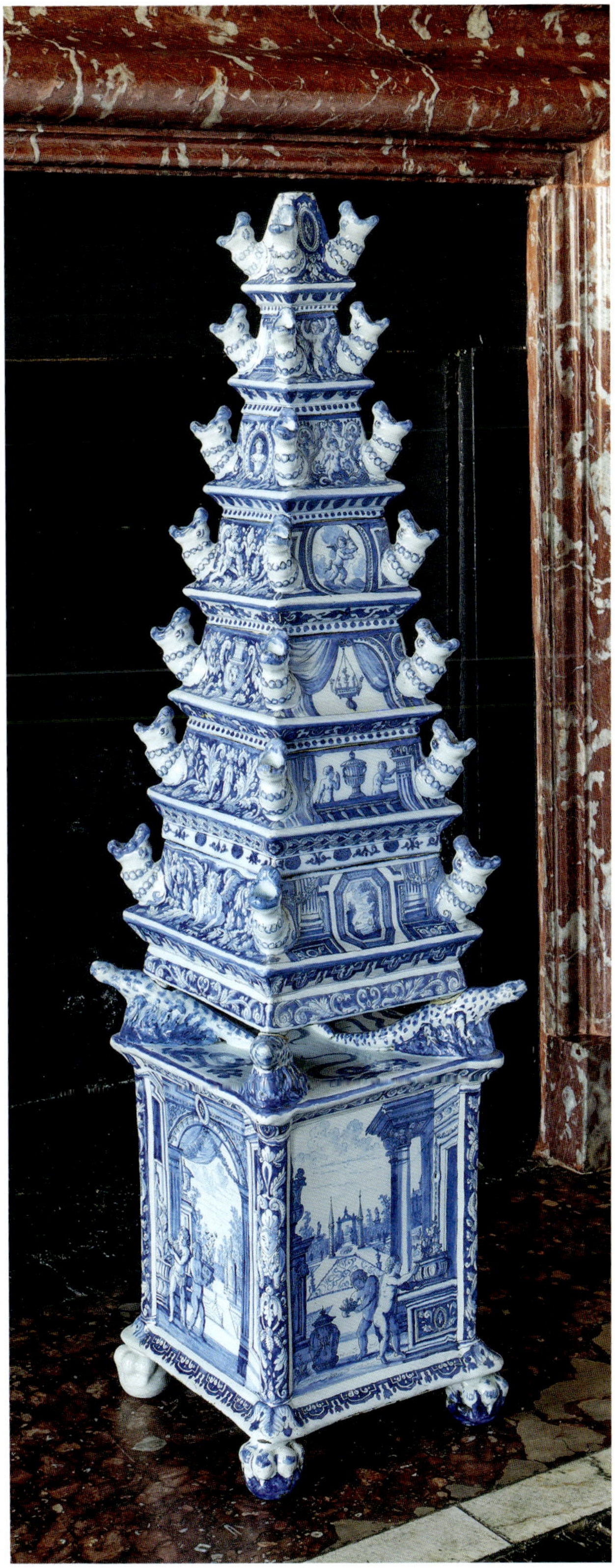

tapestries. The bases are exquisitely painted with alternating scenes of Dutch formal gardens, perhaps after engravings or drawings by Romeyn de Hooghe, and may have resembled similar schemes and cascades at Dyrham Park. They would have looked magnificent with the four serpent-form spouts on each tier filled with colourful flowers.

Hanging in the Ante Hall are two identical, large blue-painted Delftware tiles or plaques, *c.* 1670–90, depicting exotic vegetation and wildlife, each mounted in a contemporary, probably Dutch, black and gold frame (fig. 73). The scenery, with a conspicuous coconut, pineapple and banana palm tree, evokes the topography and rich produce of South-east Asia, with a pagoda or porcelain tower in the distance. The image, in fact, represents Guandong province in southern China and is taken from an engraved plate in Johan Nieuhof, *Het gezantschap der Neêrlandtsche Oost-Indische Compagnie aan den grooten Tartarischen Cham* (Amsterdam, 1665), a record of a Dutch trade mission to China, 1655–57, later translated into English by John Ogilby as *An Embassy from the Dutch East India Company to the Grand Tartar Cham, Emperor of China* (London, 1669).

Nieuhof's lavishly illustrated publication documented the mission sponsored by the Dutch East India Company, and was the first commercial eye-witness account of Asia. For almost a century, it defined China for Europeans and inspired many inventive chinoiseries on pottery and lacquer ware. The subject-matter would have appealed to Blathwayt, the former Secretary to the Lords of Trade and Plantation of the British Overseas Empire, with responsibility for the New World, who clearly took an interest in profitable

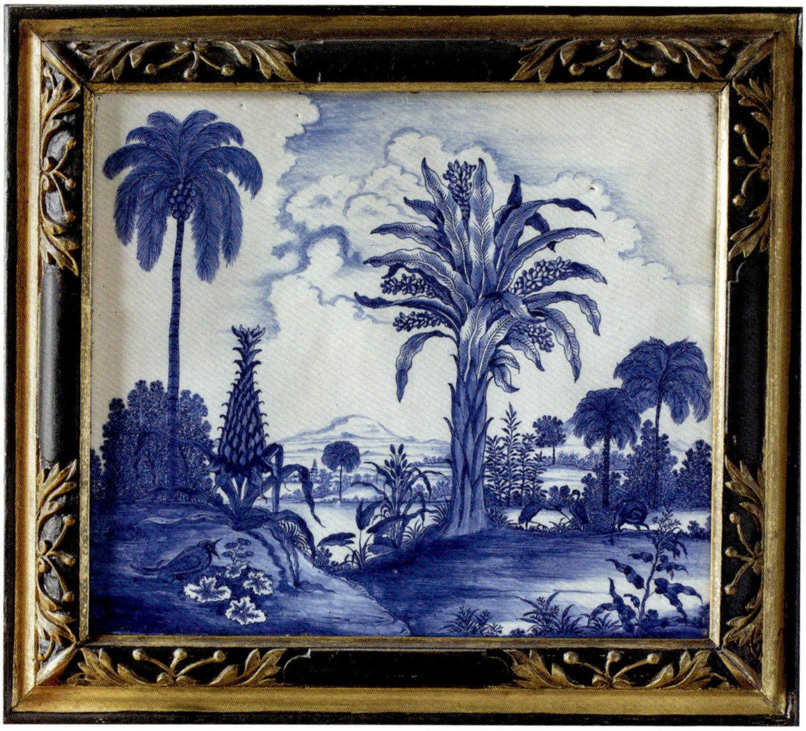

FIG. 73
One of a pair of tiles or plaques, tin-glazed earthenware, Delft, The Netherlands, unmarked, *c.* 1670–90
Framed, 43.5 × 48.0 cm
National Trust, Dyrham Park, Gloucestershire (NT 452247)

luxury goods, both personally and professionally. The tiles, which are not listed in the 1710 inventory, first appear as '2 Delf Pictures' in Mrs Blathwayte's Room in the inventory of 1742, prepared following the death of his son, also William (1688–1742).[4]

Other properties with Delftware include Belton House, Lincolnshire; Blickling Hall, Norfolk; Erddig, Wales; Lytes Carey Manor, Somerset; Saltram House, Devon; Tatton Park, Cheshire; and Uppark House, West Sussex. At Kingston Lacy, in Dorset, owned by the Bankes family (see p. 14), there is a typical three-piece Delftware garniture (a set of matching vases), comprising a large jar and two bottles, *c.* 1695 (fig. 74). Their shapes recall Chinese porcelain of the 1630s, no longer imported following China's official ban on trade in 1657. The decoration, too, was inspired by these earlier wares – hunters on horseback and scholars in conversation, and a rare depiction of the Buddha Maitreya in an imagined heaven surrounded by monks. The last is after an engraving by Jacob van Meurs, published in the travel account by Olfert Dapper (*c.* 1635–1689), *Beschryving Des Keizerryks Van Taising Of Sina* (Description of the Empire of Taising of China) (Amsterdam, 1670), and provides evidence that Chinese woodblock prints were available in the Netherlands at this date.

The garniture matches an entry in the meticulous account book kept by Margaret Bankes (d. 1730), wife of the MP John Bankes (1665–1714), who recorded on 26 September 1698: 'Payd for a large delph jar & 2 bottles £3.00.00'.[5] For over a century it has sat above a contemporary Dutch burr-walnut cabinet-on-stand with so-called 'seaweed marquetry', *c.* 1700–10, inscribed with the names of otherwise unrecorded journeymen, Jan Roohals and I. Hoogeboom. With the death of Queen Mary II in 1694 and the increasing numbers of Chinese porcelains imported for sale in England in the 1690s, the market for luxury Delftware quickly abated.

FIG. 74
A three-piece garniture, tin-glazed earthenware, Delft, The Netherlands, unmarked, *c.* 1695
Height 70.4 cm and 60.0 cm
National Trust, Kingston Lacy, Dorset (NT 1250639)

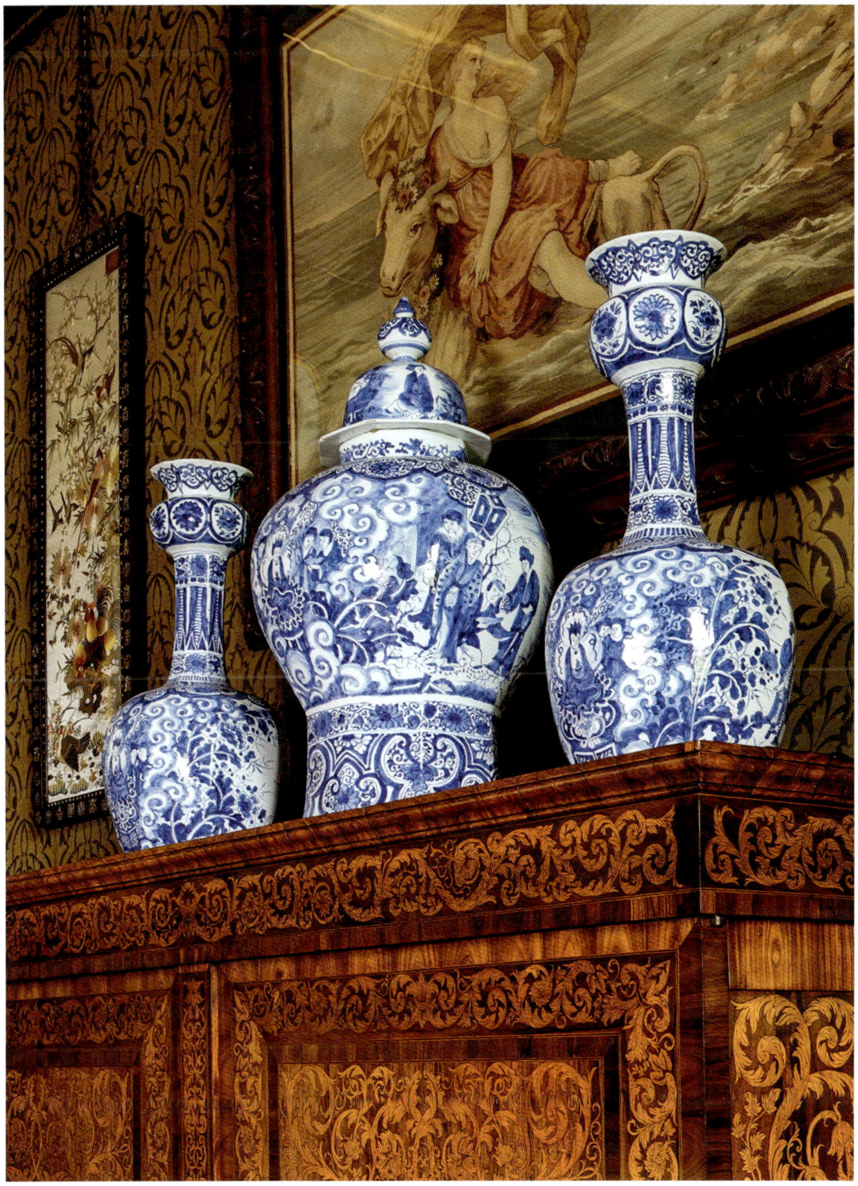

NOTES

1 See Ferguson 2016, pp. 43–53.
2 See Lambooy 2014, pp. 231–48.
3 See Ressing 2000, pp. 1–32.
4 Gloucestershire Archives, Gloucester, Dyrham Park Archives, Blathwayt Family, D1799/E256, Inventory, with valuation, of the household goods at Dyrham, 1742.
5 Ferguson 2016, p. 52.

15

GABRIEL METSU (1629–1667)

The Duet ('Le corset bleu'), *c.*1660

Oil on panel, 39 × 29 cm
Signed, at the bottom of the sheet of music: *G. Metsu*
National Trust, Upton House, Warwickshire – The Bearsted Collection (NT 446725)

PROVENANCE
Probably the Lambert Witsen sale, Amsterdam, 25 May 1746, lot 4; bought by Maniére at the Pierre-Louis Randon de Boisset sale held by Pierre Remy and others in his house in rue Neuve des Capucines, Paris, 27 February and following days, 1777, lot 81; bought by J.-B.-P. Le Brun at the Charles Destouches sale, Paris, 21 March 1794, lot 42; bought by Nicolas Lerouge at the Le comte Wautier sale, Paris, 9 June and following days, 1797, lot 11; bought by Pierre Joseph Lafontaine for Michael Bryan on behalf of George Hibbert of Clapham at the François-Antoine Robit sale, Paris, 11–18 May 1801, lot 70; Hibbert sale, Christie's, 13 June 1829, lot 65, to Joseph Neeld, Grittleton House, Wiltshire; with John Neeld, 1st Baronet in 1878; by whom sold to Baron Lionel de Rothschild in the winter of 1878–79; by division to his son, Alfred de Rothschild, in 1882; bequeathed by him to Almina, Countess of Carnaervon; from whom acquired by Knoedler, London, and sold to Walter Samuel, 2nd Viscount Bearsted in 1924; given by him to the National Trust in 1948

EXHIBITED
In Trust for the Nation, National Gallery, London, 1995–96, no. 65; *New Light on Old Masters*, Upton House – Squash Court Gallery, 2013

SELECTED LITERATURE
Laing 1995, no. 65; Waiboer 2012, pp. 88, 224–25, no. A–82

The Duet, dated *c.* 1660, is among the highlights of Gabriel Metsu's mature work. The painting demonstrates the utter perfection of his rendering of various materials. It takes its title from the elegant young woman who holds a musical score – on which the painter placed his signature, upside down – and is apparently about to sing to the accompaniment of the lute played by the young man. Her colourful attire immediately attracts attention – a gleaming satin dress and a blue velvet jacket trimmed with white fur along the edges and cuffs. This blue jacket is such a striking feature that it provided the painting with a name, *Le corset bleu*, when it was engraved as part of the celebrated collection of Pierre-Louis Randon de Boisset (1708–1776) in Paris.[1] The woman's white head-cloth conceals most of her curls. Her feet rest on a foot-warmer. She has pushed aside the costly Persian carpet in order to lean on the table, where a large glass of wine is within reach. Completely immersed in her thoughts, she stares straight ahead, avoiding the gaze of the man behind the table. Looking towards her, he sits on the table while tuning his lute. The hilt of his sword is just visible at left.

The woman's lapdog is depicted in the foreground, looking at its mistress, as if providing commentary on the scene. We can only speculate about the relationship between the woman and the man: are they already married, or still courting? The presence of a lute is significant, for emblem literature and contemporary painting both portrayed it as the instrument most evocative of love. In the course of his career, Metsu produced a number of thematically related compositions, in which men attempt to attract the attention of women making music. Sometimes the import of such pictures is fairly obvious. In Metsu's *Woman at the Virginal with a Man Offering a*

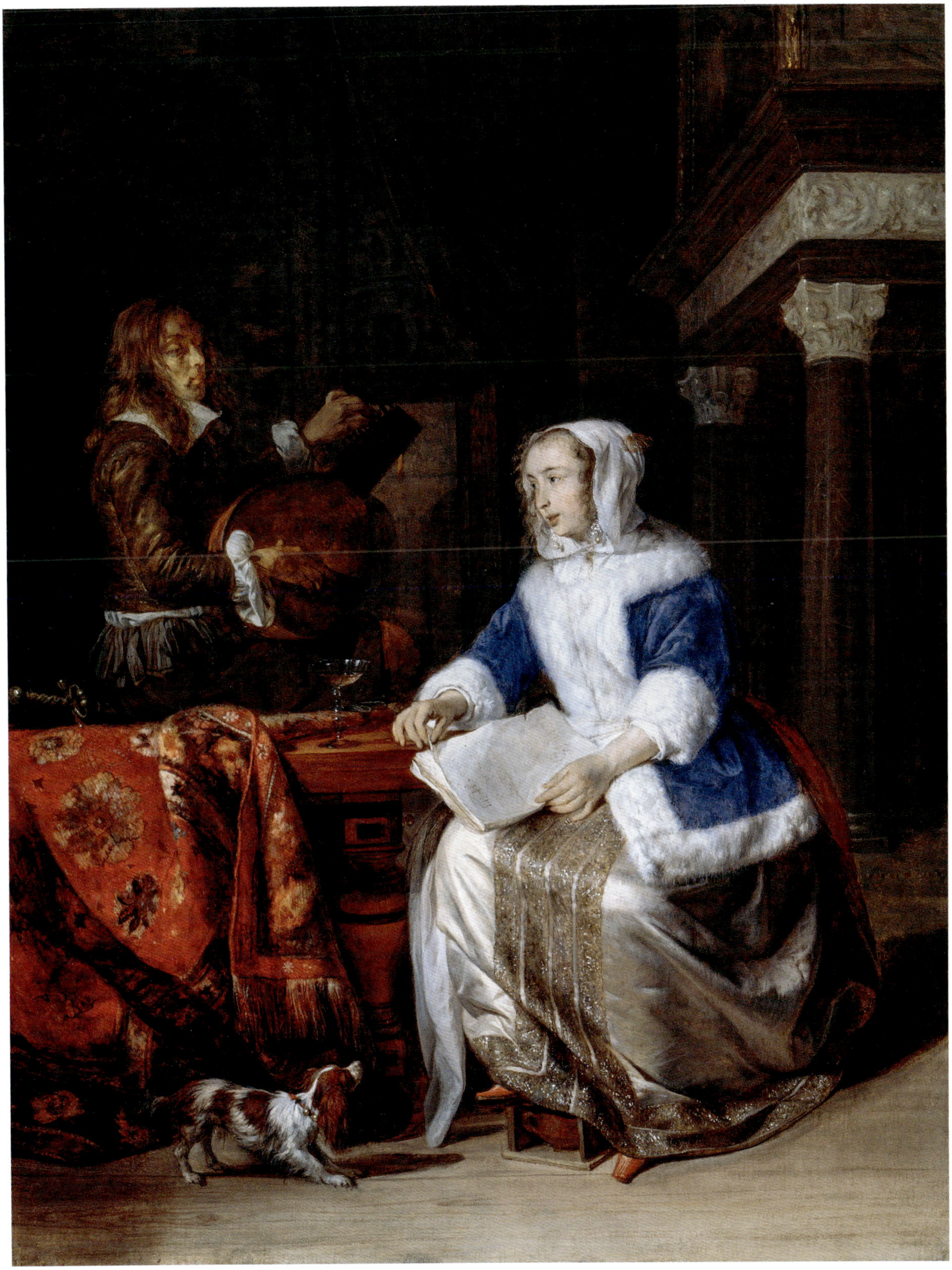

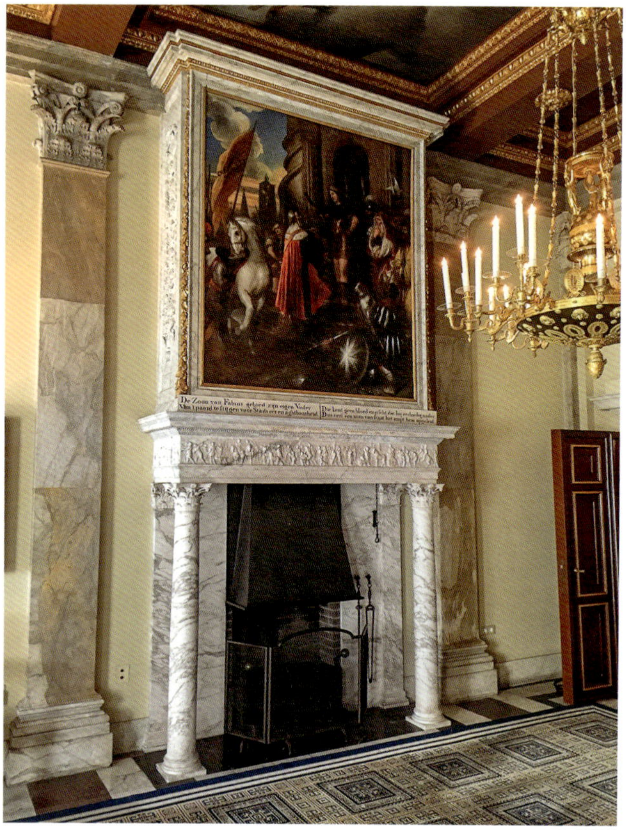

FIG. 75
Artus Quellinus (1609–1668)
Chimney in the former Burgomasters' Chamber, 1654 (the overmantel is a history painting of 1656 by Jan Lievens)
White marble
Amsterdam, Royal Palace

Drink (London, English Heritage, Ranger's House), for example, the woman seems to be in two minds about the man's offering.[2] Should she accept the glass of wine and, implicitly, his love? *The Duet* is a variation on the theme of courtship, inviting the viewer to wonder about the woman's availability.

These people are members of the social elite, indicated by their splendid clothing and the room's luxurious furnishings. Behind the figures, a large tapestry has been pulled aside to reveal the open door behind it, allowing us a view of the rest of the house. The scene depicted on the tapestry is difficult to identify. The most striking feature of this sumptuous interior is the chimneypiece at right. Metsu based it on the monumental example in the Burgomasters' Chamber of the newly completed Amsterdam Town Hall (fig. 75). Designed by Jacob van Campen, this building (now the Royal Palace on Dam Square) had been festively inaugurated in 1655 and was considered by the city's inhabitants to be one of the Seven Wonders of the world. From around 1660 the Amsterdam painter Pieter de Hooch produced several paintings that feature rooms in the town hall.[3] Apparently Metsu, also a resident of Amsterdam, was similarly impressed by the building's grand interior, since he included its richly decorated chimneypieces in at least eight other genre scenes, including a painting in the Mauritshuis (fig. 76).[4] The chimneypiece depicted in this painting was created for the town hall in 1654 by the Flemish sculptor Artus Quellinus.[5] Metsu faithfully reproduced its general design, including the sculptured frieze, but left out its figures, horses and chariots. He also took some liberty with the colour scheme, by painting the load-bearing marble columns and other elements of the chimneypiece in red, whereas the original was executed entirely in white marble. The biggest change to the original setting involved the overmantel. The Royal Palace still has a large history painting of 1656 by Jan Lievens hanging here, but Metsu replaced it with a blurry scene that was never meant to be legible.

Dutch genre painting reached its apex in the third quarter of the seventeenth century, the period in which this work originated. Artists such as Gerard ter Borch (cat. 3), Gerrit Dou, Pieter de Hooch (cat. 10), Frans van Mieris the Elder, Jan Steen (cat. 20) and Johannes Vermeer were working in a number of different cities in Holland, but they seem to have been very well informed about one another's work.[6] The luxurious atmosphere of *The Duet* is related to several high-life scenes by Ter Borch, a very influential

FIG. 76
Gabriel Metsu (1629–1667)
A Young Woman Composing a Piece of Music, c.1664
Panel, 58 × 44 cm
The Hague, Mauritshuis (94)

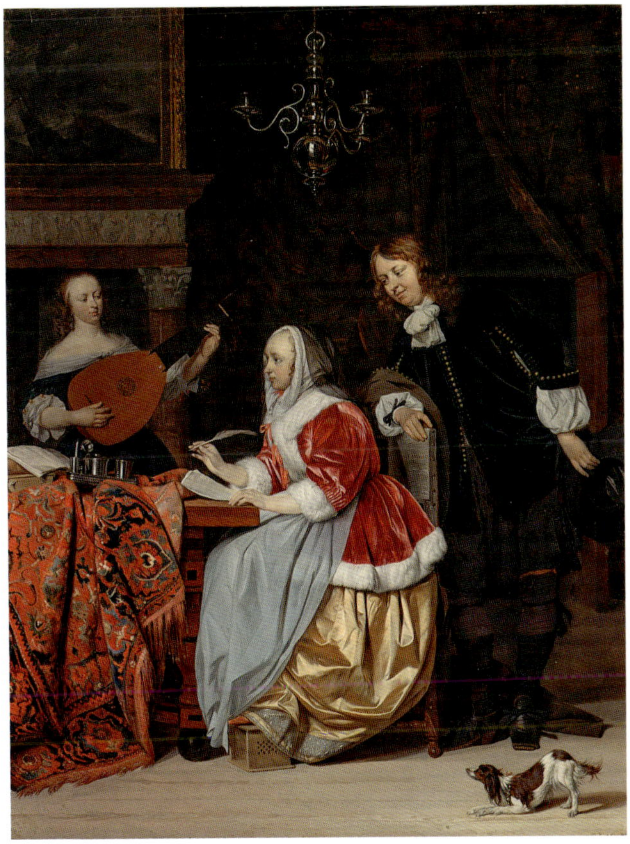

master.[7] For artistic and commercial reasons, Metsu continually engaged with the latest trends, which resulted in an oeuvre that displays great diversity in style and subject-matter. He also continued to adapt his technique. His earliest works are painted in rather broad brushstrokes that betray the influence of his Utrecht teacher Nicolaus Knupfer, as well as that of another Utrecht painter, Jan Baptist Weenix. After moving from his native city of Leiden to Amsterdam in 1654, Metsu began to work in the smooth and meticulous manner of the Leiden 'fine painters'. The elegant scene discussed here is generally thought to have originated in the last years of his life. On stylistic grounds it can be dated to around 1660, a time when Metsu was working in an extremely refined technique.[8] His brushstrokes are so subtle that they can be detected only by scrutinising the paint surface. The refined rendering of the clothing worn by the woman recalls the work of Frans van Mieris the Elder (see fig. 93, p. 171). Like Metsu's central figure, the women in Van Mieris's paintings are often dressed in fur-trimmed, red velvet jackets and dresses of satin. His finely painted work was tremendously popular.[9] Metsu probably hoped to capture a share of this market by imitating his successful colleague's technique as closely as possible. The art-historical literature of the seventeenth century stresses that a good painter must be able to make a distinction between various fabrics and materials. For example, the Leiden painter Philips Angel stated in his *Lof der Schilder-Konst* (In Praise of Painting), published in 1642, that 'a painter worthy of praise should be able to render this variety in the most pleasing way for all eyes with his brushwork, distinguishing between harsh, rough clothiness and smooth, satiny evenness'.[10] Metsu succeeded admirably in fulfilling this requirement. The elements in the foreground are highly finished, generally built up in opaque paint layers with successive glazing, whereas the background is essentially sketchy and more thinly painted. The contrast between the treatment of the two faces illustrates this clearly: the man's features are loosely and economically applied with translucent glazing, whereas the woman's face is built up more gradually with opaque highlights.[11] Scenes of this type could command large sums of money. Metsu would certainly have been able to insist on a high price for this painting, as indicated by research into the market for his work in the seventeenth century.[12] Unfortunately, though, nothing is known about the first owners of *The Duet*.[13] The work's provenance cannot be traced back

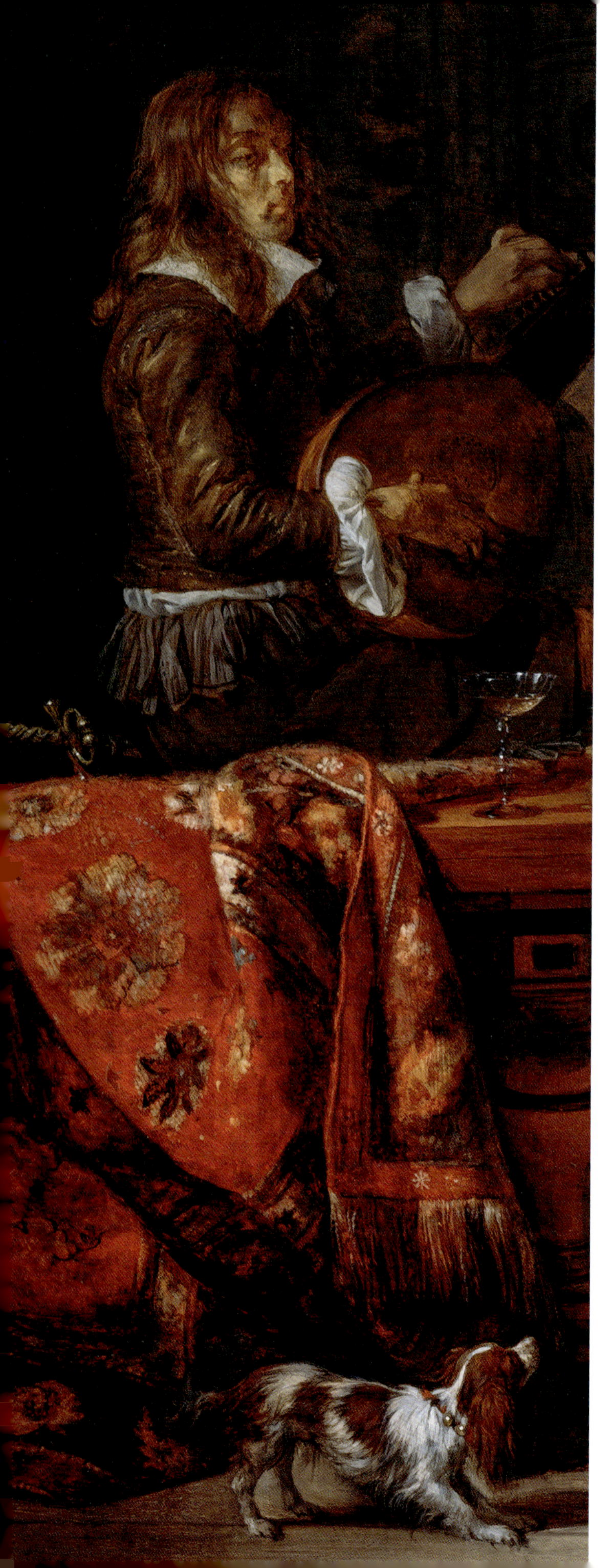

further than 1746, when the work was described in an Amsterdam sale catalogue as 'a woman wearing a satin dress, who makes music with a gentleman, tender and first-rate by Gabriel Metsu'.[14] After passing through the hands of various owners in France, one of whom had it put in its splendid Rococo frame, *The Duet* came into the possession of Lionel de Rothschild and his heirs in the winter of 1878, after which it was purchased in 1925 by Walter Horace Samuel, 2nd Viscount Bearsted (1882–1948). In 1948, he bequeathed it as part of Upton House to the National Trust, together with paintings by such artists as Jan Lievens, Pieter Saenredam and Jan Steen (cat. nos. 14, 19, 20). QB

NOTES

1 Laing 1995, p. 178.
2 Waiboer 2012, no. A–129; Buvelot in Van Suchtelen, Buvelot *et al.* 2016, p. 140, fig. 19d.
3 See Goossens in Peeters, Sutton, Goossens *et al.* 1997, nos. 18–20.
4 Q. Buvelot in Van Suchtelen, Buvelot *et al.* 2016, no. 19.
5 Goossens in Peeters, Sutton, Goossens *et al.* 1997, p. 81, fig. 21a.
6 See Waiboer *et al.* 2017.
7 Waiboer 2012, p. 88 and fig. 26.
8 Waiboer 2012, pp. 88, 224 (*c.*1659–62).
9 Buvelot in Van Suchtelen, Buvelot *et al.* 2016, p. 140.
10 Angel 1642, p. 55; Q. Buvelot in Van Suchtelen, Buvelot *et al.* 2016, p. 140.
11 As observed by Louisa Goldsmith, in an examination report of the Hamilton Kerr Institute, Cambridge, January 1995 (kept in the painting's files).
12 On the early owners of Metsu's work, see P. Roelofs in Waiboer *et al.* 2010, pp. 96–125.
13 For the full provenance, see Waiboer 2012, p. 224.
14 For the original Dutch of the quotation, see Waiboer 2012, p. 224.

16

CORNELIS VAN POELENBURCH (1594/95–1667)

Landscape with Tobias and the Angel, c.1625

Oil on panel, 36.8 × 53.3 cm
Signed lower centre: *C.P.*
National Trust, Osterley House, Middlesex – Property of the Earldom of Jersey Trust, on loan to Osterley House
(NT 773373)

PROVENANCE
Probably in the Robert Child collection at Osterley House in 1782; thence by descent

LITERATURE
Sutton *et al.* 1988, p. 407. fig.3; Sluijter-Seijffert 2016, pp. 109–10, note 118

The Italianate Dutch painter Cornelis van Poelenburch was born in Utrecht, the son of a Catholic canon. Around 1617, after training under Abraham Bloemaert, he travelled to Italy, where he stayed for ten years. His small-scale, colourful and highly finished Roman *campagna* landscapes with ruins, populated with nymphs, or with biblical or mythological figures, were immensely popular. His work was internationally acclaimed, and he was collected by patrons such as Prince Frederick Henry of Orange (1584–1647), Cosimo II de' Medici (1590–1621) and Charles I. The English king invited Poelenburch to London, where he worked intermittently between 1637 and 1641; and the crown paid £60 per annum for the rent of 'sevall houses and gardens situate in Orchard Streete ... Westm[inster] for the vse of and dwellings of Cornelius Van Polenburgh and Alexander Keyrinx two Dutch Painters'.[1] British patrons were eager to acquire Poelenburch's work for the adornment of the walls of their cabinet rooms, and pictures by him can still be found in many private, as well as public, British collections.

In Rome, Poelenburch was a founding member of the Bentvueghels ('Birds of a Feather'), a *schildersbent*, or artists' society, mostly made up of Dutch and Flemish painters working in that city, where his membership nickname was 'Satiro' (satyr). He was influenced by the work of the German painter Adam Elsheimer, who died before his arrival in Rome, and by the Flemish painter Paul Bril, the president of the city's Accademia di San Luca, with whom he sometimes worked.

Poelenburch probably painted *Tobias and the Angel,* the picture that is now at Osterley Park in Middlesex, in Rome about 1625. At first the subject of the picture appears to be the bucolic scene in the middle of the composition, where a goatherd can been seen, playing on a recorder as he rides a donkey down a slope from behind a rocky outcropping, following a pair of goats. However, behind him in the distance is the true subject, the diminutive figures of Tobias and the Angel from the biblical story (Book of Tobit: 5.5–6 and 6.2–9), which was a popular subject in Dutch painting in the seventeenth century. The composition is similar to other examples of Poelenburch's work from this time, where the viewer's eye is taken from a dark foreground towards central figures or animals before finally reaching the subject of the picture, illuminated in the background, with a further landscape brightly lit up in the distance. In the present picture we see two figures, walking away from us – the Archangel Raphael, in the guise of a human, leading Tobias, holding a fish he has just caught in the River Tigris, off to the city of Rages

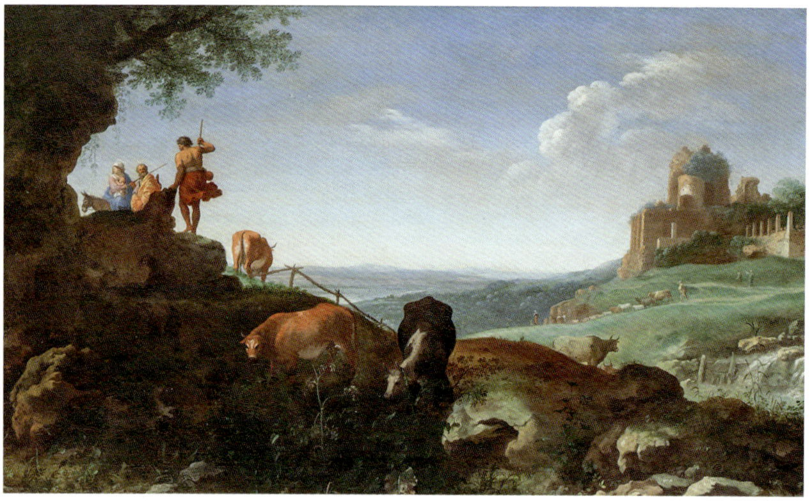

FIG. 77
Cornelis van Poelenburch (1594/95–1667)
Landscape with the Flight into Egypt, 1625
Oil on panel, 45 × 74 cm
Utrecht, Centraal Museum (inv. 8391)

(Ray, in modern-day Iran). For example, the painting is comparable in style and in the conception of its design to Poelenburch's *Flight into Egypt*, dated 1625,[2] formerly in the collection of the Marquess of Bute and now in the Centraal Museum, Utrecht[3] (fig. 77), and to *Moses Striking the Rock* (Palazzo Pitti, Florence)[4] and *The Annunciation to the Shepherds* (Musée de la Chartreuse, Douai),[5] all painted around the same time.

Poelenburch painted at least three other pictures of this subject, in works in the collections of Brodie Castle (National Trust for Scotland), the Palazzo Pitti in Florence and the Musée d'Art et d'Histoire in Geneva.[6] He is also said to have copied one of Adam Elsheimer's two pictures of the same subject.[7] Likewise, there are at least three copies of the Osterley picture, including a version that was formerly in the collection of Lord Lee of Fareham, co-founder of the Courtauld Institute of Art, London (sold at Christie's, 24 March 1961, lot 81).[8] The present picture was in the collection of the banker and politician Robert Child (1739–1782), where it was recorded, in the Breakfast Room at Osterley, in 1782. It has stayed in the family collection, by descent, and is currently on loan from the Earldom of Jersey Trust to Osterley House. DT

NOTES

1 Wood 2000–01, p. 125; R. P. Townshend, 'Alexander Keirincx's Royal Commission of 1639–1640', in Roding *et al.* 2003, pp. 138 and 148, note 9.
2 See Harwood *et al.* 2002, p. 76, no. 4.
3 Centraal Museum, Utrecht (8391).
4 Palazzo Pitti, Florence (1890–1220).
5 Musée de la Chartreuse, Douai (295).
6 Inv. 97, 8262 and 1827–2 respectively.
7 Sluijter-Seijffert 2016, pp. 109–10, note 118.
8 Sluijter-Seijffert 2016, p. 297, no. 22.

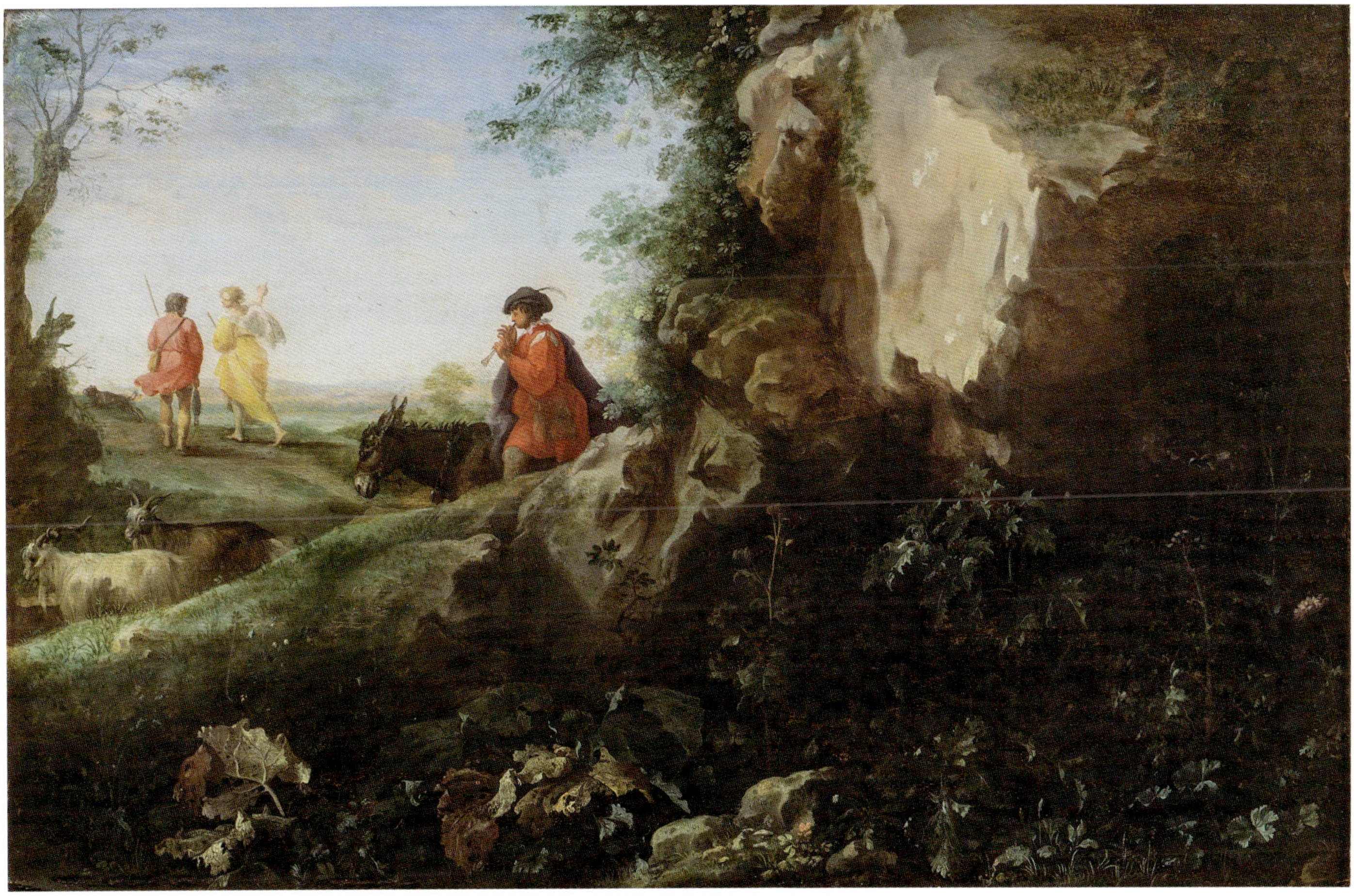

CAT. 16

Furniture and Interiors

CHRISTOPHER ROWELL, NATIONAL TRUST FURNITURE CURATOR

HIDDEN AWAY AT THE ARGORY IN COUNTY Armagh, Northern Ireland, is a Dutch ebony (*ebbenhout*) cabinet inlaid with engraved mother-of-pearl (*parlemoer*) flowers (fig. 78), which was identified in 1998 as the work of Herman Doomer,[1] a specialist Amsterdam *ebbenhoutwerker*, and Rembrandt's frame-maker and client.[2] Dating from around 1640, it is a masterpiece in the so-called auricular style.[3] Called *kwab* or *kwabwerk* in Dutch – '*kwab*' means lobe, dewlap or flabby tissue – this bizarre decoration is named in English after the auricle or convoluted cartilage of the human ear. The broken pediment of the Argory cabinet is reminiscent of a pair of shark fins, terminating surreally in turtle heads. Within the pediment, in an upright oval auricular frame, is a marquetry 'painting' of mother-of-pearl flowers inlaid in an ebony ground, which is clearly influenced by Japanese art.[4]

The auricular style was promulgated by Dutch craftsmen, designers and engravers, particularly by the Utrecht silversmiths Adam and Paul van Vianen. Adam's son, Christiaen, worked for both Charles I and Charles II. His auricular silver rosewater basin (Victoria and Albert Museum, M.1–1918), with fantastical marine imagery, is signed, dated and marked London, 1635. Auricular design was adopted for picture frames. A British *locus classicus* is the Long Gallery at Ham House,[5] which was remodelled in 1639.[6] The earliest frame, around the portrait of *Charles I* by Sir Anthony van Dyck and studio (*c.*1638; NT 1139944), is of the type named after the Venetian architect and sculptor Jacopo Sansovino, demonstrating the Italian strand in the origins of the auricular style.[7] Sir Peter Lely's portrait

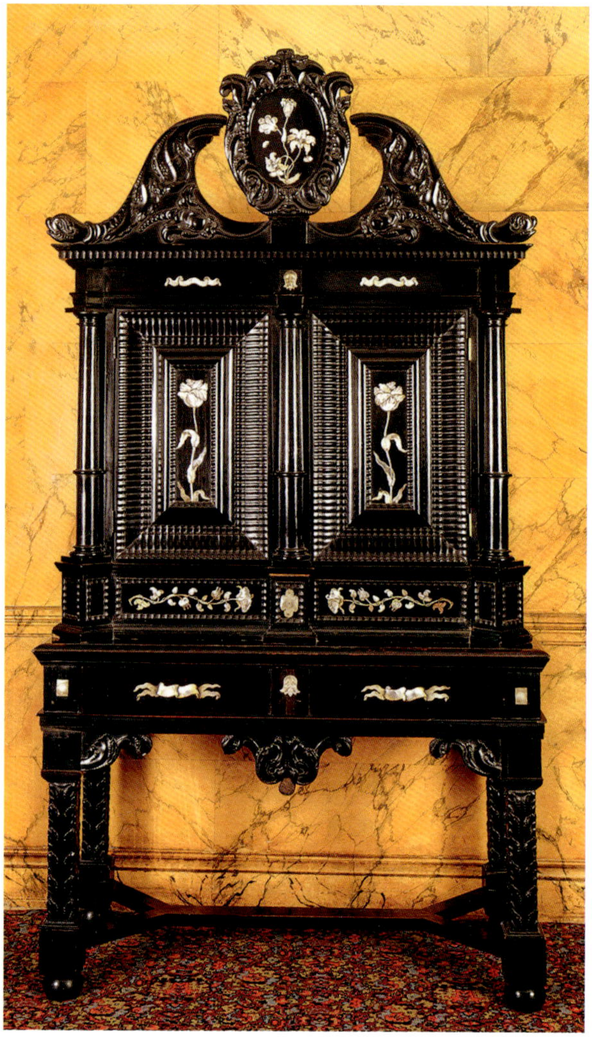

FIG. 78
Herman Doomer (*c.*1595–1650), Amsterdam
Cabinet on stand, *c.*1640,
Ebony inlaid with mother of pearl,
229.2 × 123.2 × 55.9 cm
National Trust, The Argory, County
Armagh (NT 563765)

FIG. 79
Dutch(?) carved and gilded frame, 9.8 cm wide, original to the portrait of *John Maitland, 1st Duke of Lauderdale*, by Edmund Ashfield (active from 1669, died *c.*1700), signed and dated 1674/75, pastel, 30.4 × 24.7 cm
National Trust, Ham House, Surrey (NT 1140137)

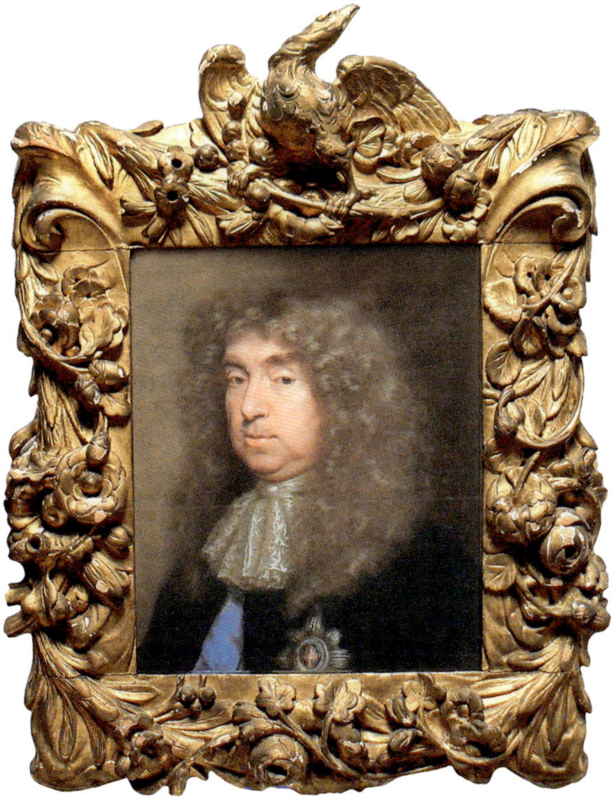

of *Lady Elizabeth Tollemache, with a Black Page* (*c.*1650; NT 1139940) is in a transitional carved and gilded auricular frame of about 1650, while his *John Maitland, 1st Duke of Lauderdale in State Robes, Wearing the Chain of the Order of the Garter* (*c.*1672; NT 1139952) has a full-blown auricular frame in which the *mouvementé* carving overlaps the sight edge. The carved and gilded frame of Edmund Ashfield's pastel portrait of the duke (signed and dated 1674/75) is probably Dutch or by a Dutch emigrant, judging by its method of construction and its close similarity to contemporary Dutch equivalents (fig. 79).[8] It is a blend of the Dutch imitative carving tradition – the eagle, acorns, berries and flowers – and the auricular.

The Green Closet at Ham House, a unique survival of a Charles I display room for smaller paintings and miniatures,[9] reminds us that frames in the seventeenth century were not necessarily gilded but often veneered in ebony or made of an ebonized wood such as pearwood (fig. 80). In 1677, thirty-eight paintings were in ebony frames and nineteen in gilt frames.[10] The ebony frames, with their elegant mouldings, are indistinguishable from their contemporary Dutch equivalents.

Ham also contains a unique cabinet possibly made in The Hague and covered throughout in ivory, partly worked in ripple mouldings (*c.*1650–60; fig. 81).[11] A larger cabinet in ebony, with a similar internal configuration of drawers, was probably also imported from The Hague (*c.*1670–72; NT 1139780). At least one table is in markedly Dutch style (*c.*1675; NT 1140049).[12] Dutch joiners and cabinet-makers were employed by the Lauderdales in the 1670s.[13]

Depictions of seventeenth-century Dutch interiors give vivid impressions both of the houses of richer citizens and of picturesque low life, whereas there is a much scarcer visual record of British equivalents.[14] The European art trade and the movement of artists and craftsmen were significant influences on both sides of the Channel. Gerrit Jensen, who was probably Dutch and seems to have trained abroad, perhaps in Paris, was made free of the London Joiners' Company in 1667, subsequently being appointed a royal cabinetmaker.[15] He made furniture inlaid with metal[16] and was responsible for the remarkable set of French-inspired silver furniture at Knole, incorporating a looking-glass and table flanked by torchère stands (1676–80; NT 130034–6).[17] Payments to him between 1672 and 1683 by John Maitland, 1st Duke of Lauderdale, suggest that he supplied several pieces of parquetry and French-style floral marquetry furniture at Ham House (*c.*1672–83; NT 1139568, etc.),[18] including a splendid bellows with silver mounts (fig. 82).[19]

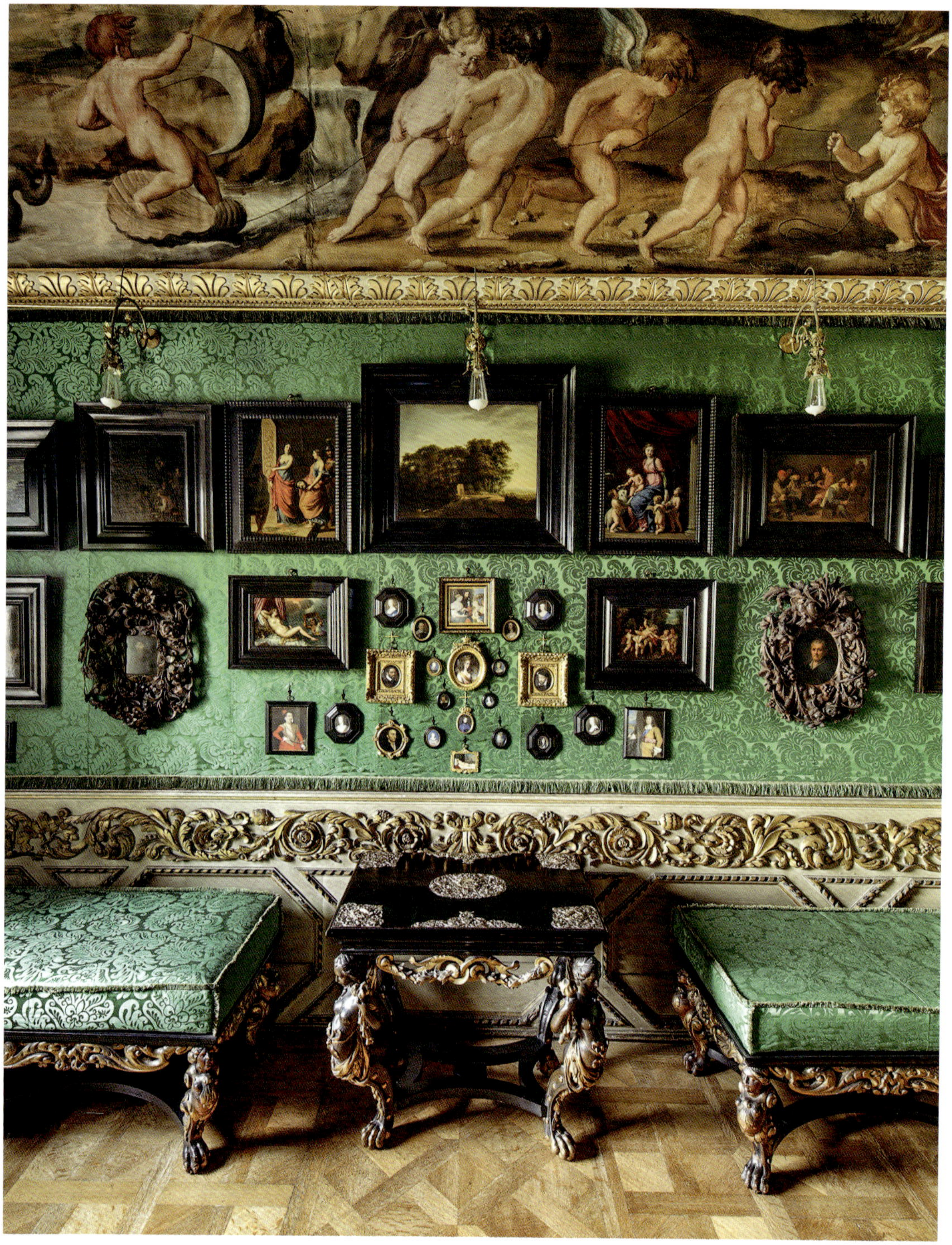

FIG. 80
The principal wall of the Green Closet, Ham House, Surrey, *c.*1639, showing a majority of ebony frames around cabinet pictures and miniatures

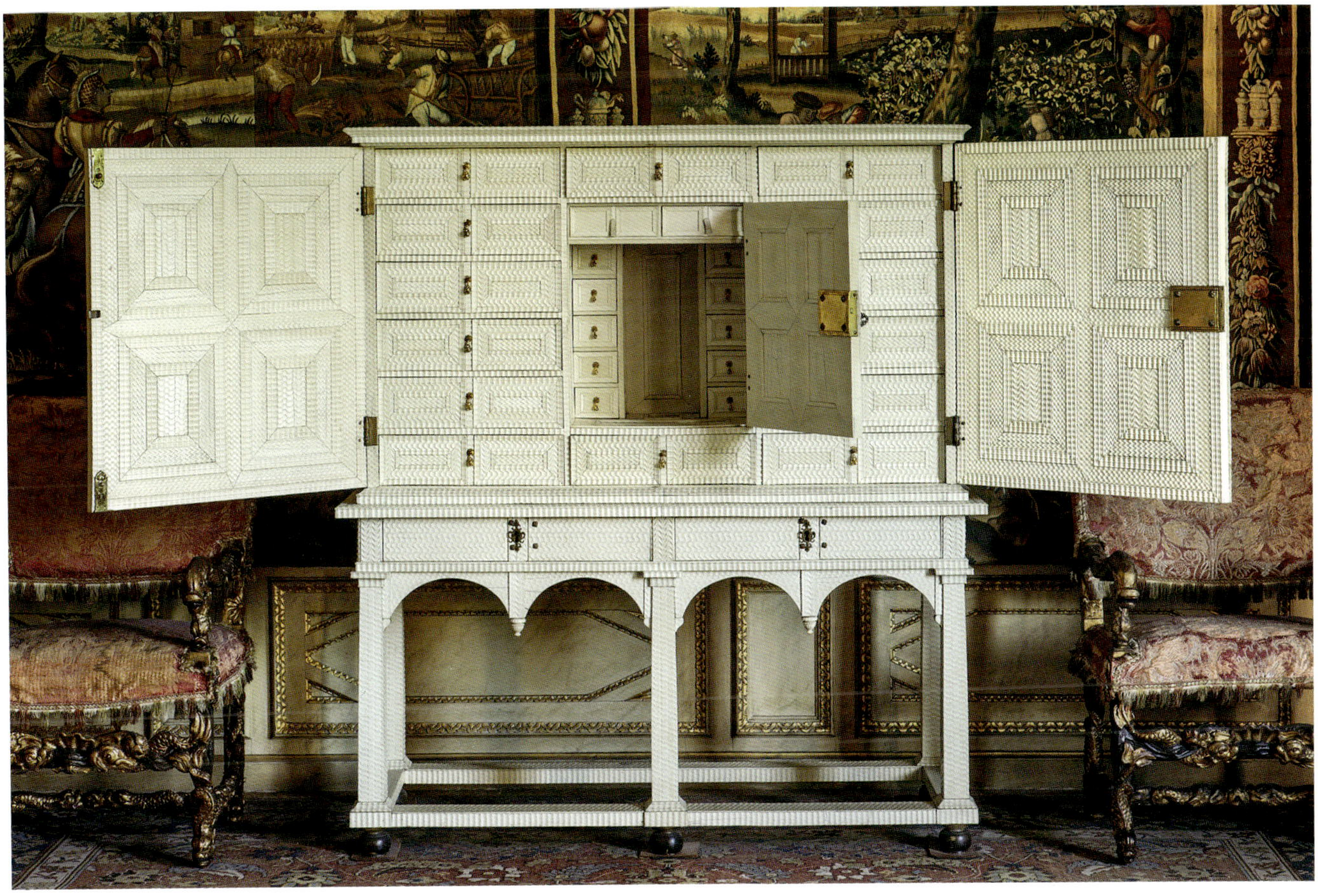

FIG. 81
The Hague (?), Cabinet on stand, *c.*1650–60
Oak veneered with ivory, 163 × 144.2 × 54 cm
The National Trust, Ham House, Surrey
(NT 1139080)

Oriental porcelain, carpets, lacquer and curiosities imported by the Dutch and British East India Companies created a craze for the Far East. These goods – loosely called 'Indian' – influenced the design of furniture, such as the 'Chinese' japanned chairs at Ham (*c.*1672–83; NT 1139867).[20] After the Glorious Revolution of 1688, Queen Mary II's love of oriental porcelain was shared by her friend Elizabeth Percy, Duchess of Somerset, who collected large blue-and-white Chinese covered jars[21] and displayed them on carved walnut stands of four different designs (*c.*1690; Petworth House, NT 483455, 485407, 485405, 485427), like the plainer equivalents at Hampton Court.[22] Dutch tulip vases, tiles (NT 452247)[23] and other forms of glazed earthenware or 'Delft' ware were also imported, such as those at Dyrham (NT 452205–6) and Erddig (NT 1145597).[24]

The Duchess of Somerset and her husband, John Seymour, the 'Proud' 6th Duke, transformed Petworth House into an English 'Versailles', employing in 1693 the Huguenot Daniel Marot, the architect of William III's Dutch royal hunting palace, Het Loo.[25] Grinling Gibbons, an Englishman born and trained in the Netherlands, was commissioned by the Somersets to produce his masterpiece, the so-called Carved Room (*c.*1692).[26] Originally, the room was half the

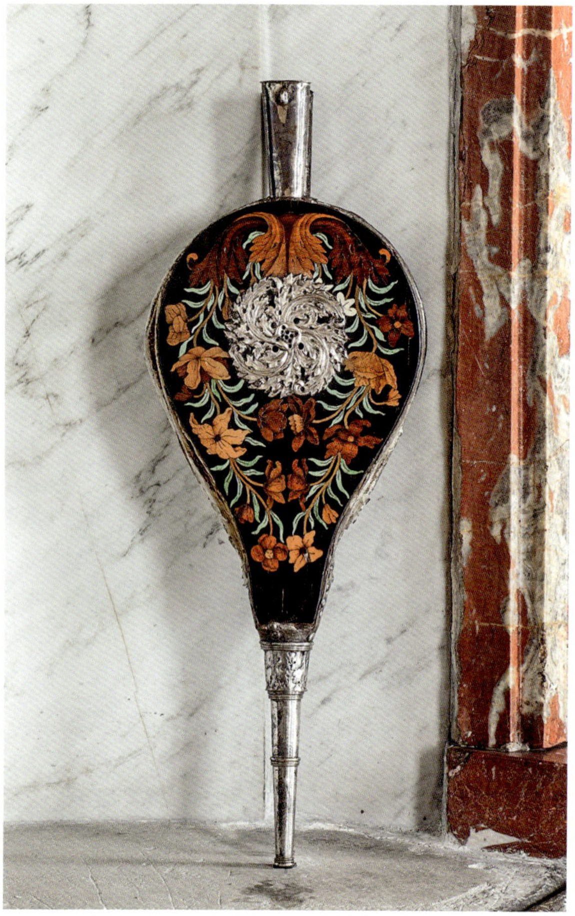

FIG. 82
Attrib. Gerrit Jensen (1634/5–1715)
Bellows, *c.*1673, wood marquetry mounted with silver, 53 × 17.5 cm, the pierced silver mount 5 cm diameter and marked *SS* for Steven Starling; the opposite side covered in silver relief
The National Trust, Ham House, Surrey (NT 1140041)

FIG. 83
Detail of the Carved Room at Petworth, *c.*1692, showing limewood carvings by Grinling Gibbons between the frames of a pair of full-length portraits by John Closterman
The National Trust, Petworth House, West Sussex

size, with the finest carvings displayed in a side light, incorporating crestings and drops around two pairs of full-length portraits (1692; NT 486184–85 and *c.*1615–20; NT 486187–88). The picture frames are hollowed out of the wood, defying the medium in airy filigree, while the crestings and drops encasing them are *tours de force* (fig. 83). The astonishing finesse of Gibbons's carvings was praised by Horace Walpole, who dubbed them 'the greatest monument of his skill'.[27]

Dutch-influenced interiors are also notable at Dyrham Park, which was built in the 1690s for the Dutch-speaking William Blathwayt (see pp. 16, 98–99 and 132–33, and cat. nos. 1 and 7). The entrance hall is lined with painted and gilded leather – of which an even grander polychrome fragment survives at Ham (Dutch, *c.*1675; NT 1140123) – a typical element of rich Dutch interiors.[28] Blathwayt acquired two panoramas by Samuel van Hoogstraten, one of which is a *trompe l'oeil* perspective dated 1662, which is set in a doorway to give the impression of rooms beyond (fig. 3, p. 17). This is truly Holland translated to England.

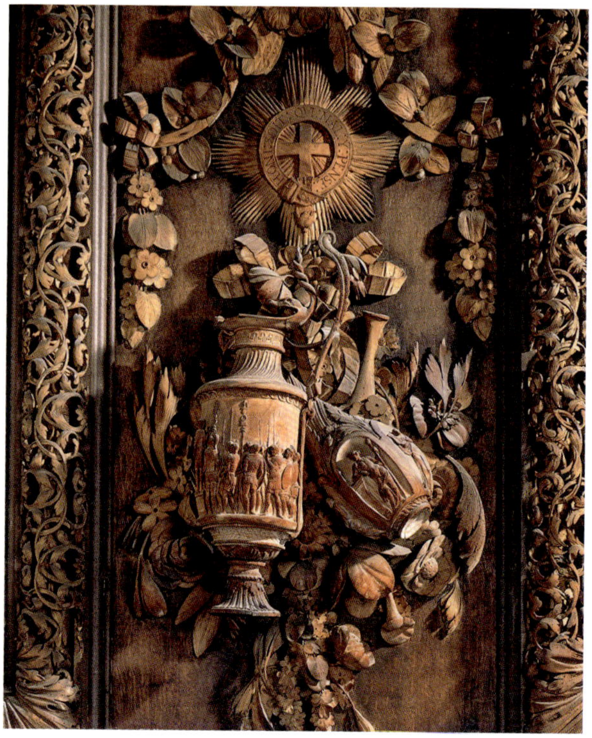

NOTES

1 Jervis 1998, pp. 42–44.

2 For Doomer, see Baarsen 1996, pp. 739–49, and Baarsen 2007, pp. 80–109.

3 For an account of the auricular style in Holland, see Baarsen 2007, pp. 124–45.

4 The foremost practitioner of these floral 'paintings' in mother-of-pearl, who may have worked for Doomer in this capacity, was Dirck van Rijswijk; see Baarsen 2007, pp. 106–09 and 192, fig. 160.

5 For the auricular frames in the Long Gallery at Ham, see J. Simon, 'Picture Framing at Ham in the Seventeenth Century', in Rowell 2013, pp. 144–57, and Simon 2014 (see also https://www.nationaltrust.org.uk/documents/picture-frames-at-ham-house.pdf).

6 For the remodelling of the Ham Gallery, see D. Adshead and C. Rowell, 'Seventeenth-Century Decorative Woodwork at Ham House', in Rowell 2013, pp. 81–82.

7 This portrait with its frame was presented in *c.*1638 by the king to his childhood friend, William Murray, later 1st Earl of Dysart, the owner of Ham House; see J. Simon in Rowell 2013, pp. 145–47, fig. 122, and Simon 2014, pp. 2 and 9.

8 See J. Simon in Rowell 2013, p. 155, fig. 138 and Simon 2014, pp. 24–25, and, for comparable Dutch equivalents around a pair of portraits by J. van der Stock, signed and dated 1676, see C.J. de Bruyn Kops in Van Thiel and De Bruyn Kops 1984, pp. 265–67, no. 75.

9 For the Green Closet see C. Rowell, 'The Green Closet at Ham House: A Charles I Cabinet Room and its Contents', in Rowell 2013, pp. 14–29.

10 Rowell 2013, p. 439.

11 Baarsen 1996 and R. Baarsen, 'Seventeenth-century European Cabinet-Making at Ham House', in Rowell 2013, pp. 194–203, at pp. 194–95 and figs. 182–83.

12 pp. 196–97 and figs. 184–85.

13 R. Baarsen in Rowell 2013, p. 197.

14 For paintings of Dutch interiors, see Fock 2001.

15 For details of Jensen's life, see Bowett and Lindey 2017, pp. 27–50.

16 Bowett 2014, pp. 103–18.

17 For the Knole set, see C. Rowell, 'Table, Mirror and Pair of Candlestands in the King's Bedchamber at Knole, Kent', in Snodin and Llewellyn 2009, p. 354, no. 166, pl. 5.74. It was made for Lady Frances Cranfield, widow of Lionel Sackville, 5th Earl of Dorset, and may bears her cipher *FCD* (Frances Cranfield Dorset). It is the sole complete set of silver mirror, table and candlestands to survive in Britain. Silver furniture was popularized by the mistresses of Charles II, being regarded as the ultimate in luxury, as at Ham; see Rowell 2013, pp. 123–24.

18 R. Baarsen in Rowell 2013, pp. 198–202.

19 T. Murdoch, 'From the Gate to the Hearth: Metalwork at Ham House', in Rowell 2013, pp. 232–47, at p. 235; the reverse of the bellows is covered in embossed silver: see ibid., fig. 222.

20 Rowell 2013, pp. 124–25 and figs. 109–10.

21 Lord Egremont Collection on loan to the National Trust; see Ferguson 2016, pp. 34–35 and 227.

22 Rowell 2012, p. 43.

23 A rare set of ceramic blue-and-white chinoiserie tile panels at Dyrham (fig. 73) were hung as pictures and retain their original, probably Dutch, black-and-gold japanned frames. The scenes are taken from Nieuhof 1665.

24 Ferguson 2016, pp. 50–51 and 228 (Dyrham tulip vases) and pp. 46–47 and 228 (Erddig garden pot).

25 For a general account of the patronage and collecting of the Duke and Duchess of Somerset, see Rowell 2012, pp. 34–49.

26 For the original Carved Room, see Esterly 1998, pp. 108–17, and Rowell 2000, pp. 19–26.

27 Walpole 1763, pp. 85–86. At Dunham Massey, the National Trust also owns Gibbons's *Deposition from the Cross* after Tintoretto (1671; NT 931239); see Esterly 1998, pp. 16–33 and figs. 7–8 and 11, and here p. 62.

28 C. Rowell, 'Leather Panels from the Marble Dining Room at Ham House', in Snodin and Llewellyn 2009, p. 352, no. 155, pl. 5.24.

17

FRANS POST (1612–1680)

A Village in Brazil, c.1675

Oil on panel, 19 × 24 cm
Signed lower right: *F. Post*
National Trust, Ham House, Surrey – The Dysart Collection (NT 1139908)

PROVENANCE
At Ham House by 1679; thence by descent; acquired by HM Government when Sir Lyonel Tollemache, 4th Baronet and Sir Cecil Tollemache, 5th Baronet gave Ham House to the National Trust in 1948; entrusted to the care of the Victoria and Albert Museum until 1990, when returned to the National Trust; ownership transferred to the National Trust in 2002

SELECTED LITERATURE
Do Lago 2007, p. 326, no. 145

In Dutch landscape painting of the Golden Age, we encounter not only motifs from the Dutch countryside, but also landscapes from beyond the borders of the United Provinces. Few artists travelled as far as the Haarlem landscape painter Frans Post. His life and work are closely bound up with his patron, Johan Maurits, Count of Nassau-Siegen (1604–1679), and hence with the origins of the Dutch colony on the north-east coast of Brazil. The Dutch seized the territory from the Portuguese in 1630 primarily for the sake of its lucrative sugar trade, since a large proportion of the sugar consumed in Europe at that time came from this region. To boost sugar production, the Dutch West India Company – a precursor of today's multinationals – appointed the successful young army officer Johan Maurits as governor general of the Dutch colony in Brazil in 1636. On 25 October of that year, the newly appointed 'governor, captain and Admiral-General' set sail for the West, where he ruled until 1644, having formed a European-style household. Johan Maurits did not view Brazil merely as a profitable dependency: he also found its population and its local plant and animal life endlessly fascinating. This explains why his retinue included not only soldiers but also natural scientists, cartographers and other researchers, and even artists, among whom were the young painters Albert Eckhout and Frans Post.[1] Never before had this part of South America been so thoroughly studied and documented. The landscapes Post made in Brazil between 1637 and 1644 – dated with the precision of Pieter Saenredam (see cat. 19), since a number of signatures include day, month and year – are the first views of the 'New World' by a European artist. The same applies to nine life-size figure pieces with prominent landscapes which Eckhout painted in the early 1640s.

The ambitious Johan Maurits used his unique collection, including the paintings he commissioned from Eckhout and Post, in a number of diplomatic 'gifts'. In accordance with the custom of the day, he always received something tangible in return. Some gifts were clearly intended to enhance his power and status, such as the twenty-one paintings by Eckhout (and three portraits attributed to him) that Johan Maurits presented to the Danish king in 1654 (now part of the collection of the Nationalmuseet, Copenhagen). On the other hand, his gift of forty-two paintings to Louis XIV seems to have been prompted by a lack of money. The gift to the French king included eighteen paintings Frans Post produced in Brazil, only seven of which are known today. His *View of the Island of Itamaracà* (fig. 84), dated 1637, is the earliest of the series.[2] This

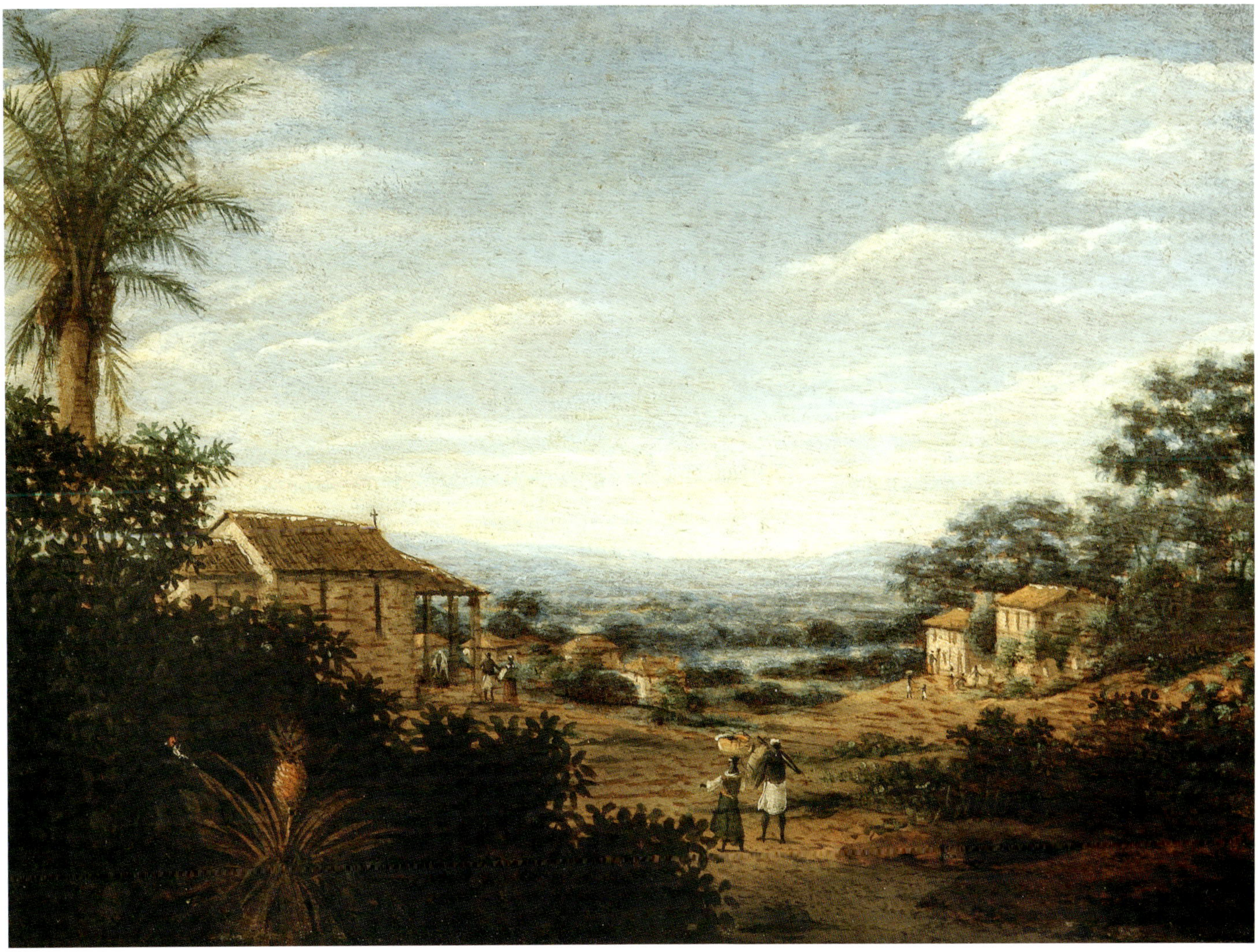

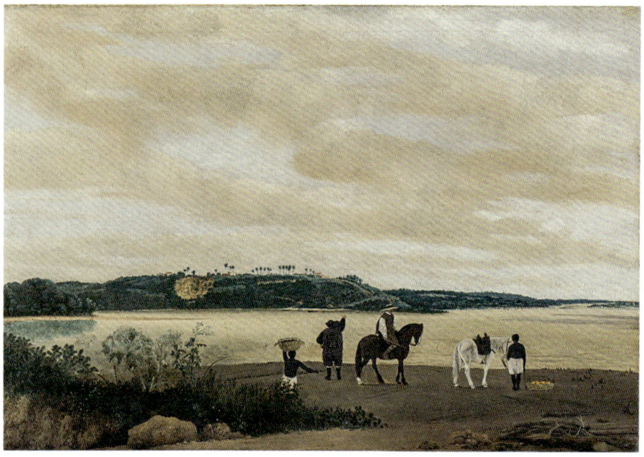

FIG. 84
Frans Post (1612–1680)
View of the Island of Itamaracà, 1637
Oil on canvas, 64 × 89 cm
The Hague, Mauritshuis (on loan from the Rijksmuseum, Amsterdam, since 1953) (915)

canvas, showing the stretch of the island that faces Rio Iguarassu, with Fort Orange and a few houses in the small town of Schoppe at far right, is characteristic of the first group of landscapes Post made in Brazil. The horizon is low, the landscape makes a flat impression, and water takes up much of the view. Only a few figures populate what is otherwise a largely empty scene, but they fulfil an essential role by intensifying the picture's air of barrenness. The seven paintings mentioned above are now in four different collections. During the upheavals of the French Revolution, the French royal collection suffered great losses, and several paintings that had belonged to the 1679 gift changed hands. *View of the Island of Itamaracà* of 1637 is now in the Mauritshuis, The Hague, on permanent loan from the Rijksmuseum in Amsterdam. The building that houses the Hague collection was commissioned by Count Johan Maurits in 1633 and designed by Jacob van Campen; perhaps it was Van Campen's assistant, Pieter Post, who introduced his brother Frans to the count.

Post's years in Brazil made such a lasting impression on him that he devoted himself exclusively to Brazilian landscapes for the rest of his life, working in his native city of Haarlem from the time of his return in about 1644 until his death in 1680. Besides documenting the local Brazilian topography, Post's work is characterised by an atmospheric quality and the spontaneous rendering of natural scenery. It can be assumed that he did not rely solely on his visual memory, but also used drawings he had made in Brazil, some of which were recently rediscovered.[3] The painter had a monopoly on views of Dutch Brazil, as the only trained artist besides Eckhout to have stayed there. His oeuvre numbers about two hundred paintings, around a quarter of which are now considered lost.[4] In Haarlem, Post abandoned his previous, somewhat monochrome tonality and turned instead to quite strong colours that greatly enhanced the appeal of his work (fig. 85).[5] These paintings were purchased by important collectors, including Stadholder Frederick Henry of Orange, who paid large sums of money for them. From about 1660 onwards, in his most prosperous period, Post started to place less emphasis on topographical accuracy and to wield his brush more loosely. The paintings made in the last ten years of his life attest to a decline in quality, evidently attributable to alcoholism, an affliction shared by other Dutch artists. It was even reported that Post experienced considerable trembling towards the end of his life.[6] His deteriorating health explains the lesser quality of *A Village in Brazil* at Ham House. Abrasion of the paint layers allows the grain of the wood to shine through the scene, which is among Post's last dozen works and was probably made around 1675. It shows some of the enslaved men and women whom the Dutch had taken from Africa to Brazil to work on the plantations and in the sugar mills.[7] The enslaved men and women who figure in nearly all of Post's paintings were no doubt part of the daily reality of the colony, where thousands of African men, women and children lived in slavery. To the left we see a small chapel with a portico bearing a cross (which appears

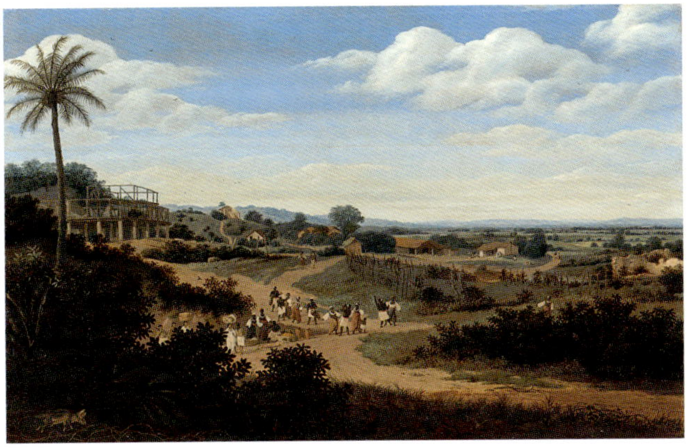

FIG. 85
Frans Post (1612–1680)
Brazilian Landscape with a House under Construction, *c.*1655–60
Oil on panel, 46 x 70 cm
The Hague, Mauritshuis, gift of Willem, Baron van Dedem to the Friends of the Mauritshuis Foundation, 2002 (1127)

in several other paintings by Post),[8] with small houses in the middle and two larger buildings at right. The *couleur locale* is determined by the palm tree to the left of the chapel and, at lower left, a pineapple plant on which a tropical bird perches.

This modest work is of great importance, not so much for its composition as for its very early and complete provenance. Its history can be traced back almost to the artist, which is exceptional for the paintings that Post produced for the free market. It was first described in the Private Closet of Elizabeth Murray, Countess of Dysart (see cat. nos. 2 and 12). In 1672 she married John Maitland, Duke of Lauderdale (see p. 58 and cat. 11), who had brought many paintings from his own collection to Ham House. An inventory drawn up in 1683 states that Post's panel was bought between 1677 and 1679, that is to say, during the painter's lifetime.[9] It is the oldest record of a painting by Post in England, where his work is still fairly rare.[10] The Royal Collection, however, has a prime example of Post's work, a painting that was acquired by King George III in 1762 as part of Joseph Smith's famous collection of pictures.[11] Like the paintings by Post that ended up in the Louvre as a result of Johan Maurits's 1679 gift, the small painting at Ham House has not left its original home for more than 330 years (see cat. 4).[12] QB

NOTES

1 Buvelot *et al.* 2004.
2 Corrêa do Lago 2007, no. 1; regarding the gift to Louis XIV, see Corrêa do Lago 2005.
3 De Bruin 2016.
4 Corrêa do Lago 2007, nos. 1–55, with additions in Buvelot 2008, pp. 116–17.
5 Corrêa do Lago 2007, no. 42.
6 Corrêa do Lago 2007, p. 80.
7 The Mauritshuis is preparing a major research project on Johan Maurits's governorship of the Dutch colony in Brazil, focusing on the history of slavery in Dutch Brazil and on Johan Maurits's reputation in his own time.
8 For example, Corrêa do Lago 2007, no. 146; see also ibid., p. 306.
9 Corrêa do Lago 2007, p. 145. As early as 1683, the painting was inventoried under another name in 'An Estimate of Pictures in Ham-house' (The Tollemache Papers, Buckminster Estate Office, MSS, no. 361): '33. An Indian Landskip of Dewit'. The number 33 is recorded on the back of the panel. Another inventory drawn up in that year does in fact mention Post as the author. See A. Laing, 'Appendix 2: Fitting Pictures to Rooms: A Re-Examination of the Ham House 'Estimate of Pictures' (*c.*1683), and its Collation with the Inventories', in Rowell 2013, p. 411.
10 Corrêa do Lago 2007, p. 339. The National Gallery, London, has a work by Post on loan from the Rijksmuseum, Amsterdam (ibid., no. 125).
11 Corrêa do Lago 2007, no. 18.
12 The seventeenth-century frame of ebonized wood and ebony veneer is probably original.

18

REMBRANDT VAN RIJN (1606–1669)

Self-portrait, Wearing a Feathered Bonnet, 1635

Oil on poplar panel, 91.2 × 71.9 cm
Signed and dated lower right: *Rembrant/ f. 1635*
National Trust, Buckland Abbey, Devon – The Samuel Collection (NT 810136)

PROVENANCE

Possibly in the collection of Baron von Eck und Hungerbach until 1679; acquired by Prince Joseph Wenzel I of Liechtenstein, Vienna, by 1767; by descent to the Princes of Liechtenstein, Vaduz, until at least 1948; with Edward Speelman, London, 1960s; Harold, Baron Samuel of Wych Cross; acquired by the National Trust as a gift from the estate of the Edna, Lady Samuel of Wych Cross in 2010

EXHIBITED

Rembrandt Revealed, Buckland Abbey, Devon (2014–15); *Am I Rembrandt?*, Dulwich Picture Gallery (2016–17)

SELECTED LITERATURE

Vosmaer 1868, p. 508; Bode 1883 , pp. 411, 576, no. 131; Dutuit 1881–85, III, p. 50, no. 141; von Wurzbach 1886, no. 26; Michel 1893, pp. 215, 560; Bode and de Groot 1898–1900, III (1899), no. 168; Moes 1897–1905, no. 6693, p. 33; de Groot 1907–28, VI, 1916, no. 584, pp. 285–86; Valentier 1908, p. 150, no. 174; Bredius 1935, no. 25; Gerson 1968, no. 171; Lecaldano 1969, p. 103, no. 164; Tümpel 1986, no. A 64; Bruyn *et al.* 1989, III, no. C 92; Slatkes, 1992, p. 378, no. 251; Wright 1982, no. 24, p. 41, pl. 51; Van de Wetering 2005, IV, p. 234; Duffy-Zebellos and Fletcher 2014, pp. 32–39; Van de Wetering 2014, pp. 545–46, no. 134

This portrait of Rembrandt was signed and dated *1635* by the celebrated artist the year he and his wife, Saskia van Uylenburgh, moved to the fashionable Nieuwe Doelenstraat in Amsterdam. By the mid-1630s Rembrandt was running a successful, in which some of his assistants worked on copying his self-portraits. This led to confusion about the authorship of the Buckland picture, previously attributed to Govaert Flinck, a prized pupil of the master. The present work, however, is visually typical of Rembrandt's self-portraits of the mid-1630s – painted during this period of wealth and acclaim, before financial strains and family losses would reveal a heartbreaking melancholy about the sitter's face in later self-portraits.

The picture was bought by the property developer and philanthropist Harold, Baron Samuel of Wych Cross (1912–1987), who left the majority of his important Dutch and Flemish picture collection to the City of London, where it can be seen in the Mansion House, cared for the by the Guildhall Museum and Art Gallery. Of the remainder of the collection, a provision of the will of Samuel's widow, Edna Nedis, Lady Samuel (1918–2008), left three pictures to the National Trust and two others were accepted by the British Government in lieu of inheritance tax, transferred to the National Trust and allocated directly to Buckland in 2010. The pictures accepted in lieu were Willem van de Velde the Younger's *Dutch Shipping in a Heavy Swell with a Small Hoeker* and *A Dutch Three-Master and a Boier in Stormy Weather*, and the pictures donated were the Flemish painter David Teniers the Younger's *Peasants Dancing outside a Tavern,* the Haarlem painter Adriaen van Ostade's *Interior of an Inn*, and the portrait of Rembrandt, thought to be by one of his students until its recent rediscovery as an autograph self-portrait and subsequent addition to the large group of approximately forty pictures he painted of himself.[1]

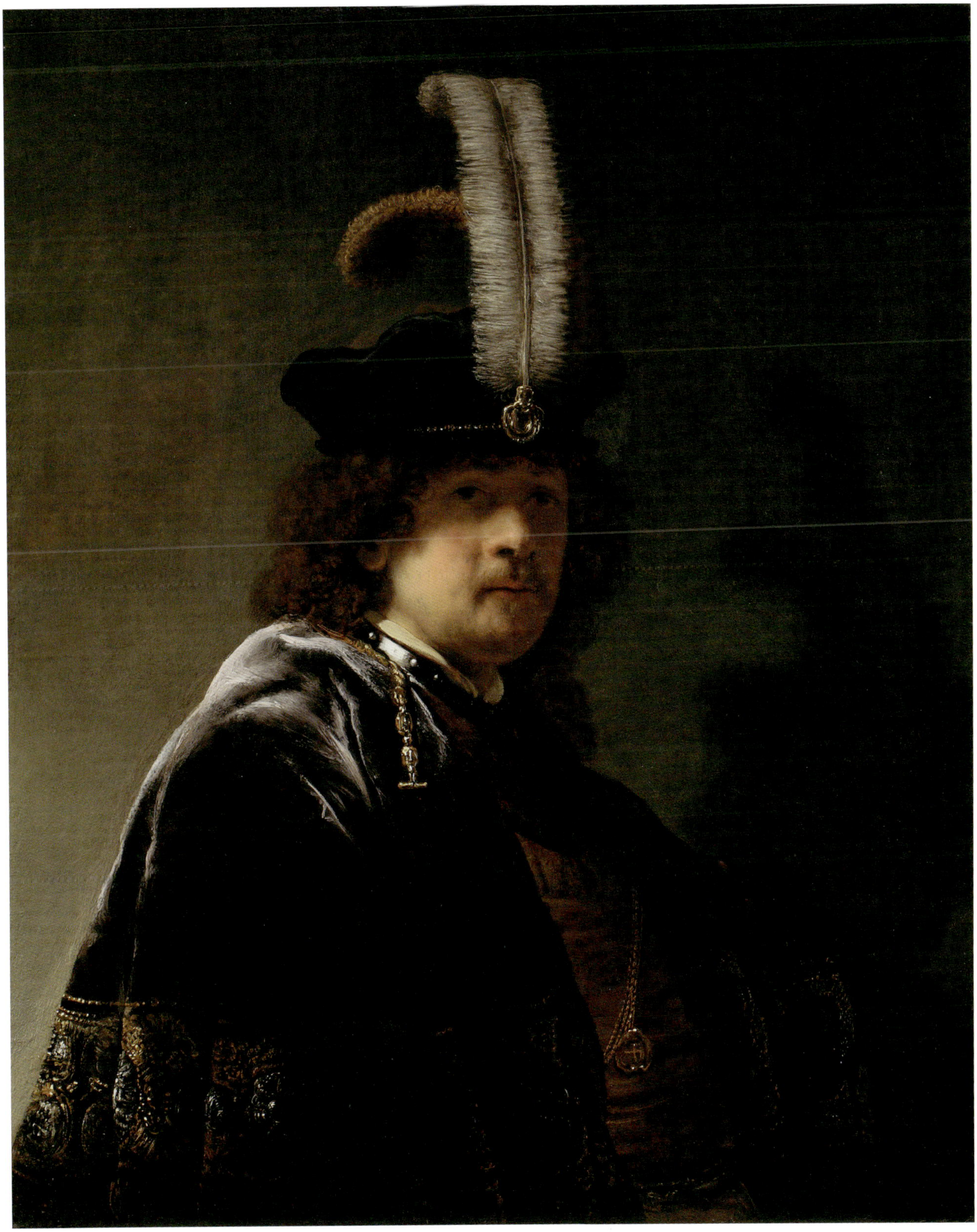

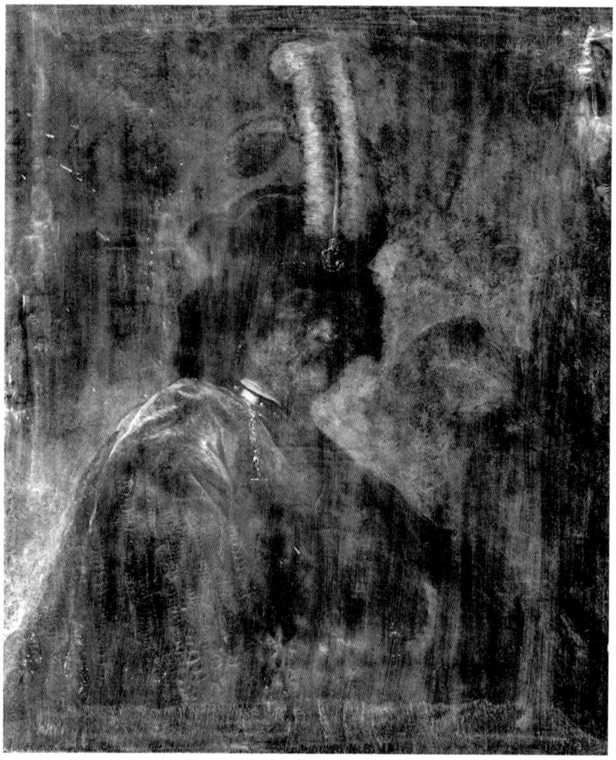

X-ray of cat. 18

In the eighteenth century the portrait was in the collection of the Princes of Liechtenstein. It was kept in Vienna until the annexation of Austria into Nazi Germany in 1938, after which it was transferred with other works of art from the collection to the family's castle at Vaduz in Liechtenstein, where it remained until at least 1948. At some point after that it was sold, and it was subsequently with the London picture dealer Edward Speelman, in the 1960s, from whom Lord Samuel bought it.

While the picture is one of Rembrandt's many self-portraits painted over his long career, it is also an example of a *tronie*, a popular type of figurative painting that depicted people in costume, playing some sort of role, pulling faces or revealing human emotions, or appearing as stock characters such as an old man or a young maid. As opposed to sitters in a true portrait, in a *tronie* 'the identity of the sitter appears to have been of secondary importance'.[2]

Rembrandt's fanciful costume is meant to appear as generically old-fashioned, rather than identifying him as playing a particular role, and as such it gives the self-portrait an air of timelessness, although his old-fashioned velvet bonnet, decorated with large ostrich feathers, is reminiscent of the sixteenth century. He also wears a gorget, a piece from a suit of armour used for protecting the wearer's throat, although he is not necessarily meant to be playing the role of a soldier – nor is he meant to be a member of a *schutterij*, or civic guard, who sometimes wore gorgets as part of their dress (Rembrandt's 1656 inventory shows that he owned a gorget, which he used as a studio prop).

In the portrait Rembrandt wears lovelocks, a particularly aristocratic fashion for growing a long lock of hair down one side of the face, something that there is no evidence for the artist doing. Rembrandt instead presents himself as an unidentifiable character, gazing out at the viewer with his arms akimbo. The left arm jutting out towards the viewer, as well as the gorget and the feathered hat, can all be seen in other works by Rembrandt from around this time, including the 1634 etching *Self-portrait with Plumed Cap and Saber* (Rijksmuseum, Amsterdam) and in the 1636 painting *The Standard Bearer* (private collection), suggesting the artists was pleased with the appearance of this particular pose.[3]

The representation of Rembrandt in the Buckland picture can also be seen reproduced in etchings the artist made for his 1634 grisaille painting *Ecce Homo*, or *Christ before Pilate* (National Gallery, London), and it was copied by other artists, appearing as a drawing amongst other objects on a table in the Dordrecht

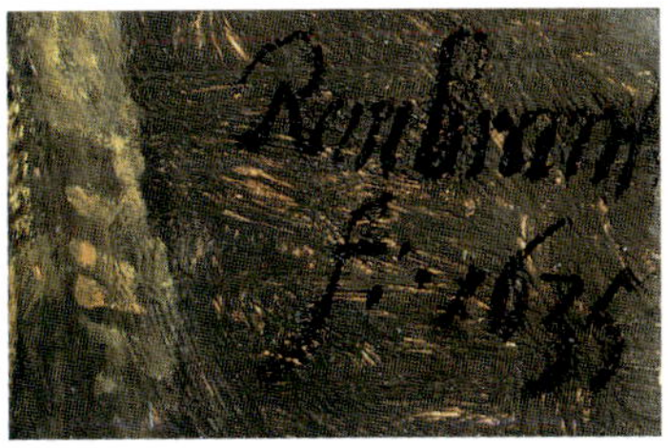

Signed and dated: *Rembrant f. 1635*

painter Abraham Susenier's *Vanitas Still Life with a Skull, Feathers, an Overturned Rummer, a Sculpture and a Portfolio of Drawings* (private collection), or in a 1791 mezzotint by Johann Peter Pichler.

TECHNICAL ANALYSIS

The possibility that the portrait was painted by Rembrandt himself was suggested by Professor Ernst van de Wetering, who had seen the painting previously as part of the Rembrandt Research Project. The Research Project team had decided that the painting was most likely to have been painted by one of his pupils. Subsequently, however, a greater understanding of Rembrandt's self-portraits and advances in technical analysis led to further consideration of its attribution, and Van de Wetering encouraged the National Trust to clean the painting and undertake technical research to identify the type of wood, the materials and technique, the authenticity of the signature, clarification of certain aspects of the earlier x-ray and any evidence from infra-photography related to changes in the development of the painting.

Microscopic examination of the cell structure of thin wood sections identified the timber panel as a member of poplar/willow group *Salicaceae*.[4] Whilst oak was the more common panel material, there are at least seven known paintings by Rembrandt on poplar.[5] Paint analysis and XRF (x-ray fluorescence) concurred that the pigments were typical of Rembrandt's palette. Paint analysis also confirmed that the signature and date were contemporary and not added at a later date.

The x-ray image proved most interesting, as it clearly revealed Rembrandt's alterations discerned by Van de Wetering in an earlier x-ray. In the current x-ray, the presence of a white cuff indicates that he may have originally intended to have his proper left sleeve visible, with his hand hidden under the cloak. The infra-red photograph showed areas of reserve above the bonnet and along its proper left side.[6]

After the conservation treatment, a slight circular impression in the paint layer in the lower right corner was clearly visible. Correspondence with the Liechtenstein Princely Collections confirmed that this was likely to be from the Liechtenstein seal of 1733, now lost but affirming the painting's provenance to the collection. DT & CS

NOTES

1 Discussed in Van de Wetering 2014, pp. 545–46, no. 134.
2 De Winkel 2006, p. 137.
3 See Berger, Jr. 2000, pp. 282–84.
4 Ian Tyers, 'Wood identification of a panel painting: Self Portrait with a White Feathered Bonnet, Rembrandt', *Dendro-Chronological Consultancy Report 668*, January 2014.
5 Written communication between Porfessor Ernst van de Wtering and Christine Slottved Kimbriel (Hamilton Kerr Institute), 2014.
6 Technical analysis undertaken by the Hamilton Kerr Institute and the National Gallery, London.

Prints

DAVID A.H.B. TAYLOR, NATIONAL TRUST CURATOR OF PICTURES AND SCULPTURE

The National Trust's collection includes a huge number of works on paper, many of which were made by Dutch artists working in Britain in the seventeenth century, responding to this prolific period of artistic output in the British Isles and demonstrating the rise in print culture in the British Isles. These engravers and mezzotinters often reproduced painted portraits in printed form, thus satisfying an eager market for images of famous men and women, which were collected for various reasons, ranging from displaying connoisseurial tastes to showing allegiance towards the sitter in the portraits. Engraved copies of portraits became increasingly popular in the seventeenth century, and they were a commodity that could be acquired across the social classes, including simpler versions of such copies that were sold cheaply.

Some paintings in the Trust's collection have likewise been the source for printed reproductions. Through this medium paintings became widely disseminated as images, increasing the fame of the picture and the original artist, as prints were cheaper and easier to produce (once the plate had been prepared). In the late seventeenth century there was a great fashion for engraved views of country houses and estates.

The portraits of celebrated royal, political and religious figures became highly sought after. One such figure was the young Charles II (1630–1685) during the years of the Commonwealth when his restoration to the throne was hoped for by many, but was by no means a foregone conclusion. As such Charles's portrait was produced in huge numbers, not least as prints after painted portraits. One such portrait, by the Dutch artist Gerrit van Honthorst (see cat. 9), was painted in The Hague while Charles was in exile there (fig. 86). It probably shows Charles as Prince of Wales when he arrived in the city in 1648, before news of his father Charles I's execution the next year had reached the Continent. The portrait was probably painted in Honthorst's studio and it appears have been a commission from Charles's aunt, Elizabeth Stuart, Queen of Bohemia (see cat. 9), who left it, amongst other pictures, to William Craven, 1st Earl of Craven (see p. 104). It stayed in the Craven collection, by descent, whence it was acquired by HM Treasury and transferred to the National Trust in 1968, and it is now on display at Ashdown House, Oxfordshire.

The portrait shows the king in armour, holding a commander's baton, and it serves to provide a very positive image of the exiled Charles for those wanting to see the Stuart monarchy restored. Accordingly, there was great currency in the reproduction of the portrait – various painted copies were made, but it was easier to reproduce in printed form.[1] A particularly fine head-and-shoulders version was engraved in 1650, once Charles had (in name) become king, by Cornelis de Visscher (fig. 87), a celebrated portrait draughtsman and engraver from Haarlem, who, despite dying in his thirties, produced over two hundred engravings. His superb engraving of Charles includes his titles as king (albeit in exile) in a Latin inscription, reminding viewers of his right to rule. The inscription also includes the words '*cum privilegio*', which reveals that it was produced with Charles's consent, thus making it an official, authorised image of the king in waiting.

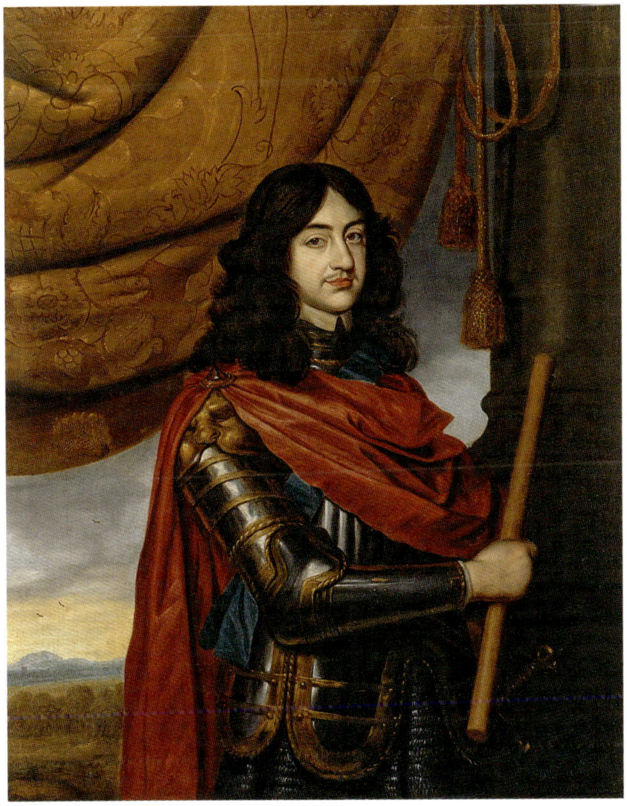

FIG. 86
Studio of Gerrit van Honthorst (1592–1656)
Charles II, as Prince of Wales, *c.*1648
Oil on canvas, 120.7 × 95 cm
National Trust, Ashdown House, Oxfordshire
(NT 493059)

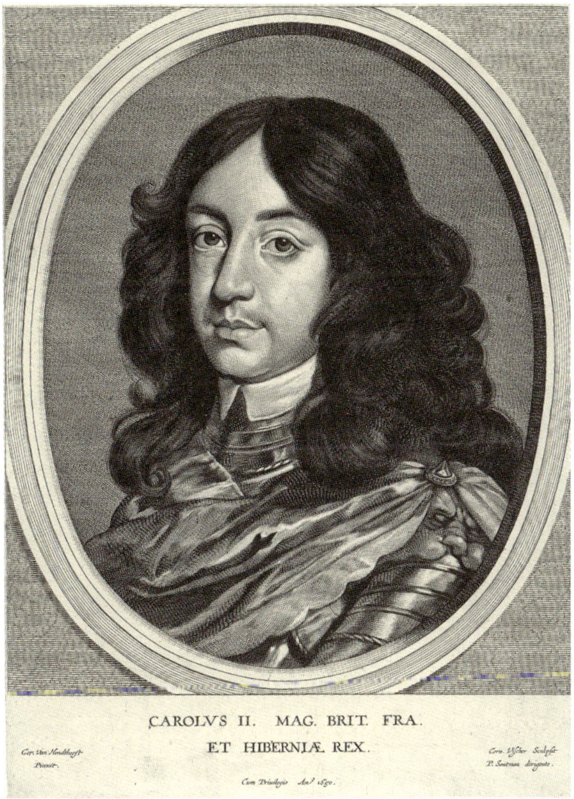

FIG. 87
Cornelis Visscher (1529–1558)
after Gerrit van Honthorst (1592–1656)
Charles II, 1650
Line engraving on paper, 355.6 × 292.1 mm
National Galleries of Scotland (SP II 21.18)

One form of printmaking that became an English speciality was the mezzotint, a type of printmaking produced by working over a copperplate with a toothed tool called a rocker to roughen the surface of the plate, which would then be polished in areas to create an image. The result was a watery effect, quite unlike line engraving, making it ideal for recreating the half tones of skin when copying painted portraits, and it enabled mezzotinters to modernise the reproduction of painted portraits in England.

Prince Rupert (see cat. 22), who 'in the Netherlands ... was trained in etching, like many children of the nobility at this time',[2] practised mezzotinting and championed the art form in England, where he produced the famous *Little Executioner* in 1662,[3] but the best mezzotinter in London was the Dutch artist Abraham Blooteling. He came to England in the period following the Anglo-Dutch Wars when there was an influx of Dutch artists to the British Isles, including the Van de Velde family of seascape painters (see cat. 21). He was apparently invited to England in 1673 by Prince Rupert, and he arrived with his student and brother-in-law Gerard Valck. Eventually he split his time between London and Amsterdam, and worked as a publisher as well as an engraver. During his career he produced some of the finest printed reproductions of painted

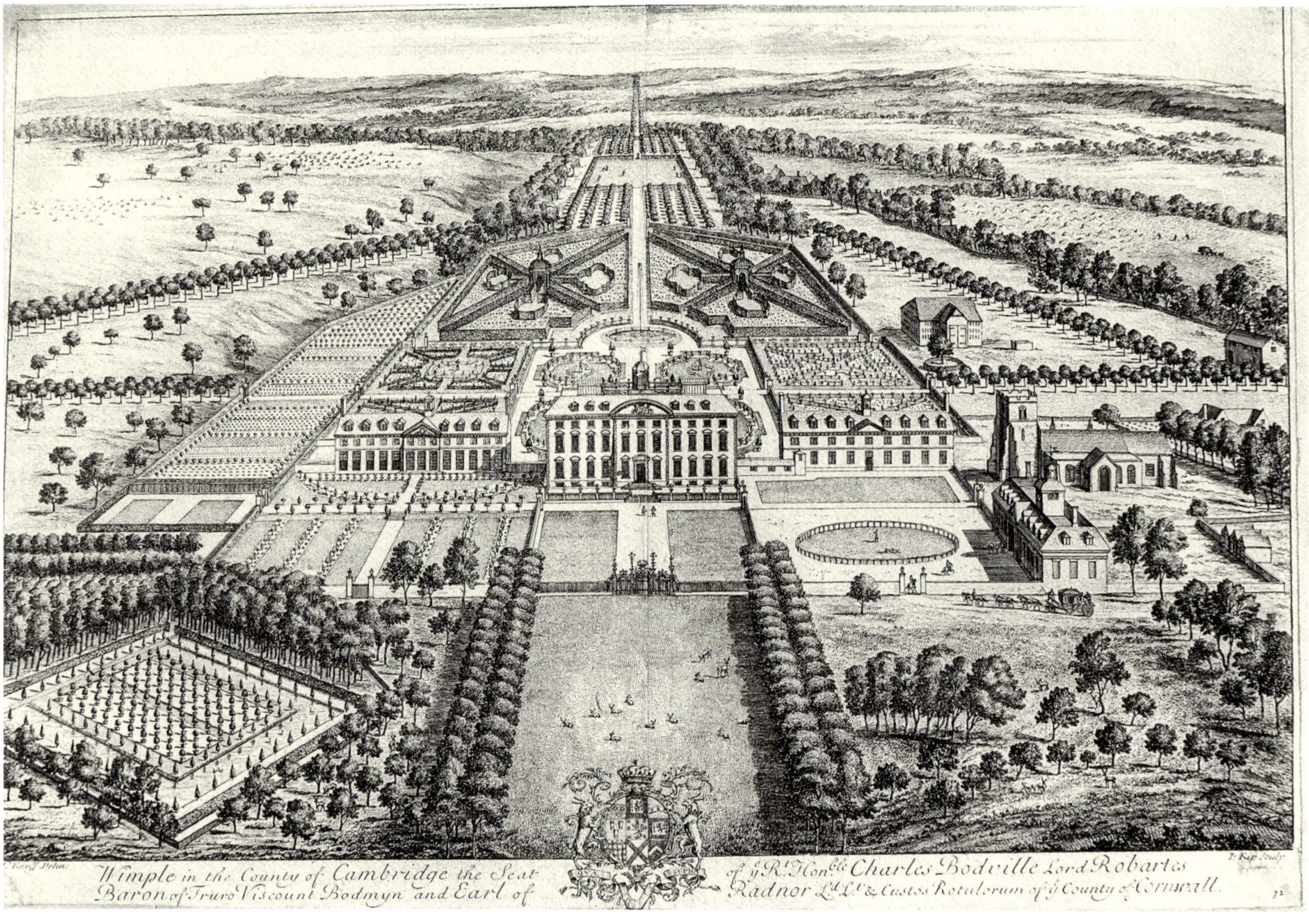

portraits ever seen in England, including large-scale images of the king and other members of the royal family. He was consequently held in high regard, and worked closely with Peter Lely (see cat. 12), who had also encouraged the younger artist to come to England in order to reproduce his works. This transactional relationship meant that Blooteling's fame in England was assured by copying the images of the most celebrated sitters that Lely, the king's official painter, painted; Lely's portraits were, in turn, seen by a larger audience than just his rich patrons and their circles.

An example of Blooteling's mezzotint of Prince Rupert is at Moseley Old Hall in Staffordshire (NT 477191); another, an engraving of Charles II's illegitimate son James Scott, Duke of Monmouth and Buccleuch (1649–1685) is at Fenton House in London (NT 1448630), and an engraving of Edward Stillingfleet, Bishop of Worcester (1635–1699), is at Felbrigg in Norfolk (NT 1396990). A rarer example of one of Blooteling's non-portrait engravings is the print after Jacob Jordaens's *Childhood of Jupiter*, at Calke Abbey in Derbyshire (NT 286596).[4]

While portraits dominated the print market in England after the Restoration, other genres were reproduced, including satirical prints, images of natural history, and landscapes. The type of combined landscape and architectural view that depicted aristocratic country houses within their estates became highly fashionable towards the end of the seventeenth century and into the next. The best-known artists

FIG. 88
Johannes Kip (*c.*1653–1722)
View of Wimpole Hall, Cambridgeshire, 1707
Engraving on paper, 342 × 485 mm
National Trust, Wimpole, Cambridgeshire
(NT 206324)

producing such works in England were the Dutch draughtsman and painter Leendert Knyff and his fellow-countryman the engraver Johannes Kip, who had travelled to England to work after the Glorious Revolution. They collaborated on a number of works, specialising in topographical bird's-eye views of palaces and country houses and their gardens.

In 1707 they published the monumental *Britannia Illustrata* (or *Views of Several of the Queens Palaces also of the Principal Seats of the Nobility and Gentry of Great Britain*), a survey of country houses comprising eighty such images, engraved by Kip after drawings by Knyff. It includes one of Wimpole Hall in Cambridgeshire (fig. 88), which was bequeathed to the National Trust by the owner, Elsie Bambridge, in 1976.[5] These large, detailed, fold-out folio illustrations reveal the developing taste for formal gardens in England, including those influenced by Dutch antecedents following the assumption of the throne by William III and Mary II. They also provide an insightful visual record for viewers in the twenty-first century, showing lost houses and gardens, seen from the air, and for imagining building schemes that were never realised. The engraving of Wimpole, for example, includes a new design scheme for the house, possibly by Christopher Wren, that was intended but never built. As a record 'it is vital to an understanding of the evolution of the house, gardens, and surrounding landscape .... Kip's engraved view is our only visual key to the cumulative improvements by successive owners.'[6]

NOTES

1 Honthorst painted two portrait 'types' of Charles II: painted copies of the Ashdown House type include one in the Warwick County Council collection and a head-and-shoulder version in the Bayerische Staatsgemäldesammlungen–Alte Pinakothek, Munich (no. 3902).
2 Griffiths 1998, no. 142, p. 211.
3 British Museum, 1849,1003.134.
4 The original Jordaens picture is in the Louvre (inv. 1405).
5 *Britannia Illustrata* was commissioned and sold by the London bookseller David Mortier (1673–1728), who was also Dutch.
6 Adshead 2007, p. 17, no. 3.

19

PIETER SAENREDAM (1597–1665)

Interior of the Church of St Catherine, Utrecht, c.1660

Oil on panel, 117 × 96 cm
National Trust, Upton House, Warwickshire – The Bearsted Collection (NT446733)

PROVENANCE
Johan Steyn sale, Haarlem, 28 April 1711, lot 14; Vincent van der Vinne sale, Haarlem, 29 March 1775, lot 86; sale Drouot, Paris, 9 February 1928, lot 46; thence with W.E. Duits, Amsterdam, and Jacques Goudstikker, Amsterdam; acquired there by Walter Samuel, 2nd Viscount Bearsted by 1929; given by him to the National Trust in 1948

EXHIBITED
The Bearsted Collection, Whitechapel Gallery, London, 1955, no. 24; *Saenredam: La fachada occidental de la iglesia de Santa Maria de Utrecht*, Museo Thyssen-Bornemisza, Madrid, 2008–09, no. 10

SELECTED LITERATURE
Schwartz and Bok 1989, p. 276, no. 130; Q. Buvelot in Buvelot and Buijs 2002, p. 132; G. van Heemstra, 'The Upton House Saenredam: Conservation and Technique', in Van Asperen de Boer and Helmus 2000, pp. 88–103; Van Heemstra and Marchant 2000, pp. 69–88; L.M. Helmus in Helmus *et al.* 2000–01, pp. 273–75, no. 64; Helmus *et al.* 2002, pp. 273–75, no. 64; Helmus and Wuestman 2008–09, p. 70, no. 10

Pieter Saenredam spent his entire working life in Haarlem, where he enrolled as a master in the local painters' guild in 1623. Although he also painted a few exteriors of churches (and occasionally other old buildings), he focused mainly on church interiors.[1] His earliest exploration of this genre is a design of 1627 for a print by Jan van de Velde the Younger, which was published the following year in Ampzing's description of the city of Haarlem. In 1628 Saenredam also completed his first painting of a church interior, that of the church of St Bavo in Haarlem (Los Angeles, The J. Paul Getty Museum).[2] It was possibly his contemporary and friend Jacob van Campen – designer of buildings in classicist style, such as the Mauritshuis in The Hague (fig. 99, p. 183) and the Royal Palace in Dam Square in Amsterdam – who stimulated Saenredam to make countless, mostly true-to-life depictions of Romanesque and Gothic churches.[3] This painter-architect had also contributed to Ampzing's 1628 publication and had painted Saenredam's portrait that same year. Interestingly, the only 'modern' or contemporary church that Saenredam portrayed was the New Church (Nieuwe Kerk) in Haarlem, which Van Campen designed. Saenredam's teacher in the field of perspective was most likely the surveyor Jan Wils, though Van Campen must also have taught him a thing or two in this regard.

Starting in 1632, Saenredam undertook a number of study trips to various Dutch cities, including an extended stay in Utrecht in 1636, when Haarlem was struck by a plague epidemic. It was in this period that he documented the interior of many old churches in Utrecht in a large number of drawings that reveal his exactitude, devotion and seriousness.[4] One of the churches Saenredam visited in Utrecht was the church of St Catherine; this convent church, built by the Carmelites from 1468 onwards, is still standing. The turbulent history of the church includes a time, after the Reformation, when it was used for secular purposes, even to quarter soldiers. A Scottish-English congregation worshipped in the building from 1622 to 1625, then, after its refurbishment as a church in 1635–36, services were held there for members of the Dutch Reformed Church, starting in June 1636.

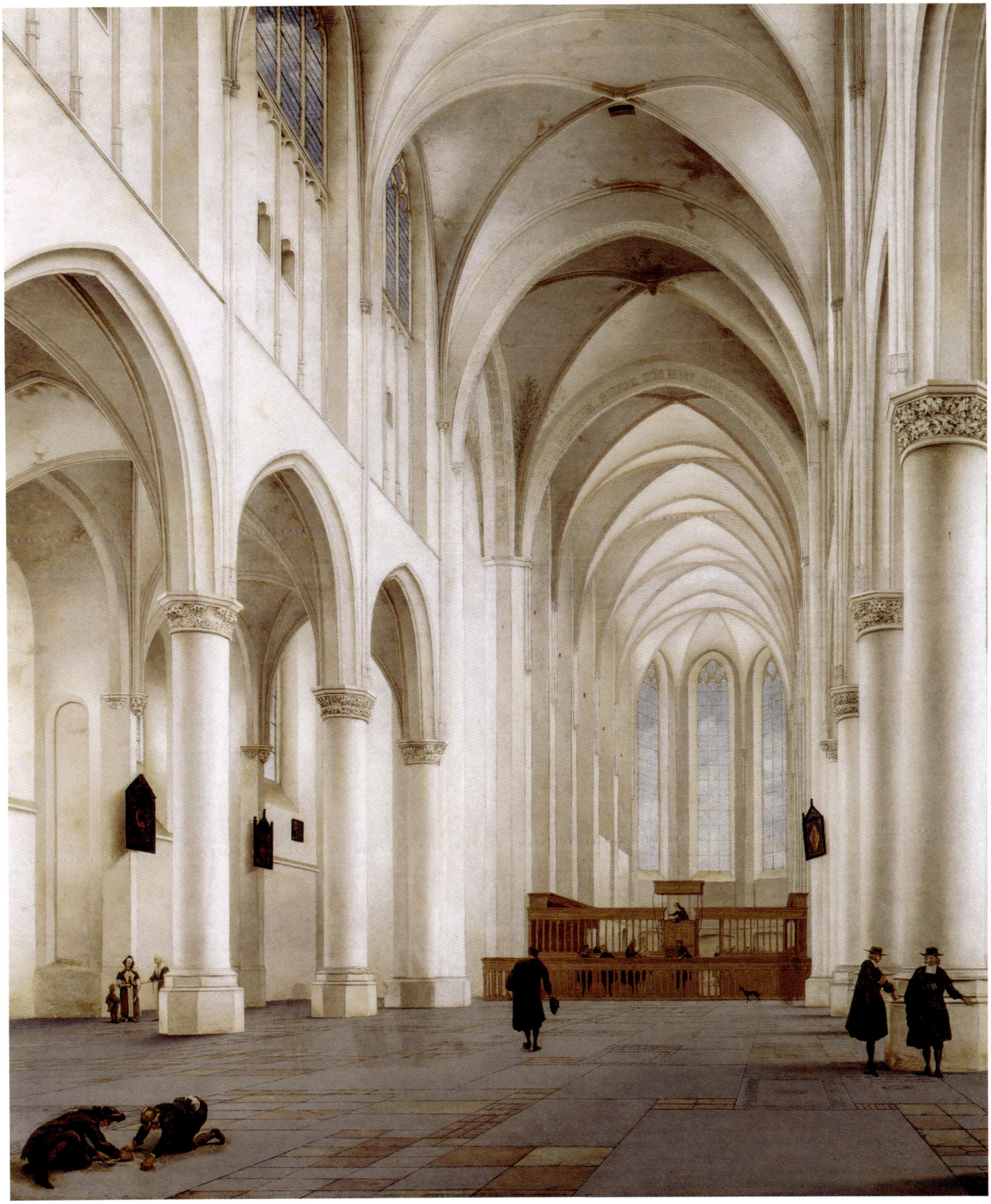

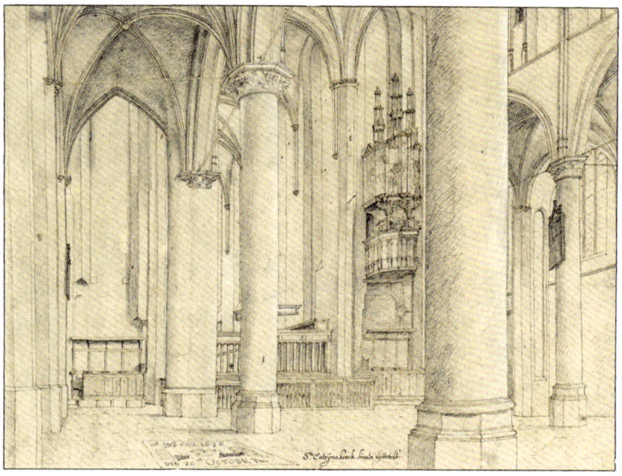

FIG. 89
Pieter Saenredam (1597–1665)
Interior of the Church of St Catherine, Utrecht,
2 October 1636
Pen and brown ink, black chalk, washed, graphite, 378 × 507 mm
Utrecht, Het Utrechts Archief
(28599)

Several months later, Saenredam made drawings of the interior, three of which survive. The artist was a very meticulous person with a painstaking and precise working method, and he almost always dated his on-site sketches. Two of the three sheets are dated 2 October 1636 and 20 October 1636, respectively (figs. 89 and 90). The third sheet, containing a study of the transept of the church, must also have originated during this period.[5] Only much later in his career, however, did Saenredam produce the present painting of the nave and choir of the church of St Catherine, which is one of his larger panels and the only painting he made of this church. Although it is neither signed nor dated, the attribution to Saenredam has never been in doubt.

On grounds of style and dendrochronological evidence, the painting cannot have originated before *c.*1660 and therefore must date from the last years of Saenredam's life.[6] It is based largely on the sketch made on 20 October 1636, preserved in the Utrecht archives (fig. 90).[7] Saenredam transformed the horizontal format of the drawing into a vertical format for the painting. To realise this, he omitted the pillar at far right, consequently doing away with most of the view of the right aisle. This meant that the choir was no longer in the centre of the composition, but to the right of middle, giving rise to an ingenious composition which, compared with the drawing, has gained much in terms of persuasiveness and spatial coherence. The latter quality is due in part to the church's beautiful floor, which is not depicted in the drawing but playfully executed in the painting. In the midst of the dominant grey of the floor tiles and tombstones, Saenredam's characteristic light grey and light pink tones catch the eye. This passage could almost be seen as a harbinger of modern, abstract painting. The command of the brush and the tonality of the subdued palette testify to the great artistry of this painter, whose extremely evocative church interiors reveal, on closer inspection, countless subtle details, even in the whitewashed walls and pillars. Whereas some passages display opaque layers of paint, others are more transparent, allowing the warm tone of the panel to influence the viewer's perception of the painting.[8] The most colourful passages are formed here by the blue of the partly cloudy sky, which is visible through the windows of the nave and the choir. For the blue Saenredam used costly ultramarine, a pigment obtained from lapis lazuli, a semi-precious stone.[9] At the height of the window at far left is a striking detail, a pigeon perched on the edge of the triforium; this rather inconspicuous bird is already present in the preparatory study mentioned above. This sheet also contains a Latin text, still in situ in the church, on which Saenredam based the inscription he painted on the triumphal arch above the choir screen, which states that the vault of the choir was completed in 1524.[10]

Quite a bit is known about the genesis of this painting: for example, infrared reflectography has

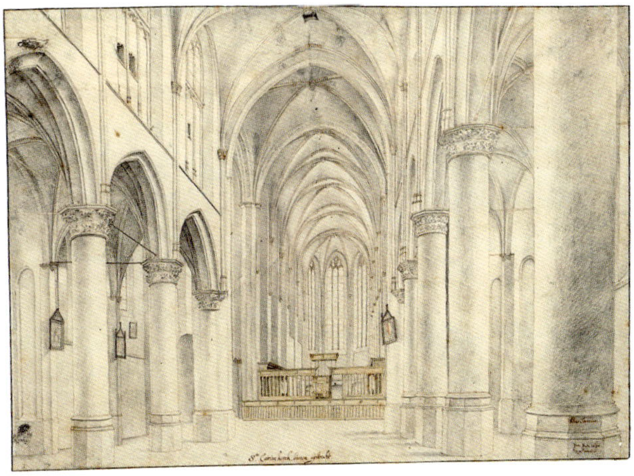

FIG. 90
Pieter Saenredam (1597–1665)
Interior of the Church of St Catherine, Utrecht,
20 October 1636
Pen and brown ink, black and white chalk,
305 × 401 mm
Utrecht, Het Utrechts Archief
(28621)

revealed an extremely precise underdrawing that served as the basis of the scene.[11] The underdrawing, which shines through the paint layers here and there, must have been prepared with the help of a construction drawing such as those Saenredam usually made. This now lost drawing (of the same size as the painting) was probably transferred to the panel by blackening the back of the paper with chalk and then tracing over the most important lines. The impression made on the prepared panel made it possible to translate the drawn interior into an oil painting. A close comparison of the on-site sketch and the panel shows that Saenredam corrected the spatial proportions in the painting. He shifted the vanishing point of the composition somewhat with respect to the drawing: on the sheet, the vanishing point is indicated by a circle drawn around a point on the uppermost moulding of the baptistery screen; in the painting, the vanishing point is on the same moulding, but more to the right. Precisely in this spot is a tiny hole left by the pin to which Saenredam attached a thread to check the perspective,[12] a method observed in the work of other seventeenth-century artists, not only other painters of church interiors but also genre painters such as Johannes Vermeer.[13]

In Saenredam's paintings, characterised by peace and harmony, the people are always subordinate to the architecture, and this painting is no exception. A number of figures enliven the composition, which is dominated by massive pillars, walls and vaults. At far left stand two women and a child, in the middle is a man seen from the back, and two gentlemen converse at right. Several figures are clustered around the choir screen, where a sermon is being delivered from the pulpit. This pulpit is centrally located in front of the choir screen and the baptismal enclosure – all installed in 1635–36, not long before Saenredam visited the church.[14] The chandeliers, acquired in 1649, do not appear in the painting. In the foreground two young men liven things up a bit: kneeling on the floor, where they have spread out a piece of paper, they seem to be tracing the decoration or text on a tombstone.

During the restoration of the painting, completed in 1998 by Geraldine van Heemstra at the Hamilton Kerr Institute in Cambridge, a disturbing, badly yellowed layer of varnish was removed, thus revealing the cool palette and many interesting, previously unobserved details.[15] To begin with, it became apparent that the figures had been added only after completion of the architectural interior. Infrared reflectography even showed that other figures had originally been depicted that were presumably removed or overpainted by Saenredam himself – a phenomenon that is not unique in his oeuvre, having been observed in his interior view of the church of St Bavo in Haarlem (London, National Gallery).[16] In the painting discussed here, there was initially a group of three figures (to the left of the middle, at the height of the conversing gentlemen), and two more adults, which Saenredam overpainted (to the right of the baptistery screen and the dog). A close look reveals the contours of these two groups, shining through the paint layers. The present figures were not painted by Saenredam. They are traditionally attributed to Isaak van Nickelen, another Haarlem artist, who is referred to as the author of the figures in the oldest description of the painting, recorded in 1711, when it was sold at auction from the collection of the earliest known owner, Johan Steyn (1649–1708), a former magistrate of Haarlem.[17] In fact, a close comparison of the figures clearly shows that they were not all painted by the same hand, which means that a third painter must have contributed to this work. That this staffage was indeed applied only after the death of Saenredam in 1665 is apparent from the figures' dress. Their costumes, shoes and hats conform to later fashions, as does the hair style of the woman at far left and the periwig of the pastor in the pulpit.[18]

Saenredam was long a favourite of eighteenth-century collectors and art dealers. Later he was somewhat forgotten, however, and did not become the object of renewed attention until the late nineteenth century.[19] At first his rehabilitation was confined mainly to his drawings, which were considered more important than his paintings. But several publications on Saenredam and the first monographic exhibitions brought about a turning point in the appreciation of his paintings in the 1920s and 1930s. It was in this period that Walter Horace Samuel, 2nd Viscount Bearsted (1882–1948) bought the present painting. That was remarkably early and remarkable in any case, because Saenredam's painted oeuvre is not very large. As a result of Bearsted's extremely generous donation, this rare painting, along with the rest of the collection at Upton House, became the property of the National Trust in 1948.[20] QB

NOTES

1 Schwartz and Bok 1989; L.M. Helmus in Helmus *et al.* 2000; see also Giltaij and Jansen 1991.
2 Schwartz and Bok 1989, no. 55.
3 Q. Buvelot in Buvelot and Buijs 2002, p. 154.
4 Helmus *et al.* 2000; Helmus *et al.* 2002.
5 Schwartz and Bok 1989, p. 276; De Groot in Helmus *et al.* 2000, nos. 63, 65, 66.
6 L.M. Helmus in Helmus *et al.* 2000, p. 275.
7 De Groot in Helmus *et al.* 2000, no. 63.
8 Van Heemstra 2000, p. 97.
9 Van Heemstra 2000, p. 97.
10 De Groot in Helmus *et al.* 2000, p. 272.
11 Van Heemstra 2000, p. 96.
12 Van Heemstra 2000, pp. 96 and 98, fig. 8.
13 J. Giltaij, 'Scientific examination of the underdrawing of seventeenth-century architectural painters', in Van Asperen de Boer and Helmus 2000, pp. 32–55; J. Wadum, 'Vermeer in Perspective', in Wheelock *et al.* 1995, pp. 67–78.
14 De Groot in Helmus *et al.* 2000, p. 270.
15 Van Heemstra 2000; see also Van Heemstra and Marchant 2000.
16 Van Heemstra 2000, p. 103.
17 Schwartz and Bok 1989, pp. 236, 319 note 18, 322 note 23; L.M. Helmus in Helmus *et al.* 2000, pp. 273, 275; Q. Buvelot in Buvelot and Buijs 2002, p. 132.
18 Van Heemstra 2000, pp. 102–03; L.M. Helmus in Helmus *et al.* 2000, p. 273.
19 Schwartz and Bok 1989, pp. 247–51; L.M. Helmus in Helmus *et al.* 2000, p. 15.
20 Paintings by Saenredam, which are a rarity in public collections in the United Kingdom, can be found in the National Gallery, London; Kelvingrove Art Museum, Glasgow; and the Scottish National Gallery, Edinburgh (Schwartz and Bok 1989, nos. 43, 58, 63, 127).

20

JAN STEEN (1626–1679)

The Tired Traveller, c.1660–61

Oil on panel, 32 × 25 cm
Signed lower right: *JSteen* (JS in ligature)
National Trust, Upton House, Warwickshire – The Bearsted Collection (NT 446735)

PROVENANCE
Possibly in the collection of Victor-Amédée de Savoie, Prince de Carignan but not in his sale, 18 June 1743; bought by Bernard Pinney at the J. F. Tuffen sale, Christie's, 11 April 1818, lot 100; in the collection of Sir Simon Clarke by 1819; bought at his sale by Henry Bevan, Christie's, 9 May 1840, lot 100; entered the collection of Alfred de Rothschild between 1884 and 1902; by descent to his daughter Almina, Countess of Carnarvon; with Knoedler, London, in 1924, from whom acquired by Walter Samuel, 2nd Viscount Bearsted; given by him to the National Trust in 1948

EXHIBITED
The Bearsted Collection, Whitechapel Gallery, London, 1955, no. 29; *New Light on Old Masters*, Upton House – Squash Court Gallery, 2013

SELECTED LITERATURE
Braun 1980, p. 102, no. 123; Q. Buvelot in Buvelot, Hilaire and Zeder 1998, pp. 192, 194

Jan Steen's large oeuvre of around four hundred paintings displays a very wide range of subjects and styles. Among his genre scenes, his standard repertoire features taverns, inns and brothels, and he invariably shows a penchant for attractive women. Whereas most of his compositions of this type include a dozen or more figures, this small inn scene from Upton House depicts only two, a young woman and a resting traveller, to whom she hands a glass of red wine. This wine glass, which the woman holds by the foot, is literally and figuratively the heart of the composition. The man has interrupted his walk in the countryside to sit down and rest on a half-barrel in the shady garden of an inn. This somewhat older man is obviously charmed by the young servant girl, judging from his eager look and slightly expectant pose, with one hand on the table and the other on his knee. His real intentions, however, are apparent from the freshly plucked rose, which he has laid upside-down on the table. Although the deeper meaning of this motif is uncertain, the rose seems to refer directly to the woman. The figures' facial expressions speak volumes, for the man's hopeful and extremely avid glance seems not to be reciprocated by the young woman, who keeps a straight face. In any case, the man is more interested in her than in the wine she proffers: indeed, he pointedly refrains from touching the glass. The intimacy of the encounter is heightened by the triangular composition formed by the juxtaposition of the man and woman, who incline towards one another in this close-up scene. The vine-covered pergola above them closes off the composition at the top, which intensifies the already intimate character of the scene. Clearly, some form of love is involved here, whether or not of a fleeting nature.

Men and women flirting is a motif that occurs frequently in Steen's work. In fact, the Musée Fabre in Montpellier has an earlier version of this composition in which Steen unmistakably depicted the same figures (fig. 91).[1] Steen's oeuvre contains quite a few variants of this kind, which usually display some literal repetitions.[2] In the Montpellier painting, too,

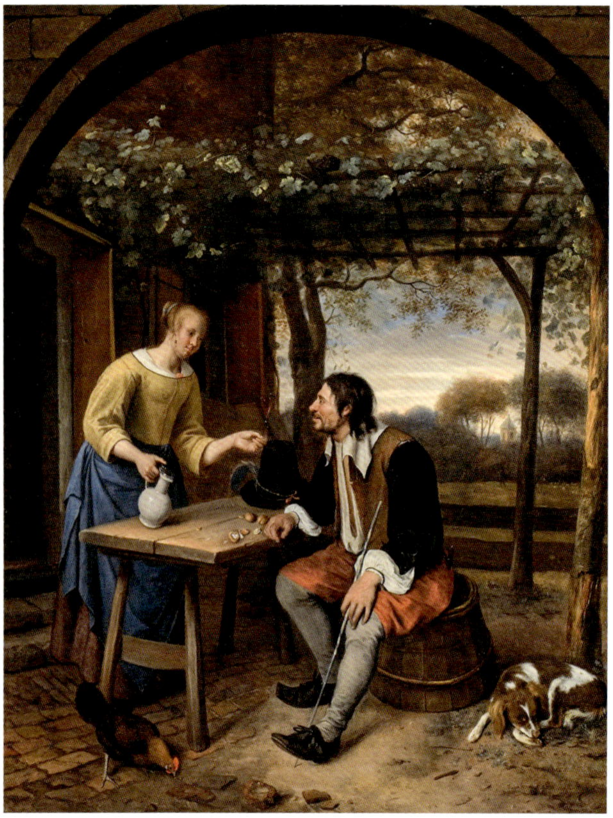

FIG. 91
Jan Steen (1626–1679)
The Rest before an Inn, *c.*1659–60
Oil on panel, 55 × 41 cm
Montpellier Agglomération, Musée Fabre,
bequest of Antoine Valedau, 1836 (836-4-55)

the glances of the man and woman intersect. This first version has no rose on the table but walnuts instead, one of which is cracked. It cannot be a coincidence that Steen gave this half-walnut the form of a heart. This striking motif calls to mind an old Dutch saying: 'If one has the nut, one must crack it'.[3] In other words, one must seize the opportunity, and the man in Steen's painting does not need to be told twice. The figures are given more space in the Montpellier version, and the composition is framed at the top by an arched stone gate rather than vines. On the basis of this *trompe-l'oeil* motif, which Steen first used in paintings dating from 1659,[4] the painting in Montpellier is generally dated to the years 1659–60. The considerably smaller version discussed here probably originated a little later, presumably around 1660–61.[5] In 1660, Steen moved with his family from Warmond (near Leiden) to Haarlem, where he became a member of the local painters' guild the following year. Earlier on, he had rented a brewery in Delft, probably as a means of earning money, since painting did not always provide him with a livelihood.

In the later version, the accessories have been kept to a minimum, but in the first version the man and woman are portrayed full-length, with the striking detail that the man casually lets his walking stick rest against his foot and knee. This stick has disappeared completely from the later version. It is possible that the maidservant is based on a lost preparatory study, given that she appears in this pose not only in the paintings in Montpellier and Upton House but also in an inn interior by Steen that can be dated to the same period.[6] In the first version in Montpellier, we see more of the figures and also more of the landscape. For example, there are three more figures on the grass in the background, and, immediately behind them, a church tower. Because Steen zoomed in less on the principal figures in the Montpellier version, we also see the entrance door and the window of the inn (the point of the open shutter appears precisely above the wine glass), and in the foreground a chicken snatching the remains of food by the table and a dog sleeping next to a tree at right. Both panels testify to Steen's painstaking attention to the details of the clothing and the play of light on such objects as the earthenware wine-jug with a pewter lid. Comparison of the technique of these two paintings reveals that the brushwork of the first version in Montpellier is smoother and more refined than that of the later version in Upton House.[7] Remarkably, differences between these two paintings can be discovered in the smallest details, such as the

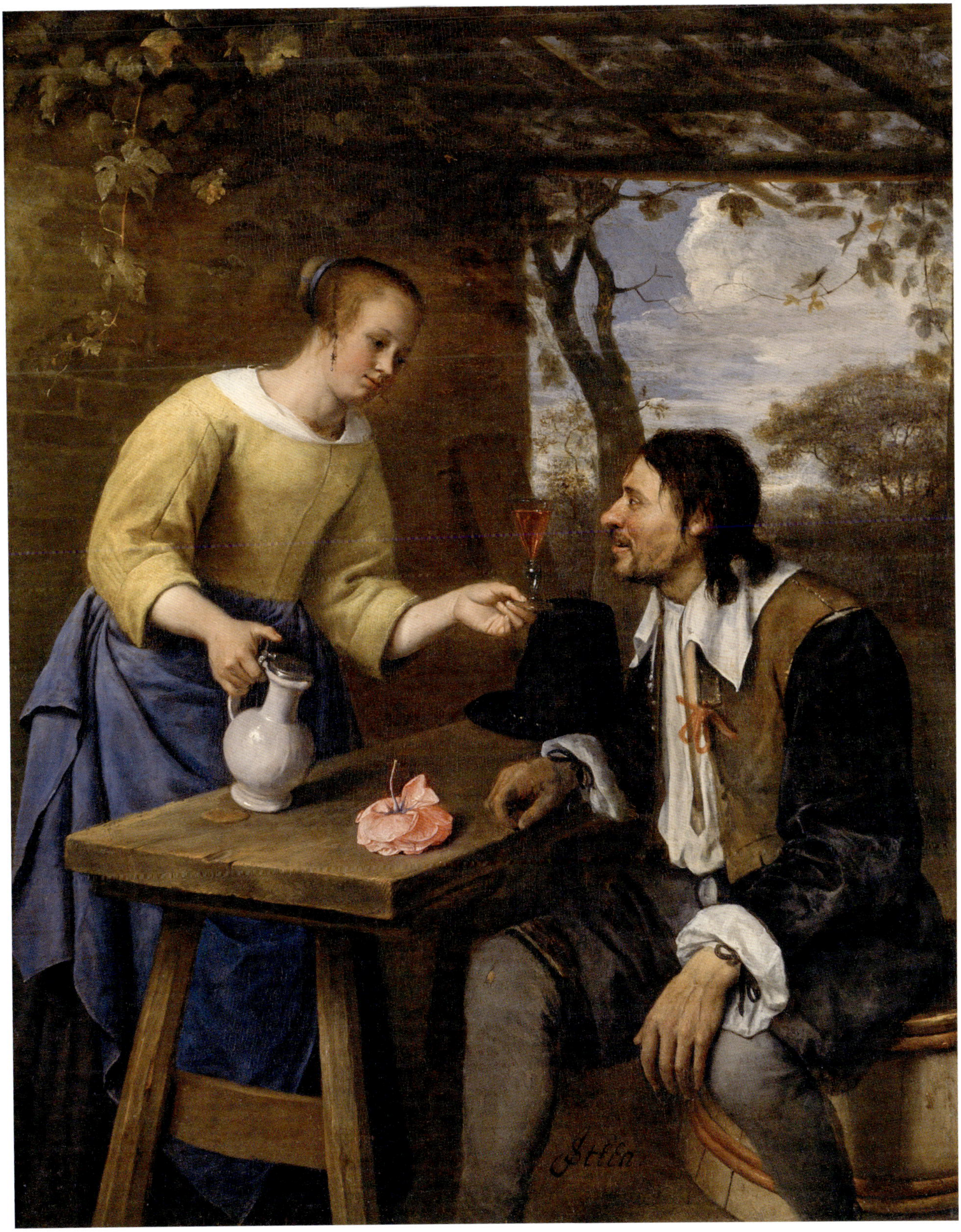

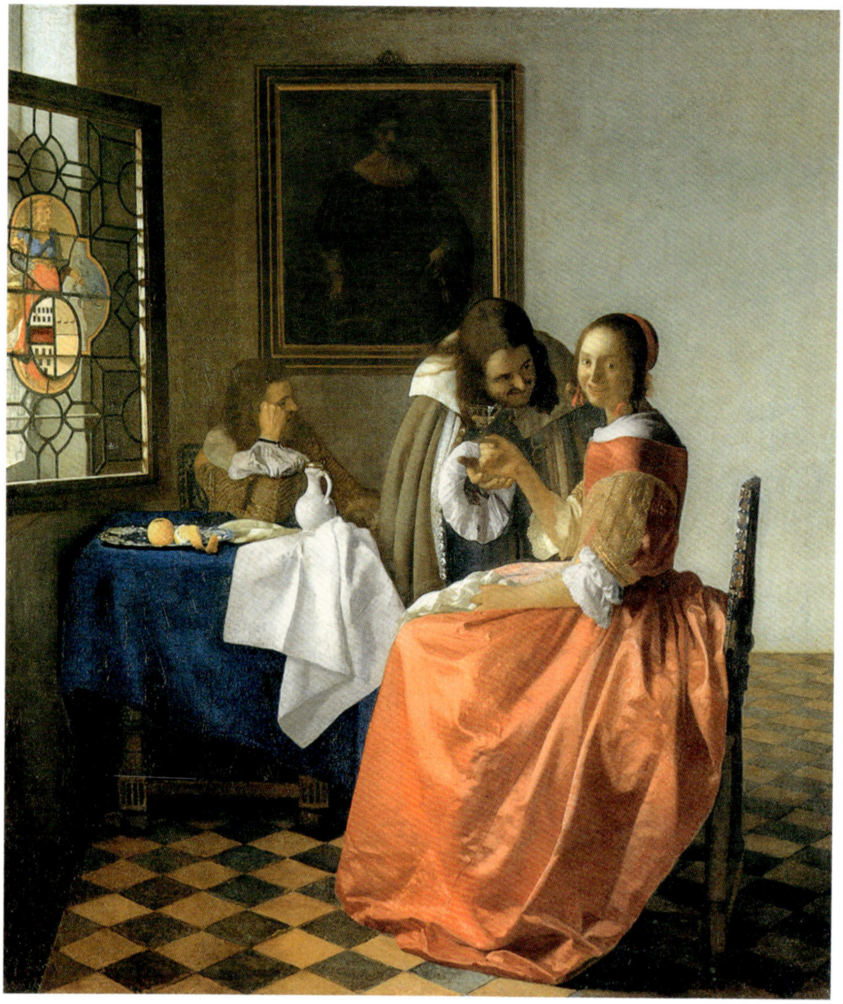

FIG. 92
Johannes Vermeer (1632–1675)
Young Woman with a Wine Glass, c.1660–61
Oil on canvas, 78 × 67 cm
Braunschweig, Herzog Anton Ulrich-Museum (316)

man's hat, which lies on the table. In the Montpellier painting, his hat is decorated with a feather on a splendid chain, two details that are missing in the later version. Yet the later version has a detail, a hole in the knee of the man's trousers, that is lacking in the earlier version.

In seventeenth-century Dutch genre painting, proffering a glass of wine is a routine means of establishing contact between a man and a woman. There are plenty of examples in the work of such famous genre painters as Gerard ter Borch (cat. 3), Pieter de Hooch (cat. 10), Gabriel Metsu (cat. 15) and Johannes Vermeer (fig. 92).[8] In the work by Vermeer, there is actual physical contact: the man's hand touches the woman's after giving her a glass of wine – an expressive gesture that serves as a link between the figures, like the wine glass in Steen's painting. It is striking that Steen's paintings in Montpellier and Upton House are clearly derived from compositions by the Leiden 'fine painter' Frans van Mieris, a close friend of Steen who often painted similar flirting couples in the same period. Whenever wine is not the principal motif, both Steen and Van Mieris show us a man offering oysters to a woman, a variation on the age-old theme of seduction (fig. 93). The traditional, rather neutral title of the present painting by Steen,

FIG. 93
Frans van Mieris the Elder (1635–1681)
The Oyster Meal, 1661
Oil on panel (arched top), 27 × 20 cm
The Hague, Mauritshuis, gift of Sir Henry Deterding, 1936 (819)

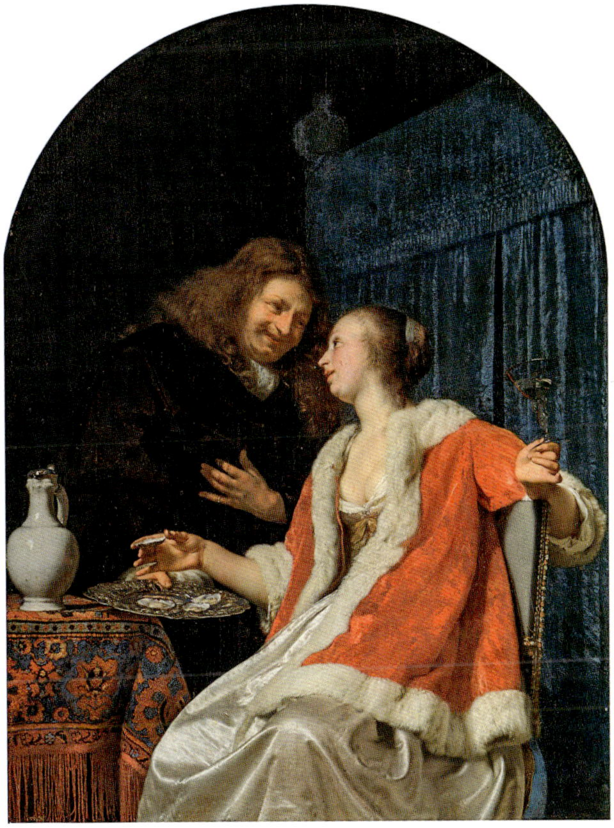

The Tired Traveller,[9] is a typically Victorian characterisation of a scene that is much less innocent than it seems. This amusing picture has always been loved by collectors. After belonging to Alfred de Rothschild (1842–1918) and passing by descent to his daughter Almina, Countess of Carnarvon, the painting was sold through a London art dealer in 1924 to Walter Horace Samuel, 2nd Viscount Bearsted MC, who bequeathed his collection of paintings as part of Upton House to the National Trust in 1948 (see also cat. nos. 14, 15, 19). QB

NOTES

1 Buvelot 1998, pp. 192–95, no. 52.
2 See Buvelot 1998, pp. 196–99, no. 53; Van Suchtelen 2010, pp. 54–55.
3 Buvelot 1998, p. 195, note 10.
4 E.g., the painting dated 1659 in The National Gallery, London; reproduced in Perry Chapman, Kloek and Wheelock 1996, no. 10.
5 W.T. Kloek in Chapman, Kloek and Wheelock 1996, p. 144. A later copy after the Steen at Upton House was sold in New York, Sotheby Parke Bernet, 19 March 1981, lot 7, repr. (see Buvelot 1998, p. 195, note 9).
6 Rose-Marie and Eijk van Otterloo Collection; see Kloek in Chapman, Kloek and Wheelock 1996, p. 145.
7 Several pentimenti – by the man's right foot, for example, and at his hand on the table – can be discerned with the naked eye in the painting at Upton House.
8 See Q. Buvelot in Waiboer *et al.* 2017, pp. 164–73.
9 See Smith 1829–42, IV, p. 36, no. 112 (and IX, pp. 514–15, no. 107).

21

WILLEM VAN DE VELDE THE ELDER (*c.*1611–1693)

*The Battle of Texel (Kijkduin), 11/21 August 1673, the Engagement of the Two Fleets, c.*1673

Oil on canvas, 114.3 × 184.2 cm
National Trust, Felbrigg Hall, Norfolk – The Windham Collection (NT 1401180)

PROVENANCE
Purchased by William Windham II by 1752; thence by descent; bequeathed by Robert Wyndham Ketton-Cremer to the National Trust in 1969

Sea pieces by the Van de Veldes and their followers represented an important aspect of the English eighteenth-century taste for Dutch painting, and were an 'essential ingredient' of English country house picture hangs.[1] William Windham II (1711–1761), custodian of Felbrigg Hall in the mid-eighteenth century, was an avid collector of marine pictures, and counted among his collection six 'Van de Veldes'. The majority are medium-sized views of ships navigating stormy seas, now regarded as studio works, but the 1764 inventory also lists two large Van de Veldes for which the attribution has stood the test of time.[2] These are identified as two views of the Battle of Texel – the present picture by Van de Velde the Elder, and that by the Younger now in the ownership of the National Maritime Museum, though kindly on loan to Felbrigg. The Battle of Texel, known in Dutch history as the Battle of Kijkduin, was the last battle of the three Anglo-Dutch wars, and the only one to which Van de Velde the Elder was not an eyewitness. Nonetheless, the artist brings an air of credibility to his account of the action in this picture, crowded as it is with a level of detail that attests to a highly sophisticated understanding of the intricacies of sea battles built up over decades as a first-hand, seaborne observer.[3] The painting shows the battle shortly after the crucial moment when Sir Edward Spragge, commander of the English fleet, transferred from his flagship, the *Prince*, seen in the centre left foreground with its main and mizzen masts decimated to mere stumps, to the *St George*; Spragge's new ship, indicated by the large blue flag at its main, is glimpsed starboard bow view at the centre right of the composition, somewhat obscured by the stern of a Dutch ship and the clouds of cannon fire. The *St George* too would be destroyed only an hour later and Spragge was drowned in his attempt once again to transfer ships.[4]

Between them, Van de Velde father and son painted numerous views of the battle. Windham's versions would have been complementary: about the same size, and with very similar frames, they probably hung on either side of the doorway to the drawing room.[5] The treatment of their respective subjects is likewise complementary, demonstrating much of the difference between the two artists: aside from depicting different moments in the same battle, the present picture, with its bird's-eye viewpoint, evenly distributed lighting and proliferation of detail is more documentary in nature, while its counterpart, with its lower viewpoint (as if painted from an observing vessel), dramatic lighting, and emphasis on atmospheric effects, provides a more poignant reflection on Spragge's demise.[6]

It was in the turbulent years around the Battle of the Texel that the Van de Veldes relocated to England, where they went on to make the most of the emergent London art market, answering (but by no means fulfilling) the growing demand for marine painting.[7]

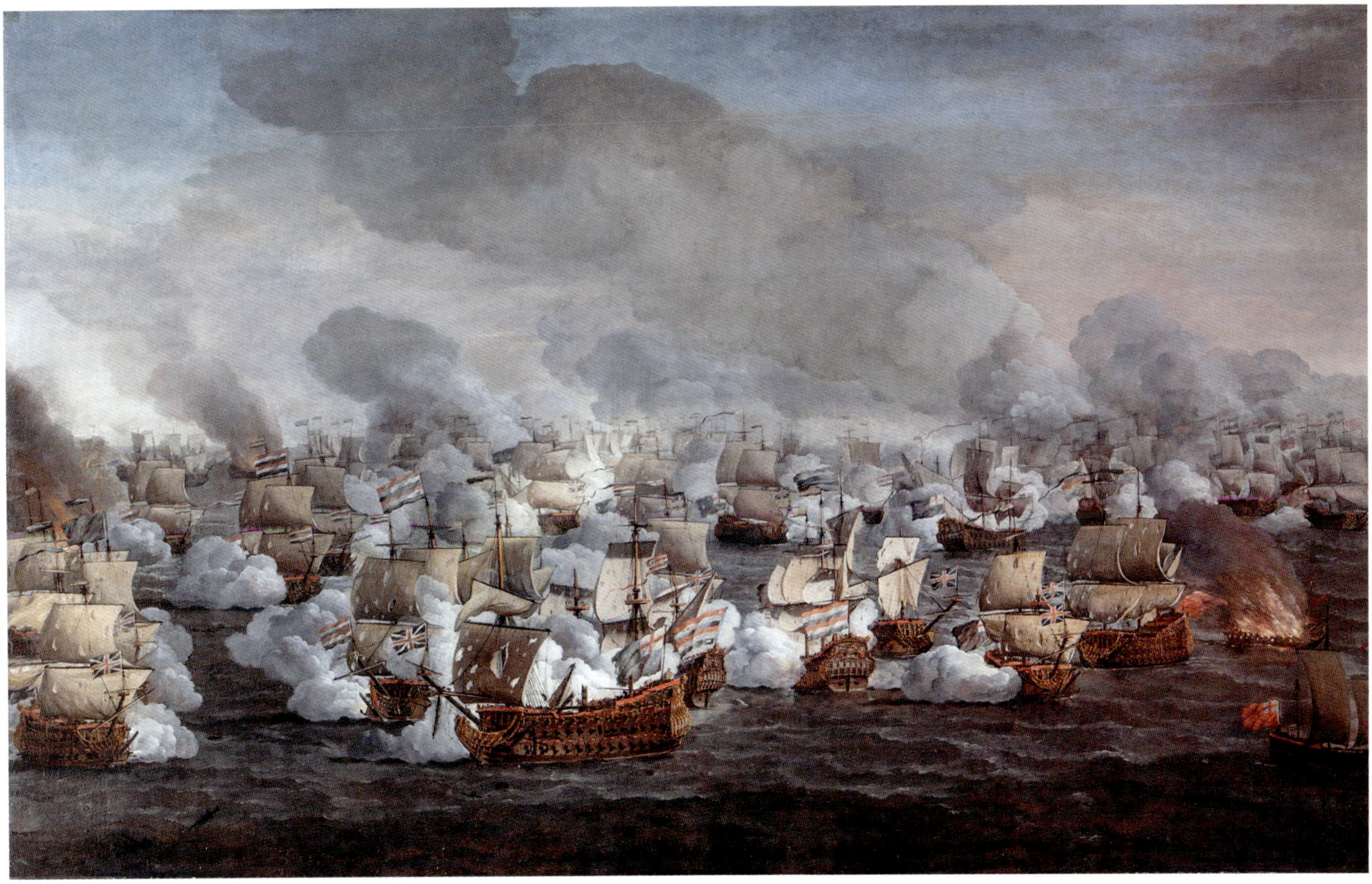

This demand persisted throughout the eighteenth century, and the present picture may have been bought by Windham – its first recorded owner – in London.[8] In the absence of any documentation, however, there remains the possibility that the picture was purchased on the Grand Tour, as was the case with many such sea pieces that have ended up on the walls of English country houses. Windham completed the Tour in 1738–42, returning home via Holland, where it seems reasonable to assume – though again impossible to prove – that he purchased a significant part of his Dutch and Flemish pictures.[9]

As an enthusiastic and competent seafarer and helmsman, who 'could, and did build vessels, and navigate them himself',[10] Windham regarded his Van de Veldes, particularly his two largest, as more than merely obligatory elements in a demonstration of the fashionable taste for Dutch pictures.[11] An indication of how greatly Windham prized his largest Van de Veldes is given by two letters from 1752 in which – ironically, but indicative of someone who knew only too well the treacherous waters of the East Anglian coast – Windham instructs his agent to send him 'my great V. Velde' by land, as 'I cannot trust [it] to the seas'.[12]

As Merlin Waterson has demonstrated, the backdrop of the North Sea would have loomed large at Felbrigg, located only a couple of miles from the north coast of East Anglia.[13] In the later eighteenth century, William Windham II's son, William Windham III (1750–1810), had a wood planted on the Felbrigg estate as a buffer against the northerly winds, but also to make a feature of the sea. A late eighteenth-century guidebook describes the setting to visitors, shortly after the wood had been planted:

> *From the upper part of the wood the sea presents itself, but not in so striking a manner as it will from the new plantation, which in a few years will conceal that pleasing object from the eye, and then at once display all its awful majesty. Mr Windham's plantations are designed to answer two purposes, to ornament and belt round his park, and to extend his great woodland scene nearer the sea, towards which, at two miles distance it forms a grand bulwark, and from which he looks down an easy declivity, over a bold shore, to an unlimited prospect on the German ocean.*[14]

While William Windham II was not able to enjoy his son's transformation of the landscape, the fact that from the coastline near Felbrigg one could have looked out eastwards across the sea broadly in the direction the island of Texel would surely not have been lost on him. AG

NOTES

1 Bryant 2003, p. 86.
2 Norfolk Record Office, WKC 7/181/464 X 5.
3 On the possible sources for the Van de Veldes' depictions of the Battle of the Texel, see Robinson 1958, p. 79.
4 For the comprehensive account of the scene, see Robinson 1990, I, pp. 186–87. There is a related drawing of the composition in the National Maritime Museum which shows a number of the key ships in similar positions, though at a slightly later point in the battle. See Robinson 1990, I, p. 187, no. 143, and Robinson 1958, p. 80, no. 409.
5 Robinson 1990, I, p. 188, no. 143.
6 Waterson 1986, pp. 904–05.
7 Johns 2016, p. 21.
8 Robinson 1990, I, p. 187, no. 143.
9 Ketton-Cremer 1962, p. 121; Moore 1985, p. 128.
10 Hardinge 1816, p. 27.
11 See Waterson 1986, pp. 904–05.
12 Norfolk Record Office, WKC 7/179/464 X 5. It is unclear whether the 'great V. Velde' refers to the present picture or the National Maritime Museum picture. See Robinson 1990, I, p. 188, no. 143, and Waterson 1986, pp. 904–05.
13 Waterson 1986, p. 904.
14 Norwich 1795, pp. 229–30.

22

SIMON PIETERSZ VERELST (1644–1721)

Prince Rupert of the Rhine (1619–1682), *c*.1680–82

Oil on canvas, 26 × 102 cm
Signed upper left: *S. Verelst F.*
National Trust, Petworth, West Sussex – The Egremont Collection (NT 486254)

PROVENANCE
Purchased by 3rd Earl of Egremont from the sale of Giovanni Battista Cipriani, Christie's, 24 Mar 1786, lot 102; thence by descent; accepted by HM Treasury from John Wyndham, 6th Lord Leconfield and 1st Lord Egremont in lieu of death duties in 1956; transferred to the National Trust in 1990

This portrait shows the handsome Civil War hero Prince Rupert of the Rhine (1619–1682) not as the epitome of the dashing cavalier during the reign of his uncle Charles I but as an older man, portrayed after the restoration of his cousin, Charles II. Painted throughout his life by various Dutch artists, such as Michiel Jansz van Miereveld, Rembrandt van Rijn, Gerrit van Honthorst, Cornelis van Poelenburch and Peter Lely, the prince also had a personal interest in art and science, and was associated with the development of the mezzotint printmaking process (his most famous mezzotint is the so-called *Little Executioner*, made in 1662). He is shown here in his fifties, a figure of respect within the extended Stuart family – a member of the House of Lords, a Privy Councillor, 'General at Sea and Land' and a romantic reminder of a long-gone age.

The artist Simon Pietersz Verelst portrayed Prince Rupert in a fashionable wig and wearing the ceremonial robes of the Order of the Garter, the ancient and noble chivalric order, awarded to the prince in 1642 by Charles I. By being portrayed in its robes he was displaying his position in society and his allegiance to the Stuart monarchy, the family of his mother, Elizabeth Stuart, Queen of Bohemia (see cat. 9). Rupert's slightly contorted pose is typical of Verelst's work, as is the attention to detail, such as the depiction of the marble pedestal that he leans against, and the characteristic way the artist paints light falling on the various materials of his opulent costume, including on the threads of the huge tassels or in the folds of his voluminous shirt.

Verelst came from a family of artists from The Hague. He was the son of Pieter Hermansz Verelst, who was a pupil of Gerrit Dou's, and the brother of Herman and Johannes Verelst, who both also worked in London, and the uncle of Cornelis and Maria Verelst. He studied at The Hague's Confrerie Pictura, which his father had co-founded, and soon afterwards moved to London.

He is probably best known as a flower painter, specialising in carefully observed depictions of abundant blooms in glass vases, with which he delighted patrons and collectors after he arrived in England in 1669. His most famous admirer was Samuel Pepys, who visited Verelst's studio on 11 April 1669 and commented in his *Diary* on the realism of some dew drops on a leaf in one of the artist's paintings, which the artist offered to sell him: 'a Dutchman, newly come over, one Evarelst, who took us to his lodging close by, and did shew us a little flower-pot of his doing, the finest thing that ever, I think, I saw in my life; the drops of dew hanging on the leaves, so I was forced, again and again, to put my finger to it, to feel whether my eyes were deceived or no. He do ask 70l. for it: I had the vanity to bid him 20l.; but a better picture I never saw in my whole life; and it is worth going twenty miles to see it.'

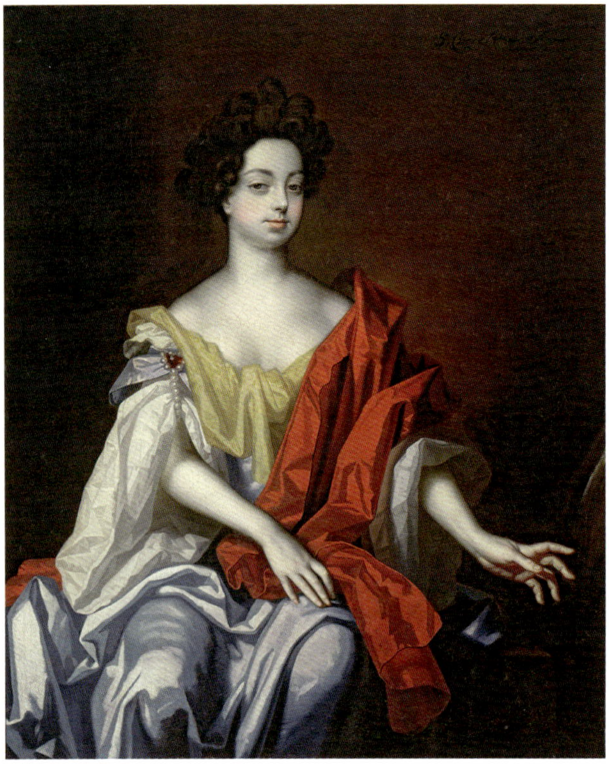

FIG. 94
Simon Pietersz Verelst (1644–1721)
Eleanor ('Nell') Gwyn (1651–1687), *c.*1680–85
Oil on canvas, 122 × 96 cm
The Royal Hospital, Chelsea, London (inv. 384)

Verelst supposedly turned to portrait painting with the support of the Duke of York, the future James II (1633–1701) and George Villiers, 2nd Duke of Buckingham (1628–1687), and he was one of many successful portraitists attached to the court during the 1670s, for a while becoming a highly fashionable artist to sit for. He painted several members of the royal family, including Charles II[1] and Mary of Modena, Duchess of York (1658–1718).[2] He also painted at least three of the king's mistresses, the most famous of whom was the comic actress Eleanor ('Nell') Gwyn (1651–1687). He appears to have been particularly associated with her, and, like other women at court using specific portraitists, she probably commissioned him as a means to promote herself. He painted her on a number of occasions (as in fig. 94), as well as painting Charles Beauclerk, 1st Duke of St Albans (1670–1726), one of her two sons by the king.[3]

According to the engraver and antiquary George Vertue, Verelst 'grew very proud & conceited. & scorn'd all other masters',[4] apparently calling himself the 'God of Flowers'.[5] After a successful career in England as both a flower painter and a court portrait painter, he eventually 'went mad and fell on hard times'.[6] DT

NOTES

1 Royal Collection (RCIN 409151).
2 Yale Center for British Art, New Haven (B1979.19).
3 The portrait of Charles Beauclerk, 1st Duke of St Albans, is in a private collection.
4 Vertue 1930–47, I, p. 32.
5 Thieme-Becker 1907–50, XXXIV (1940), p. 238.
6 Karst 2013–14, p. 47, no. 1.

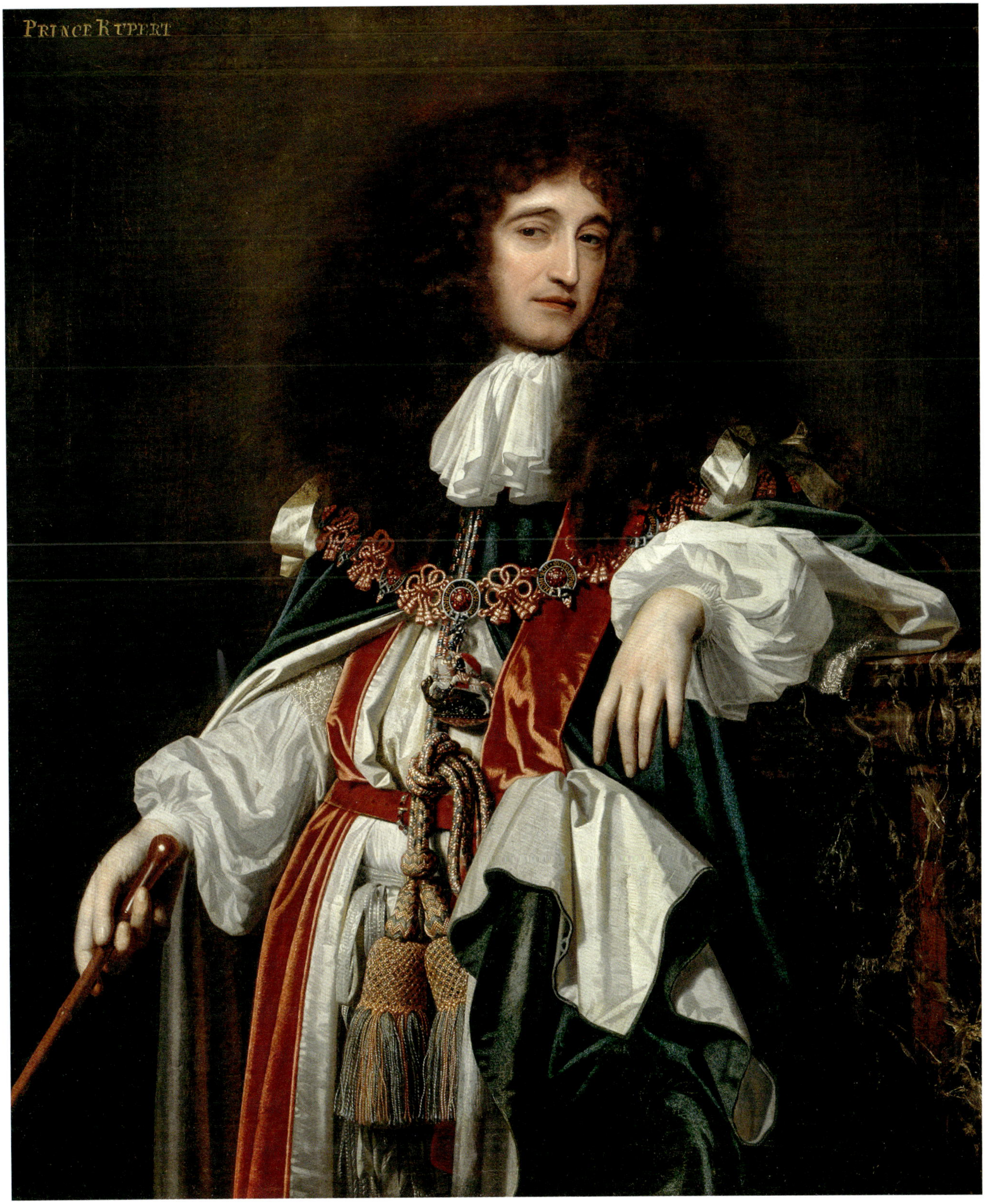

CAT. 22

Dutch Paintings from the Collection of Sir Thomas William Holburne

AMINA WRIGHT, SENIOR CURATOR, THE HOLBURNE MUSEUM

IN 1868, VISITORS TO THE *National Exhibition of Works of Art* in Leeds were given a privileged glimpse of three dozen items from the collection of Her Majesty the Queen. In the gallery of German, Flemish and Dutch Old Masters on the first floor, they would have been charmed by 'the most attractive' of Van Dyck's depictions of Queen Henrietta Maria, and intrigued by his triple portrait of Charles I. Alongside them were pictures lent by such distinguished collectors as the Baron de Ferrières, the Duke of Devonshire, and Sir Thomas William Holburne (1793–1874).

Holburne's contribution to this area, no. 778 in the catalogue, was a 'Violin Player' by 'Gerard Dou', which had been removed from a mahogany case in his front drawing room in Bath for the exhibition. The so-called 'portrait of himself by Gerard Douw' has since been identified as a copy of the 1653 original now in the Liechtenstein Collection. Today it hangs in the new extension galleries of the Holburne Museum in Bath in an evocation of the Victorian collector's drawing room.

By the 1860s, Sir William Holburne was becoming known nationally as a collector: in 1867 we find him listed as a member of the newly founded Burlington Fine Arts Club alongside such luminaries as Ruskin, Lord Leighton and Baron Ferdinand de Rothschild. He must have been a passionate collector: his butler Harry Pattington regularly told the tale of 'a little fracas' over the purchase of some silver spoons in a Bath shop, in which Sir William exchanged insults with a rival and received a 'blow in the face' that drew blood.

Unlike his near neighbour the great connoisseur William Beckford, Thomas William Holburne was not born into great wealth or privilege. He was the younger of two sons. Although the family had earned a baronetcy through their ancestor's endeavours on the battlefield, they lived in ordinary town houses in Bath, far away from their castle at Menstrie near Stirling, which had long since been sold. Following in the footsteps of his grandfather Admiral Francis Holburne, William entered the Royal Navy as a Volunteer aged eleven. That year, 1805, saw him fighting on board HMS *Orion* at the Battle of Trafalgar. During these busy years of warfare against Napoleon, he travelled widely; meanwhile, his brother Francis, a soldier, died in the Peninsular War.

William retired permanently from the Navy in 1820, on inheriting his father's estate and title. In 1824, the young Sir William, now 6th Bt, set out to gain the gentleman's education he had never received: he travelled first to Italy, then returned over a year later to Bath via Germany and the Netherlands, visiting Antwerp, Amsterdam, The Hague and Brussels. There is little to suggest that he brought any paintings back from his journey through Holland, but his interest in them would have been nurtured by visits to galleries and dealers.

Holburne's collecting is marked by two characteristics, a love of the small and finely wrought, and a conservative taste, particularly where pictures are concerned. By the 1860s, British art collections were more typically being created by industrialists and the urban middle classes with a preference for work by their contemporaries. Sir William owned few paintings made in his lifetime; his taste for Old Masters was very much that of his aristocratic predecessors, particularly George IV. Visits to his wealthy Yorkshire cousins, the Earls of Harewood, must also have inspired him.

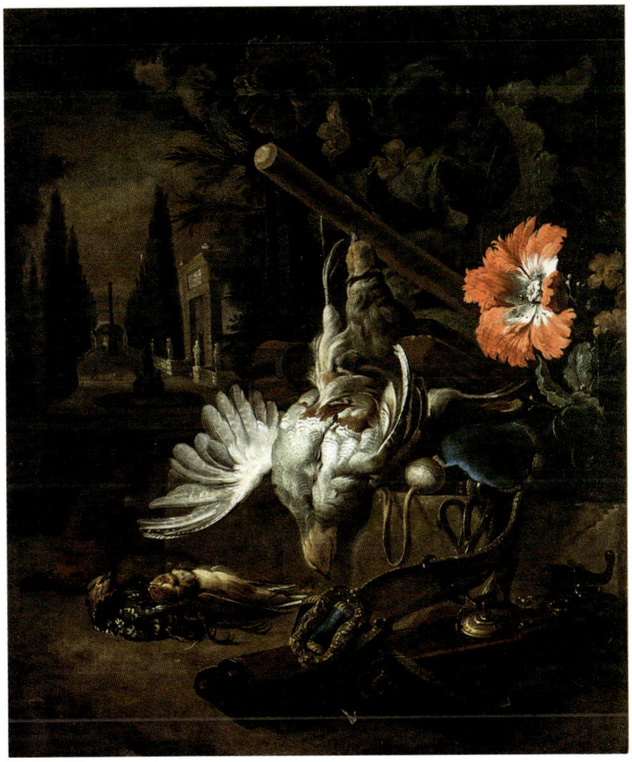

FIG. 95
Jan Weenix the younger (1642–1719)
Still Life with Game in a Garden, *c.*1690
Oil on canvas, 70.3 × 85.2 cm
The Holburne Museum, Bath (A87)

Firm evidence for the source of Holburne's pictures is very elusive, as almost nothing remains in the way of journals, letters or accounts. The collection is typical, however, both in terms of range and period, of those being sold regularly in Bath's salerooms in the 1840s and 1850s. Although Bath had, by this time, greatly declined as a fashionable resort, its art dealers and frequent auctions were nationally important. There is every likelihood that Holburne was buying, probably through an agent, from local Bath sales.

A room-by-room catalogue produced in 1867 gives us a clear sense of how Sir William displayed his paintings. It lists all the pictures in the terraced house in Cavendish Crescent that he shared with his three sisters and gives a valuable glimpse of the collection as it neared completion. The walls are dominated by works of the Dutch School: the Dutch paintings are not only more numerous, but also of better overall quality than the Italian and British ones, many of which are later copies. In 1867 some forty per cent of the paintings were Dutch.

In the ground-floor dining room, Holburne family meals were taken surrounded by still lifes of fruit, shellfish and game attributed to Weenix (fig. 95), De Heem and their Flemish contemporaries, while the family's military and naval backgrounds were celebrated through seascapes by Peeters and the Van de Veldes and battle scenes by Jan Wyck. The greatest strength of the picture collection was its cabinet paintings, both landscape and genre scenes. Some of these hung on gold wallpaper between crimson damask curtains in the drawing room, but most were in Sir William's private study with his miniature sculpture gallery of antique and Renaissance bronzes.

The Dutch landscapes hung alongside recent British works in the same genre, mostly by Holburne's neighbour Thomas Barker and his brother Benjamin, whose paintings were often so indistinguishable from those of their Netherlandish predecessors as to have been subsequently misattributed. Although there were many views of northern woods and rivers by or after such artists as Hobbema, Hackaert and Wynants, it is the Italianate cabinet pictures that stand out as some of the finest in the whole museum. Holburne was particularly drawn to the sunlit flocks of Berchem and Du Jardin, and must have paid handsomely for a signed *Landscape with Hawking Party* by Philips Wouwerman.

In contrast to these serene landscapes, Holburne also had a taste for low life: he appears to have collected etchings by and after Adriaen van Ostade, and owned a colourful early work by the Haarlem artist, *The Ballad Monger*, signed and dated 1635 (fig. 96). With a savage

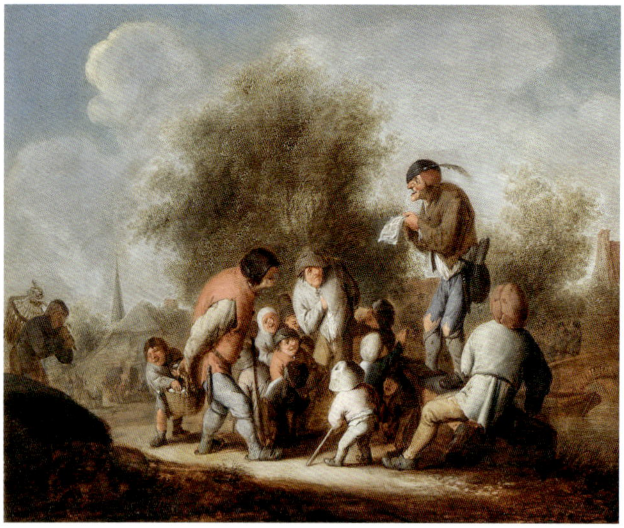

FIG. 96
Adriaen van Ostade (1610–1685)
The Ballad Monger, 1635
Oil on panel, 30.5 × 41.3 cm
The Holburne Museum, Bath (A48)

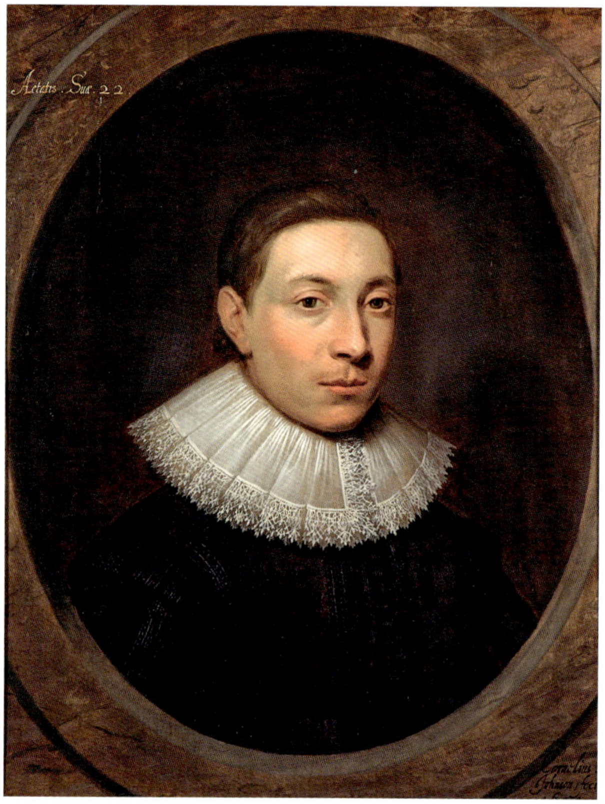

FIG. 97
Cornelius Johnson (1593–1661)
Unknown Young Man, 1620
Oil on panel, 66.7 × 49.6 cm
The Holburne Museum, Bath (A78)

Brawl by Aelbert Cuyp's uncle Benjamin, this is one of the best-loved Dutch pictures in the Holburne Museum today. A cosy couple by Hendrick Martensz Sorgh (signed and dated 1661) was originally in the collection of Sir William's wealthy aunt Catherine Cussans. In her sale at Christie's, it was coyly entitled 'Dutch Courtship': it depicts a young woman in a gloomy interior distracted from a dish of waffles by her leering companion.

The collection also includes some fine portraits, several by artists from the Netherlands working in England and Scotland. Holburne naturally preferred named sitters, the more famous the better. Wishful thinking on his part and the imaginations of unscrupulous dealers may be equally to blame for the unlikely identifications given to some of his portraits. For example, a very early portrait of an as yet unidentified young man by Cornelius Johnson, dated 1620 (fig. 97), was listed as 'A Portrait of John Milton, in his 25th year'. Milton was born in 1608.

Holburne's 'Large upright portrait of Wilmot, Earl of Rochester, in court dress [by] Sir Godfrey Kneller' is now known to be a portrait not of John Wilmot but of his far less notorious successor, Laurence Hyde, Earl of Rochester, by the Dutch Willem Wissing rather than his German rival Kneller. This spectacular image of James II's Lord High Treasurer is one of the few works in the collection for which Holburne left a verifiable provenance, having been purchased, as he noted, from the 1846 sale of the contents of Forde Abbey in Dorset.

Two large Amsterdam portraits show how tastes changed in the 1650s: an *Unknown Gentleman* by Nicolaes Eliasz Pickenoy of around 1620 is typically Dutch in its sober black costume, immaculate white ruff and plain background. Dating from around thirty years later, a *Portrait of a Lady* by Jacob Adriaensz Backer

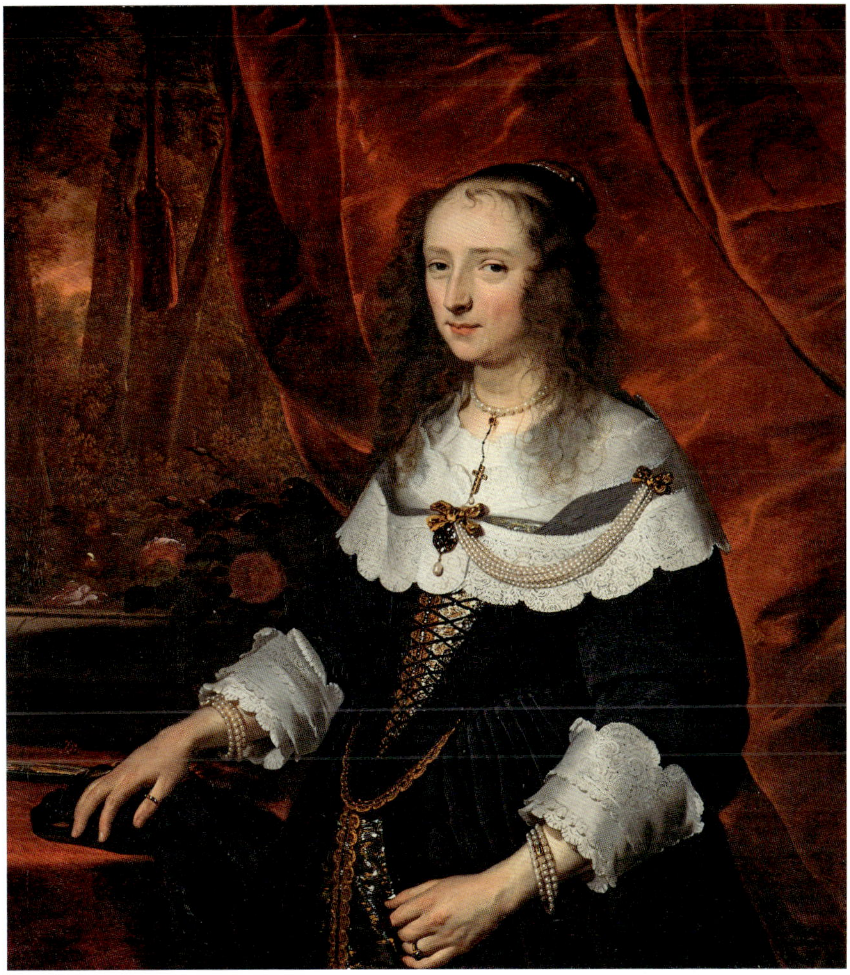

FIG. 98
Jacob Adriaensz Backer (1608–1651)
Unknown Lady, c.1650
Oil on canvas, 101.6 × 88.4 cm
The Holburne Museum, Bath (A7)

(fig. 98) shows a strong Flemish influence in the use of a landscape background with late evening light, a still life of roses on the window-ledge, elaborate jewellery and a deep red curtain that echoes the fiery sky.

Following Sir William's death in 1874 with no heirs to perpetuate the family name, his surviving sister Mary Anne Barbara appointed a Board of Trustees to place 'the extensive collection ... formed by my late brother ... in a Museum in Bath'. The Museum was intended as a memorial not only to Sir William but to the whole Holburne of Menstrie family.

Today, thanks to conservation, connoisseurship and documentation schemes like the Public Catalogue Foundation, the paintings are gradually being cleaned, researched and rehabilitated. Sir William Holburne's collection of Netherlandish works is now acknowledged to be one of the finest in the country. At the Holburne Museum today, the best of the Dutch and Flemish paintings (including three now firmly attributed to Pieter Brueghel the Younger) can be seen in context with Sir William's Anglo-Dutch furniture and exceptional silver made in Holland's Golden Age, including some of Holburne's beloved spoons. Alongside Italian and British pictures, silver and ceramics, Grand Tour souvenirs, portrait miniatures, books and mineral specimens, they represent a rare and eclectic survival of a Victorian gentleman's townhouse collection.

Royal Picture Gallery Mauritshuis, The Hague

QUENTIN BUVELOT, SENIOR CURATOR, MAURITSHUIS

Anyone who has visited the Royal Picture Gallery Mauritshuis knows what a special place it is. The collection is both remarkable for its focus and for its quality – in spite of being small, it is one of the top four in the world for Dutch paintings. The Mauritshuis is small but sumptuous, grand yet intimate, and so it is often called the gem of Dutch museums. For many, the Mauritshuis is the most beautiful museum in The Netherlands, if not in Europe. 'Mauritshuis' is the name of both the museum and the building that houses the collection. It owes its name to its first occupant, Johan Maurits (1604–1679), count of Nassau-Siegen. His palatial residence was constructed between 1633 and 1644 in the centre of The Hague, right next to the Binnenhof, the seat of Dutch government. The Mauritshuis was designed by the Dutch architect Jacob van Campen in a style inspired by classical antiquity and is perhaps the most striking example known of Dutch classicist architecture, with its strict symmetry, classical pilasters, capitals, cornices and pediments (fig. 99).

The collection has a rich history that is rooted in the holdings of the stadholders of Holland, the princes of Orange. It focuses on seventeenth-century painting from the Northern and Southern Netherlands and includes the work of such artists as Rembrandt, Vermeer, Hals and Rubens. Fifteenth- and sixteenth-century masters like Rogier van der Weyden and Hans Holbein the Younger are also represented. In addition to first-rate paintings by great masters, the collection also contains attractive works by lesser-known artists. The core of the collection was amassed by two princes of Orange, William IV of Orange (1711–1751) and his son William V (1748–1806). William IV tried to reconstruct the dispersed collection of his ancestors, Frederick Henry and Amalia of Solms. This prince inherited paintings that had once belonged to his distant cousin, King-Stadholder William III. William IV bought paintings at auctions which were known – or presumed – to have belonged to the original stadholders' collections, such as Rembrandt's 1631 *Simeon's Song of Praise*, originally acquired by Frederick Henry. William IV also made important 'new' acquisitions, such as *The Bull* by Paulus Potter. But it was his son who once again elevated the stadholders' collection of paintings to a princely level. William V had been fascinated by art from a young age and took a serious interest in collecting. He had great success at auctions, buying top-notch works such as *The Garden of Eden with the Fall of Man* by Jan Brueghel the Elder and Rubens. The purchase of the complete collection of the tax collector Govert van Slingelandt, which included masterpieces by Rembrandt and Van Dyck, was another high point in the prince's collecting career.

It was William V who first made the collection of paintings accessible to the public. In 1774 he had the paintings taken from the Stadholder's Quarters in the Binnenhof to a building on the Buitenhof that had been specially designed to accommodate the collection of over two hundred paintings. This picture gallery was open to the public at set times, which made it the first public art collection in Holland – a milestone in Dutch museum history. Twenty years later, however, the crowded walls of the Gallery were stripped of their paintings, not by order of the Stadholder, but by French troops who had invaded the Dutch Republic

FIG. 99
Exterior of the Mauritshuis, The Hague

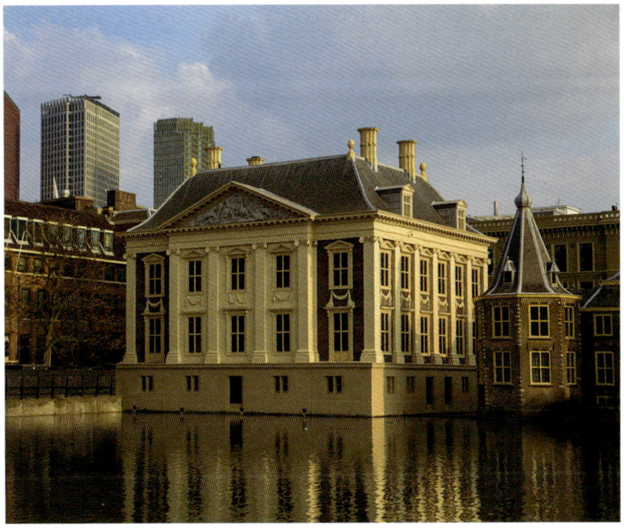

in 1795. The Prince of Orange fled to England, and his art collection was taken to the Louvre in Paris. After Napoleon's final defeat at the Battle of Waterloo, the bulk of the paintings were brought back to the Netherlands thanks to the interventions of the Duke of Wellington. William V had died by this time; his son, King William I (1772–1843), handed over the entire collection to the state in 1816 and the stadholders' paintings have been a state collection ever since – the Royal Picture Gallery.

The first director of the new museum was Johan Steengracht van Oostcapelle (1782–1846). In the summer of 1821, a start was made on moving the paintings from the Gallery to the upper floor of the recently acquired Mauritshuis, where 274 paintings were exhibited in the first years – a sizeable number, especially considering that around 250 works are on display today on two floors of the entire museum. The upper floor must have been filled to the brim. Approximately 120 of these paintings had belonged to William V's collection, but the rest had been acquired between 1816 and 1822 and included works by contemporary artists. These 'modern' masters were taken to another location in 1838, which freed up the wall space urgently needed to accommodate important acquisitions; the ground floor of the building would only became available for exhibiting paintings in 1875. King William I often played a vital role in acquiring paintings for the museum. He stipulated, for example, that Vermeer's now celebrated *View of Delft* go to the Mauritshuis instead of the Rijksmuseum in Amsterdam. Other important purchases soon followed, such as *The Lamentation of Christ* by Rogier van der Weyden, the oldest painting in the collection and still the only work in The Netherlands that is attributed to the artist. In 1828 the Mauritshuis acquired a painting that has become one of its icons, Rembrandt's *Anatomy Lesson of Dr Nicolaes Tulp* (fig. 100).

The appointment of Abraham Bredius (1855–1946) as director in 1889 ushered in a new era for the Mauritshuis. Bredius was a professional art historian with museum experience and a broad network. His keen eye and connections enabled him to make many opportune and advantageous acquisitions. In 1894, for instance, he purchased the portrait of an unknown man which he then attributed convincingly to Hans Memling. Bredius also managed to acquire *The Goldfinch* by Carel Fabritius (fig. 101). His large private fortune enabled him to make important purchases which he subsequently lent to the museum. He also succeeded in persuading a number of private collectors to lend their masterpieces to the Mauritshuis. Having such unique works on loan, many of which were being shown to the public for the first time, attracted additional visitors to the museum and insured the involvement of collectors, which often led to important bequests. The most sensational example of such a benefactor is undoubtedly Arnoldus des Tombe, who bequeathed twelve works to the museum, one of

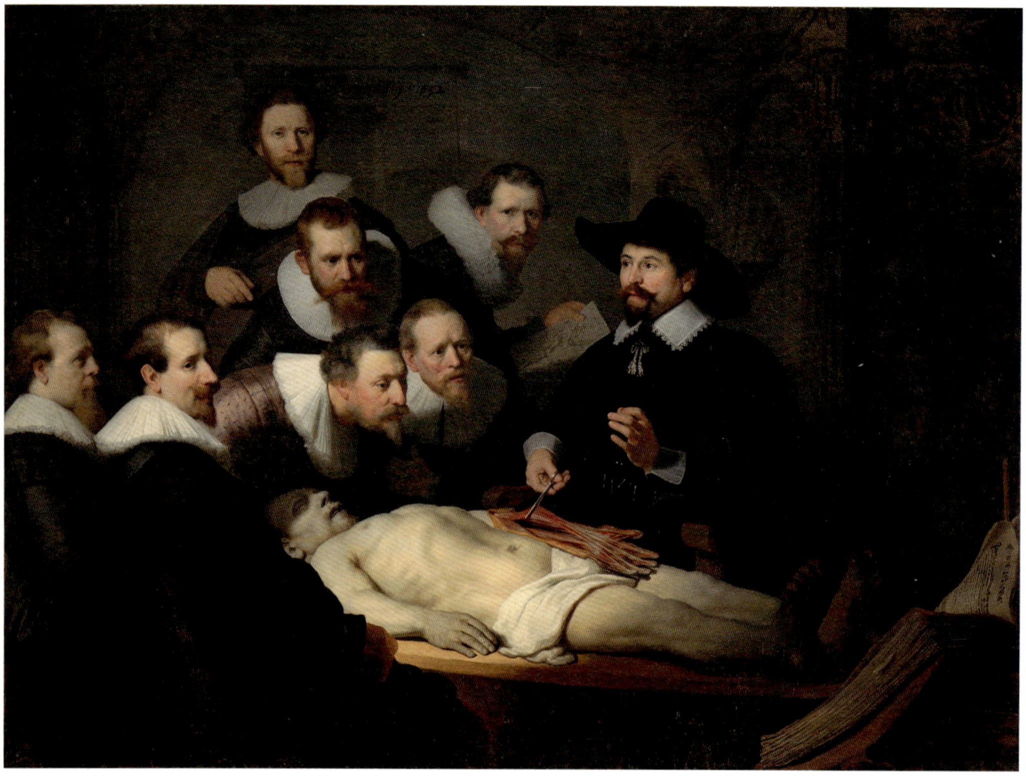

FIG. 100
Rembrandt van Rijn (1606–1669)
The Anatomy Lesson of Dr Nicolaes Tulp, 1632
Oil on canvas, 170 × 217 cm
The Hague, Mauritshuis (146)

which was Vermeer's *Girl with a Pearl Earring* (fig. 102). Bredius himself also made a sizeable bequest to the Mauritshuis – twenty-five paintings, including such highlights as Rembrandt's *Andromeda, Saul and David, Two Moors* and *Homer*.

Bredius was succeeded in 1909 by Wilhelm Martin (1876–1954), another art historian. Martin's great coup was the acquisition of a number of important paintings at the sale of the Steengracht collection, the private holdings of the Mauritshuis's first director. This is how Gerard ter Borch's *Hunting for Lice* entered the collection.

During the Second World War, the most important paintings were put in bomb-proof storerooms, so the collection survived the war largely unscathed. The liberation was followed by a very prosperous period for the Mauritshuis, which has continued to the present day. The museum's pro-active acquisitions policy has led to exceptional purchases. Its aim has always been to strengthen the heart of the collection and fill in the gaps, a prerequisite to purchase always being a painting's high quality and good condition. Above all, the Mauritshuis seeks to share with its visitors the best of seventeenth-century painting of the Northern and Southern Netherlands. This includes the great masters, but the Mauritshuis also upholds the tradition of displaying the very best work of lesser-known artists of the Dutch Golden Age, such as Dirck de Bray's *Still Life of a Bouquet in the Making*, acquired in 2011. Such exceptional purchases depend on the support of others,

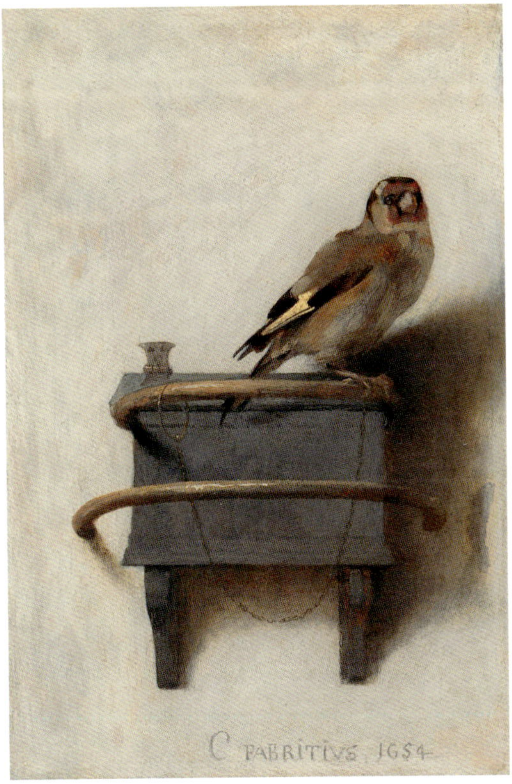

FIG. 101
Carel Fabritius (1622–1654)
The Goldfinch, 1654
Oil on panel, 34 × 23 cm
The Hague, Mauritshuis (605)

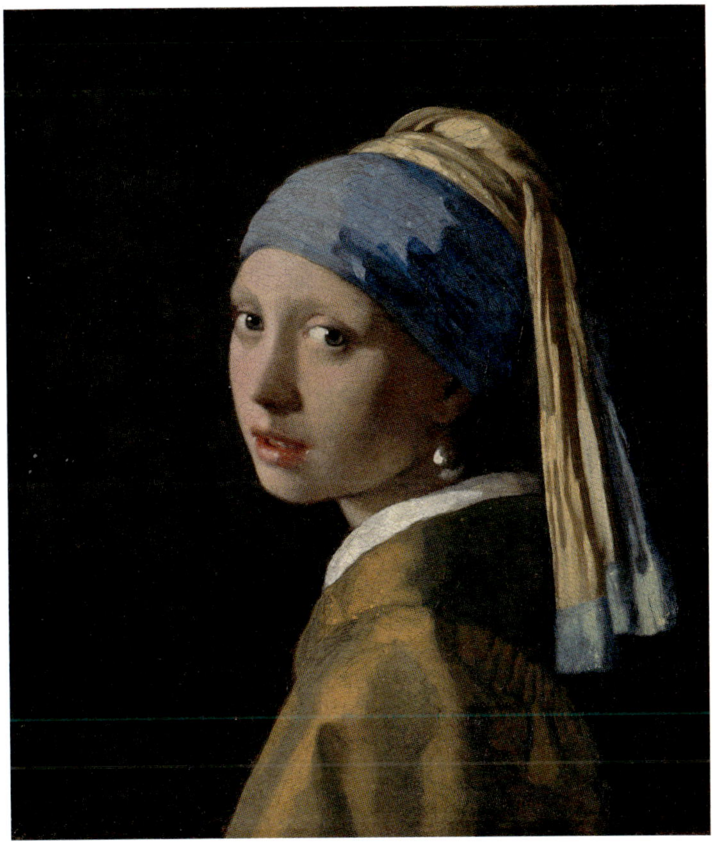

FIG. 102
Johannes Vermeer (1632–1675)
Girl with a Pearl Earring, *c.*1665
Oil on canvas, 44.5 × 39 cm
The Hague, Mauritshuis (670)

such as the Rembrandt Association, the BankGiro Lottery and individual benefactors. The support of the Friends of the Mauritshuis Foundation has also been instrumental in bringing about many important acquisitions. The purchase in 1999, for example, of Rembrandt's extraordinary *Portrait of an Elderly Man* from an English private collection was made possible by a substantial contribution from the Friends.

Today the tasks of a museum include not only acquisitions and care for a collection but also the organisation of exhibitions. The Mauritshuis, like other Dutch museums, has been organising shows with increasing frequency since the 1950s. In 1997, the Mauritshuis was able to set up its own conservation studio under the eaves of the historic building so that both conservation treatment and research can be carried out more intensely and effectively.

In the twenty-first century the Mauritshuis remains a dynamic museum with its sights set firmly on the future. In June 2014 the museum reopened after a major extension and renovation of the building. The museum is now twice as large, with modern and up-to-date visitors' facilities and with the international allure that it deserves. At the same time, the Mauritshuis has retained its distinctive and intimate atmosphere that is so characteristic of this unique location.

BIBLIOGRAPHY

Adshead 2007 D. Adshead, *Wimpole: Architectural Drawings and Topographical Views*, London 2007

Angel 1642 P. Angel, *Lof der Schilder-Konst*, Leiden 1642

Anon 1953 Anon., 'A New Rembrandt Portrait', *The Burlington Magazine*, 84, 1944, pp. 62–63

Art Treasures 1857 *Art Treasures of the United Kingdom*, exh. cat., Manchester (Museum of Ornamental Art) 1857

Baarsen 1996 R. Baarsen, 'Herman Doomer, Ebony Worker in Amsterdam', *The Burlington Magazine*, 128, 1996, pp. 739–49

Baarsen 2007 R. Baarsen, *Furniture in Holland's Golden Age*, Amsterdam 2007

Bachrach, Thijssen and Van Karnebeek-Van Roijen 1970–71 A.G.H. Bachrach, L. Thijssen, D. van Karnebeek-van Roijen, *'Shock of Recognition': The Landscape of English Romanticism and the Dutch Seventeenth-Century School*, exh. cat., The Hague (Mauritshuis) and London (Tate Gallery) 1970–71

Bakker et al. 1984 N. Bakker *et al.*, *Masters of Middelburg. Exhibition in the honour of Laurens J. Bol*, exh. cat., Amsterdam (Waterman Gallery) 1984

Bauch 1960 K. Bauch, *Der frühe Rembrandt und seine Zeit*, Berlin 1960

Beck 1972 H.-U. Beck, *Jan van Goyen, 1596–1656: Ein Oeuvreverzeichnis*, 4 vols., Amsterdam 1972, vol. 2

Beckett 1968 R.B. Beckett (ed.), *John Constable's Correspondence VI: The Fishers*, Ipswich 1968

Bedaux and Ekkart 2000 J.B. Bedaux and R.E.O. Ekkart (eds.), *Pride and Joy: Children's Portraits in the Netherlands 1500–1700*, exh. cat., Haarlem (Frans Hals Museum), Antwerp (Koninklijk Museum voor Schone Kunsten) and Amsterdam, Ghent and New York 2000

Beherman 1988 T. Beherman, *Godfried Schalcken*, Paris 1988

Bergvelt et al. 2004 E. Bergvelt *et al.*, *Hollandse meesters van een Amsterdamse bankier: De verzameling van Adriaan van der Hoop (1778–1854)*, Amsterdam and Zwolle 2004

Berger 2000 H. Berger, Jr., *Fictions of the Pose: Rembrandt Against the Italian Renaissance*, Stanford 2000

Berkvens-Stevelinck, Bots, Hoftijzer and Lankhorst 1992 C. Berkvens-Stevelinck, H. Bots, P.G. Hoftijzer and O.S. Lankhorst (eds.), *Le magasin de l'Univers: The Dutch Republic as the Centre of the European Book Trade*, Leiden 1992

Bikker, Bruijnen and Wuestman 2007 J. Bikker, Y. Bruijnen and G. Wuestman, *Dutch Paintings of the Seventeenth Century in the Rijksmuseum Amsterdam*, Amsterdam 2007, 2 vols.

Birch 1760 T. Birch, *The Life of Henry, Prince of Wales, Eldest Son of King James I*, London 1760

Bode 1883 W. Bode, *Studien zur Geschichte der holländischen Malerei*, Braunschweig, 1883

Bode and De Groot 1989–1900 W. Bode and C. Hofstede de Groot, *Rembrandt*, Paris 1898–1900

Bloemendal, Van Dixhoorn and Strietman 2011 J. Bloemendal, A. van Dixhoorn and E. Strietman (eds.), *Literary Cultures and Public Opinion in the Low Countries, 1450–1650*, Leiden 2011

Bol 1956 L.J. Bol, 'Een Middelburgse Brueghel-groep IV. In Bosschaerts Spoor,' *Oud Holland*, 71, 1956, pp. 132–53

Bol 1960 L.J. Bol, *The Bosschaert Dynasty, Painters of Flowers and Fruit*, Leigh-on-Sea 1960

Bol 1982 L.J. Bol, *'Goede onbekenden'. Hedendaagse herkenning en waardering van verscholen, voorbijgezien en onderschat talent*, Utrecht 1982

Bolten 2007 J. Bolten, *Abraham Bloemaert (c. 1565/1651): The Drawings*, Leiden 2007

Bowett 2007 A. Bowett, 'The Engravings of Daniel Marot', *Furniture History*, 43, 2007, pp. 85–100

Bowett 2014 A. Bowett, 'A Group of Metal Marquetry Tables attributed to Gerrit Jensen', *Furniture History*, 50, 2014, pp. 103–18

Bowett and Lindey 2017 A. Bowett and L. Lindey, 'Looking for Gerrit Jensen', *Furniture History*, vol. 53, 2017, pp. 27–50

Braun 1980 K. Braun, *Alle tot nu toe bekende schilderijen van Jan Steen*, Rotterdam 1980

Bredius 1935 A. Bredius, *Rembrandt Gemälde*, Vienna 1935

Brenninkmeyer-de Rooij et al. 1988 B. Brenninkmeyer-de Rooij *et al.*, *Paintings from England: William III and the Royal Collections*, The Hague (Mauritshuis) 1988

Briels 1997 J. Briels, *Vlaamse schilders en de dageraad van Hollands Gouden Eeuw 1585–1630, met biografieën als bijlage*, Antwerp 1997

Broos et al. 1990–91 B. Broos *et al.*, *Great Dutch Paintings from America*, exh. cat., The Hague (Mauritshuis) and San Francisco (The Fine Arts Museums of San Francisco) 1990–91

Bruyn et al. 1989 J. Bruyn *et al.*, *A Corpus of Rembrandt Paintings, 1635–1642*, Dordrecht, 1989, vol. 3,

Bryant 2003 J. Bryant, *Kenwood: Paintings in the Iveagh Bequest*, London 2003

Buchanan 1824 W. Buchanan, *Memoirs of Painting, with a Chronological History of the Importation of Pictures by the Great Masters into England since the French Revolution*, 2 vols., London 1824

Buijsen et al. 1998 E. Buijsen *et al.*, *Haagse Schilders in de Gouden Eeuw. Het Hoogsteder Lexicon van alle schilders werkzaam in Den Haag 1600–1700*, The Hague and Zwolle 1998

Bürger 1857 W. Bürger (Théophile Thoré), *Trésors d'art exposés à Manchester en 1857 et provenant des collections royales, des collections publiques et des collections particulières de la Grand Bretagne*, Paris 1857

Bürger 1858–60 W. Bürger (Théophile Thoré), *Musées de la Hollande*, 2 vols., Paris 1858–60

Bürger 1866 W. Bürger (Théophile Thoré), 'Van der Meer de Delft', *Gazette des Beaux-Arts*, 21, 1866, pp. 297–330, 458–575

Buvelot 2004 Q. Buvelot, *Mauritshuis: A Summary Catalogue*, The Hague and Zwolle 2004

Buvelot 2005 Q. Buvelot, *Frans van Mieris, 1635–1681*, exh. cat., The Hague (Mauritshuis) and Washington, DC (National Gallery of Art), 2005

Buvelot 2008 Q. Buvelot, 'Frans Post (1612–1680): Catalogue raisonné. By Pedro & Bia Corrêa do Lago', *The Burlington Magazine*, 150, 2008, pp. 116–17

Buvelot and Buijs 2002 Q. Buvelot and H. Buijs, *A Choice Collection: Seventeenth-Century Dutch Paintings from the Frits Lugt Collection*, The Hague (Mauritshuis) 2002

Buvelot, Hilaire and Zeder 1998 Q. Buvelot, M. Hilaire and O. Zeder, *Tableaux flamands et hollandais du Musée Fabre de Montpellier*, Paris, Montpellier and Zwolle 1998

Buvelot and Gordenker 2016 Quentin Buvelot and Emilie Gordenker (eds.), *Thank you! A Tribute to Willem Baron van Dedem (1929–2015)*, The Hague 2016

Buvelot et al. 2004 Q. Buvelot *et al.*, *Albert Eckhout: A Dutch Artist in Brazil*, The Hague (Mauritshuis) 2004

Buvelot et al. 2011–12 Q. Buvelot *et al.*, *Ilone et George Kremer: Héritiers de l'Âge d'Or hollandais*, Paris (Pinacothèque de Paris) 2011–12

Buvelot et al. 2017 Q. Buvelot *et al.*, *Slow Food: Dutch and Flemish Meal Still Lifes 1600–1640*, exh. cat., The Hague (Mauritshuis) 2017

Chong 1987–88 A. Chong, 'The Market for Landscape Painting in Seventeenth Century Holland', in Sutton *et al.* 1987–88, pp.104–20

Clarke and Foxcroft 1907 T. E. S. Clarke and H. C. Foxcroft, *A Life of Gilbert Burnet, Bishop of Salisbury*, Cambridge 1907

Colvin 1984 H. Colvin, 'Letters and Papers Relating to the Rebuilding of Combe Abbey, Warwickshire, 1681–1688', *The Walpole Society*, 50, 1984, pp. 248–309

Cornelis and Schaplehouman 2016 B. Cornelis and M. Schaplelhouman, *Adriaen van de Velde: Dutch Master of Landscape*, exh. cat., London (Dulwich Picture Gallery) 2016

Corrêa do Lago 2007 Pedro and Bia Corrêa do Lago, *Frans Post (1612–1680): Catalogue Raisonné*, Milan 2007

Corrêa do Lago and Ducos 2005 P. Corrêa do Lago and B. Ducos, *Frans Post (1612–1680): Le Brésil à la cour de Louis XIV*, exh. cat., Paris (Musée du Louvre) 2005

Crosby Ivy 1991 J. Crosby Ivy, *Constable and the Critics, 1802–1837*, Woodbridge 1991

De Bruin 2016 A. de Bruin, 'Frans Post: Animals in Brazil', *Master Drawings*, 54, 2016, pp. 292–368

De Groot 1907–28 C. Hofstede de Groot, *A Catalogue Raisonné of the Most Eminent Dutch Painters of the Seventeenth Century*, 8 vols., London 1907–28

De Groot 1911–12 C. Hofstede de Groot, 'Nieuw Ontdekte Rembrandts (II)', *Onze Kunst*, 22, 1911–12

De Meyere 2006 J. De Meyere, *Utrechtse schilderkunst in de Gouden Eeuw: Honderd schilderijen uit de collectie van het Centraal Museum te Utrecht*, Utrecht 2006

De Winkel 2006 Marieke de Winkel, *Fashion and Fancy: Dress and Meaning in Rembrandt's Paintings*, Amsterdam 2006

Dixon Hunt 1990 J. Dixon Hunt (ed.), *The Dutch Garden in the Seventeenth Century*, Dumbarton Oakes 1990

Duffy-Zebellow and Fletcher 2014 L. Duffy-Zebellos and S. Fletcher, 'Three Questioned Rembrandts re-enter the Canon: More to Come', *International Foundation for Art Research (IFAR) Journal*, 15, no. 2, 2014, pp. 32–39

Dukelskaya and Moore 2002 L. Dukelskaya and A. Moore (eds.), *A Capital Collection: Houghton Hall and the Hermitage. With a Modern Edition of Aedes Walpolianae, Horace Walpole's Catalogue of Sir Robert Walpole's Collection*, New Haven and London 2002

Dutuit 1881–85 E. Dutuit, *L'Œuvre Complet de Rembrandt*, 2 vols., Paris 1881–85

Ekkart 2000 R. E. O. Ekkart, 'Diest, Adriaen van', in *Saur Allgemeines Künstlerlexikon: Die bildenden Künstler aller Zeiten und Völker*, 92 parts, Munich 2000, vol. 27

Ekkart and Buvelot 2007–08 R. E. O. Ekkart *et al.*, *Dutch Portraits: The Age of Rembrandt and Frans Hals*, exh. cat., London (National Gallery) and The Hague (Mauritshuis) 2007–08

Esterly 1998 David Esterly, *Grinling Gibbons and the Art of Carving*, exh. cat., London (Victoria and Albert Museum) 1998

Ferguson 2016 P. F. Ferguson, *Ceramics, 400 Years of British Collecting in 100 Masterpieces*, London 2016

Fila and Dekker 2013 Jack Fila and Jeroen J. H. Dekker, *De Kunst van het Opvoeden*, exh. cat., Dordrecht (Dordrechts Museum) 2013

Fock 2001 C. Willemijn Fock (ed.), *Het Nederlandse interieur in beeld 1600–1900*, Zwolle 2001

Foster 1889 J. Foster, *Register of Admissions to Gray's Inn 1521–1889*, London 1889

Fredericksen et al. 1988–96 Burton Fredericksen *et al.*, *The Index of Paintings Sold in the British Isles During the Nineteenth Century*, 4 vols., Santa Barbara 1988–96

Frederiks 1958 J. W. Frederiks, *Dutch Silver: Wrought Plate of North and South-Holland from the Renaissance until the end of the Eighteenth Century*, The Hague 1958

Frijhoff and Spies 2004 W. Frijhoff and M. Spies, *Dutch Culture in a European Perspective: 1650, Hard-Won Unity*, 5 vols., London 2004

Gemar-Koeltzsch, Ertz and Nitze-Ertz 1995 E. Gemar-Koeltzsch, K. Ertz, C. Nitze-Ertz, *Holländische Stillebenmaler im 17. Jahhundert*, 3 parts, Lingen 1995

Gerson 1968 H. Gerson, *Rembrandt Paintings*, London 1968

Gerson 1983 H. Gerson, *Ausbreitung und Nachwirkung der holländischen Malerei des 17. Jahrhunderts*, Amsterdam 1983 (1st edn 1942)

Giltaij and Jansen 1991 J. Giltaij and G. Jansen (eds.), *Perspectiven: Saenredam en de architectuurschilders van de 17e eeuw*, exh. cat., Rotterdam (Museum Boijmans Van Beuningen) 1991

Gore 1964 F. St John Gore, *Upton House, The Bearsted Collection: Pictures*, London 1964

Graham 1716 R. Graham, *A Short Account of the Most Eminent Painters, both Ancient and Modern, down to the Present Times*, 2nd edn, London 1716

Griffiths 1998 A. Griffiths, *The Print in Stuart Britain, 1603–1689*, London 1998

Gudlaugsson 1959–60 S. Gudlaugsson, *Geraert Ter Borch*, 2 vols., The Hague 1959–60

Haak 2003 B. Haak, *The Golden Age: Dutch Painters of the Seventeenth Century*, Zwolle 2003 (Dutch edn 1984)

Hardinge 1816 G. Hardinge, *Biographical Memoirs of The Rev. Sneyd Davis*, London 1816

Harris 1978 J. Harris, 'A Bird's-Eye View of Dunham Massey', *Apollo*, 53, 1978

Harris 1979 J. Harris, *The Artist and the Country House. A History of Country House and Garden View Painting in Britain 1540–1870*, London 1979

Harwood et al. 2002 L.B. Harwood *et al.*, *Inspired by Italy, Dutch landscape painting 1600–1700*, exh. cat., London (Dulwich Picture Gallery) 2002

Haskell 1976 F. Haskell, *Rediscoveries in Art: Some Aspects of Taste, Fashion and Collecting in England and France*, London 1976

Hearn 1995–96 K. Hearn (ed.), *Dynasties: Painting in Tudor and Jacobean England 1530–1630*, exh. cat., London (The Tate Gallery) 1995–96

Hearn 2004 K. Hearn, 'Merchant Patrons for the Painter Siberechts', in M. Galinou (ed.), *City Merchants and the Arts 1670–1720*, Wetherby 2004, pp. 83–92

Hearn 2015 K. Hearn, *Cornelius Johnson*, London 2015

Heemstra and Marchant 2000 G. van Heemstra and R. Marchant, 'The Upton House Saenredam, Conservation and Technique', *Hamilton Kerr Bulletin*, 3, 2000, pp. 69–88

Hellinga 1962 W.G. Hellinga, *Copy and Print in the Netherlands. An Atlas of Historical Bibliography*, Amsterdam 1962

Hellinga 2001 L. Hellinga (ed.), *The Bookshop of the World : The Role of the Low Countries in the Book-trade, 1473–1941*, 't Goy-Houten 2001

Helmus et al. 2000–01 L.M. Helmus *et al.*, *Pieter Saenredam, het Utrechtse werk: Schilderijen en tekeningen van de 17de-eeuwse grootmeester van het perspectief*, exh. cat. Utrecht (Centraal Museum) 2000–01

Helmus et al. 2002 L.M. Helmus *et al.*, *Pieter Saenredam, the Utrecht work: Paintings and Drawings by the 17th-century Master of Perspective*, exh. cat., Los Angeles (The J. Paul Getty Museum) 2002

Helmus and Wuestman 2008–09 L.M. Helmus and Gerdian Wuestman, *Saenredam: La fachada occidental de la Iglesia de Santa Maria de Utrecht*, Madrid (Museo Thyssen-Bornemisza), 2008–09

Hofstede de Groot 1907–28 C. Hofstede de Groot, *Beschreibendes und kritisches Verzeichnis der Werke der hervorragendsten Holländischen Maler des XVII. Jahrhunderts*, 10 vols., Eslingen a.N. and Paris 1907–28

Houbraken 1718–21 A. Houbraken, *De groote schouburgh der Nederlantsche konstschilders en schilderessen*, 3 vols., Amsterdam 1718–21

Ingamells 2009 J. Ingamells, *Later Stuart Portraits 1685–1714*, London (National Portrait Gallery) 2009

Jackson-Stops 1985 G. Jackson-Stops (ed.), *The Treasure Houses of Britain: Five Hundred Years of Private Patronage and Art Collecting*, exh. cat., Washington, DC (National Gallery of Art), 1985

Jackson-Stops 1988 G. Jackson-Stops, 'The Court Style in Britain', in R. Baarsen, P.M. Johnston, G. Jackson-Stops and E. Evans Dee (eds.), *Courts and Colonies: The William and Mary Style in Holland, England, and America*, exh. cat., New York (Cooper-Hewitt Museum) and Pittsburgh (Carnegie Museum) 1988

Jacobsen 1932 G. Jacobsen, *William Blathwayt: A Late Seventeenth Century English Administrator*, New Haven and London 1932

Jacques 2002 D. Jacques, 'Who Knows what a Dutch Garden Is?', *Garden History* (Garden History Society), 30, no. 2, Winter 2002, pp. 114–30

Jacques 2017 D. Jacques, *Gardens of Court and Country: English Design 1630–1730*, New Haven 2017

Jacques and Van der Horst 1988 D. Jacques and A. van der Horst, *The Gardens of William and Mary*, Bromley 1988

Jameson 1844 A. Jameson, *Companion to the most celebrated private galleries of art in London containing accurate catalogues, arranged alphabetically, for immediate reference, each preceded by an historical & critical introduction, with a prefatory essay on art, artists, collectors & connoisseurs*, London 1844

Jansen, Ekkart and Verhave 2011–12 A. Jansen, R. Ekkart, J. Verhave, *De portretfabriek van Michiel van Mierevelt (1566–1641)*, Delft (Museum Het Prinsenhof) 2011–12

Jardine 2008 L. Jardine, *Going Dutch*, London 2008

Jervis 1998 S. Jervis, 'Ebony at The Argory: 'Een Ebbenhout cabinet met parlemoer ingeleydt'', *Apollo*, 147, April 1998, pp. 42–44

Johns 2016 R. Johns, 'After Van de Velde', in E. Hughes (ed.), *Spreading Canvas: Eighteenth-Century British Marine Painting*, exh. cat., New Haven (Yale Center for British Art) 2016, pp. 17–39

Judson and Ekkart 1999 J. Richard Judson and R.E.O. Ekkart, *Gerrit van Honthorst, 1592–1656*, Dornspijk 1999

Jowell 1977 F.S. Jowell, 'Thoré-Bürger and the Art of the Past', diss. Harvard University, Cambridge, Mass., 1977

Karst 2013–14 S. Karst, 'Off to a new Cockaigne: Dutch Migrant Artists in London, 1660–1715', *Simiolus*, 37, 2013–14

Kempski and Juang 2015 M. Kempski and S. Kuang, 'Technical Report – A Magus at a Table, Upton House', National Trust 2015

Kersten, Lokin and Plomp 1996 M.C.C. Kersten, D.H.A.C. Lokin and M.C. Plomp, *Delft Masters: Vermeer's Contemporaries*, exh. cat., Delft (Stedelijk Museum Het Prinsenhof) 1996

Ketton-Cremer 1962 R.W. Ketton-Cremer, *Felbrigg: The Story of a House*, London 1962

Kisluk-Grosheide 2000 Daniëlle Kisluk-Grosheide, 'The (Ab)Use of Export Lacquer in Europe', in Michael Kühlenthal, ed., *Ostasiatische und Europäische Lacktechniken*, Munich 2000, pp. 27–42

Kloek 1977 W. Kloek, 'Art in 17th-Century Holland', *Simiolus*, 9 1977, pp. 116–18

Kollmann 2000 S. Kollmann, *Niederländische Künstler und Kunst im London des 17. Jahrhunderts*, Hildesheim, Zurich and London 2000

Kopplin 2015 M. Kopplin (ed.), *Gérard Dagly (1660–1715) und die Berliner Hofwerkstatt*, Munich 2015

Krempel 1999 León Krempel, *Studien zu den datierten Gemälden des Nicolaes Maes (1634–1693)*, Petersberg 1999

Krist and Iby 2015 G. Krist and E. Iby (eds.), *Investigation and Conservation of East Asian Cabinets in Imperial Residences (1700–1900)*, Vienna, Cologne and Weimar 2015

Laing 1991 A. Laing, 'Whence this Clutch of Four?', *Country Life*, 185, June 1991, pp.172–3

Laing 1993 A. Laing, 'Sir Peter Lely and Sir Ralph Bankes', in D. Howarth (ed.), *Art and Patronage in the Caroline Courts*, Cambridge 1993

Laing 1995 A. Laing, *In Trust for the Nation: Paintings from National Trust Houses*, exh. cat., London (National Gallery) 1995

Lambert 1985 A.M. Lambert, *The Making of the Dutch Landscape: An Historical Geography of the Netherlands*, London, 1985

Lambooy 2014 S. Lambooy, 'Imitation and Inspiration: The Artistic Rivalry between Delft Earthenware and Chinese Porcelain', in J. van Campen and T. Eliëns (eds.), *Chinese and Japanese porcelain for the Dutch Golden Age*, Zwolle 2014

Langemeyer et al. 1974 G. Langemeyer *et al.*, *Gerard Ter Borch, Zwolle 1617 – Deventer 1681*, exh. cat., The Hague (Mauritshuis) and Münster (Landesmuseum) 1974

Lecaldano 1969 P. Lecaldano, *The Complete Paintings of Rembrandt*, London 1969

Lewis 2014 Y. Lewis, 'A Young Royalist Abroad in the 1640s: In Pursuit of "Mr John Bankes's observations on his travels"', *National Trust Arts, Buildings, Collections Bulletin*, Autumn 2014

Lloyd 2004 C. Lloyd, *Enchanting the Eye: Dutch Paintings of the Golden Age*, exh. cat., London (Royal Collection) 2004

Lloyd Williams 1992 J. Lloyd Williams, *Dutch Art and Scotland: A Reflection of Taste*, exh. cat., Edinburgh (National Gallery of Scotland), 1992

Loukes 2016 A. Loukes, *Remastered: Bosch to Bellotto – An Exhibition of Petworth's European Old Masters*, exh. cat., Petworth (Petworth House) 2016

Louw 2009 H. Louw, 'Dutch Influences on British Architecture in the Late-Stuart Period, c.1660-c.1714', *Dutch Crossing*, 33, no. 2, October 2009

Lowenthal 1986 A. Lowenthal, *Joachim Wtewael and Dutch Mannerism*, Doornspijk 1986

Luijten, Van Suchtelen, Baarsen and Kloek 1993 G. Luijten, A. van Suchtelen, R. Baarsen, W. Kloek (eds.), *Dawn of the Golden Age: Northern Netherlandish Art 1580–1620*, exh. cat., Amsterdam (Rijksmuseum) 1993

MacLaren 1991 N. MacLaren, *Christopher Brown, The Dutch School: 1600–1900*, 2 vols., London 1991

MacLeod, Marciari Alexander et al. 2001 C. MacLeod, J. Marciari Alexander *et al.*, *Painted Ladies: Women at the Court of Charles II*, exh. cat., London (National Portrait Gallery) 2001

Mandelbrote and Lewis 2004 G. Mandelbrote and Y. Lewis, *Learning to Collect: the Library of Sir Richard Ellys (1682–1742) at Blickling Hall*, London 2004

Marijnissen et al. 1992 P. Marijnissen *et al.* (eds.), *De Zichtbaere Werelt: Schilderkunst uit de Gouden Eeuw in Hollands oudste stad*, exh. cat., Dordrechts (Dordrechts Museum) 1992

McCabe 2015 I. B. McCabe, *A History of Global Consumption, 1500–1800*, London and New York 2015

McNeil Kettering 1988 A. McNeil Kettering, *Drawings from the Ter Borch Studio Estate*, 2 vols., Amsterdam 1988, vol. 2

Meijer 1996 F.G. Meijer, 'Bosschaert, Ambrosius d. J.', in *Saur Allgemeines Künstlerlexikon: Die bildenden Künstler aller Zeiten und Völker*, 92 parts, Munich 1996

Michel 1893 E. Michel, *Rembrandt. Sa vie, son oeuvre et son temps*, Paris 1893

Millar 1960 O. Millar, 'Abraham van der Doort's Catalogue of the Collections of Charles I', *The Walpole Society*, 37 1960

Millar 1963 O. Millar, *The Tudor, Stuart and Early Georgian Pictures in the Collection of Her Majesty The Queen*, 2 vols., London 1963

Millar 1964 O. Millar, *The Orange and the Rose: Holland and Britain in the Age of Observation, 1600–1750*, exh. cat., London (Victoria and Albert Museum) 1964

Millar 1978 O. Millar, *Sir Peter Lely*, exh. cat., London (National Portrait Gallery) 1978

Moes 1897–1905 E.W. Moes, *Iconographia Batava*, 2 vols., Amsterdam 1897–1905

Moore 1985 A.W. Moore, *Norfolk & The Grand Tour: Eighteenth-century travellers abroad and their souvenirs*, exh. cat., Norwich (Norwich Castle Museum) 1985

Mowl and Earnshaw 1995 T. Mowl and B. Earnshaw, *Architecture without Kings: The rise of puritan classicism under Cromwell,* Manchester 1995

Muller and Murrel 1997 J.M. Muller and J. Murrell (eds.), *Edward Norgate: Miniatura or the Art of Limning*, New Haven and London 1997

Naumann 1981 O. Naumann, *Frans van Mieris (1635–1681) the Elder*, Doornspijk 1981

Nieuhof 1665 J. Nieuhof, *Het gezantschap der Neerlandtsche Oost-Indische Compagnie, aan den grooten Tartarischen Cham, den tegenwoordigen keizer van China*... Amsterdam 1665

Nieuwenhuys 1834 C.J. Nieuwenhuys, *A Review of the Lives and Works of Some of the Most Eminent Painters*, London, 1834

Nihom-Nijstad 1983 S. Nihom-Bijstad, *Reflets du siècle d'or : tableaux Hollandais du dix-septième siècle*, Paris (Institut Néerlandais) 1983

Norwich 1795 *The Norfolk Tour: Or, Traveller's Pocket Companion, being a Concise Description of all the Principal Towns, Noblemens and Gentlemens Seats, and other Remarkable Places in the County of Norfolk*, Norwich 1795

Peeters, Sutton, Goossens et al. 1997 J. Peeters, P. Sutton, E.J. Goossens *et al.*, *Het Paleis in de schilderkunst van de Gouden Eeuw*, exh. cat., Amsterdam (Royal Palace) 1997

Peronnet et al. 1998 B. Peronnet *et al.*, *Répertoire des tableaux vendus en France au XIXe siècle: 1801–1810*, 2 vols., Santa Monica 1998

Perry Chapman, Kloek and Wheelock, 1996 H. Perry Chapman, W.T. Kloek, A.K. Wheelock, *Jan Steen: Painter and Storyteller*, exh. cat., Washington, DC (National Gallery of Art), and Amsterdam (Rijksmuseum) 1996

Portrait Groups 1960 *Portrait Groups from National Trust Collections*, exh. cat., Eastbourne (Towner Art Gallery) 1960

Public Catalogue Foundation 2013 *Oil Paintings in National Trust Properties*, 6 vols., London 2013

Purcell 2017 M. Purcell, *The Country House Library*, New Haven and London, 2017

Pyne 1819 W.H. Pyne, *The History of the Royal Residences of Windsor Castle, St James's Palace, Carlton House, Kensington Palace, Hampton Court, Buckingham House, and Frogmore*, 3 vols., London, 1819

Quodbach 2014 E. Quodbach (ed.), *Holland's Golden Age in America: Collecting the Art of Rembrandt, Vermeer and Hals (Studies in the History of Art Collecting in America, no. 1)*, New York 2014

Ressing 2000 H. Ressing, 'Delfts aardewerk in Dyrham Park', *Voormen uit Vuur*, 173, no. 4, 2000, pp. 1–32

Rikken 2008 Marrigje Rikken, *Melchior d'Hondecoeter – Bird painter*, Amsterdam 2008

Robins 1842 G. Robins, *Mr. George Robins is Honoured With Instruction to Announce for Unreserved Competition ... the Splendid Property of Every Denomination Appertaining to Shugborough Hall*, London 1842

Robinson 1958 M.S. Robinson, *Van de Velde Drawings: A Catalogue of Drawings in the National Maritime Museum made by the Elder and the Younger Willem Van de Velde*, Cambridge 1958

Robinson 1990 M.S. Robinson, *Van de Velde: A Catalogue of the Paintings of the Elder and the Younger Willem Van de Velde*, 2 vols., London 1990

Roding et al. 2003 Juliette Roding *et al.*, eds., *Dutch and Flemish Artists in Britain 1550–1800*, Leiden 2003

Roethlisberger and Bok 1993 M.G. Roethlisberger and M.J. Bok, *Abraham Bloemaert and his Sons: Paintings and Prints,* Ghent 1993

Rothschild 1897 Baron F. Rothschild, *The Red Book*, privately printed 1897

Rothwell 2000 J. Rothwell, *Dunham Massey, Cheshire,* London, 2000

Rowell 2000 C. Rowell, 'Grinling Gibbons's Carved Room at Petworth: "The most superb monument of his skill"', *Apollo*, 151, no. 458, April 2000, pp. 19–26

Rowell 2012 C. Rowell, *Petworth: the People and the Place*, London 2012

Rowell 2013 C. Rowell (ed.), *Ham House: 400 Years of Collecting and Patronage*, New Haven and London, 2013

Sambrook 2003 P. Sambrook, *A Country House at Work: Three Centuries of Dunham Massey*, London 2003

Schama 1987–88 S. Schama, 'Dutch Landscapes: Culture as Foreground', in Sutton 1987–88, pp. 64–83

Schama 1987 S. Schama, *The Embarrassment of Riches: An Interpretation of Dutch Culture in the Golden Age*, London 1987

Schneider 1932 H. Schneider, *Jan Lievens*, Haarlem 1932

Schneider and Ekkart 1973 H. Schneider and R. E. O. Ekkart, *Jan Lievens: Sein Leben und Seine Werke*, Amsterdam 1973

Schroder 2007 T. Schroder, *Renaissance Silver from the Schroder Collection*, exh. cat., London (Wallace Collection) 2007

Schwartz and Bok 1989 G. Schwartz and M. J. Bok, *Pieter Saenredam: De schilder in zijn tijd*, Maarssen and The Hague 1989 (English edn 1990)

Sebag-Montefiore and Armstrong-Totten 2013 C. Sebag-Montefiore and J. Armstrong-Totten, *A Dynasty of Dealers: John Smith and Successors 1801–1924: A Study of the Art Market in Nineteenth-Century London*, London 2013

Segal and Roding 1994 S. Segal and M. Roding, *De Tulp en de Kunst, verhaal van een symbool*, exh. cat., Amsterdam (Nieuwe Kerk) 1994

Sevcik 2015–16 A. K. Sevcik (ed.), *Schalcken: Gemalte Verführung*, exh. cat., Cologne (Wallraf-Richartz-Museum & Fondation Corboud) and Dordrecht (Dordrechts Museum) 2015–16

Sharpin 1842 E. C. Sharpin, *Death Scenes: Extracted from Biographical and Other Works*, London, 1842

Shaw 1990 B. Shaw, 'Pieter van Roestraeten and the English 'vanitas'', *The Burlington Magazine* 132, 1990, pp. 132–36

Shawe-Taylor 2010 D. Shawe-Taylor, *Dutch Landscapes*, exh. cat., London (Royal Collection) 2010

Shawe-Taylor and Buvelot 2015–17 D. Shawe-Taylor and Q. Buvelot, *Masters of the Everyday: Dutch Artists in the Age of Vermeer*, exh. cat., London (Queen's Gallery), Edinburgh (Queen's Gallery) and The Hague (Mauritshuis) 2015–17

Shawe-Taylor and Rumberg 2018 D. Shawe-Taylor and P. Rumberg (eds.), *Charles I: King and Collector*, London (Royal Academy) 2018

Sikkens-De Zwaan 2002 M. Sikkens-De Zwaan, 'Magdelena Poulle (1632–99): A Dutch Lady in a Circle of Botanical Collectors', *Garden History* (Garden History Society), 30, no. 2, Winter 2002, pp. 206–20

Simon 2014 J. Simon, *Picture Frames at Ham House*, The National Trust, 2014

Simpson 1953 F. Simpson, 'Dutch Paintings in England before 1760', *The Burlington Magazine*, 95, 1953, pp. 39–42

Sitwell 2015 C. Sitwell, 'Revelations through Science: 'A Magus at a Table' by Jan Lievens at Upton House', *National Trust Arts, Buildings, Collections Bulletin*, Autumn 2015

Slatkes 1992 L. J. Slatkes, *Rembrandt. Catalogo completo dei dipinti*, Florence 1992

Slive et al. 1989–90 S. Slive *et al.*, *Frans Hals*, exh. cat. Washington, DC (National Gallery of Art), London (Royal Academy of Arts) and Haarlem (Frans Hals Museum) 1989–90

Sluijter-Seijffert 2016 N. Sluijter-Seijffert, *Cornelis van Poelenburch, 1594/5–1667, The Paintings*, Amsterdam 2016

Smith 1829–42 J. Smith, *A Catalogue Raisonné of the Works of the Most Eminent Dutch, Flemish, and French Painters*, 8 vols. and supplement, London 1829–42

Smith 1860 T. Smith, *Recollections of the British Institution for Promoting the Fine Arts in the United Kingdom; with some Account of the Means Employed for that Purpose and Biographical Notices of the Artists who have Received Premiums &c, 1805–1859*, London 1860

Snodin and Llewellyn 2009 M. Snodin and N. Llewellyn (eds.), *Baroque 1620–1800: Style in the Age of Magnificence*, exh. cat., London (Victoria and Albert Museum), London 2009

Standen 1980 E. A. Standen, 'English Tapestries 'after the Indian Manner'', *Metropolitan Museum Journal*, 15, 1980, pp. 119–42

Stoesser-Johnston 2002 A. Stoesser-Johnston, 'Robert Hooke and Holland: Dutch influence on his architecture', *Bulletin KNOB*, 99.2000.4, 2002, pp. 121–37

Stourton and Sebag-Montefiore 2010 J. Stourton and C. Sebag-Montefiore, *The British as Art Collectors: From the Tudors to the Present*, London 2010

Strong 2000 R. Strong, *The Artist and the Garden*, New Haven and London 2000

Sumowski 1983–90 W. Sumowski, *Gemälde der Rembrandt-Schüler*, 5 vols., Landau/Pfalz 1983–90

Sutton 1980 P. C. Sutton, *Pieter de Hooch: Complete Edition*, Oxford and New York 1980

Sutton 1992 P. C. Sutton, *Dutch & Flemish Seventeenth-Century Paintings: The Harold Samuel Collection*, London 1992

Sutton 1998 P. C. Sutton, *Pieter de Hooch 1629–1684*, exh. cat., London (Dulwich Picture Gallery) and Hartford (Wadsworth Atheneum) 1998

Sutton 2002 P. C. Sutton, *Dutch & Flemish Paintings: The Collection of Willem Baron van Dedem*, London, 2002 (with a supplement published in 2012)

Sutton et al. 1987–88 P. Sutton *et al.* (ed.), *Masters of the 17th Century Dutch Landscape*, exh. cat., Amsterdam (Rijksmuseum), Boston (Museum of Fine Arts) and Philadelphia (Museum of Art) 1987–88

Taylor 2002 D. A. H. B. Taylor, 'Ravenous Covetousness: Sir Peter Lely's portraits of the Duchess of Lauderdale', *History Scotland*, 2, no. 2, 2002

Taylor 2012 D. A. H. B. Taylor, 'Lely in Arcadia: religious, pastoral, musical and mythological themes in Peter Lely's subject pictures', in C. Campbell (ed.), *Peter Lely: A Lyrical Vision*, exh. cat. London (Courtauld Gallery) 2012

Ter Molen 1984 J. ter Molen, *Van Vianen. Een Utrechtse familie van zilversmeden met een internationale faam*, Rotterdam 1984

Thieme-Becker U. Thieme and F. Becker, *Allgemeines Lexikon der bildenden Künstler von der Antike bis zur Gegenwart*, 37 vols., Leipzig 1907–50

Thornton and Tomlin 1980 P. Thornton and M. Tomlin, 'The Furnishing and Decoration of Ham House', *Furniture History*, 16, 1980

Tomlin 1982 M. Tomlin, *Ham House*, London 1982

Tümpel 1986 C. Tümpel, *Rembrandt in Selstzeugnissen und Bilddokumenten*, Amsterdam 1986

Valentiner 1908 W. R. Valentiner, *Rembrandt des Meisters Gemälde*, Berlin 1908

Valentiner 1921 W. R. Valentiner, *Rembrandt: Wiedergefundene Gemälde*, Stuttgart and Berlin 1921

Van Asperen de Boer and Helmus 2000 J. R. J. van Asperen de Boer and L. M. Helmus (eds.), *The Paintings of Pieter Jansz. Saenredam (1597–1665): Conservation and Technique*, Utrecht 2000

Van der Ploeg and Vermeeren 1997–98 P. van der Ploeg and C. Vermeeren (eds.), *Princely patrons: the collection of Frederick Henry of Orange and Amalia of Solms in The Hague*, exh. cat., The Hague (Mauritshuis) 1997–98

Van der Vinde 2007 L. van der Vinde, *Children in the Mauritshuis*, Zwolle 2007

Van de Wetering 2005 E. van de Wetering, *A Corpus of Rembrandt Paintings IV: Self-portraits*, Dordrecht 2005

Van de Wetering 2014 E. van de Wetering, *A Corpus of Rembrandt Painting VI: Rembrandt's Paintings Revisited – A Complete Survey*, Dordrecht 2014

Van der Willigen and Kinkelder 1993–98 A. van der Willigen and M.C. Kinkelder, 'Dictionary of Dutch and Flemish Landscape and Marine painters working in oils, active before 1725', typescript 1993–98 (RKD, The Hague)

Van der Willigen and Meijer 2003 A. van der Willigen and F. G. Meijer, *A Dictionairy of Dutch and Flemish Still-life Painters Working in Oils, 1525–1725*, Leiden 2003

Van Gelder 1953 (1) [J.G. van Gelder] Editorial: Dutch Pictures at the Royal Academy', *The Burlington Magazine*, 95, 1953, p. 34

Van Gelder 1953 (2) J.G. van Gelder, 'Rembrandt and his Circle', *The Burlington Magazine*, 95, 1953, pp. 34–39

Van Strien 1998 K. van Strien, *Touring the Low Countries: Accounts of British Travellers*, Amsterdam 1998

Van Suchtelen 2010 A. van Suchtelen, *Jan Steen in the Mauritshuis*, The Hague 2010

Van Suchtelen 2015 A. van Suchtelen, *Dutch Self-Portraits of the Golden Age*, exh. cat., The Hague (Mauritshuis) 2015

Van Suchtelen et al. 2001 A. van Suchtelen *et al.*, *Holland Frozen in Time: The Dutch Winter Landscape in the Golden Age*, exh. cat., The Hague (Mauritshuis) 2001

Van Suchtelen, Buvelot et al. 2016, A. van Suchtelen, Q. Buvelot *et al.*, *Genre Paintings in the Mauritshuis*, The Hague and Zwolle 2016

Van Suchtelen and Wheelock 2008–09 A. van Suchtelen and A.K. Wheelock, *Dutch Cityscapes of the Golden Age*, The Hague (Mauritshuis) and Washington, DC (National Gallery of Art) 2008–09

Van Thiel and De Bruyn Kops 1984 P.J.J. van Thiel and C.J. de Bruyn Kops, *Prijst de Lijst*, exh. cat., Amsterdam (Rijksmuseum) 1984

Van Westrheene 1856 T. van Westrheene, *Jan Steen*, The Hague 1856

Vertue 1930–47 G. Vertue, 'Note Books', *Walpole Society*, 6 vols., London 1930–47

Vosmaer 1868 C. Vosmaer, *Rembrandt Harmensz. Van Rijn, sa vie at ses oeuvres*, The Hague 1868

Waagen 1854–57 G. Waagen, *Treasures of Art in Great Britain: Being an Account of the Chief Collections of Paintings, Drawings, Sculptures*, 3 vols. and supplement, London 1854 and 1857

Waiboer et al. 2010 A.E. Waiboer *et al.*, *Gabriël Metsu*, exh. cat., Dublin (National Gallery of Ireland), Amsterdam (Rijksmuseum) and Washington, DC (National Gallery of Art), 2010

Waiboer 2012 A.E. Waiboer, *Gabriel Metsu: Life and Work: A Catalogue Raisonné*, New Haven and London 2012

Waiboer et al. 2017 A. Waiboer *et al.*, *Vermeer and the Masters of Genre Painting: Inspiration and Rivalry*, exh. cat., Paris (Musée du Louvre), Dublin (National Gallery of Ireland) and Washington, DC (National Gallery of Art), 2017

Walpole 1763 H. Walpole, *Anecdotes of Painting in England*, vol. III, London 1763

Walpole 1849 H. Walpole, *Anecdotes of Painting in England; with some Account of the Principal Artists; and Incidental Notes on other Arts*, 3 vols., London 1849

Walpole 1937–83 H. Walpole, ed. W.S. Lewis, *The Yale Edition of Walpole's Correspondence*, 48 vols., New Haven 1937–83

Waterhouse et al. 1952–53 E. Waterhouse *et al.*, *Dutch Pictures 1450–1750*, exh. cat., London (Royal Academy) 1952–53

Waterhouse 1994 E.K. Waterhouse, *Painting in Britain 1530–1790*, New Haven and London 1994

Waterson 1986 M. Waterson, 'Brigantines and Battle-Pieces: Marine Pictures at Felbrigg, Norfolk - II', *Country Life*, 18 September 1986, pp. 904–06

Wegener 1995 U.B. Wegener, 'Bloemaert, Abraham', in *Saur Allgemeines Künstlerlexikon: Die bildenden Künstler aller Zeiten und Völker*, 92 parts, Munich 1995, vol. 11, pp. 547–48

Wenley 2015 R. Wenley *et al.*, *Flinck in Focus. A Question of Identity in 17th-century Dutch Portraiture*, exh. cat., Birmingham (Barber Institute of Fine Arts) 2015

Westermann 2001 M. Westermann, ed., *Art & Home, Dutch Interiors in the Age of Rembrandt*, exh. cat., Denver (Denver Art Museum) and Newark (Newark Museum) 2001

Wheelock et al. 1995 A.K. Wheelock *et al.*, *Johannes Vermeer*, exh. cat., Washington, DC (National Gallery of Art), and The Hague (Mauritshuis) 1995–96

Wheelock 2001–02 A.K. Wheelock, *Aelbert Cuyp*, exh. cat., Washington, DC (National Gallery of Art), London (National Gallery) and Amsterdam (Rijksmuseum) 2001–02

Wheelock et al. 2004 A.K. Wheelock *et al.*, *Gerard ter Borch*, exh. cat., Washington, DC (National Gallery of Art), Detroit (Institute of Arts) and Amsterdam (Rijksmuseum) 2004

Wheelock 2008–09 A.K. Wheelock, *Jan Lievens: A Dutch Master Rediscovered*, exh. cat., Washington, DC (National Gallery of Art), Milwaukee (Milwaukee Art Museum) and Amsterdam (Rembrandt House), 2008–09

Wheelock 2014 A.K. Wheelock, 'Pieter de Hooch/ The Bedroom/1658/1660', *Dutch Paintings of the Seventeenth Century*, NGA Online Editions, https://purl.org/nga/collection/artobject/1172

White 1982 C. White, *The Dutch Pictures in the Collection of Her Majesty the Queen*, Cambridge 1982

White 2015 C. White, *Dutch Pictures in the Collection of Her Majesty the Queen*, London 2015

White and Buvelot 1999–2000 C. White and Q. Buvelot (eds.), *Rembrandt by Himself*, exh. cat., London (National Gallery) and The Hague (Mauritshuis) 1999–2000

Winiewicz-Wolska 2001 Joanna Winiewicz-Wolska, *Malarstwo holenderskie w zbiorach zamku królewskiego na Wawelu*, Krakow 2001

Wood 2000–01 J. Wood, 'Orazio Gentileschi and Some Netherlandish Artists in London: The patronage of the Duke of Buckingham, Charles I and Henrietta Maria', *Simiolus*, 28, 2000–01

Worsley 2002 G. Worsley, *England's Lost Houses*, London 2002

Wright 1982 C. Wright, *Rembrandt Self-Portraits*, London 1982

von Wurzbach A. von Wurzbach, *Rembrandt Galerie*, Stuttgart 1886

PROPERTY GAZETTEER

Ascott House (cat. 5)
Wing, near Leighton Buzzard, Buckinghamshire, LU7 0PR

Ashdown House (cat. 9)
Lambourn, Newbury, Oxfordshire, RG17 8RE

Buckland Abbey (cat. 18)
Yelverton, Devon, PL20 6EY

Castle Ward (cat. 13)
Strangford, Downpatrick, County Down, BT30 7BA

Dunham Massey (cat. 6)
Altrincham, Cheshire, WA14 4SJ

Dyrham Park (cat. 1, 7)
Dyrham, near Bath, Gloucestershire, SN14 8HY

Felbrigg Hall (cat. 21)
Felbrigg, Norwich, Norfolk, NR11 8PR

Ham House (cat. 2, 4, 11, 12, 17)
Ham Street, Ham, Richmond, Surrey, TW10 7RS

Osterley Park (cat. 16)
Jersey Road, Isleworth, Middlesex, TW7 4RB

Upton House (cat. 14, 15, 19, 20)
near Banbury, Warwickshire, OX15 6HT

Polesden Lacey (cat. 3, 10)
Great Bookham, near Dorking, Surrey, RH5 6BD

Petworth House (cat. 8, 22)
Petworth, West Sussex, GU28 9LR

PHOTOGRAPHIC CREDITS

Front cover, pp. 6, 137, 140, 163 National Trust Images/Christopher Hurst; frontispiece, back cover, figs. 6, 7, 17, 18, 26, 45, 48, 56, 62, 64, 80, 81, 82, 86, pp. 65, 69, 78–79, 91, 142, 177 National Trust Images/John Hammond; figs. 1, 3, 4, 5, 9, 38, 46, 47, 51, 52, 61, 63, 66, 67, 88, pp.13, 53, 83, 107, 115, 116, 119, 127, 151, 169, 173 National Trust Images; fig. 2, 55, p. 103 National Trust Images/Derrick E. Witty; fig. 8 National Trust Images/Angelo Hornack; figs. 10, 68, 69 Mike Fear © National Trust/Waddesdon Manor, The Rothschild Collection (Rothschild Family Trust); pp. 29, 130, 155, 156, 157 National Trust Images/Chris Titmus; figs. 11, 14, 25, 28, 65 Royal Collection Trust/© Her Majesty Queen Elizabeth II 2018; fig. 12 National Portrait Gallery, acquired with help from the Art Fund, 1965; figs. 13, 15, 35, 43 © Rijksmuseum; figs. 16, 19, 20, 75, 84, 85, 93, 99, 100, 101, 102 Mauritshuis, The Hague; figs. 21, 27, 44 © The Trustees of the British Museum; figs. 22, 53 The National Gallery, London; fig. 23 Staatliche Museen zu Berlin, Nationalgalerie; fig. 24 Museum of Fine Arts, Boston, Rose-Marie and Eijk van Otterloo Collection; pp. 50–51, 57, fig. 79 National Trust Images/Christopher Warleigh-Lack; fig. 29 National Gallery of Canada, Ottawa; fig. 30 National Trust Images/Matthew Hollow; fig. 31 National Trust Images/Simon Harris; fig. 32, 83 National Trust Images/Andreas von Einsiedel; fig. 33 National Trust Images/Simon Tranter; fig. 34 National Trust Images/Nick Meers; fig. 36 Frits Lugt Collection, Fondation Custodia; fig. 37 Centraal Museum, Utrecht, on loan from the Cultural Heritage Agency of the Netherlands, Amersfoort; fig. 39 Haags Historisch Museum, The Hague, on loan to the Boerhaave Museum, Leiden; figs. 40, 41, 49 National Trust Images/Robert Thrift; fig. 42 English Heritage, Kenwood House, The Iveagh Bequest (46); fig. 50 Victoria and Albert Museum, London; fig. 54 National Trust Images/Simon Buckley; fig. 57 The Fitzwilliam Museum; fig. 58 Philadelphia Museum of Art, Gift of Anthony N. B. Garvan, 1983; fig. 59 Washington, D.C., National Gallery of Art, Widener Collection; fig. 60 National Trust Images/Jonathan Buckley; fig. 70 National Trust Images/Robert Harris; fig. 71 Scottish National Portrait Gallery, Edinburgh; pp. 129, 131 National Trust Images/Angelo Hornak; figs. 72, 74 National Trust Images/Robert Morris; fig. 73 National Trust Images/Chris Lacey; fig. 76 Royal Palace, Amsterdam; fig. 77 Centraal Museum, Utrecht; fig. 78 National Trust Images/W. Anderson-Porter; fig. 87 National Galleries of Scotland; figs. 89, 90 Het Utrechts Archief; fig. 90 Het Utrechts Archief; fig. 91 Montpellier Agglomération, Musée Fabre, bequest of Antoine Valedau, 1836; fig. 92 Braunschweig, Herzog Anton Ulrich-Museum; fig. 94 Royal Hospital Chelsea, London, UK / Bridgeman Images; figs. 95, 96, 97, 98 Holburne Museum, Bath